Goblet d'Alviella

The Contemporary Evolution of Religious Thought

in England, American and India

Goblet d'Alviella

The Contemporary Evolution of Religious Thought
in England, American and India

ISBN/EAN: 9783337264253

Printed in Europe, USA, Canada, Australia, Japan

Cover: Foto ©Lupo / pixelio.de

More available books at **www.hansebooks.com**

THE CONTEMPORARY EVOLUTION

OF

RELIGIOUS THOUGHT.

THE CONTEMPORARY EVOLUTION

OF

RELIGIOUS THOUGHT

IN

ENGLAND, AMERICA AND INDIA,

BY

COUNT GOBLET d'ALVIELLA,

PROFESSOR OF COMPARATIVE THEOLOGY IN THE UNIVERSITY OF BRUSSELS AND
FORMERLY MEMBER OF THE BELGIAN HOUSE OF REPRESENTATIVES.

"Notre siècle a vu des mouvements religieux aussi extraordinaires que ceux d'autrefois, mouvements qui ont provoqué, au début autant d'enthusiasme, qui ont déjà eu, proportion gardée, plus de martyrs et dont l'avenir est encore incertain."—E. RENAN, *Les Apôtres.*

TRANSLATED

BY

J. MODEN.

NEW YORK:
G. P. PUTNAM'S SONS,
27 & 29, WEST TWENTY-THIRD STREET.
1885.

TO

EMILE DE LAVELEYE,

WHO EVEN IN THE HEAT OF THE STRUGGLE FOR THE PROGRESS

OF THE HUMAN MIND HAS NEVER SEPARATED

RELIGION AND LIBERTY.

TRANSLATOR'S PREFACE.

When this work first came under my notice, I was struck with its calm judicial tone, its fine catholicity of spirit, and above all with its comprehensive grasp of the bearing of modern science upon ultimate religious beliefs. To trace the changes of religious thought and note their inter-dependence, their "evolution," in the life of two great races, during the most eventful period in the history of the human mind, is certainly no small undertaking, and yet it was one which, as it seemed to me, the Author had successfully accomplished. And although I was fully aware that a large proportion, possibly, indeed, the majority of those likely to be interested in a question of this kind, were, in all probability, able to read the work in the original, it still appeared to me and to friends on whose judgment I relied, that so important a book ought to be translated for the sake of those less versed in the French language and yet in full sympathy with the subject. The present translation is the result, which I now offer to the English-speaking public on both sides of the Atlantic.

In the performance of my self-imposed task, I have sought to reproduce not only the thought, but, as far as possible, the spirit of the work. It is for others to say how far I have succeeded in this attempt. The one great pre-requisite for the task I have certainly possessed —sympathy with the subject. This sympathy has extended to the historical and critical as well as to the more philosophical parts of the book; but at the same time I must confess to having felt a special interest in the chapters which treat of Mr. Herbert Spencer's philosophy and of the attempt that is being made by Mr. Savage and others to reconcile religious faith with the Philosophy of Evolution, and to thus base the life of the soul upon the consciousness of the Absolute, that indestructible rock which the wildest storms of scepticism can never wear away.

As the reader will observe, I have added several notes, which in one or two cases are of considerable length. It has appeared to me desirable to make at least some mention of whatever within my own knowledge was calculated to throw any direct light upon the text of the work, or to bring its critical examination down to a later date. Hence the notes in reference to certain new books; to the Spencer-Harrison controversy; to the most recent phases of the Brahmo Somáj movement; and to other matters likely to prove of interest to the reader or give greater value to the book. My having made no reference to Dr. Martineau's recently published work—"Types of Ethical Theory"— may seem either an exception or an omission on this head. But the book in question appeared too late for mention in those chapters where the high position and extensive influence of its author are considered; and then again, though a great and most important work, it has but an indirect bearing upon the evolution of religious thought and does not come, therefore, within the strictly legitimate scope of this book.

Those who read with interest what is said in these pages on the progressive modification and development of religious thought in England, America, and India, may possibly regret that the Author did not at least extend the scope of the work to Germany. This regret, indeed, was expressed to me, the other day, by Professor Pfleiderer, of Berlin, who spoke most highly of what Count d'Alviella has actually accomplished. It may be remarked, however, that the book would not have possessed, in such case, the unity which now characterises it, and that the field is still open for the application of a similar method of critical observation to the various Protestant countries of the Continent—Germany, Holland, Switzerland, and Sweden.

To the merely superficial observer of the present condition of religious thought there often comes a feeling of dread or of exultation, according as he is at the positive or negative stage of belief and clings to religion or would see it destroyed. But he who looks around upon the religious opinions of his fellows in the spirit of this book or ponders over the changes of belief it describes, will find no cause for either despondency or sceptical triumph. He will see that though the form of religion changes the substance remains; and he will be led to believe, or strengthened in the conviction, that religion can no more die out of the heart of man, in his race capacity, than gravitation can disappear from the physical world. As the soul's perception of the underlying Reality, as its consciousness of relationship and affinity to the mysterious Power in whose Immensity the Space-universe is embosomed like a mote in the sunbeam, it is not only an abiding but the grandest, because the ideal and governing factor in man's spiritual being. Chained to the phenomenal by his intellect, it is in and through religion alone that he is brought into practical relationship with the Absolute. It is true he becomes conscious of Transcendent Existence by the processes of the intellect, but it is only in love and aspiration—only in the consciousness of that " Eternal Mystery" to which Herbert Spencer ascribes religion or from the sense of absolute dependence to which Schliermacher traced it, or, indeed, from the perception of God in the moral law as taught by Kant, that the human blends with the Divine, and the soul of man passes into the infinite and partakes of its rest and fulness. To every open mind the universe with its wondrous commingling of atoms and mysterious onflowing instants, is a revelation of the Eternal in Space and Time. And with the thought that thus perceives the Supreme Being, behind the world, there comes the feeling, the "emotional consciousness" which is a personal realization of Him. For reverence is born of what the mind recognises as great, vast, sublime. And in this way the soul passes from the visible to the invisible, from the phenomenal to the real.—But not simply as the correlative of great thoughts is the Divine life given, for it flows into every young soul and enshrines itself in opinions that seem absolutely true when erroneous, and inspires a confidence that claims fullest knowledge where knowledge is impossible. Innumerable souls thus live before God—souls that could never reach Him if clear intellectual vision were needed to do so. Nothing, indeed, is more marvellous than this second or higher form of instinct which makes even intellectual error subservient to the continuance of spiritual truth in the human heart. Thus the imperishable treasure of the soul's life is always contained in an earthen vessel supplied by the intellect. Moulded, fashioned and conditioned according to the needs of the mind in all its multiform stages of progress, that is to say enshrined in a thousand mythological or theological forms, this sense of God the Infinite manifests itself as faith, as religion; and men cling to it in certain phases of their growth as a mother clings to her child, and at other times they spurn it as a worthless thing because an awakening mind has shown them it is not identical with some special form of belief, as they have earnestly or even passionately taken it to be.

Now the preception of this truth is the key that unlocks every system of faith and discloses the spiritual power which may be associated with the crudest opinions, showing us that though absolute truth is not the heritage of man the harmony of sincerity is made absolute and suffices for the life of the soul. Hence it enables us to understand the origin and influence of the great religions of the past as they are revealed to us by Comparative Theology, and it will enable the reader to rightly estimate the changes of religious thought which are taking place to-day in our midst—changes which this work describes and attempts to account for by carrying the great law of Evolution into that domain of human experience which was so long regarded as a separate province of the mind, but is now seen to be nothing more than its bright upper and heavenward side.

Leicester, July, 1885.

CONTENTS.

	PAGE
INTRODUCTION	1

PART I.

CHAPTER I.
THE PROGRESS OF FREE INQUIRY IN ENGLAND SINCE THE REFORMATION ... 13

CHAPTER II.
THE PHILOSOPHY OF EVOLUTION AND THE CRISIS OF THEISM ... 35

CHAPTER III.
THE PROGRESS OF THOUGHT IN ORTHODOX PROTESTANISM ... 57

CHAPTER IV.
ENGLISH UNITARIANISM ... 81

CHAPTER V.
RATIONALISTIC CONGREGATIONS BEYOND THE PALE OF CHRISTIANITY ... 103

CHAPTER VI.

COMTISM AND SECULARISM 129

PART II.

CHAPTER VII.

THE GENESIS OF UNITARIANISM IN THE UNITED STATES ... 153

CHAPTER VIII.

THE TRANSCENDENTAL MOVEMENT—EMERSON AND PARKER ... 167

CHAPTER IX.

FREE RELIGION AND THE RELIGION OF ETHICS 183

CHAPTER X.

COSMISM AND THE RELIGION OF EVOLUTION ... 209

PART III.

CHAPTER XI.

THEISM IN CONTEMPORARY INDIA 225

CHAPTER XII.

THE SOCIAL REFORMS OF THE BRAHMO SOMÁJ ... 241

CHAPTER XIII.

THE ECLECTICISM OF THE BRAHMA DHARMA IN ITS STRUGGLE
 WITH HINDU MYSTICISM 257

CHAPTER XIV.

SYNCRETISM OF THE NEW DISPENSATION 273

CHAPTER XV.

BRAHMOISM AND THE RELIGIOUS FUTURE OF INDIA ... 291

SUMMARY AND CONCLUSION.

INTRODUCTION.

UNATTACHED to any Church, but in moral and intellectual sympathy with all who, either as representatives of a religious organization or otherwise, are seeking to reconcile religion and reason, I have been engaged, for several years past, in studying the various attempts which are being made by the English, the Americans, and the Hindus, to solve what Professor Tyndall calls "The problem of problems of our age." It is the result of these studies that I now offer to the public.

I could have wished to extend my work to all those countries where an attempt is also being made to ensure a rational satisfaction to the religious sentiment; but, taking into consideration the magnitude of such an attempt, I have thought it wise to restrict myself to those peoples whom special circumstances have permitted me to more closely observe. There is, moreover, an exceptional interest in studying the conflict between religion and science among the Anglo-Saxon nations, who, on both sides of the Atlantic, are regarded as forming at once the most religious and the most practical race of the modern world.

Those who read this work to the end will see how it is that, without destroying the unity of the subject, I have been able to connect, with a sketch of religious progress in England and the United States, an exposition of the religious reform now being carried on in India by the different schools of Brahmoism. There is, in short, a movement of emancipation going on among the Hindus, which, while retaining its originality in the presence of European influences, represents none the less the indirect action of Anglo-Saxon culture on the spirit of the old Hindu philosophy.

It is in no sectarian or proselytizing spirit that this work is written. I have been influenced neither by a desire to secure acceptance for any one of the systems of belief which I have sought to explain, nor by an assumption that I am capable of offering any new solution of the problem. My sole aim has been to furnish some few materials for the history of Rationalism in the second half of the nineteenth century. I have, therefore, specially applied myself to collecting facts and to summarizing documents, adding, at the same time, my own views on the ground of general criticism.

I may even go so far as to say that I should be greatly embarrassed if, at the outset, it were necessary for me to decide between the relative claims of the religious doctrines which are described in this volume. Whenever I have watched the working of the different systems on the spot, whenever I have found myself in personal relation with their principal representatives, or have been able to study them in the works of their most authoritative interpreters, I have been struck much more forcibly by the unity of principle pervading them than by the diversity of form they possess.

Why not avow it, even at the risk of being taxed with indifference or ever-changing opinions by those who do not understand me? I was little short of feeling myself a Unitarian when with Dr. Martineau in England, or with Mr. Savage in the United States; a Theist with Mr. Voysey; a Transcendentalist, at Boston with Theodore Parker; a believer in the Divinity of the Cosmos, at New Bedford with Mr. Potter; a Humanitarian, at New York with Mr. Adler; and even a Brahmoist, at Calcutta with the leaders of the Brahmo Somaj. To say the least, if I had been born in any one of these systems of belief, in all probability, I should have remained in it, because it would have presented no barrier to my moral and intellectual development.

I may say, therefore, with Montaigne: "C'est icy un livre de bonne foy, lecteur." But I should also add that it is not only a book written in good faith, but also one that has resulted from sympathy with the subject. When a man is closely connected with the struggles of political factions in his own country, he feels a certain pleasure in transporting himself into a calmer and healthier atmosphere, where he may express himself free from the reservations or the party spirit of electoral and parliamentary controversy. All the writers who have considered the progress of the conflict between the modern spirit and Roman orthodoxy, from the higher levels of thought—as Renan, Renouvier, de Laveleye, Castelar, and Mariano—have pointed out the disadvantages, and even the dangers which accompany any form of destruction in religious matters, without a corresponding process of reconstruction. This consideration, grave as it is, would not influence me, if it were a question of defending the essential conditions of our civilization, the independence of individual judgment, the claims of science or the exercise of public liberty, against the assumptions of any church. But however resolved I may be to persevere in such a course as this, I cannot, in the presence of the disappointments and embarrassments which it reserves for us, restrain a feeling of envy for the wisdom of those more fortunate peoples with whom attempts at religious reconstruction go hand in hand with the progress of dogmatic demolition. Hence, though I have attempted to give to this work an impartial and impersonal character, it bears the impress of a large and perhaps the best part of my own individuality.

Some time since, Mr. Gladstone, in describing the various currents of religious thought which prevail in the modern world, divided them into two classes, according as their adherents admit or deny the moral government of Providence and the sanctions of a future life.[1] In the first of these groups he placed the partizans of Papal infallibility, together with those who attribute to their Church a divine origin (Episcopalians, Old Catholics and members of the Greek Church) as well as the various Evangelical sects, the Universalists, the Unitarians, and also the majority of Theists. In the second division—characterized as the negative school—he classed Sceptics, Atheists, Agnostics, Secularists, Pantheists, Positivists, and the believers in a revived Paganism.

Now this classification is perfectly justifiable for those who occupy, as Mr. Gladstone does, a definite philo-

---

1. *The Courses of Religious Thought*, by the Right Hon. W. E. Gladstone, in the *Contemporary Review*, of June, 1876.

sophical stand-point. But on the more general ground where I have taken up a position, it is not so much the nature of the religious ideas, which has to be considered, as their flexibility, that is to say the extent to which those who accept them admit the right of free inquiry in relation to their adoption or rejection. I came to the conclusion, therefore, that the best course I could persue, would be to describe in succession the condition of the various churches and schools of religious thought by arranging them, as far as possible, in the order of decreasing dogmatic opinion. On the other hand, since my purpose is less that of describing any given religious organization than of tracing the course of its evolution, I have also deemed it useless to dwell upon such facts as the eccentricities of certain American sects, the practices of the Salvation Army and the like, which have often occupied public attention, but which, as it seems to me, mark either a retrograde tendency or a deviation from the general course of religious development.

I have thought it desirable to commence the first part of the work with a sketch of the progress which free inquiry has made in England since the reign of Henry the Eighth; in seeing by this means how the present has sprung from the past, the reader will be the better able to anticipate how the future will flow out of the present.

Nor has it seemed to me less indispensable to devote a special chapter to a description of the influence exercised upon the religious sentiment by the scientific philosophy of the age, which is everywhere tending to predominate in the higher strata of modern thought.

It will be thus seen that the present conflict between religion and reason, is not confined to the peoples of our continent; while at the same time it will become apparent how the leading minds of the Anglo-Saxon race have set about solving this great problem, without sacrificing the respective claims of either of the two parties in the conflict.

The chapters which follow contain an exposition of the progress of religious thought in the various denominations of Great Britain, from the Anglican Church to orthodox Positivism and indeed to the rudimentary worship of the Secularists, passing in review the evangelical sects, the Unitarians, the pure Theists and other rationalistic communions.

The second part of the work is principally devoted to the United States. I explain in it how the Unitarian movement sprang up there from the original Puritan orthodoxy by a gradual but by no means illogical evolution, and how, after having passed through the phase of Transcendentalism, it has produced numerous organizations which border on the limits of pure Theism or even extend to Agnosticism, some indeed realizing, to a certain extent, the type of a Church of Humanity without any dogmatic barriers whatever, and others attaching themselves more or less closely to the recent philosophy of evolution.

The object of the third part is to show how contact with European culture has produced in India a breaking up of the old systems of Polytheism on the one hand, and on the other an eclectic Theism, due to a synthesis of the religious progress made by the two races. But I also endeavour, at the same time, to show how the mysticism, always latent in the Hindu character, threatens to paralyse all attempts to start the mind of that people along the less demonstrative course of European religious life. I have further taken into consideration what are likely to be the general results, in the future, of this action and re-action between the two principal branches of the great Aryan family.

Finally, a concluding chapter contains a statement of what modern criticism has left of the old beliefs, and seeks to foreshadow the kind of religious re-construction for which this residuum of belief may yet serve in the future.[1]

If in our day the religious sentiment is often regarded as incapable of a new season of bloom, and even destined to a more or less early disappearance, it is because the present conflict between faith and free inquiry is held to be fundamental and definitive. Religion, it is urged, pre-supposes the supernatural, which reason excludes. It is necessary, however, to come to a clear understanding as to the meaning of the terms employed in such a statement as this. If by the supernatural the anti-natural is meant, that is to say a violation of the order revealed in nature, in a word the miraculous, then I readily admit that it must be henceforth abandoned as utterly irreconcileable with the requirements of every

---

1. Several chapters of this book have appeared, at various intervals, in the form of articles published in the *Revue des Deux Mondes*. But it will be readily understood that I have not been able to unite them in a continuous narrative, like this work, without considerable modifications, in order to embody such information as may have been necessary, respecting the changes which are always taking place in the factors of religious evolution. The chapters which relate to England and India have been, as it were, completely re-written.

system of philosophical thought. But if the term supernatural simply stands for the super-sensible, or what is above nature, or, indeed, to speak more correctly, what is above reason, then there is nothing in science which can proscribe it. M. Littré himself, speaking in the name of the Positive Philosophy, declares that it is perfectly legitimate for anyone to transport himself into the "transrational," if he is so disposed, in order to form there such ideas respecting the origin and purpose of things as may please him best; and Mr. Herbert Spencer does not hesitate to affirm that the conception of an Omnipresent Power transcending the limits of knowledge is the supreme outcome both of science and religion.[1]

In order to see that reason and religion are not necessarily in antagonism, it will suffice to remember that they belong to two different provinces of the human mind. Philosophy, making use of the materials furnished by observation, formulates a conception of the universe. This conception the religious sentiment takes possession of, in order to dramatize, color and idealize it; and, while seeking in it the symbol of the Unknowable, which remains as the residiuum of all synthetic philosophy, we also project into it a human element, which sends back to us an echo of our aspirations towards the Infinite and the Absolute. Doubtless, a conflict cannot fail to arise between free inquiry and what appears to be the religious sentiment as soon as any such dramatized conception of the Cosmos ceases to correspond with the requirements of science, which may have

---

1. Littré, Trans-rationalism in the *Revue Positive* of January, 1880. Herbert Spencer, *First Principles*, Chapter v.

gradually become hostile to it. Still, in reality, the hostility, under these circumstances, is simply between two scientific conceptions, the more ancient of which, having become antiquated by the progress of knowledge, has not been rejected by religion. Now, this elimination is only a question of time. Experience teaches us that, after a greater or less period of oscillation and groping about for a new support, the religious sentiment always succeeds in freeing itself from its antiquated forms, and adopts an explanation of the universe more in conformity with the revelations of science and the aspirations of contemporary society.

It is certainly quite possible that the dogmatic element in religion may have to play a more and more restricted part in the future. A strong tendency is daily gaining ground, especially in the Protestant churches, to no longer look for the test of religion in this or that confession of faith, but in obedience to what the celebrated English critic, Mr. Matthew Arnold, has spoken of as "A Power, not ourselves, that makes for righteousness." When God is thus reduced to an ideal, of which the moral and physical order constitutes the permanent manifestation, the first duty that presents itself to us is to search for the laws by which the Divinity reveals His action—a course dictated by the very attributes of reason; and the second is to adapt our conduct to those laws—and it is just here that religion most unquestionably retains a great mission in the development of humanity.

It will perhaps be objected that this is to confound religion with morality? Morality, I answer, addresses itself to the judgment only; it is therefore inadequately armed, as Auguste Comte so clearly understood, to struggle against passion and selfishness in the domain of sentiment and imagination. Ethics, philosophy, sociology, or whatever else we please to call the application of reason to the discovery of the laws of our individual destiny, and the conditions of our collective existence, may reveal to us the practical requirements of duty; but this sense of duty needs to be animated with life by religion, that is to say realized in all its fulness.

Von Hartman has said that religion is the *popular* conception of the ideal. He should have called it, however, its *living* conception, for regarded from this point of view, there is no one who does not need religion, and thus understood, the religious sentiment is not only rational, it is also as indestructible as reason itself.

I may add that the chief thing for general peace of mind and the progress of ideas, is less that of attracting the Churches to Rationalism, than to the adoption of liberal principles; less that of getting them to accept views in harmony with modern science, than of inducing them to recognize the absolute right of the individual to think for himself, and thus winning them over to a belief in the constant possibility of religious progress.

It is undeniable that we are now passing through an acute crisis of religious belief. If we do not wish to render it more intense and prolong its duration, it is imperative upon us to strip ourselves of every prejudice and put aside all intolerance, as well with regard to existing beliefs as in respect to those opinions offered in place of them. This attitude of mind, indeed, is not only commanded by the necessities of the present transition, it recommends itself to us, moreover, as the result of the entire movement of contemporary thought. Each day the conviction is growing stronger—on the one hand that the human mind cannot reach the supreme reality except by means of imperfect symbolism—on the other, that all the forms of religious thought are the product of natural causes embodying, side by side with unavoidable errors, an element of truth, and that they are subject to the law of progress.

It is this that the Platonic philosopher Maximus of Tyre caught a glimpse of, as early as the Second century of our era, when he characterized all the forms of faith as powerless efforts directed towards the same lofty ideal.

It is this that has been placed in the clearest light by one of the most recent and at the same time most advanced sciences of the age—Comparative Theology.

If the present work should have no other result than the confirmation of this double position, which is inseparable from all impartial, sympathetic and fruitful criticism, I shall not consider that I have written in vain.

PART I.

CHAPTER I.

THE PROGRESS OF FREE INQUIRY IN ENGLAND SINCE THE REFORMATION.

Sunday in England—A picture of religious life in London—Number and variety of sects—Odd practices—Open-air preaching—The teaching thus communicated—The political character of the reform effected by Henry VIII.—The elements which favoured its extension among the masses—The influence of foreign refugees: Ochino, Acontius and Corrano—Persecution of the Dissenters under the Tudors and Stuarts—The Latitudinarians: Chillingworth and Jeremy Taylor—Relation between the increase of sects and the progress of toleration—The Puritan movement in the seventeenth century—Development of Latitudinarian ideas under the Restoration—Secularization of philosophy and science—Locke and the sensational school—Attempts to base the validity of Revelation on the authenticity of miracles—English Deism: Lord Herbert of Cherbury and his successors—The decline of this school—The general predominance of Utilitarianism in the theology of the eighteenth century—The mystical reaction of the Wesleyans—Coleridge and German idealism—The application of symbolism to the interpretation of Christian dogmas—The convergence of scientific and historical researches towards the negation of the supernatural—Progress of Rationalism among the sects open to theological change—Contemporary Theism—Professor F. W. Newman and Miss F. P. Cobbe—Growth of religious liberty in British legislation—The slow but steady progress of reform—The parliamentary oath and the blasphemy laws.

The majority of foreigners who visit England seem to regard Sunday as a day on which all the wheels of social existence are stopped. It would be more correct to say, that, with the English, secular life gives place everywhere to religious life on one day of the week. And however little we attempt to examine this new phase of activity, we shall find in it, especially in the large towns, an inexhaustible source of original impressions and fruitful observations. It is, indeed, a necessary study for anyone who would get at the root of the English character, and judge of the British nation under all its aspects.

The variety and exuberance of religious phenomena presented by London to-day are such as have not been witnessed since the time when sophists and theologians encumbered the streets of Alexandria.

The London Post Office Directory of 1882 gives a list of 1,231 places of worship belonging to about thirty distinct sects;[1] but as this list refers merely to congregations domiciled in their own buildings, it must be supplemented by all the religious organizations which hold their meetings in private rooms, as well as by the services which are held in the open air, in such places as the parks, the public squares, and even under the arches of the railway viaducts.[2]

It will be seen that people of all tastes and temperaments can find abundant satisfaction for their religious wants. If they are fond of imposing ceremonies and a gorgeous ritual, combining all the resources of æsthetics, the Roman Catholic Church, the Greek Church, the Ritualistic and Irvingite Churches vie with each other in attracting them by their pomp and symbolism. If they desire to connect their religious aspirations with a respect for free inquiry, they have only to make a choice from a whole series of congregations, whose beliefs extend from Christian Rationalism to religious services without a God. If they wish to see curious phenomena or extraordinary spectacles, they have but to follow some crowd which is burying itself in a hall with bare walls and no other fittings than a platform and a number of benches. It is, perhaps, a meeting of the Tabernacle Ranters which they have entered, whose eccentricity will show itself in innumerable Hallelujahs! as a sign of their appreciation of the prayers and discourse of their improvised preacher; or it may be our visitors have fallen in with a gathering of those Shakers or Jumpers who, in the midst of the English life of this nineteenth century, recall the contortions of St. Medard and the Dancing Dervishes of the East. If they care to venture, in company with one of the initiated, into a sort of cavern, where there reigns a mysterious obscurity, they will perhaps hear the existence of God denied between the singing of two mystic hymns, but they will thus have an opportunity of holding communion with the spirits of Jesus and Mahommed, if not of calling forth the shades of their grandmothers.

Here stands an immense Tabernacle, which resembles a theatre. You will find in it from five to six thousand persons fixing their looks

---

1. The Directory for 1884 shows an increase of 40 in the two years.—*Translator*.

2. Paris contains 169 places of worship, taking into account the congregations in private buildings and the dissenting sects : that is to say, one place of worship for every 17,000 inhabitants, whereas London possesses one for about every 2,000.

in a meditative attitude upon a minister, who, assisted by two deacons, is plunging successively into a deep tank of clear water young men clothed in a kind of dressing-gown and young girls in long bathing-gowns of white flannel. Elsewhere, you may see worshippers of both sexes begin the communion service by exchanging the kiss of peace. Or, again, in another place, some fifty worthy people are to be seen sitting with a placid and becoming countenance and waiting patiently for the influence of the Holy Spirit. Your presence will not in any way disturb their pious ecstasy; a proper bearing is all that is required of you, and then the worshippers will not even appear to perceive your intrusion.

Suddenly a flourish of loud trumpet-like notes bursts forth in the neighbouring street. Music, and military music, on the Sunday! It is a detachment of the Salvation Army marching to its barracks, with officers of the fair as well as the stronger sex at its head, singing hymns to put the Devil to flight and firing circulars and pamphlets at the miserable sinners who have been attracted by the sound of the band.

At length it is evening, and, the services being over, the public thoroughfares are thronged with worshippers who have poured forth from innumerable chapels, whose gables are, in many cases, in a line with the fronts of the houses. There is nothing, however, disorderly about this large and motley crowd which lines the principal streets. These latter are dimly lighted by long rows of lamps that are eclipsed on the week-days by the gas from the shop-windows. No vehicle disturbs the pedestrians. Here and there some gin-palace or shop for the sale of eatables throws a dazzling ray of light from its half-open door. By the side of the foot-ways hand-carts or barrows are wheeled along, and fruit-sellers deal out their goods from them by the light of a flickering candle, which throws over the countenance of the purchaser a reflection not unlike that seen in Rembrandt's pictures.

At each corner of the street, groups may be seen around some open-air orator. Here, a Methodist preacher, with a long beard and extravagant gestures, is trying to excite the religious feelings of his auditors by pathetic appeals, garnished with edifying anecdotes. Or, here again, two representatives of rival sects are confounding each other in turn by Biblical arguments, with a degree of calmness and moderation not always to be witnessed in Parliamentary debates. Sometimes a whole group, at the bidding of its improvised minister, will sing a hymn, whose modulated words drown the noise of the crowd. Gradually all disperse; the streets become empty, and the policeman, the emblem of the State which never rests, is soon in sole possession of the great sleeping town.

As to myself, it was almost entirely as an idler in search of novelty that, some ten years ago, I undertook a series of visits to various London congregations. I certainly came into contact with more than one extravagance and more than one absurdity, in carrying out this purpose; but the smile which may have been brought to my lips, quickly died away from a feeling of general respect for the sincerity of conviction which everywhere showed itself, and of special sympathy for the efforts of those who in various ways were labouring to bring the religious sentiment into harmony with the general progress of civilization. At all events it is to this first comprehensive view of the innumerable subdivisions of English Protestantism that I am indebted for some idea of the importance of the great religious reform inaugurated by Luther, and as yet incomplete.

The introduction of Protestantism into England was notoriously a work of political policy rather than of religious conviction. It is true the Roman clergy had rendered themselves as odious to the masses by their abuses as they had done to the Crown by their pretensions, while the old leaven of the Lollards, which was fermenting still in the heart of the nation, could not fail to make the people favourable to a movement that promised to realize all the hopes and aspirations of Wycliff—that Protestant of the Reformation's dawn. But whilst the popular element inclined towards extreme views of the Reformation, the official element of the nation,—that is to say the King, the Court, the judicial functionaries, and the members of the Universities,—desired to retain a sort of Catholicism without the Pope, in which the Sovereign would exercise supreme authority over the religious affairs of the nation. Thus the Thirty-nine Articles, which have formed since 1562 the constitutional basis of the English Church, embody all the doctrines contained in the canon of Scripture, as well as the Apostles', the Nicene, and the Athanasian creeds. The ritual was minutely drawn up in the *Book of Common Prayer*, which substituted the national idiom for the Latin language; and an eagerness was shown to maintain the whole of the ancient ecclesiastical organization, with the simple difference, for the most part, that the King took the place of the Pope at the head of the hierarchy.[1] The new Church maintained the assumption of its predecessor as to Apostolical succession, and there was nothing, not even the title of "Catholic," which it did not lay claim to in face of the Roman Church.

In point of fact, the human conscience had merely exchanged tyrants by this shifting of supremacy. Every established form of religion implies State heresies, which the Civil Power must repress as infringements of public order. The celebrated Parliamentary leader, Pym, who took so active a part in the fall of Charles I., does not profess in this matter any other ideas than those of Henry VIII. "It belongs to Parliaments," said he, "to establish true religion and to punish false."[2] But if, in the accomplishment of this duty, the State sometimes acts as cruelly as the Church itself, it is never as suspicious in its search for heresies nor as rigorous in their repression; it seldom seeks to penetrate to the tribunal of conscience, but contents itself generally with a nominal submission. The Reformation, moreover, could not escape in England, any more than elsewhere, the application of its central principle, which consisted of setting up the authority of the individual conscience; and from the very fact that it represented a compromise between the extreme opinions of the period, it had to resist opposite tendencies, alike hostile to free inquiry, the one arising from the literal interpretation of a traditional text, the other consisting of the assumed infallibility of a living authority. In short, the Reformation, having commenced among the enlightened classes and being closely bound up with the life of the governing aristocracy, had to maintain, at one and the same time, respect for individual culture and a certain repugnance for all kinds of fanaticism.

---

1. Henry VIII. once caused three Lutherans and four Catholics to be drawn to the place of execution on the same hurdle, because they were all guilty of denying his supremacy. The only difference was that the former were hanged and the latter burned.—*Vide*, Neal, *History of the Puritans*.

2. J. J. Tayler. *A Retrospect of the Religious Life of England*. 2nd Edition. London, 1876. Page 116.

During the reign of Edward VI., England offered an asylum to all who had been exiled from their native land, on religious grounds, without regard to sect or race. As early as 1549, indeed, Archbishop Cranmer, who had already invited from the Continent a certain number of scholars and theologians of the reformed school, to aid in the re-organization of the English Universities, constituted a Church for foreigners, which was shortly afterwards divided into four branches, formed respectively of Flemish, Walloons, Italians, and Spaniards. The liberal spirit which had already shown itself in this small community, especially among the exiles of Italian and Spanish origin,[1] could not fail to strongly re-act, were it only by the works of their theologians, upon the religious ideas of those with whom they had found safety and independence.

Among the first Italian Protestants who took refuge in England, in or about the year 1547, was an old Capucine monk from Sienna, Bernard Ochino, who had largely contributed to the progress of the Reformation in his own country. Greatly in favour at the Court during the reign of Edward VI., he was obliged to flee into Switzerland at the death of that monarch, and shortly afterwards being proscribed from all Protestant communities, in consequence of his Socinian opinions, he died, in a state of wretchedness, in a small village of Moravia, at the age of 76. But, though banished from England, he left behind him numerous sympathisers, and more than one person in the foreign Churches, both able and willing to carry on his work—notably Jacques Acontius, a lay member of the Italian

---

[1]. Among the Italians the Reformation had assumed a more intellectual direction than elsewhere, and this need not be a matter of astonishment to those who bear in mind the social atmosphere created by the Renaissance. The dogma of the Trinity, that great mystery of orthodox Christianity, had first of all to bear the assault of rational criticism. In 1531, a Spanish Doctor, Michel Servetus, who had studied at the University of Padua, and whose tragic end is well known, wrote that the nature of God is indivisible, and that the persons of the Trinity are simply modes of the divine activity. This species of Pantheism, which was re-stated by Sabellius, spread rapidly through the conventicles held during the next twenty years in the north of Italy, with the more or less disguised toleration of the Venetian Republic. It is even stated that, about 1546, some forty persons belonging to the most enlightened classes of Society, formed at Vicence an Association for the restoration of "Christian Monotheism." It seemed as if Italian Protestantism was about to extend the Reformation principles to their utmost limits from the first, when there suddenly burst forth that storm of re-action which swept it clean away from the whole Peninsula.

Church, who, in drawing up a list of the doctrines necessary for salvation, omitted to inscribe therein the doctrine of the Trinity, and Antoine Corrano, the minister of the Spanish Church, who, suspended from his functions on account of his extra-Trinitarian beliefs, was none the less made a canon of St. Paul's.[1]

It was doubtless not judicious to attack the official dogmas too openly—to pass on, for instance, from extra-Trinitarian to anti-Trinitarian opposition—since it was possible that the State, once roused, would speedily show the difference, and that, too, with all the cruelty of the age. Witness those unhappy Anabaptists or Arians, who, from George Van Parris, in 1551, to Edward Wightman, in 1611, perished—as Servetus had done, and for the same crime—in flames kindled by Protestant hands. But these intermittent persecutions were powerless to arrest the progress of ideas, and the ashes of the last Socinian martyrs were scarcely cool before Arminian doctrines—those near neighbours of Arianism—had already begun to leaven the opinions of the Anglican clergy.

The Dutch sect of Arminians or Remonstrants did not confine themselves, as the reader may be aware, to a simple rejection of the dogma of predestination and that of the absolute equality of the three Divine Persons; they also raised the standard of religious toleration against the narrowness of Calvinistic theologians. Meanwhile, their broader views were brought into England by a former chaplain of the English Embassy in Holland, John Hales, who had been present at the discussion of the Council of Dordrecht, and who, forcibly impressed by the reasoning of Episcopius, had even at that time, to use his own expression, "bid John Calvin good night." Having connected himself, on his return to England, with one of the most distinguished men of the day, Lord Falkland—"whose house," says an author of that period, "looked like the University itself by the company that was always found there"—he formed, with Chillingworth, Jeremy Taylor, and some other young clergymen, the nucleus of what is still known as the Latitudinarian party in the English Church.

---

1. G. Bonet-Maury. *Des Origines du Christianisme Unitaire chez les Anglais.* I. Vol. Paris, Fishbacher. 1881. (This work has been translated into English by the Rev. E. P. Hall, and published by the British and Foreign Unitarian Association.—*Translator*.)

The position taken up by John Hales—a very bold one for the period—was that sincere error is not a crime, and that, consequently, "differences of opinion" should not be repressed by force. Even more: he laid down the principle which was destined to make liberal Protestantism triumphant. "If we were not," said he, in one of his sermons, "so ready to launch anathemas at each other, we should be united in heart, though separated in expression of opinion, which would be to the advantage of all. It is unity of spirit in the bonds of peace, and not identity of conceptions, which the Holy Spirit demands."[1]

Chillingworth's *Religion of Protestants*, published in 1637, and a few years later Jeremy Taylor's *Liberty of Prophesying*, were perhaps even more serviceable to the cause of toleration and religious progress than the sermons of John Hales. Still, both these authors accepted the absolute authority of the Bible. "The Bible, and the Bible only, is the religion of Protestants." Such is the very sentence which Chillingworth uses as the foundation of his argument when he attacks the confessions of faith arbitrarily imposed either by churches or individual theologians. But all three insist on this point: that the sense of the Scriptures is to be freely determined by individual judgment. Chillingworth's contention was that those who are mistaken and those who are not mistaken in matters of doctrine, may be alike saved. And he was so persuaded of the goodness of God, he said, that if all the errors charged against Protestants in the entire world could be concentrated in himself, he should be less shocked at all these errors united than at the idea of asking forgiveness for them.

Jeremy Taylor, on his part, shows the necessity of a constant recourse to the authority of individual reason. The authority of reason he held to be the best judge. Each man must determine, by and for himself, the nature of the truth revealed in the Scriptures. God, he declared, had no right to demand from us perfect freedom from error, but He had the right to demand that we should seek to avoid it. He who did not resolve to seek truth for himself, virtually gave himself up with indifference to the acceptance of truth or error. Might we not suppose these to be the words of Channing, uttered some two centuries afterwards?

Among the factors which contributed to the progress of religious liberty in England, we must recognize, side by side with the Lati-

---

1. Tulloch *Rational Theology in England in the Seventeenth Century*.

tudinarian tendencies which thus showed themselves in the Established Church, the multitude of sects which, from the time of Edward VI., strove to carry out, beyond the pale of Anglicanism, the logical evolution of the Protestant Reformation. Within fifty years, indeed, English Protestantism passed through, in a reverse direction, so to speak, all the stages which the Christian Church, as a whole, had required several centuries to cross in order to attain its complete development in the Roman hierarchy. It was, in the first place, the rejection of the Papal supremacy which gave birth to the Anglican Church. Afterwards, those proscribed by Queen Mary, who, during their exile, had come into contact with the Calvinists of the Continent, clamoured during the reign of Elizabeth for the introduction of the Presbyterian organization, which placed the government of the Church in assemblies of ministers and elders. The Presbyterians, however, merely sought to reform the National Church by the suppression of the Episcopate and the Liturgy. But the Independents soon arose, and they, repulsing all interference of the Civil Power in questions of ecclesiastical organization, demanded absolute freedom for the individual congregations, as well in their relations to each other as in their common relation to the State. At length, the Anabaptists, the Quakers, the Seekers, the "Fifth Monarchy Men," and the other sects which sprang up during the troubles of the first Revolution, endeavoured to suppress all kinds of ecclesiastical functions in order to give free scope to individual inspiration, in imitation of those primitive assemblies which the Acts of the Apostles show us under the influence of the Holy Spirit.[1]

This curious manifestation of Atavism finds an explanation in the increasing desire to literally follow the Scriptures, not only in matters of doctrine, but also in the method of ecclesiastical organization. This exclusive respect for the letter of Scripture had, it must be admitted, nothing in common with the spirit of free inquiry, nor even with the principle of religious toleration; for, as a matter of fact, the greater part of the sects which sprang from the Puritan movement, have shown themselves more opposed to the progress of Rationalism than the Anglican Church. But, in asserting their claim to the right of existence, they thereby strongly promoted the general liberty.

---

1. J. J. Tayler. *A Retrospect of the Religious Life of England.* Page 126.

By their very multiplicity they could not fail to develop the habit of constant recourse to individual judgment in matters of belief. For at least a certain number of their congregations, indeed, the absence of any standard of doctrine or discipline, together with the centrifugal force which removed them more widely every day from traditional Christianity, could not fail to insensibly facilitate their transition to opinions more and more advanced and to soon lead them, both in logic and in boldness, beyond the restrained audacity of the Latitudinarian party, whom the Articles of the Anglican Church held in check. It is these circumstances which gave birth to Unitarianism.

The persecutions directed against the Dissenters by the two first Stuarts merely served to multiply the number of sects and to call forth the energy of their adherents. At about the time of the earlier Revolution, Thomas Edwards, the author of the *Gangræna*, stated that there were in England 176 distinct sects; and when, after the passing triumph of the "Saints' Republic," England returned into the fold of royalty and Anglicanism, the Dissenters remained none the less an element which had to be considered in all the future religious, intellectual, and political movements of the English nation.

At the Restoration, an outbreak of licence succeeded the excess of social rigour which prevailed in the preceding period, as is usually the case after every too abrupt or exaggerated reform. This re-action, of which Hobbes was the principal representative in philosophy, could not be other than favourable to the cause of intellectual liberty. Hobbes, it is true, after having destroyed the very foundation of all religion, of all morality, and of all liberty, entrusted to the Sovereign the absolute right to determine the religious opinions, as well as the public and private duties, of his subjects. But, in the very heart of the Established Church, the Latitudinarian party had resumed their work of emancipation, with the Glanvils, the Hookers, the Berkeleys, and other theologians of the same school, to whom Mr. Lecky, an author by no means favourable, as a rule, to the Anglican Church, attributes the honour of having been the true founders of religious liberty in England.[1]

But we must not forget that, as early as the seventeenth century, the direction of the intellectual movement ceases to belong exclusively

---

1. W. Lecky. *History of the Rise and Influence of Rationalism in Europe.* Vol. II., page 72.

to the theologians. First of all, it is Lord Bacon who establishes the experimental or inductive method, and thus opens the way to the Sensational School. Then comes Locke, who seeks to explain all mental phenomena by the impressions made on the senses and by the association of ideas. Lord Bacon carefully separated religion from philosophy; Locke, however, did nothing of the sort, but even claimed to submit the truth of Christianity to the test of his method. In his celebrated work on *The Reasonableness of Christianity*, he maintains that the human mind, shut up, as it is, in the phenomenal world, cannot of itself attain to the full possession of religious truth. This truth must, therefore, be communicated to us by an external revelation. But by what means are we to recognize the authenticity of this supernatural communication? By miraculous signs, Locke answers, whose historical occurrence cannot be called in question. Now this condition, he adds, is exactly met by the Christian Revelation, which rests on the fulfilment of prophecy and the history of miracles. Still, it is for reason to examine these credentials, and to determine, by the aid of its common processes, the exact meaning and extent of the revelation.

Now there is no difficulty to seize upon the weak point of this argument, which entrusts the proof of supernatural Christianity to historical documents. But criticism, which was then merely in its infancy, especially in its application to religious history, justified the illusion that exegesis might become the most valuable ally of Biblical orthodoxy. The Bible, up to that time, had been regarded among Protestants as the very word of God, addressing itself directly to the souls of believers. No one would have previously dared to apply to the Pentateuch, to the Prophecies, the Gospels, or even to the Acts of the Apostles, the critical process employed in the study of a profane author; and it would have been regarded as sacrilege, not only to discuss the date of their composition or the personality of their authors or compilers, but even to take into account the part played by the surrounding circumstances of time, place, passion, and prejudice. By dissipating this atmosphere of traditional inviolability in the interest of religious truth, Locke paved the way for the great critical movement which was destined, not, indeed, to confirm the miracles of the Bible, as the author of *The Reasonableness of*

Christianity sincerely supposed, but, on the other hand, to eliminate the supernatural from Christianity, while, at the same time, it conceded the fullest respect for its moral and spiritual elements.

Side by side with Locke and the Sensational School, but in this case beyond the lines of Christianity, the Deistical School took up the defence of natural, as against revealed, religion. This movement originated with Lord Herbert of Cherbury, who has been called the Father of English Deism. Its doctrines were based entirely on the beliefs which its author considered common to the whole human race. For instance: the existence of God; the act of worship embodied in prayer; the forgiveness of sin by repentance; and, finally, the immortality of the soul, with the sanctions of a future life. This was to apply to religion itself the synthetic method which Acontius had adopted in order to obtain the fundamental and essential doctrines of Christianity from the beliefs common to different churches; only, in opposition to Acontius, Lord Herbert did not hesitate to threaten with damnation those who refused to accept his five articles of faith. Illustrating another inconsistency, more than one example of which is to be met with in the history of the human mind, this philosopher, who denied the Biblical revelation, believed he had himself been honoured by a special revelation; and he was accustomed to relate, in all sincerity, that, having one day cast himself on his knees to ask God whether he should do right in publishing his book, he received the divine *imprimatur*, by means of a sweet and distinct sound, which bore no resemblance to any of the sounds of earth.

It was this doctrine of a natural Monotheism which was developed successively by Blount, Shaftesbury, Woolston, Tindal, Chubb, Collins, and Bolingbroke. Some of these writers openly attacked the different forms of traditional Christianity; others, however, simply sought to develop the principles of Deism in the direction of the special philosophical schools to which they belonged. But whatever favour their works may have enjoyed among the superior classes, it was chiefly the negative side of their doctrines which gained them adherents, and we have no knowledge of any attempt to organize a system of worship on the basis proposed by Lord Herbert or his successors.[1]

---

1. It is impossible to regard in a serious light the description which Collins gives us in his *Pantheisticon* of a society which dined together periodically in order to treat of religious opinions at dessert, while they at the same time made use of an

Besides, nothing could well be less calculated to excite religious feeling than this cold Theodicy, which made of God a skilful mechanic, external to the world and unnecessary for sustaining the order of things. In France, where Deism was imported by Voltaire and developed by Rousseau, it furnished a philosophy for the movement which was coming into existence against all the abuses of the old *régime*, and it may be said, in spite of the failure of Robespierre, and later, of the Theophilanthropists who attempted to organize it into a system of worship, that it was the real religion of the French Revolution. But reduced to maintaining its ground in England as a pure speculation, it soon succumbed under the double attack of positive religion and critical philosophy. By the second third of the century it had fallen into a state of rapid decay, and gradually all the representatives of British science or literature, of any distinction, took up a position among its adversaries.[1] For whilst Middleton, Butler, and Paley called to the support of a more or less liberalized theology, all the resources of criticism, science, and contemporary metaphysics, Hume developed his universal scepticism, the penetrating logic of which was as merciless in its bearing upon the claims of Deism as it was in relation to traditional Christianity. With Gibbon the last representative of the school founded by Lord Herbert of Cherbury, was destined to disappear.

Never has there seemed to be more complete harmony between reason and Christianity than during the second half of the eig' teenth century. Locke held undisputed sway both as a theologian and a philosopher. Faith presented itself as no longer due to a restriction of free inquiry, but as a consequence of scientific demonstration. Theology had exclusive recourse to the method of induction, the theory of innate ideas was proscribed, and intuition discredited as tainted with mysticism. It was by external observation that henceforth the existence of God and the action of Providence were to be demonstrated. It was only by making an appeal to the historical proofs supplied by miracles that any attempt was to be made to establish the validity of the Christian revelation, the immortality of the soul, and the obligations of morality.

esoteric liturgy (v. Ed. Sayous—*Les Deistes Anglais* et le *Christianisme depuis Toland jusqu' a Chubb*. 1. Vol. Paris, Fishbacher. 1882.

1. H. Taine. *Histoire de la litterature Anglaise*, t. iii, page 160.

But, at the same time, it would be impossible to find a better example to show that the triumph of theology is not always that of religion. All true spirituality seems wanting at this period. In the eyes of the ruling class, worship is nothing more than a kind of police arrangement, the official church is simply an institution to regulate public morals; and no one is scandalized by seeing its ministers adopt the common-place life of the country squire. Its prelates, moreover, only occupy themselves in securing the favour of the Court, and in playing the wit at the expense of the last of the Deists. The enlightened section of the public have come to regard any manifestation of religious fervour as a morbid symptom, or, at least, as a sign of bad taste. The same feeling extends even to the Dissenting sects who, having attained to a position of relative freedom, are the prey of a sort of religious Positivism equally removed from indifference and enthusiasm.[1]

This state of things arose from the fact that though the Sensational theology answered to the utilitarian tendencies of the age, it could create none of the emotional and idealistic manifestations which play so large a part in the genesis of the religious sentiment. As early as the first half of the century, Wesley and Whitfield had given the signal of a re-action by bringing into prominence the mystical aspects of Christianity and by specially insisting upon the greatness of the sacrifice accomplished by Jesus. Still, their religious method, which substituted the living and concrete figure of the traditional Christ for cold metaphysical abstractions, had, from its deficiency in rational elements, but a slight hold upon the educated classes who had formed their convictions in the school of Locke. It was only, indeed, at the beginning of the nineteenth century, when Coleridge had attacked Sensationalism with new weapons, that a system better fitted to satisfy the deeper aspirations of the religious consciousness was seen to spring up among liberal theologians.

Coleridge, who was the son of an Anglican clergyman, passed through Unitarianism before taking orders in the Established Church. But he was, above all things, an adept in German idealism, which he had had an opportunity of studying during his residence at the

---

[1]. Thomas Erskine May. *Constitutional History of England.* Vol. III., page 82.

different German Universities in 1799, and which he did not cease to teach and spread in England for more than twenty-five years. The influence of his writings on the succeeding generation was enormous; it can only, indeed, be compared with that of Carlyle, that grand and fantastic genius, who, in turn, has aimed such rude thrusts at the Sensational theology of the preceding century.

The philosophical system of Coleridge rests entirely on the distinction between reason and understanding. Adopting the theory of Kant, that man possesses in reason, thus regarded, a special organ for placing himself in contact with the absolute realities of the moral and spiritual world, he concluded therefrom that God has not limited Himself to entering into relations with mankind by a merely local and temporary revelation, but that He never ceases to speak to us directly by the voice of conscience, which is the interpreter of pure reason. Not that Coleridge called in question the Biblical revelation, but it was the conformity of this revelation with the absolute laws of religion and morality, which seemed to him the best proof of its authenticity.

The consequences of this doctrine will be readily seen. On the one hand, by recognizing in every man a divine element, it allowed the fundamental dogma of the Incarnation to be no longer regarded as a local and unique occurrence, and one very difficult of reconciliation with the most characteristic attributes of the Divine Nature, but as a symbol of permanent and universal communion between God and humanity. On the other hand, it brought back the attention of the churches from the previously absorbing thought of a future life to a consideration of the best means for improving the present world. And, further, by regarding miracles as a possible consequence rather than as a necessary proof of divine activity, it tended to make reason, and not Scripture, the supreme standard of truth. The historical details of the Biblical tradition thus fell back into secondary importance; so much so, that even the verification of defects and errors in the compilation of the sacred books could not henceforth weaken the great moral and religious truths of Christianity.

During the ages of religious fervour, it was to Scripture that an appeal was made for the solution of all scientific problems. The most striking instance of this naïve faith is, perhaps, the celebrated treatise, written in the sixth century, by the monk, Cosmas, in order to prove, among other applications of the Bible to geography, that the earth could only be a parallelogram having a length equal to twice its breadth, for this irrefragable reason that such was the form of the Mosaic Tabernacle, and that St. Paul speaks somewhere of the earth as a tabernacle. Gradually, however, the rights of science were timidly advanced, in cases where it neither directly nor indirectly conflicted with theology. At a later period, an absolute independence was supposed to be simultaneously conceded to the two rivals; not, indeed, by giving to each of them a separate sphere, but by attributing to them, respectively, the supremacy according as a question was regarded from a scientific or a religious point of view. The same individual, for instance, might admit, as a scientist, that the earth revolved round the sun; as a religious man, that the sun turned round the earth. The disciples of Descartes, again, had a right to maintain, as philosophers, that the mechanism of the universe is to be explained by exclusively physical causes, and as Christians, that they did not believe anything of the kind. Still such contradictions, however unconsciously they may occur, are too clear a violation of the unity of the human mind not to prove detrimental to orthodoxy, as soon as the progress of knowledge begins to converge towards the negation of the supernatural.

Now, since the first blow which Capernicus gave to the cosmogony of the Bible, there has never ceased to be a growing antagonism between the affirmations of science and the letter of Revelation. The earth, which the Scriptures had made the centre of creation and the place where God had thought it right to offer himself up as a sacrifice for the redemption of humanity, saw itself suddenly relegated, by the marvellous generalizations of the Newtons and Laplaces, to the rank of a secondary satellite,—a grain of cosmic dust lost in the immensity of the universe. Then came the science of Geology, which, in the hands of the Playfairs and the Lyells, not only overthrew the received interpretation of Gensis, but at the same time destroyed the central doctrine of Calvinism, by carrying back the ravages of suffering and death far beyond the first sin of the first man. Concurrently with these changes, parallel discoveries took place in all branches of positive knowledge, which led to an indefinite extension in the action of the general and permanent laws of nature, and reduced to this extent the sphere given up to accidental rule and, consequently, to miraculous agencies. Even in the question of religion itself, for instance, there is not a system of belief whose formation, growth, decay, and disappearance has not been explained as due to natural causes by a new science, which has thus given to all forms of faith a place in the intellectual and moral development of humanity, and, as a matter of course, has reduced historical Christianity to a mere stage or passing form of our religious evolution.

Such is the undoubted conclusion to which impartial researches in Biblical criticism have led. Locke thought he had found in exegesis the best support for a belief in the supernatural origin of Christianity. The Tübingen school began the demolition of this castle in the air, and it may be confidently affirmed that there is hardly a stone of it left standing. Not only have the miracles and prophecy lost all credence from a historical point of view, but, further, the authenticity of the Gospels has shared the fate of the tradition which attributes the Pentateuch to Moses. And just as it has become a settled conviction that the introduction of Monotheism among the Hebrews was of late occurrence, so critics have succeeded in discovering, in the most venerable documents of the primitive church, traces of the Greek and Oriental elements which entered into the formation of Christianity. Thus, while Revelation found itself in antagonism with the increasing progress of the Natural Sciences, it saw itself deprived of the testimony of history, which remained, to a certain extent, its last citadel.

Once introduced into England, this double current, which is, at the same time, critical and affirmative, could not fail to exercise a profound influence upon the philosophical and religious ideas of the most enlightened minds. Even Protestant theology could not escape its action. "The tendencies of scientific and of historical research being thus in the same direction," says Dr. Martineau, one of the most distinguished and impartial writers upon religious subjects in England,[1] "and meeting with no adequate counteraction from conservative resistance, a general disposition is manifested among churches open to theologic change, no longer to lay stress on the miraculous

---

1. The Introduction to the 2nd Edition of J. J. Tayler's *Retrospect of the Religious Life of England*, page 36.

elements of early Christian tradition, to regard them as rather weakening than strengthening the authority of the narrative, and to frame a conception of the origin of Christianity which shall not be dependent on their abjective reality. . . . Even, however, among the conservative theologians a significant silence respecting the 'signs and wonders' on which they (the stories of the bodily resurrection and ascension of Christ) rest indicates that the old emphatic appeal to them is known to be out of keeping with the feeling of the time, and can no longer be hopefully urged." For a long time past, the theologians who are still faithful to the old beliefs have sought to avoid embarrassment by the hypothesis that miracles do not necessarily imply the violation of natural laws: that they may simply be the result of a higher law hitherto undiscovered by the investigations of science. This is what Mr. Lecky calls meeting the Rationalists half way.[1]

These compromises, however, of which Coleridge had set the example, could not arrest the progress of those who, like Carlyle, desired to apply the method of Rationalism with rigorous logical consistency. As early as the second third of this century, German idealism produced in England a school which openly rejected Revelation in favour of the principle of pure Theism. Between the Deists of the eighteenth century and the Theists of the nineteenth there is this great difference, however, that while the first formulated a mechanical conception of the universe, and made of God a Being external to creation, the second make the principle of divine immanence in the universe the basis of religion, and consequently regard reason and conscience as alike organs of the divine in man.

The principal representatives of these doctrines in England to-day are Professor F. W. Newman and Miss F. Power Cobbe. "Their pure Theism," says Dr. Martineau,[2] "is so noble a product of the most capable thought and truest inward experience that, if it only were an historic instead of a private gift, and could come to men as inspiration instead of reason, it would regenerate the world."

Professor Newman's work, *The Soul: its Sorrows and Aspirations*, although published thirty years ago, has remained the standard exposition of the methods and doctrines which characterise English Theism.

---

1. Lecky. *History of Rationalism in Europe*. Vol. II., page 178.
2. Introduction to the 2nd Edition of the Rev. J. J. Tayler's work, page 38.

As to Miss Cobbe, who has equally given herself up to the claims of subjective idealism, she has known how to unite a power of philosophical reasoning, rare enough in her sex, with a liveliness of imagination and a warmth of sentiment which give to her style a special and peculiar charm.

This school, which owes its origin to Kant, through the intermediate agency of Coleridge and Carlyle, remains to-day as young and vigorous as ever. Based upon pure reason, freed from all compromise with revealed theology, and accepting a metaphysical system which is sufficiently in harmony with the positive sciences to follow the current of their discoveries without inconsistency, and even sometimes to draw new arguments from them, it tends more and more to take the lead in resisting the encroachments of those recently propounded doctrines which are shaking the foundation of natural religion and even attacking the principles hitherto regarded as the basis of philosophy and of morals. To say the least, it possesses the great merit of having been the first to demonstrate, by the mere fact of its existence, the possibility of reconciling the religious sentiment, and even a certain degree of mysticism, with the unlimited exercise of free inquiry.

The emancipation thus gradually secured in the domain of opinion could not fail to produce a corresponding effect in the laws of the land. From the earliest period of the Reformation, men of generous sentiments had raised their voices in favour of the largest religious toleration. But freedom of religious opinion was a conception too much in opposition to the received ideas of the age for it to have the least chance of making itself heard by the Government and, above all, by the people themselves. Among the various Protestant nations, England is perhaps the one in which this liberty was first practically enjoyed, but it is also that in which the principle has been slowest to secure recognition as a question of legal right—an inevitable result of that condition of things in which the subjection of the Church to the State makes of all heresy, according to the theory of Hobbes, an act of insubordination to the institutions of the country.

It is hardly two centuries ago since the statute, *De haeretico comburendo*, was abrogated. At the Restoration, all meetings of more than five persons for the purpose of worship, except at the Parish

Church, were prohibited under pain of imprisonment and transportation. No Nonconformist minister could approach a town or municipal borough within a radius of five miles; no Dissenter could teach even in a private school. The crime of heresy grew blacker in proportion as the heretic deviated from the official type in the matter of doctrine and worship. The profession of Unitarianism was regarded as blasphemy; a Roman Catholic could neither acquire nor inherit property without abjuring his faith. Towards the end of the Restoration period fifteen hundred Quakers perished in prison. The forms and ceremonies of the State, as a civil institution, were identified with the sacraments of the Established Church. No citizen could hold any public office if he had not taken the communion during the year, and, to avoid deception in this matter, a law was passed for punishing Dissenters who might present themselves at the communion service of an Anglican Church.[1]

A relaxation of these rigours commenced at the Revolution of 1688, when Anglicans and Dissenters joined hand in hand to overthrow the throne of the Stuarts. Still it was only at about the end of last century that England resolutely entered upon the course of toleration. To-day, as Lord Coleridge recently stated, the acquittal of Mr. Bradlaugh, who had been prosecuted on the charge of blasphemy for his attacks upon Christianity,[2] has made it clear that the Christian religion has ceased to be identical with the laws of the country.

All denominations have now secured the legal right to existence, as well as to the possession of their churches, schools, and the like, as ordinary property, while they are perfectly free to spread their views by teaching and preaching. No one can be compelled to take part in

---

1. Thomas Erskine May. *The Constitutional History of England.* Vol. III., page 76.

2. Messrs. Foote, Ramsey, and Kemp have been less fortunate in an analogous case. But it appears that the caricatures published in the *Freethinker* were possessed of a bearing which distinguishes them completely from the attacks made upon Christianity by Mr. Bradlaugh. Thus Mr. Bradlaugh and Mrs. Besant both stated, in the course of the trial, that they had ceased to take part in the propagandism of the *Freethinker* from November, 1881, in consequence of the coarse nature of its drawings (v. *Inquirer* of the 28th of April, 1883). Still it may be objected that if Messrs. Foote, Ramsey, and Kemp were really guilty of a breach of public morals, they should have been prosecuted by an appeal to the Acts which punish such an offence, and not by calling into play superannuated Statutes, which misleads the public mind with regard to the nature of the offence, and also as to the motives which ensured its condemnation.

any form of religious worship or even to assist in its maintenance. The Universities have been prohibited, except as regards degrees confirmed by the theological faculty, from making attendance at their lectures or the sitting for degrees, dependent upon any kind of theological opinions. All distinctively denominational teaching has been excluded from the Board or rate-supported schools; and voluntary schools, subject to State inspection, can no longer obtain grants except when their religious teaching is made optional by the use of the "conscience clause," and given beyond the hours of ordinary school work. The State, in its civil capacity, has provided for the registration of births and marriages apart from the intervention of the parish clergyman, and even without any religious service whatever. The Burials' question, which is complicated by the claims of ecclesiastical property, received a partial solution in the Bill of 1879, which conceded to Dissenters the right of burial in the parish church-yards by their own ministers; and everything leads to the belief that, before long, the matter will be definitively settled by the removal of all distinction between the consecrated and the un-consecrated portions of the cemeteries. And, finally, not only is the form of a man's religious belief no longer permitted to influence his rights as a citizen, but, further, with the exception that Atheists are still excluded from Parliament, all civil and military posts are tenable, irrespective of whether those who hold them profess any religious opinions or not.

Those reforms—which the Declaration of the Rights of Man, and other modern Constitutions of the same type, have sketched out with a clear and general import in a few lines—represent in England the difficult and complex labour of several generations. There is not one of these measures which before becoming law, was not successively rejected in several parliamentary sessions, if not in several Parliaments, by insensibly decreasing majorities. There is not one of them which was not introduced as a partial measure, applicable first to one sect and then to another, till at last by a continued extension it assumed the character of a general principle.

This characteristic method of English legislation is specially illustrated in the question of the Parliamentary Oath. In France, in Belgium, and indeed in the majority of constitutional states, the invocation of the divinity, as yet retained or but partly suppressed in judicial affairs, has long since disappeared from the political oath.

The English, on the other hand, have, for practical purposes, readily conceded to witnesses in the courts of justice, the right to pledge themselves to truth by the oath of their choice, or even to confine themselves simply to a solemn affirmation. As regards the Parliamentary Oath, however, they have only consented to widen the terms of the formula by small extensions, made after long periods of resistance and under the continued pressure of public opinion.

Thus, for instance, the proposal to abolish the Test Act, which rigidly excluded every Dissenter from the Legislature by imposing upon him an oath involving adhesion to the Established Church, was first made in Parliament during the session of 1787. It was not till 1828, however, that the measure was passed for the relief of Protestant Nonconformists; and not till the following year for the Roman Catholics. Henceforth Parliament was accessible to any one who was willing to swear allegiance to the Crown on the true faith of a Christian. In 1833, the election of Mr. Pease led to the right being granted to the Quakers, and the Moravian Brethren with other separatists, to substitute a simple affirmation for the oath, which is what English Liberals claim to-day on behalf of those who cannot conscientiously make a direct or indirect appeal to the Deity. As early as 1830 a special form of the Oath was demanded on behalf of the Jews; it was not obtained, however, till 1858, after Parliament had several times annulled the election of Mr. Lionel de Rothschild, who was each time re-elected by the city of London. The "true faith of a Christian" did not survive this new breach, and a readjustment of the general formula, which was adopted in 1866, extended its application to all Theists, whatever their special opinions respecting the Supreme Being.

The reader will remember the conditions under which the question has been raised afresh by the return of Mr. Bradlaugh to Parliament. Personal objections to the junior member for Northampton, have doubtless had much influence in the rejection of the Bill which proposed to substitute a simple declaration of allegiance for the existing Oath. But when we call to mind the precedents of Parliamentary history, and when at the same time we reflect upon the insignificant majority which threw out Mr. Gladstone's Affirmation Bill, we may safely predict that many sessions of Parliament will not pass before this last barrier to liberty of conscience has been removed from the Legislature of England.

CHAPTER II.

THE PHILOSOPHY OF EVOLUTION AND THE CRISIS OF THEISM.

What is at stake in the conflict between religion and science—The idea of development in contemporary philosophy—Increasing generality of the laws which explain the different groups of phenomena—Darwin and his Theory of the origin of species—Stuart Mill and the relativity of human knowledge—The union of this doctrine with evolution—Herbert Spencer's postulate: the Persistence of Force—Extension of the evolution hypothesis to all orders of phenomena—The affirmation of the Unknowable as an absolute and unconditioned Reality—The relation of this doctrine to the religious sentiment—Mr. Gladstone's humorous remark—The theory of evolution in antagonism with Christian orthodoxy—Huxley's *Lay Sermons*—Tyndall's Belfast address—Rapid progress of evolution—The Agnostics—The religion of the future, according to the author of *Ecce Homo*—Scientific attempts to reconcile the essential principles of Theism with the doctrine of evolution—Dr. Carpenter's theory referring force to volition—Mr. W. Graham and finality in evolution—The opinions of Matthew Arnold and Balfour Stuart—Distinction between the scientific theory of evolution and its philosophical application—The metaphysical systems which, according to Mr. J. Sully, may be legitimately grafted upon the theory of evolution—Theological attempts to maintain the principles of Theism with the sacrifice of the First Cause—Dr. Martineau's thesis—Religious opinions in the different strata of English society.

Up to the present, we have seen the attacks of reason merely directed against the intervention of the supernatural, whilst the verdict of philosophy and history in condemning the pretensions of Revealed Religion, has had no other result than the confirmation of Natural Religion. But at about the middle of this century a current of ideas was set in motion, which threatens to sweep away the very foundations of Theism. No one can close his eyes to the evidence of this crisis, which relates to questions incomparably more important for the moral and religious future of society, than the authenticity of the prophecies, and the credibility of the miracles, the direct or the indirect inspiration of the Scriptures, the possibility of the Incarnation, and the necessity for Redemption. What is now at stake is the personality, the wisdom, the goodness, and the power of God; the reality of a First and a Final Cause, the immortality and, indeed, the very existence of the soul, the freedom of the will and the idea of duty.

These beliefs have doubtless long been proof against all attacks: the Materialism of Hobbes, the Sensationalism of Condillac, the Scepticism of Hume, and the Atheism of Feuerbach have in turn blunted their arms in assaults upon them. But now it is a question of a combatant incomparably more redoubtable, inasmuch indeed as this new enemy presents himself exclusively in the guise of scientific armour. I am speaking here of the philosophy of evolution.

Thus, as M. Taine remarks with regard to Carlyle, in his fine work on English Literature, we are living in a current of ideas, which having its source in Germany, impregnates to-day the philosophy, the literature and the science of the whole western civilization. This is the tendency to introduce into everything the principle of development, of *entwickelung*, or according to the definition of the eminent French critic—of the mutual dependence which connects the terms of a series of events, and binds them all to some abstract property, conceived of as common to the whole series.[1]

Exclusively philosophic at the commencement with Leibnitz, Kant, Fichte, and Hegel, this doctrine has received from the experimental method the most striking confirmation which it has ever been the lot of any speculative system to obtain. All the scientific discoveries made within the last fifty years—and these are sufficiently astonishing to justify the enthusiasm, if not the infatuation, of our age with regard to what comes under the head of the positive sciences—have never ceased to converge towards a synthesis which explains all the phenomena of nature by inherent causes, and refers them to a few laws that are becoming more and more general.

Astronomy, for instance, has long since taught us, by its nebular hypothesis, that the heavenly bodies must have been formed from primitive cosmic matter by the simple effect of an initial impulse, and without the ulterior intervention of any external agent whatever. To the law of gravitation, which thus suffices to explain the development of our solar system, the physical sciences have added the no less fruitful hypothesis of the persistence of force, or rather of the conservation of energy.[2] Chemistry has established the identity of the

---

1. H. Taine, *Histoire de la Littérature Anglaise*. t. iv., p. 283.

2. Mr. Herbert Spencer does not appear to allow that there is any real difference between "force" and "energy," as many scientists suppose, though, as he says, "To our perceptions this second kind of force differs from the first kind as being

inorganic elements that enter into the composition, not only of all bodies belonging to this planet, but also of all those with which the space-traversing power of the spectroscope makes us acquainted; while, at the same time, it has enabled us to foresee the possibility of reducing these elements themselves to a single substance. Morphology has shown the prevalence of unity of structure among all living beings, from the cell in a free condition up to the most complicated organism in the scale of life, progress being measured, to a certain extent, by diversity and complication of organic function. Biology, moreover, has compared the physiological changes which take place in the nerve-centres of all the creatures possessed of a brain, either for the translation of thought into action or in its production by external agency.

Natural history, again, after having destroyed the artificial barriers raised between the various species, has revealed, at least among the superior animals, the germ or outline of faculties hitherto thought to be the exclusive monopoly of the human race; whilst, on the other hand, Anthropology has traced the origin of civilization from a state of barbarism bordering on animality. And, just as Embryology has shown us the gradual passage of the human embryo through the whole hierarchy of inferior organic forms, so Palæontology has discovered an analogous gradation in the fauna and flora of the different ages of the earth. Finally, Geology, by attributing to our globe a past which is to be measured by incalculable myriads of ages, has supplied to the believers in the continuity of the development of the world the material necessary for the formation of systems, such that the astonishing multiplicity of the effects produced therein might not be out of keeping with the unity of the cause and of the process giving rise to them.

It was Mr. Darwin who first drew from these discoveries a scientific confirmation of the hypothesis, already formulated by Lamarck and Goethe, and then resumed in England by Chambers in his *Vestiges of Creation*, of the unity of origin among living beings. In 1858, Darwin brought before the Linnean Society of London, simultaneously with Mr. Wallace, the theory of natural selection, which attributes the variation of species to the action of these two general laws: the universality of the struggle for life assuring the survival of the fittest

not intrinsic, but extrinsic." He also prefers the word "Persistence" to "Conservation." (*First Principles*, p. 190.)—*Translator.*

(that is those best adapted to the conditions of their environment), and heredity or the power which all living creatures possess of transmitting their individual characteristics by means of generation. During the following year he published his celebrated work on the origin of species, in which he places humanity itself within the scope of the development theory, in opposition to the views of Mr. Wallace, who contended that it was impossible to explain, on the principle of natural selection, the existence of certain faculties proper to the human mind, such as the power of generalization and abstraction.

The funeral honours in which the Anglican clergy took part when Mr. Darwin's remains were interred in Westminster Abbey, prove the toleration of the Broad Church party, but not the orthodoxy of the illustrious scientist. In reality, as long as the history of the earth did not condemn the hypothesis of sudden and distinct creations, the adherents of the Biblical tradition were able to reconcile to a greater or less extent, by dint of laboured ingenuity, the narrative of Genesis with the revelations of Palæontology. But the theory which derived all living nature, man included, from one or at least a few rudimentary organisms, by a sort of continuous development, and under the influence of inherent causes, is absolutely irreconcilable with the hypothesis of a creation in several acts, or even with a miraculous intervention in the progress of life on the globe. Darwin, however, made no allusion to this aspect of the question.[1]

Still in showing the chain of natural phenomena, by which organic matter has successively assumed the richest and most varied forms of life, Darwin did not reach the origin of life itself, and still less the origin of the world. The alternative he laid down was not between creation and evolution, but between organic creation by means of evolution and that same creation regarded as due to the successive intervention of an external Power. Hence he did not hesitate to declare that his doctrine, so far from excluding the existence of a First Cause, furnished a more rational and a more elevated conception of such a cause, from the mere fact that in place of a capricious, arbitrary, or powerless God, compelled to return to his work several times in order to bring it to perfection, it substituted a Supreme Being, who, from

---

[1]. See his letter to a German student, which was published in the *Academy* of November 4th, 1882. "As far as I am concerned," he says, "I do not believe that any Revelation has been made."

the first, gave to his creative work the forces and laws required to ensure its regular and progressive development.[1] In a not dissimilar manner, the new doctrine confined itself to displacing the old conception of a final cause and to presenting that idea under conditions incomparably grander than the teleological combinations of Paley and his followers. It doubtless became henceforth inadmissible to seek finality in the separate processes of nature; but nothing had occurred to prevent its being ascribed to the general end towards which the world might be regarded as advancing by its own inherent forces, or, indeed, of placing it in the law governing the evolution. In short, Darwin refrained from seeking the relation between mind and matter, and confined himself to establishing the truth that special physical modifications correspond to certain modifications of the intellectual faculties.

The Sensational Psychology, again, having been revived by the Positivist method, led to analogous conclusions in the works of Mr. J. S. Mill. "The Positive mode of thought," said the author of *Auguste Comte et le Positivisme*, "is not necessarily a denial of the supernatural: it merely throws back that question to the origin of all things. . . . Positive Philosophy maintains that within the existing order of the universe, or rather of the part of it known to us, the direct determining cause of every phenomenon is not supernatural, but natural. It is compatible with this to believe that the universe was created, and even that it is continuously governed, by an Intelligence, provided we admit that intelligent Governor adheres to fixed laws."[2]

In the philosophical system of Mr. Herbert Spencer, we arrive at the point of convergence between the current of scientific ideas which I have just analysed, and the Positivist psychology of Stuart Mill. It is from the former that that philosopher borrowed the materials with which he has constructed his synthesis of the universe; from the latter that he obtained his categories of the Knowable, which comprehend all phenomena and their relations, and of the Unknowable,

---

1. *Origin of Species*, 6th Ed., p. 269.

2. *Auguste Comte and Positivism.* London, 1865. In his three *Posthumous Essays on Religion*, Stuart Mill is still more affirmative. For instance, on page 174 he says, "There is a large balance in favour of the probability of creation by intelligence."

which applies to *Noumena*, to the Absolute, to being in itself, to the inner or essential nature of force, matter, and motion, of time and space, and even of consciousness itself. Nor does he stop here; for, while on the one hand he extends Darwin's hypothesis to the totality of phenomena, in order to explain the development of organic nature, on the other he suppresses the necessity of a First Cause by suppressing all limit of time to the action of the forces manifested in the universe. The importance this doctrine has acquired renders it necessary that I should pause to consider it at some length.

In common with Mill and Hamilton, Spencer shows that the human mind is powerless to free itself from the limitations of time and space, and that consequently it can know nothing either of substance or of a First Cause. And though a real correlation must doubtless be admitted between the objects of thought and the conceptions we form of them, still this agreement can never furnish us with more than symbols of the reality: that is to say, images which represent in an imperfect manner the things for which they stand. It is, therefore, within the phenomenal and the relative that a scientific explanation of the universe is to be sought.[1]

Now, some ultimate principle is necessary upon which to hang the whole chain of scientific reasoning. This starting point, at once logical and scientific, is found in the *persistence of force*, with its corollaries that matter is indestructible and motion continuous. Setting out from this principle, Spencer reaches the conclusion that all the material elements of our universe must have existed at some period or other in the form of attenuated matter: that is, in an incoherent, indeterminate, and homogeneous state. In virtue of the action and re-action which the atoms of this matter exerted upon each other, they at last began to move around certain centres of gravity, in the form of nebulæ possessed of a gyratory motion. But this was only the first stage in the evolutionary process. The three laws which Spencer deduces from the persistence of force—the instability of the homogeneous, the multiplication of effects, and segregation or the law of co-ordination—permit him to define the entire process of evolution as "An integration of matter and concomitant dissipation of motion,

---

[1] Mr. Spencer's *First Principles* appeared in 1862. It may be stated that all his earlier productions were but preliminary to this volume, just as his subsequent works form its systematic development.

during which the matter passes from an indefinite, incoherent homogeneity to a definite, coherent heterogeneity, and during which the retained motion undergoes a parallel transformation."[1]

Evolution, however, reaches a fatal term in equilibrium or the condition of equality between the forces which act upon the aggregate from without and the force which this opposes to them. On the other hand, no equilibrium can be definitive, since every aggregate is exposed to the action of external forces in a universe of ceaseless activity, and one in which all the motion given off by compounds in the process of evolution must be absorbed by neighbouring bodies and exercise upon them a disintegrating action. Every part of the universe must, therefore, pass through a period of integration, and then one of disintegration, analogous to the alternate phases of creation and dissolution which fill eternity, in the Brahminic Pantheism, and are dependent upon the waking and sleeping states of Brahma. "Apparently," says Spencer,[2] "the universally co-existent forces of attraction and repulsion . . . produce now an immeasurable period, during which the attractive forces predominating cause universal concentration, and then an immeasurable period, during which the repulsive forces predominating cause universal diffusion—alternate eras of evolution and dissolution."

This eternal rhythm is not, however, restricted to cosmical phenomena; it measures the existence of ephemeral things as well as the duration of a nebula. The only difference in the two cases consists in the length of the cycle, which is proportionate to the aggregates it comprises. Spencer seeks to demonstrate how this double process of evolution and dissolution suffices to explain, not only the production of inorganic phenomena, but also the hierarchy of organic beings: the appearance of the cell; the variation of species; the transition from vegetable to conscious, rational and moral life; the formation of society; the vicissitudes of history; and finally all the results of social and intellectual activity. The fluctuations of the Exchange are thus subject to the same law as the passage of a comet; while the victories of Alexander and the works of Shakespeare are reducible to the same factors as the Falls of Niagara and the spots on the sun. Human society, by dint of modification and specialization, will thus attain to a

---

1. *First Principles.* 4th Edition, page 396.
2. *First Principles,* p. 537.

state of equilibrium which will be "the establishment of the greatest perfection and the most complete happiness."[1] This Millenium, however, will be only one of the last steps towards universal dissolution. The last term of evolution is immobility or equilibrium; then comes dissolution—the doom of the species as well as the individual, and indeed of all which is only a compound of matter and motion : *Pulvis es, in pulverem reverteris !*

Still it would not be correct to conclude from this that Spencer sees in mere matter and motion the last word of philosophy. On the contrary, he rejects Materialism with perhaps even greater emphasis than Spiritualism. It would be easier, he says, to transform what we call matter into what is regarded as spirit than to carry out the opposite process, which is absolutely impossible. But no interpretation can enable us to advance beyond our symbols. In his opinion, indeed, matter and motion, to which he reduces all things, are only manifestations of the force which reveals itself in consciousness, and this force itself is only to be regarded as "a certain effect of the Unconditioned Cause, as the relative reality indicating to us an Absolute Reality, by which it is immediately produced."[2]

This Unconditioned and Absolute Reality, whose existence Spencer demonstrates by the same argument which serves to establish the relatitivity of our knowledge, thus becomes the ultimate goal at which all science ends. "Though the Absolute cannot in any manner be known, in the strict sense of knowing, yet we find that its positive existence is a necessary datum of consciousness; that so long as consciousness continues, we cannot for an instance rid it of this datum; and that thus the belief which this datum constitutes has a higher warrant than any other whatever."[3]

Now it turns out, according to our philosopher, that the fundamental idea of religion equally consists in the affirmation of this Absolute and incomprehensible Power, which is without limits in either time or space, and of which the Universe is but the manifestation:—"Not only is the omnipresence of something which passes comprehension, that m st abstract belief which is common to all religions, which becomes the more distinct in proportion as they develop, and which remains after

---

1. *First Principles*, p. 517.
2. *First Principles*, p. 170.
3. *First Principles*, p. 98.

their discordant elements have been mutually cancelled; but it is that belief which the most unsparing criticism of each leaves unquestionable —or rather makes ever clearer."[1] It is therefore "in this deepest, widest, and most certain of all facts," that the ultimate reconciliation of science and religion may and should be found. So long as religion is content to remain within the sphere of the Unknowable, Spencer sees in it the expression of a "supreme verity," and he believes that in the future, as in the past, it will prevent men "from being wholly absorbed in the relative or immediate."[2]

He goes so far, indeed, as to admit that whilst purifying themselves more and more through the influence of science, the symbolic conceptions of the Absolute will continue indefinitely to occupy the human consciousness and inspire religion,—"very likely there will ever remain a need to give shape to that indefinite sense of an Ultimate Existence, which forms the basis of our intelligence."[3] It will simply have to be remembered that every notion thus framed is "merely a symbol, utterly without resemblance to that for which it stands."[3]

Now, although Spencer explicitly rejects Pantheism equally with Theism and Atheism, his "indeterminate" conception of an "Absolute Reality," such that all the phenomena of nature are but its manifestation or veil, ends none the less, however little we may translate it into metaphysical terms, in a Pantheistic conception of the universe. It is true he drops the name of God and substitutes for it the term Unknowable, which affords him the double advantage of not being compromised by metaphysical associations and of constantly reminding him of the incomprehensible character of the Supreme Reality. But in rigidly refusing to define this Unknowable he treats it as *Being* and as *Power*; he ascribes to it immanence, unity, omnipresence, and unlimited persistence in time and space; he assigns to it the laws of

---

1. *First Principles*, p. 45.
2. *First Principles*, p. 100.
3. *First Principles*, p. 113. These concessions are unpalatable to a number of Continental Evolutionists, who have condemned them as the result of the influence unconsciously exercised upon Mr. Spencer's mind by his Protestant surroundings. Without staying to discuss the force of this argument, we may state that it would be easy to turn it against these critics themselves, by remarking that the reason why they abjure the religious sentiment with so much bitterness, even within its own province, is because they are influenced by a re-action from the prejudices which prevail in their Catholic surrounding, or which they may have long retained from early education.

nature as modes of action; and, finally, with respect to both external and internal phenomena, he regards it as sustaining the relation of substance to manifestation, and even of cause to effect. If, therefore, Spencer deviates from pure and simple Pantheism, it is merely in so far as this confounds God with the universe, while our philosopher sees in the Unknowable not only the substance of the world and the immanent cause of all its phenomena, but, over and above this, a transcendent Power which surpasses all definition.

In this respect, indeed, he is more of a Theist than of a Pantheist even, and it need be no matter of astonishment that certain of his disciples have based upon his doctrine a genuine development of mysticism. Speaking of the religious bearing of his philosophy, he says: "In the estimate it implies of the Ultimate Cause, it does not fall short of the alternative position, but exceeds it. Those who espouse this alternative position, make the erroneous assumption that the choice is between personality and something lower than personality; whereas the choice is rather between personality and something higher. Is it not just possible that there is a mode of being as much transcending Intelligence and Will, as these transcend mechanical motion? It is true that we are totally unable to conceive any such higher mode of being. But this is not a reason for questioning its existence; it is rather the reverse. Have we not seen how utterly incompetent our minds are to form even an approach to a conception of that which underlies all phenomena? Is it not proved that this incompetency is the incompetency of the Conditioned to grasp the Unconditioned? Does it not follow that the Ultimate Cause cannot in any respect be conceived by us because it is in every respect greater than can be conceived?"[1]

Still whatever may be the value of these declarations, the sincerity of which no one can doubt, Mr. Spencer's views were too much opposed to the current theological ideas, as regards both natural and Revealed religion, not to raise a violent storm among theologians, while they at the same time led to exaggerated hopes with the enemies of every religious idea. In vain did these views present a new sphere for the religious sentiment by setting forth the mystery of the Unknowable, the greatness of its manifestations, the inflexible action of its

---

1. *First Principles*, p. 109.

laws and the eternal rhythm of the forces revealing its power. They none the less replaced the personal and conscious God of the traditional theology by a Being deaf, blind, and indifferent to human misery, or at least so far removed from man that no direct relation could any longer be conceived to exist between the two terms of the religious equation; and thus there seemed to disappear that sentiment of a direct communication between the soul and its Author, which forms not only the central principle of Protestantism, but also the essential basis of Theism. As Mr. Gladstone once asked in an academical address: does not Mr. Spencer's scheme of reconciliation between religion and science resemble the proposal of a man who wishing to free himself from an intruder, should say, " My house has two sides to it and we will share them—please to take the outside?"

No one certainly can deny that Mr. Spencer's doctrine leaves room for the two great and indispensible factors of all religion: the belief in a mysterious Power and a sense of dependence upon that Power. But if it maintains dependence, does it not suppress obligation; does it not, indeed, destroy the idea of duty, which has become an element henceforth inseparable from the religious sentiment? Besides, what will remain not merely of the soul, if the very personality of the individual be only an ephemeral ebb and flow of psychological states; but even of consciousness itself if this be nothing more than motion transmuted by its environment and by hereditary tendencies?[1]

Mr. Spencer's speculations seem to have been met at first by a conspiracy of silence. In 1864, an able writer, M. Aug. Laugel, in giving an analysis of the works of the thinker whom he called "the last of the English metaphysicians," wrote thus in the *Revue des Deux Mondes*:—"In the midst of universal indifference, Mr. Herbert Spencer has remained persistently attached to the study of philosophy.

---

1. It may be stated here that Mr. Spencer, while holding that force existing as motion, light, or heat, is transmutable into modes of consciousness, and that personality, though "a fact beyond all others the most certain, is yet a thing which cannot be truly known at all,"[1] says:—" How can the sceptic who has decomposed his consciousness into impressions and ideas explain the fact that he considers them as his impressions and ideas? Or once more, if, as he must, he admits that he has an impression of his personal existence, what warrant can he show for rejecting this impression as unreal while he accepts all his other impressions as real? Unless he can give satisfactory answers to these queries, which he cannot, he must abandon his conclusions, and must admit the reality of the individual mind."[2]   (1) *First Principles*, p. 65.   (2) *Ibid*, p. 64.—*Translator*.

It has doubtless required from him heroic courage and a rare spirit of independence in order to devote himself to severe studies which can merely secure for him a few isolated followers. With the intellectual power, the fertility of resource, and the almost encyclopædic variety of knowledge with which his works abound, Mr. Spencer, if he had consented to walk in the beaten track, would have certainly obtained all those marks of public favour which English society delights to shower upon those who serve it as it wishes to be served. He has chosen, however, to condemn himself to poverty, and, what is still harder to bear, obscurity."[1]

There was never, perhaps, a prediction more fully based upon probabilities, never one more completely belied by events. Mr. Spencer's doctrine was not of a kind that could long remain hidden under a bushel, and whatever fears it might inspire in its adversaries, they were compelled to take account of it. Its early experiences were stormy. The controversy reached its height in 1874, when Professor Huxley published his *Lay Sermons*, in which he strongly contended for the rights of reason, and when Dr. Tyndall delivered his celebrated Belfast address as President of the British Association. The latter, while fully recognizing with Mr. Spencer the independence of the religious sentiment in the sphere of the Unknowable, advanced a claim for the ancient doctrine of atoms, and denied the right of theologians to explain the origin of the universe. This was more than enough to call down all the thunders of English orthodoxy upon the head of the speaker, and there were fanatics who went so far as to threaten him with the old and unrepealed statutes against the detractors of the Divinity. Writing the following year, he said he had often been compelled to remark with sadness that the way in which men are influenced by what they call their religion, forms a striking display of that corrupt nature which they assert religion is specially intended to modify or restrain.

The very violence of these attacks could but favour the spread of the doctrine they were intended to stifle. It is very interesting to follow the course of the controversy in the Reviews of the day. For several years the conflict raged. Mr. Spencer himself took part in it by means of numerous articles, while at the same time he continued

---

1. Aug. Laugel, Les etudes philosophiques en Angleterre (*Revue des Deux Mondes*, of the 15th February, 1864).

the publication of his works. To-day a great calm prevails on the subject, at least in the upper regions of English thought. Not only has the doctrine of evolution obtained a place in the sunshine of British respectability, but it is tending more and more, under one form or another, to permeate the philosophy and even the religion of the country.

Above and beyond its immediate disciples, it has secured a large measure of support in two groups which are daily becoming more numerous in the world of letters: practical men who look upon the time devoted to metaphysical or religious question as so much loss to the service of humanity, and the indifferent, who, without attacking any form of religion, are none the less desirous of being as little occupied with it as possible, and who are happy to meet with a philosophy which justifies their indifference. It was in relation to the attitude of these two classes that the word *Agnosticism* was invented some fifteen years ago, which, as its etymology shows, stands for the absence of knowledge. And this Agnostic or know-nothing way of treating religious questions has even become the fashion in certain sections of society, and many a one, who would be embarrassed to explain why he does so, calls himself an Agnostic to-day just as he might have called himself a "Freethinker" two centuries ago, or a Puseyite a generation or two since.

This state of things, which, however little it may extend itself, would seem destined to lead the more educated classes to a new interregnum of positive faith, induced Professor Seeley, one of the most distinguished members of the University of Cambridge, to publish a work in 1882 in which he attempted to describe the bearing and influence of the religious sentiment among his fellow-countrymen. According to this work, which produced a considerable sensation,[1] if we take the three elements severally able to furnish a religious ideal: the love of the true, or Science, the perception of the beautiful, or Art, the idea of duty, or Morals, it is only the third which finds satisfaction in Christianity to-day. Science—that is to say the religion of the Absolute, or of Law, which even when it proclaims itself Atheistical admits the existence of a God whom it names the Unknowable, the Cosmos, or the Universal Order—has ceased, in effect, to concede to

---

1. *Natural Religion*, by the author of *Ecce Homo*. London: Macmillan & Co. 1882.

that mysterious Reality the attributes of personality, foreknowledge, goodness and justice, or to lend it an existence distinct from the world, and recognise in it the nature of a First Cause. In the same way Art, that is the religion of Nature, revolts more and more against Christianity whose moral rigidity and æsthetic indifference it denounces.

A large number of scientists confine themselves to the criticism of the dominant theology, and abstain from making any affirmation as to the future of religion. There are some even who discount the fall of every system of faith.[1] But there also exists an important section who, "while it rejects Christianity, proclaims religion to be the highest of all things, and looks forward to a great renewal of its influence." This party, however, is divided as to the form of religion which is to be substituted for Christianity. Some believe that humanity is destined to become the object of worship; others, again, consider that the hour of Pantheism has struck, and "the time when the supernatural tyrant of the universe must give way to the universe itself." Then, again, there are differences of opinion as to the form this Pantheism will assume, and "often it may be observed that the purer, sweeter worship which is promised to us is pictured as a revival of Greek Paganism."[2]

These aspirations are by no means irreligious. The only real irreligion, and it is to be met with in the Church as well as beyond its pale, is, on the one hand, the presumption characteristic of men too infatuated with their own importance to subordinate their personality to the natural order of things; and, on the other hand, the attitude of those who are too absorbed in the trivialities of life to rise to the conception of principles and laws. Now such is not the case either with science or art, which, in common with Christian morality, condemn this double tendency in the name of their respective ideals. Let these three elements be combined and we shall possess, it is contended, a system of religion that will restore peace and spiritual union to modern society, which is now threatened with anarchy. "The natural religion of which we are in search," says the author, "will in-

---

1. The author of *Natural Religion* remarks (Preface to the 2nd Edition) that "it is not the greatest scientific authorities that are so confident in negation, but rather the inferior men who echo their opinions and who live themselves in the atmosphere, not of science, but of party controversy."

2. *Op. Cit.*, 2nd Edition, p. 73.

clude a religion of humanity as well as a religion of material things. It will retain at least the kernel (of Christianity), if it rejects the shell . . . . But along with this transfigured Christianity, only in a subordinate rank, it will include the higher Paganism, or in other words the purified worship of natural forms." And this is not all. It will preserve the worship of the principle of unity, whether the object of this worship be called Nature or God.

This system, which the author names the religion of culture, in the German sense of the word, will possess its Church and its clergy. This church will consist of the vast communion of those who are inspired by the ideals of the culture and civilization of the age, and its clergy, as educators of the people, will be subject to no restrictions of creed, but merely required to fulfil the moral and intellectual conditions suited to their office. Will the existing churches be able to adapt themselves to this transformation, or will the world be compelled to create some new organism as the vehicle of these new aspirations? There are few signs, except in England and America, of any such power on the part of Christianity. And even in these two nations, if the Church is to become the spiritual citadel of civilization, it must hasten to open its doors to new ideas and to renounce every exclusive dogma.

Professor Seeley asserts[1] that he has placed himself in his work at the standpoint occupied by the extreme school. If, however, we examine the situation from a more general point of view, it is seen that a great number of superior men refuse to admit the impossibility of reconciling the principles of spiritual religion with the doctrine of evolution.

There are some who, like the eminent physiologist, Dr. W. B. Carpenter, himself one of the first to accept, and almost a precursor of evolution, earnestly declare, as the result of their researches, that mind and will form the very basis of evolution.[2]

---

1. Preface to second edition.
2. "Science points to the origination of all power in mind." (*On Mind and Will in Nature*, in the *Contemporary Review*, 1872.) During the same year, Dr. Carpenter closed his Presidential Address at the Brighton meeting of the British Association in the following words: "For while the deep-seated instincts of humanity and the profound researches of philosophy alike point to mind as the one and only source of Power, it is the highest prerogative of science to demonstrate the unity of the Power which is operating through the limitless extent and variety of the universe, and to trace its continuity through the vast series of ages that have been occupied in its evolution."—See also on the subject, Lecky, *History of Rationalism in Europe*, I. Vol., p. 286.

Others again—such as Mr. W. Graham, in his remarkable work, *The Creed of Science* (London, 1881), which is written with the utmost impartiality and displays the highest powers of reasoning—seek to demonstrate that the philosophy of evolution possesses as its logical corollary, not a foreseen and desired aim, but a purpose progressively pursued by the Unknowable Power of Herbert Spencer. Mr. Graham thinks, moreover, that this purpose must be rational, that is to say, in conformity with what we regard as the rational order of things. "Otherwise," says he, "we cannot conceive any explanation of the past course of evolution, save chance, and we can have no guarantee that the future course of development will be controlled otherwise than by chance."

There are those, too, who lay an emphasis on the moral bearing of this purpose, and, in imitation of Matthew Arnold, conceive of the action of the Unknowable as a stream of tendency which makes for the Good and the Beautiful. And, further, there are some like Professors Tait and Balfour Stewart who, returning by means of modern science to the speculations of Neo-Platonism, affirm that it is impossible to admit the principle of continuity in the development of the universe, unless we assume the existence of an invisible universe, of which the visible order of things is in some sort a projection or sensible condensation.[1]

But I must stop here. For if I undertook to enumerate all the attempts which have been made to reconcile the philosophy of evolution with the principles of Theism, I should never finish my task. It will suffice for me to show how, according to the reasoning of an ardent champion of evolution, Mr. J. Sully, the theory in question can be legitimately held in connection with the most diverse metaphysical systems of thought, and even with the old doctrines of Natural Religion. In an article of a very exhaustive kind, which was published in 1878, in the eighth vol. of the *Encyclopædia Britannica*,

---

[1]. The *Unseen Universe*, the book in which the views of Professors Tait and Balfour Stewart are expounded, though treating of matters of an abstract nature and addressing itself exclusively to cultivated minds and indeed to scientists, has passed through a tenth edition in England and has hardly yet ceased to be a subject of controversy. Having been recently translated into French, however, and published by the firm of Germer-Baillière in their "Bibliothèque Philosophique," it has scarcely obtained an honourable mention in the special press of the country. This circumstance is characteristic of the difference in intellectual tendencies which prevails among the two peoples.

by Professor Huxley and Mr. Sully, the latter defined the theory of evolution as "the highest generalization respecting the order of phenomena in time," and, being such and such only, he considers it powerless to furnish a scientific explanation of the cause, purpose, or nature, either of the substance which furnishes the materials evolved, or of the process itself.[1] Thus the Positivist who desires to adhere to the actual data of science may accept evolution, maintaining, in doing so, that the limitations of the human mind will for ever restrict man to the knowledge of phenomena. The empirical idealist, on the other hand, may regard the theory as one that formulates "the order of sensations, actual and possible, of conscious minds."[2] Or, again, evolution is in equal harmony with all those philosophical doctrines "which regard the higher or more complex forms of existence as following and depending on the lower and simple forms, which represent the course of the world as a gradual transition from the indeterminate to the determinate, from the uniform to the varied, and which assume the cause of the process to be immanent in the world that is thus transformed."

It may not be without interest to briefly mention, at this stage of our inquiry, the principal philosophical systems which, according to the learned contributor to the *Encyclopædia*, may be legitimately grafted upon the theory of evolution. This theory, he remarks, attributes objective existence to nothing beyond motion and force. But, at the same time, the law of the conservation of energy attests that, beneath all the variations of phenomena, there is something real that exists as the substance of these manifestations. What is the nature of this reality? Here science gives place to the interpretations of philosophy, which may be classified in the following manner :—

(1) Dualistic solutions. Here evolution progresses simultaneously in the physical and spiritual orders, the coincidence between the

---

1. Professor Huxley wrote the strictly biological and Mr. Sully the general and philosophical part of the article.—*Translator*.

2. It is notorious that for empirical idealism, all the phenomena to which we attribute an objective existence, are only the projection and the reflection of our subjective sensations. Mr. Spencer maintains that if this theory were true evolution would be a dream. Mr. Sully however expressly asserts that the doctrine may be formulated in idealistic as well as in realistic terms. This latter is also the opinion of Professor Huxley, who, in his *Life of Hume*, insists upon the point with still greater emphasis.

two series of phenomena remaining unexplained or being attributed to arbitrary intervention.

(2) Monistic solutions in which mind is looked upon as a property or manifestation of matter (Materialism); where matter is made the outcome of mind (Spiritualism); or in the third place when mind and matter are taken to be the opposite sides of one and the same mysterious reality (Monism proper).

The field of hypotheses becomes still more extended when it is a question of finding the cause of evolution. Here we meet with:

(a) The systems in which a mechanical interpretation predominates —that is to say the theory that all changes are fatally determined by their antecedents (Determinism). This conception is generally connected with materialistic views as to the origin of the universe and the nature of man. It is also found, however, allied with doctrines which explain the development of life and consciousness, either by according to the primordial monads certain elementary psychical properties, or by referring mind and matter to a spiritual substance (mind-stuff) as the ultimate Reality behind the world. The difficulty of regarding matter as the source of conscious life, has equally led to the conception of the primordial substance under a quasi-material form, which, though inaccessible to our senses, has given rise to the material elements by a species of condensation.

(b) The systems in which the teleological conception predominates; in other words, those in which the evolutionary process is supposed to be directed by a tendency towards a rational end, a tendency which is known in the schools by such names as the vital or plastic principle, cosmic force or Nature personified. Following Aristotle, some of these schools of thought admit that the mind is the formative principle of the organism. Others endow the universe with a soul, and speak of nature as its visible body; they thus obtain a spiritual principle as the directive agency in the evolution of the material world. When this principle is looked upon not only as the creative cause, but also as the original source of life and consciousness, we possess in it a form of Pantheism which makes of the world a divine incarnation. "The full development," adds Mr. Sully, "of this way of regarding the world and its evolution, as the work of a spiritual principle aiming towards an end, is to be found in certain doctrines of objective idealism, which resolve all material existence into a mode of mental

existence: will and thought. These theories simplify the conception of evolution to the utmost, by the identification both of the substantial reality which enters into all parts of the world-process, and of the *rationale* of all parts of the process itself. In the systems now referred to, the mechanical idea is wholly taken up into the teleological. Purpose is the highest law of things, and it is one purpose which manifests itself through all stages of the world—evolution in the region of inorganic nature, of organic life, and of human history.

(c) The systems which combine the two preceding categories and which are generally based upon a monistic ontology. They present themselves, either as universalistic conceptions, when they see in evolution a double manifestation of the activity of a single substance (the Divine reason or principle of necessity), or as individualistic conceptions when they attribute this double manifestation to the increasing activity of an indeterminate number of elements endowed with motion and sensibility.

Although the theory of evolution claims to explain, by the action of the senses, the formation in the human mind of such ideas as time and space, it does not condemn the doctrine which attributes these conceptions to a transcendental origin. "It may however be maintained," remarks Mr. Sully, "that the idea is not even suggested by experience; if so, it would follow from the evolution theory that its present persistence represents a permanent mental disposition to think in a particular way. Even then the question would remain open, whether the permanent disposition were an illusory or trustworthy tendency, and in deciding this point the doctrine of evolution appears to offer us no assistance."[1]

We may mention incidentally that Mr. Sully admits the justice of the reproach so often urged against the evolution philosophy, that it preaches a morality destitute of a due sanction:—"Among other results this doctrine may be said to give new form to the determinist theory of volition and to establish the relativity of all moral ideas, as connected with particular stages of moral development. It cannot, as Mr. Sidgwick has shown, provide a standard or end of conduct, except to those who are already disposed to accept the law *sequi naturam* as the ultimate rule of life."

---

[1]. *Encyclopædia Britannica*, 9th Edition, Vol. VIII., p. 772.

It is generally thought that the doctrine of evolution has given a deadly blow to the belief in the existence of a Creator and to the doctrine of the immortality of the soul. Mr. Sully asserts in the following words that nothing of the sort has occurred:—"Mr. Spencer considers the ideas of evolution and of a pre-existing mind, incapable of being united in thought. Yet according to others the idea is by no means incompatible with the notion of an original Creator, though it serves undoubtedly to remove the action of such a Being further from our ken." "At first sight it might appear that the doctrine as applied to the subjective world, by removing the broad distinction between the human and the animal mind, would discourage the hope of a future life for man's soul. Yet it may be found after all, that it leaves the question where it was. It may perhaps be said that it favours the old disposition to attribute immortality to those lower forms of mind, with which the human mind is said to be continuous. Yet there is nothing inconsistent in the supposition that a certain stage of mental development qualifies a mind for immortality, even though this stage has been reached by a very gradual process of development. And if, as it might be shown, the modern doctrine of evolution is susceptible of being translated into terms of Leibnitz's hypothesis of indestructible monads which include all grades of souls, then it is clearly not contradictory of the idea of immortality."[1]

In short, according to Mr. Sully, the theory of evolution is able to to accommodate itself to almost all kinds of philosophical hypotheses as to the origin and essence of the universe, with the exception of those systems of thought which see in the order of the world either an increasing imperfection, as with the Gnostics, or a series of arbitrary creative acts, like those described in the Book of Genesis.

On the other hand, the Theism based upon rational principles has gradually recovered from the effects of the shock which the new philosophy gave it, and we have even seen theologians showing that Theism can do without a First Cause, as well as without supernatural interventions, in the explanation of the universe. "There is no longer hope," writes Dr. Martineau, in the Introduction to the Rev. J. J. Tayler's work on *The Religious Life of England*,[2] "of finding a birth-

---

1. *Op. Cit.*
2. *A Retrospect of the Religious Life of England*, 2nd Edition, p. 32.

day for matter, for laws, for species, for planets, or even for man; and no longer despair of comprehending all known phenomena within the probable range of an admitted natural order. . . . God is conceived, not as 'First Cause' prefixed to the scheme of things, but as Indwelling Cause pervading it; not excluded by Second Causes, but coinciding with them while transcending them—as the One everliving Objective Agency, the modes of which must be classified and interpreted, by science in the outer field, by conscience in the inner. This change of conception is due to the lessened prominence of mechanical ideas and the advance of physiology to a dominant position, substituting the thought of life working from within for that of transitive impulse starting from without. Under this higher form of religious thought, all need entirely ceases of reaching a creative epoch when the divine "Fiat" went forth, and prior to which was an eternal solitude of God: or of finding tasks accomplished which are beyond the resources of the known method of the world: or of insisting on gaps in the continuity of being, which only paroxysms of Omnipotence could overlap; and the breakdown, therefore, of the old proofs on these points leaves Theism quite unharmed. The modern science does not even disturb us with a new idea, for 'evolution' is only growth; it merely raises the question *how* far into the field of nature that idea can properly be carried—a question surely of no religious significance. . . . The Unity of the Causal Power, which is all that the spreading network of analogies can establish, cannot possibly be unwelcome to those who regard it all as the working of one mind."

It is further worthy of note, that Scepticism has not as yet reached the masses of the English nation. Even in the sphere of literature and art it is probable that the majority believe in a sort of vague Theism, susceptible of being transformed into positive faith or into cavilling unbelief, according to the development of character, or the pressure of external circumstances. It is nothing more than we might expect therefore that positive faith should continue to predominate in the masses, and even among the middle classes. There is hardly any exception to this, save among the workmen of the towns, who are always more or less hostile to the idea of attendance at public worship; but even their indifference seems to have been largely encroached upon, of late, by the revivals of the Methodists and the zeal of the

Salvation Army. And finally, the fact must not be overlooked that the Churches, at least in the greater part of the Protestant denominations, are seeking to keep abreast of the ideas of the age; and these attempts form one of the most interesting features of the religious evolution I have undertaken to describe.

CHAPTER III.

THE PROGRESS OF THOUGHT IN ORTHODOX PROTESTANTISM.

The English Protestant sects according to the Census of 1881—The English Church: its organization, its resources, its strength, and its privileges—Its religious parties—The theological narrowness and philanthropical activity of the Low Church party—The High Church party—The reactionary significance of the Puseyite movement—Anglican Ritualism and the conquests of the Roman Church—The formation of the Broad Church section: its symbolic and critical schools—The noise made by *Essays and Reviews*—Bishop Colenso and the Pentateuch—The increasing tendency to explain miracles by natural causes—The decline of dogma—Opposition to the Athanasian Creed—The false position of the leaders of the Broad Church party—The eventual revision of the Thirty-nine Articles—The movement for the separation of Church and State—Probable results of Disestablishment in England—Statistics of the orthodox Nonconformist sects—Methodists—Baptists—Presbyterianism in Scotland and in England—Congregationalists—The sects of less importance—The general character of Dissent—The growth of ideas in the narrowest of the orthodox sects—Schisms and expulsions—The progress of Rationalism in the Churches accessible to theological change—The enfeeblement of the Sectarian spirit—The *Evangelical Alliance*—The united action of the Churches in moral and philanthropical efforts—The barrier of creeds.

"If there were but one religion in England," said Voltaire, "its despotism would have to be feared; if there were only two they would cut each other's throats; but as there are thirty they live together in peace and happiness." Still, Voltaire did not estimate the sects beyond the pale of the Establishment as more than a twentieth part of the nation, and he thought they were all destined to be swallowed up by their great rival. Up to the present, however, events have been far enough from justifying his prediction. According to the official returns of 1882, there existed in England and Wales 186 sects, twelve of which had arisen during the preceding year, whilst only a single one had disappeared during the same period.[1] It is worthy of remark, however, that many of these denominations differ merely in name, purpose, or organization. Thus of the twelve new communions which were formed between the 1st of September, 1881, and the 31st of August, 1882,

---

1. *Whitaker's Almanack* for 1885 gives the number as 197.—*Translator.*

eight were simply separate orders connected with the military forms so oddly introduced into religious propagandism by the Salvation Army. These new orders are the Army of the King's Own, the Christian Army, the Gospel Temperance Blue Ribbon Army, the Holiness Army, the Hosannah Army, the Redeemed Army, the Royal Gospel Army, and the Salvation Navy. Among the four others there are two which appear to be purely evangelical associations,—the Christian Evangelists and the Christian Pioneers; the third is a rationalistic society, the Aletheans; and the last a Calvinistic organization, the Calvinistic Independents.

Then, again, a certain number of particular sects may represent but a single sub-division of one of the great branches of Protestantism. Thus, the Methodists figure in the returns as consisting of seventeen denominations, the Baptists form fifteen, and the Anglicans themselves nine. This arises from the fact that certain associations (formed for moral and religious purposes) claim the character of distinct sects, in order to avail themselves of the privileges which the law grants to ecclesiastical bodies. Such, for example, are the Association for the Defence of the Bible, the Evangelical Association of Missions to Workmen, and the Christian Young Men's Association.

Taking into account these circumstances, we may estimate the number of sects, properly so called, at about thirty, which is, indeed, a tolerably respectable figure for a population of about twenty-six millions. It may be added, on behalf of those who think they see in this diversity of form a source of weakness for the religious sentiment, that according to the same statistics England possessed on the 1st of September, 1882, 21,864 places of worship, or 712 more than 1881.[1]

Before passing on to a description of these different sects, it will perhaps be of interest to reproduce the following statistics, which furnish *data* more or less approximative respecting the different kinds of religious belief that prevail in the various countries where the Anglo-Saxon language is spoken.[2]

---

[1]. This number had risen to 23,341 by the beginning of 1885.—*Translator*.

[2]. The figures and information given in this chapter are borrowed for the most part from *Whitaker's Almanack* for 1883; from the *Encyclopædia Britannica*, 9th Edition, Vol. I. to XIII.; from the *Encyclopédie des sciences relegieuses*, published under the direction of M. F. Lichtenberger; and lastly from a useful compilation by Mr. William Burder, *A History of all Religions*. Philadelphia, 1873 (Parts IV. and V.)

Episcopalians	20,500,000
Methodists	15,500,000
Roman Catholics	14,100,000
Presbyterians	10,300,000
Baptists	8,050,000
Congregationalists	6,000,000
Unitarians	1,000,000
Persons belonging to other sects, Freethinkers, or those with no known belief	11,350,000[1]

The Episcopal Church, which ceased to be the established religion of Scotland in 1689, and of Ireland in 1871, has lost, even in England, all those of its privileges which are inconsistent with the civil and political equality of the people. Still it remains the National Church *par excellence*, the Church of England, the only one which the State supports and regulates. Not only do its ministers take part in public ceremonies in their official capacity, but even more, it shares in the legislation of the country by means of its Bishops, who sit in the House of Lords. Regarded as the sole heir of the property bequeathed to the Roman Church in England before the Reformation, it is alone capable of possessing and inheriting property in the interest of religion, apart from the exceptions formally established by law in favour of certain special sects. On the other hand, it remains subject to public authority, which regulates its organization, watches over its discipline, names its leaders, and possesses the right to define its creeds. It is the aggregate of these privileges and obligations which constitutes what is spoken of as the Establishment of the Anglican Church.

In 1871 the Established Church possessed sixteen thousand places of worship. Its members, estimated at thirteen millions in England, belong, on the one hand, to the aristocracy, the upper middle classes, and the members of the Universities, and, on the other, to the rural population of the greater part of the country. The labouring and artizan classes of the towns generally hold aloof from its services, and this explains the encouragement which a certain number of the High Church clergy have given to the practises of the Salvation Army.[2]

---

1. These hypothetical statistics are slightly varied in their application to 1885.—*Translator*.

2. The publication of the secret instructions of the Army, as well as the exaggerated form of its pious eccentricities, has of late greatly alienated the sympathies of

Finally, in some of the rural districts where Dissent predominates, and specially in Wales, its members form but a very small minority of the population. Its riches are immense; its annual revenue amounts to some six millions sterling, more than two-thirds of which is fixed income, the remainder being the result of voluntary effort.[1]

The Anglican Church is subdivided into two ecclesiastical provinces — Canterbury and York — which are presided over by two archbishops who receive £15,000 and £10,000 a year respectively. Under these archiepiscopal chiefs there are thirty-three bishops whose incomes range from £2,000 to £10,000 a year; thirty deans who receive from £700 to £3,000; eighty-five archdeacons; six hundred and thirteen rural-deans, and finally about thirteen thousand five hundred beneficed clergymen who are assisted by an army of curates.[2] The members of the Episcopal Bench are chosen by the Crown. Presentation, however, to the spiritual charge of a parish, belongs in the majority of cases to the largest proprietor of the district, as a legal right. This is called the right of presentation to a living, and it is by no means a rare thing to see the clerical office put up for sale at a public auction and adjudged to the highest bidder.

The legislative power of the Church resides in Parliament. It is true, there exists, in each of the two ecclesiastical Provinces, an annual assembly or Convocation, constituted by the high dignitaries of the Church and by delegates from the rank and file of the clergy. But this clerical parliament of two Houses has little more than a deliberative power, and it may even be suspended or dissolved by an Act of Parliament. The Convocation of Canterbury, for instance, was virtually suspended in 1717 on account of the sympathy which its principal members showed for the Stuarts; and it was not officially reconstituted till 1860.

---

the English Episcopate. In one of the sittings of the Upper House of Convocation, held on the 10th of May, 1883, the tendency of the movement was keenly criticised by the Bishops of Oxford, Rochester, Hereford, Chichester, and Lichfield. The last-mentioned prelate related, as the most recent eccentricities of the Salvationists in his diocese, that at Derby one of their captains had promised, by means of public bills, to stand on his head for ten minutes and preach the gospel. "And what is more," added his Lordship, "he kept his word."

1. This estimate of the income of the Established Church is too small; eight millions would probably be nearer the mark.—*Translator.*

2. The number of Bishops and other dignitaries mentioned here is corrected up to 1885.—*Translator.*

This hierarchical and centralizing organization has not prevented the English Church from being always distracted by contending parties, among which it has been compelled to establish a compromise. At present these divergent tendencies are respectively represented by the High, Low, and Broad sections of the Church.

The Low Church or Evangelical party which has developed itself along the lines traced out by Wesley and his Anglican followers, is closely related in doctrine to the sects which carry their reverence for the Scriptures to Bibliolatry and lay special stress upon the doctrines of Redemption by the blood of Christ. Low Churchmen, who chiefly belong to the middle classes, have played an important part in all the great philanthropical movements of English society, since the close of the last century, as for instance in the agitation for the Abolition of Slavery, the Temperance Cause, the various associations for the moral and material improvement of the lower classes, and the organization of Foreign Missions. It would be unjust, moreover, to disregard the claims which the members of this party possess, upon the gratitude of the public, for their activity in the foundation of schools, hospitals and various kinds of asylums. But the narrowness of its theological views weakens its influence, which pulpit ministrations that turn almost exclusively on the flames of Hell and the Merits of the Atonement, are but little calculated to raise and strengthen. Hostile alike to Rationalism and to Ritualism, this party established in 1865 an organization entitled the Church Association, with a view to meet the expenses of prosecutions for heresy before the ecclesiastical Courts of the country. It is worthy of note that some of its partizans have continued their evolution in the direction of the Evangelical sects. Thus there was founded in 1849, the Free Church of England, which numbers at present forty congregations. Another Church, due to an analogous movement, but of American origin, the Reformed Episcopal Church, has also been extending itself in England since 1873, at the expense of the Low Church party.

Now whilst the Low Church section of the clergy bases its teaching on the essentially Protestant principle of Justification by Faith, the High Church party, on the other hand, insists upon the authority of the Apostolic tradition, as this is embodied in the universal Church. This re-actionary and ritualistic school received a powerful impulse from the romantic movement which passed over Great Britain, as well as the rest of Europe, about 1830. A group of distinguished young men belonging to the University of Oxford, which has long personified in England, not only high literary culture, but also the most conservative social and religious tendencies—Dr. Pusey, Dr. Newman, the poet Keble, and Mr. Froude (the brother of the historian)—sought, by a series of small publications, which rapidly became popular under the general title of *Tracts for the Times*, to extend to religious institutions the fashion which prevailed everywhere else as a return to the conceptions and customs of the Middle Ages. In reality, this movement, which was destined to become associated with the name of Dr. Pusey, was far more than a simple return to the ancient liturgies and symbols of the Church. Its promoters, under the pretext of attributing to the traditions of the first six centuries the authority which the Reformed Churches merely concede to the decisions of the first Councils, set about extolling the invocation of the saints, the worship of the Virgin Mary, the re-establishment of the Mass, the celibacy of the clergy, auricular confession, the dogma of the Real Presence, the Roman doctrine of the sacraments, and finally, and above all, the supernatural prerogatives of the priesthood considered as a necessary agency between the worshipper and God.[1]

Ritualism has maintained its ground in the Established Church, where it shows itself chiefly to-day in the Gothic style of its architecture, in the richness of its sacerdotal vestments, and in the complicated symbolism of its ceremonies. It specially predominates in the Episcopal Church of Scotland, as a natural re-action against the Puritan baldness of the Calvinism which constitutes the doctrine of the Established Presbyterian Church. It is only a tenth of the Anglican clergy who are members of the *English Church Union*. But the most logical and

---

[1]. The position taken up by English Ritualism is almost identical with that of the Old Catholic party of Germany, since both profess a sort of Catholicism without acknowledging the Papacy. Still it is said that when Dr. Döllinger made advances to the Episcopal Church, with a view to some common ground of action, the Ritualists met his proposal with great reserve, if not with downright coldness. This circumstance arose from the fact that the two movements sprang from opposite tendencies of thought. Puseyism, for instance, is the starting point of a retrograde course, while Old Catholicism, on the other hand, is the commencement of a forward movement in the order of the evolution of the human mind. Thus their actual nearness of views is like the proximity of two trains advancing in opposite directions.—(*Vide* Moncure Conway, *A Study on the Lives of Sterling and Maurice.*)

courageous partizans of the Tractarian movement did not halt midway in their retrogressive career, which, originating in a mistrust of modern civilization, tended to the very heart of the Ecclesiasticism of the Middle Ages. Hence, within ten years of the publication of the *Tracts for the Times*, Dr. Newman, the most distinguished of the Puseyites, finished his evolution in the arms of the Roman Church, as Carlyle somewhere says, "like a child who has roamed all day on a silenced battlefield, going back at night to the breast of his dead mother."

Dr. Newman is now a Cardinal, and the numerous conversions which followed his, not only in the ranks of the Anglican clergy, but from among the aristocracy, might have led to the supposition that a large section of English society was on the road to Canossa. Some of the advocates of scepticism in England have even applauded this movement as a confirmation of their favourite theory, that between Catholicism and irreligion there is no halting-place. But it seems that, like the Roman Church itself, they mistook their hopes for reality. Since its complete emancipation in Great Britain, Catholicism has specially directed its attention to the restoration of the rich and governing classes to its fold. Favoured by a certain fashion, it has succeeded in a few exceptional cases, which made a great noise at the time; but it may be safely affirmed that the mass of the nation has not been even touched.[1]

Turning to the Latitudinarian or liberal section of the Anglican clergy, we find that it has formed, since the days of Coleridge, what is now called the Broad Church party. Coleridge, who, before his

---

1. It would be of interest to determine whether the much-talked-of conversions of a few distinguished persons have not been amply compensated for by the losses of Romanism, in favour either of Protestantism or of Freethought. In 1780 the Catholics numbered only 70,000 in England, Scotland, and Wales; in 1880 they possessed more than 1,300,000 adherents. But in estimating the value of these figures, account must be taken of three distinct factors: *(1)* The natural development of the old Catholic families; *(2)* the Catholics of foreign origin and their descendants; *(3)* the Catholics of Irish origin who have immigrated into England. This last factor alone accounts for about half the total number. Mr. G. F. Rawlinson, indeed, goes so far as to maintain, in a statistical statement published in 1874, in the *Geographical Magazine*, that the conversions effected by Catholicism in England since the commencement of the century, do not compensate for its losses, if regard be had to the general increase of the population. At all events, it is an undeniable fact that the number of Catholics in England and Wales, which in 1854 amounted to 4·24 of the population, represented only 4·61 in 1866, and no more than 4·44 in 1877.—(*Vide, Encyclopedia Britannica*, under the heading *England*.

return to the Established Church, had re-habilitated a theory of the Trinity, after the manner of Schelling, saw his method of dogmatic interpretation accepted with all the greater eagerness by the enlightened champions of Anglican doctrines, because the theology of the day had been roused to the need of adjusting itself to the requirements of German idealism, and because the miraculous elements of Christianity were beginning to lose their hold upon public opinion. There was then seen to gradually rise a new form of Alexandrian mysticism, at once Christian and rationalistic, which made the divine immanence the central principle of Christianity; enlarged the idea of Revelation to such an extent as to make of it a permanent and general gift of humanity; and, finally, opened the door to the conception of an unlimited development of religious beliefs.

The principal result of this theology has been the ever-increasing importance of Biblical exegesis. Even during the first half of the century, Dr. Arnold paved the way to larger views, but without throwing down the gauntlet to orthodoxy. It was only in the following generation that the conclusions of German criticism really penetrated into the English Church. In 1860, for instance, seven distinguished writers, five of whom were clergymen, published, under the title of *Essays and Reviews*, a volume which embodied the following scheme of thought:—(1) The necessity of reform in theology by the application of the historical and critical method to the science of religion; (2) Emancipation from the literal and supernatural authority of the Bible; (3) Adhesion to the principle of development of religious beliefs in opposition to the assumed fixity of dogma.[1]

This publication, which spread, under the ægis of the Establishment, the boldest results of contemporary criticism, caused a lively state of feeling in all the sections of Anglicanism; the evangelical press denounced the innovators with the utmost vehemence, and more than two thousand clergymen demanded their expulsion from the Church. Dragged before all the ecclesiastical courts, the bold writers were none the less ultimately acquitted by the Privy Council, and this adjudication, followed some years later by the acquittal of Bishop Colenso, who had laid a sacreligious hand on the unity and antiquity of the Pentateuch, gave at last to religious criticism the right of abode

---

1. *Vide*, in the *Revue des Deux Mondes* of June, 1875, an article by M. Albert Reville, on *Liberal Anglicanism*.

in Anglican theology.[1] One of the essayists, Dr. Temple, is now Bishop of Exeter;[2] and another, Professor Jowett, has been recently made Vice-Chancellor of the University of Oxford.

It has been said that the Broad Church party forms but a brilliant staff without a following. But this group of superior and learned men exercise none the less a profound influence on the general tone of Anglican theology. It is to them that the latter owes its increasing repugnance to insist upon the miraculous aspects of religion, as well as its tendency to explain the origin and development of Christianity without recourse to supernatural agencies.

Even the rationalistic criticism of the school which has sought to free itself from embarrassment, by mutilating the Biblical narrative in order to obtain from it a meaning in conformity with the affirmations of science, finds itself completely antiquated to-day. "There were and are—said Dean Stanley at the funeral of Sir Charles Lyell—two modes of reconciliation which have each totally and deservedly failed. The one attempts to wrest the words of the Bible from their real meaning, and force them to speak the language of science; and the other attempts to falsify science in order to meet the supposed requirements of the Bible."

The time has passed in which all was regarded as saved when the "days" of Genesis had been transformed into geological periods, when the alleged priority of light to the sun had been explained as due to the thickness of the atmospheric vapours which prevailed during the early ages of the earth's history, and when the most questionable passages of the Old Testament were interpreted as allegories possessed of a lofty morality. Even Dr. Arnold went so far as to declare that there is a poetic element in the earlier pages of Sacred History, and there are but few eminent theologians in the English Church to-day,

---

1. I know of few signs more significant of the progress made by public opinion in this matter than the dinner given in honour of Professor Kuenen, when that eminent Dutch critic was invited by the managers of the Hibbert Trust to deliver a series of lectures on the growth of the great systems of religion. All shades of religious opinion in England were represented at the banquet, from Agnosticism to Catholicism, inclusive of Jews, Unitarians, and ministers of the Established Church. Mr. Moncure Conway, who, as one of the guests, described this banquet with much humour in a contribution to the Boston *Index* of June the 15th, 1882, justly observes that it marks an entire revolution of theological opinion.

2. At the beginning of 1885 Dr. Temple was elevated to the See of London, as successor to Dr. Jackson.—*Translator*.

who do not regard the Biblical narrative as the fruit of an inspiration which, though certainly divine in its source, has been registered by human and therefore fallible interpreters.

Thus the bishop, who presided over the recent Anglican Congress held at Melbourne in Australia, said, in his inaugural address, that we should seek to state the whole truth respecting the Bible, and not leave any room for the accusation of the opponents of religion, who charge us with refusing to admit that there is a human element in the sacred books.[1] From this position to that of regarding the Gospels and the rest of the New Testament as forming a work superior in quality, but identical in kind to the religious literature of other ancient peoples, there is but a step which it is easy for a school of theologians to take, who consider the incarnation of the Divine in human consciousness as a natural and universal fact.

Even the intervention of Providence in the course of human affairs or in the evolution of natural phenomena has been openly called in question in the Established Church. The American journal, the *Index*, of the 15th of June, 1882, rightly mentioned, as a sign of progress in the ideas of the clergy, the fact that an Australian bishop had just previously refused to authorize the use of public prayer for rain, alleging that atmospheric changes are regulated by the laws of nature, and that if the piously disposed desired a remedy for drought, they would do well to improve the system of irrigation.

It is noteworthy, moreover, that the dogmas of the churches are following in the train of the Miracles. Speaking generally the doctrines of the Fall and of the Atonement are as far as possible passed over in silence by the Broad Church clergy. As to the doctrines not formally mentioned in the Thirty-Nine Articles, such as Eternal Punishment, the existence of a Personal Devil and the like—these they do not hesitate to contradict and at times condemn. Between the Trinity as it is conceived of by Dr. Martineau among the Unitarians, and by the late Dean Stanley among the Anglicans, there is scarcely the thickness of the paper on which the Thirty-Nine Articles are written, and age has terribly thinned that venerable document.[2]

---

1. *Times*, January 4, 1883.

2. Compare Dr. Martineau's pamphlet, *The Three Stages of Unitarian Theology* (1st Edition, London, 1879), with an article published by Dean Stanley in the *XIX. Century* of Aug., 1880, under the title of *The Creed of the Early Christians*.

Hence we need feel no astonishment that a minister of the Anglican Church, the Rev. C. Maurice Davies, when describing the heterodox congregations of London, should have hesitated to characterise the general position of Unitarianism by this term, "except for etymological reasons." "Between them, he adds, and some of our more advanced clergy in the Establishment, there is little difference."[1] The *Christian Standard*, an orthodox journal, has spoken out still more explicitly on the subject. "Unitarians," he said in September 1876, "have possession to a great extent of the pulpits of the Church of England. Broad Churchism is an interchangeable phrase for Unitarianism," and this in many cases known to ourselves." It is true the *Christian Standard* is an organ of the Dissenters, but its sincerity is shown by its hastening to state that, in Nonconformist, as well as in Anglican pulpits, there are a considerable number of Unitarians, that is to say men who profess Unitarian opinions.

Such is the general situation which the Bishop of Rochester recently characterised by professing his profound satisfaction that the Church was each day becoming broader and more liberal. Still it is a question that may be asked, how sincere minds are able to reconcile this breadth of opinions with their acceptance of the doctrines which serve as the official basis of the Establishment. It is clear, indeed, that the existing beliefs of the Broad Church party are in antagonism to the spirit if not to the letter of the Thirty-Nine Articles.[2]

The learned Dean of Westminster presents the doctrine of the Trinity there as a formula expressive of the comprehensiveness and diversity of the Divine Essence. According to him, the Three Persons are simply the three revelations, the three modes by which God manifests himself in turn, in nature, in history, and in the human soul. In illustration of this he says—"There are in the sanctuaries of the old churches in the East, on Mount Athos, sacred pictures intended to represent the doctrine of the Trinity. As the spectator stands on one side he sees only the figure of our Saviour on the Cross; as he stands on the other side, he sees only the Heavenly Dove; as he stands in front he sees only the Ancient of Days, the Eternal Father."—It needed less than this to make Calvin send Servetus to the stake.

1. *Heterodox London*, Vol. I., p. 311.

2. Since this work was written, three books have been published in England which may be advantageously mentioned here as bearing on the subject. Taking them in their chronological order, there is first *Natural Law in the Spiritual World*, by Professor Drummond, a work which has caused some considerable stir in the theological world from its bold attempt to rehabilitate Calvinism in the guise of modern science. The author says in his preface: "The real problem I have set myself may be stated in a sentence. Is there not reason to believe that many of the laws of the Spiritual World, hitherto regarded as occupying an entirely separate

It would be a mistake, however, to see in this logical inconsistency simply the effect of material considerations, or any want of moral courage. Such weaknesses are doubtless to be met with in the Anglican Establishment, as well as in all other Churches; but a suspicion of the kind cannot for a moment be entertained of such men as Stanley, Temple, Rowland Williams, Kingsley, and Colenso. The truth is, that with the Broad Church clergy the sentiment of religious communion predominates over all questions of dogma. Their

---

province, are simply the laws of the Natural World? Can we identify the natural laws, or any of them, in the spiritual sphere?"—So much for the problem; here is what the reader is told as to the need of its solution—"The effect of the introduction of Law among the scattered phenomena of nature has simply been to make science, to transform knowledge into eternal truth. The same crystallising touch is needed in Religion. Can it be said that the phenomena of the Spiritual World are other than scattered? Can we shut our eyes to the fact that the religious opinions of mankind are in a state of flux? And when we regard the uncertainty of current beliefs, the war of creeds, the havoc of inevitable as well as idle doubt, and the reluctant abandonment of early faith by those who would cherish it longer if they could, is it not plain that the one thing thinking men are waiting for is the introduction of Law among the phenomena of the Spiritual World? When that comes, we shall offer to such men a truly scientific theology. And the reign of Law will transform the whole Spiritual World, as it has already transformed the Natural World."—But no sooner does Professor Drummond set about solving the problem of which he thus speaks, than he shows he is far from being the strong and faithful guide the words just quoted would lead everyone to suppose. In short it is soon seen that he makes shipwreck on the rock of false analogies; and that influenced by prejudice he has cast aside the calm caution of the scientific spirit and become a theological dogmatist. "Why a virtuous man," he says, "should not simply grow better and better until in his own right he enters the Kingdom of God, is what thousands honestly and seriously fail to understand. Now Philosophy cannot help us here. Her arguments are, if anything, against us. But Science answers to the appeal at once. If it be simply pointed out that this is the same absurdity as to ask why a stone should not grow more and more living till it enters the organic world, the point is clear in an instant." Surely, however, this illustration involves the astounding assumption that man is not an organic whole; that spiritual phenomena are not a part of his being, as well as mental. And where is the proof of such an assumption? The Law of Biogenesis, which is here taken as typical of the theological doctrine that "the spiritual man is no mere development of the natural man," but "a new creation born from above," merely asserts that organic life is a thing apart in nature. But it does not show that a plant or one of the inferior animals cannot attain to the perfection of its being without the importation of some principle foreign to its essence, and by a process beyond the lines of its organic development. Besides, what is false to Philosophy cannot be true to Science, since, as Mr. Herbert Spencer explains, Philosophy is merely the science of sciences.

The second of the works in question—*The Mystery of the Universe our Common Faith*—is by a London clergyman, who is a Prebendary of St. Paul's, and the author of one or two works which have been well received in the orthodox section of the theological world. The aim and scope of the book will be best

dream is that of an ecclesiastical organization broad enough to comprise all the forms of Christianity, from Unitarianism, which would in reality strengthen their own tendencies, to the most orthodox Dissenters, who would swell the ranks of the Low Church party, while the Ritualists might be allowed to follow their special preferences for an ornate service.

In support of this view, they contend that such a state of things constitutes the true function and the sole justification of an Established Church. That a church cannot be a truly National Church if it is not sufficiently comprehensive to satisfy all the spiritual wants of the nation and to concentrate all the resources of the religious sentiment, on what Mr. Matthew Arnold calls "the promotion of goodness," that is, the moral improvement of society. Which therefore is the

---

understood from the following words:—"The suspicion that verified science and the articles of our Common Faith are at variance, causes mistrust concerning those dogmas which Holy Scripture requires us to believe: mistrust—painful as to the present, and perilous as to the future. So to employ science as to throw light on the physical constitution of the universe, and bring out clearly the great facts and doctrines which accord our intellectual and emotional experience, is the emphatic requirement of this generation from our thinkers. Unification of all knowledge in one verified system, a philosophy that combines theology and philosophy, that reveals the Mystery of the Universe, is not beyond the power of human reason; in any case we may pursue it as an ideal . . . . Spirit is not the sublimate of matter. Vast and various departments of being lie within one domain of existence. All forces are the radii of one Energy, all divergences start from one centre. Love is a force not less constraining than gravity : each in its own sphere of operation. The agency, everywhere at work, is the symbol of the One Living Presence: the source of all power and life and order. Theology declares this truth in one language ; science in another. The Word and Work, without confusion, testify to mystery ; to the one Principle underlying all things, present everywhere."—This promises well, but Mr. Reynolds's book, like *Natural Law in the Spiritual World*, is extremely disappointing. He does not really grasp the spirit of science—truth for its own sake—nor does he employ its methods. Here are one or two illustrations of this : " It was not the whole Trinity which became personally united with our nature (in Christ), but the Word which was made flesh ; so that two natures, the Divine and human, became one Person : the Eternal son is the Incarnate Son. . . . . The two natures so formed one person—sustained by food, yet omnipotent ; requiring outward light, though inwardly possessed of the glory of Godhead —that we find the human aspect wholly man and discern our brother ; we discover the Divine reality and worship God. . . . Moses, dwelling in a land of sun-worshippers, experiencing every day the power of that sun, could neither be ignorant nor forgetful of the influence of solar heat and light in promoting vegetation. That he should speak of vegetation, as apart from that influence—vegetation wholly different to that which Egypt and the Wilderness produced—can only be accounted for by a knowledge surpassing his time, advancing from nature to nature's God. As giving a statement of creation that accords with accurate modern science,

right course for them to take? Should they quit the Establishment, because they find themselves in antagonism with certain details of a constitution elaborated more than three centuries ago, in a current of religious thought which has disappeared to-day; or indeed stay in its ranks, in conformity with the true spirit of the institution, in order to maintain therein the right of free inquiry and, perhaps, prepare in this way the return of England to religious unity, but, this time, by means of liberty and progress?

This reasoning does not lack a certain force and the conception it involves is not without grandeur, although it finds no place for the

---

he is a man most wonderful. . . . It (the Bible) touches on every science, is wholly unscientific, yet has never been proved in error."—These short extracts suffice to denote the position Mr. Reynolds occupies. His book, indeed, though rich in the best materials and marked by great inspirational power, is by no means fitted to perform the task it claims to accomplish.

The third of the works alluded to in this note—*The Scientific Obstacles to Christian Belief: Boyle Lectures for 1884*, by Canon Curteis, Professor of New Testament Exegesis in King's College, London, is a much higher order of production. Though specially designed to establish the truth of the doctrines of Christianity, and therefore necessarily of a controversial character, it is written with a degree of spiritual insight and philosophical candour, which is calculated to make it the starting-point of a new era in the English Church. The author sees that something must be given up, and he is willing to surrender many of the old outworks, as for instance the necessity for the belief in Miracles, in order that the citadel of spiritual truth may be the more readily defended and retained. In relation to the sceptical spirit of the age, his words are:—" We possess, on the one hand, an analysing, subdividing, restless questioning power in the Intellect; we have, on the other hand, a formative, simplifying, synthetic power in the Imagination. The movements of the intellect are rapid, incessant, mordant, disintegrating, and, by themselves, merely destructive. Interminable and illimitable investigation is their proper function; and without their salutary check forms of thought once established, would remain eternally fixed; customs and dogmas and formulæ once accepted would refuse all change and all purification . . . . Thus the work of the pure Intellect is throughout analytical and discriminative. And whenever weary of its eternal investigations, it would pause and clothe with shapeliness and beauty its heaps of crude materials, it is obliged at once to awaken its companion and to borrow help from the Imagination." With respect to the question, why should "That only which satisfies the *human mind* be regarded as true?" Canon Curteis says:—" This, as everybody knows, is the standing question of Philosophy. And it were well that it should now-a-days be answered out of hand, and be finally laid to rest. For after all that has been written and thought and said for ages upon the subject, there really can no longer be any reasonable doubt about the answer, nor any hesitation in affirming plainly that *the human mind has nothing whatever to do with absolute and outside truth;* that it is but a mirror constructed to image forth the universe in a manner impressive and useful and delightful to us; and that its presentment is *relative*, not absolute truth. And since we can never get behind ourselves, cannot see except with the eye, nor think

Catholics or for the adherents of religious organizations beyond the lines of Christianity, such as Jews, Theists, and Comtists. Even as early as the seventeenth century, Chillingworth justified his entrance into the Church, by alleging that it was sufficient for a clergyman to adhere in a general way to the doctrines of the Establishment, and that he accepted the Thirty-Nine Articles as a treaty of peace. But it is none the less true that if Politics live by compromises, because they depend upon the accommodation of doctrines to facts, Religion which operates exclusively in the sphere of principle, demands from its very nature, sincerity of conviction and the logic of character.

Whatever sympathetic feeling may prompt us to interpret the constitution of a Church in the broadest sense, we must admit that neither conscience nor thought can develop itself freely, so long as they are constantly coming into collision with a compulsory creed. The situation, indeed, is becoming more and more false, within the pale of the Church, for those who, having renounced the supernatural, desire to preach what they actually believe, and to no longer teach what they have ceased to believe. They are incessantly drawn on, in spite of themselves, to making compromises, which, if they do not lead to the falsification of the expression of thought, none the less produce unconscious subtleties. Numerous decisions, given by the ecclesiastical courts, have shown, moreover, even in recent days, that there are limits to free inquiry in the Established Church; and though Bishop Colenso escaped all condemnation for heresy, this was due to a flaw in ecclesiastical legislation, which did not contemplate having to pronounce judgment upon the opinions of a bishop.

The remedy for this false position would be found in the suppres-

---

except with the brain, it is obvious that the very first and most essential act in all our mental work must be an act of pure Faith—*faith* in the sufficiency of our faculties, *faith* in the approximate veracity (for all practical purposes) of our mental mirror, *faith* in the gift we possess of interpreting all things in terms of our own mind, complete in its triple functions of Intellect, Imagination, and Conscience."
—It is easy to see the importance of this far-reaching principle, both as regards the evolution of religious thought and the claims of Scepticism. Those who accept it must give up dogmatising about what lies beyond the ken of human faculty, and remember, with Mr. Spencer, that all our conceptions of God, as the Ultimate Existence, are merely symbols; while the negative dogmatist will find it equally opposed to his unfortunate habit of measuring the depths of the universe by the sounding-line of his own surface-bound conceptions.—*Translator*.

sion of all declaration of allegiance to dogmatic Christianity. As early as 1772, more than 250 clergymen and eminent laymen of the Church of England, petitioned Parliament in order to obtain its sanction that the admission to Holy Orders should not necessitate a subscription to the Thirty-Nine Articles. The Episcopal Church of Ireland entered upon this permissive course from the moment of the rupture of its relations with the State, by suppressing obligatory adherence to the damnatory clauses of the Athanasian Creed. The Episcopal Church of America has gone a step further than this by omitting the creed in question from its liturgy. Hence it may be confidently stated, that the disappearance of the creed at present implied in the Thirty-Nine Articles is simply a matter of time.[1] The only question is whether this reform will take place before the destruction of the Establishment, that is, the dissolution of the bond which unites the Church to the State ; and here we come to another of the principal problems which the present condition of Anglicanism presents.

The official status of the Established Church was calculated, as a matter of course, to provoke attack from both Dissenters and Freethinkers. Some forty years ago, this opposition assumed the form of an Anti-State Church Association, which has become to-day the Society for Liberating Religion from State control, or simply the Liberation Society. As a matter of fact, the agitation for the separation of Church and State has lost something of its intensity since the disappearance of the privileges of the Anglican Church, with regard to marriages, funerals and public education. Still political circumstances may, at any moment, give a new impulse to this movement, and it is very doubtful whether even the Abolition of the Thirty-Nine Articles would prevent its final triumph ; for if the Establishment became broad enough to embrace all the sects of Protestantism, it would even then be questionable whether they would consent to enter it.[2]

---

1. The *Inquirer* of the 31st of March, 1883, stated that a parish meeting of St. James's (West Derby), had just previously passed a resolution requesting the minister to no longer recite the Athanasian Creed during the services, and pledging themselves to pay the costs of any prosecution which might be undertaken against him.

2. There are many thoughtful men of liberal tendencies in the Nonconformist communions who believe the cause of truth and the interests of civilization would be far better served by reforming the Church, and making it really National, than by destroying it as an Establishment.—*Translator*.

But it may be asked whether the Episcopal Church would not have more to gain than to lose in the disruption of its connection with the State. It would doubtless have to give up a portion of the immense wealth which it monopolizes to-day. Still, is it really necessary in order to preserve the vitality or even the *prestige* of that Church, that it should have at its head an Episcopal Body whose annual income amounts to about £160,000, apportioned to but little over thirty members? In England, however, reforms generally proceed by means of compromise; it is, therefore, highly probable that the Church would be allowed to retain, over and above the fabrics themselves, a part of its revenues, proportionate to the number of its members and the extent of its requirements. If, moreover, some of its privileges should disappear, this need not diminish its vitality or limit its usefulness; for in what respect could its true religious interests be served by the maintenance of parochial charges without congregations, as in villages where almost the entire population belongs to Nonconformist communions?

On the other hand, if its prelates have to give up their seats in the House of Lords, if its liturgy is no longer allowed to exclusively figure in public ceremonies, will not the Church gain in return for this, an independence, well worth the loss of a certain amount of wealth and some few honours? Is it not an absurd spectacle to see its religious beliefs regulated in the last resort by Parliament, in which there are Dissenters, Catholics, Jews and Agnostics, and where to-morrow there will doubtless also be Atheists?

It will certainly be felt as a hardship after having been the Church of England, to be nothing more than one of the sects of English Protestantism. Still these sects have shown by their example that, even in the matter of faith, liberty is superior to protection, since in spite of persecution, poverty, social discredit and inferiority of resources and talent, they have succeeded in equalling, if not in surpassing, by the number and activity of their adherents, the powerful religious organization which had, as the heritage of its predecessor, the monopoly of the higher education, the patronage of the ruling classes and the support of public authority. There exists, moreover, a fact which should reassure the Episcopal Church of England, as to the religious consequences of Disestablishment. In Ireland, where the Establishment was suppressed on the 1st of January, 1871,[1] the Episcopal Church, which numbered only 11·9 of the whole population, had increased by the end of 1880 to 12·3 per cent. or 635,670 members, the entire number of inhabitants being estimated in 1881 at 5,159,839 persons.

The part which the Established Church has not succeeded in playing among the lower classes has devolved chiefly upon the Dissenting sects, born of the anti-dogmatic and anti-formalist inspiration which constitutes the popular characteristic of Protestantism.

The Methodists, though of recent origin, form to-day the most important of the sects. Methodism sprang from the evangelical movement which was commenced by John Wesley in 1739, in the very heart of the English Church. Its adherents, who were estimated at 76,978 in the year 1791, when Wesley died, consist to-day of about 800,000 active members in Great Britain, with something like a million-and-a-half of children in its Sunday schools. The denomination is divided into several secondary bodies, such as Wesleyans, Primitive Methodists, Methodists of the New Connexion, United Methodists, &c. Each of these organizations is governed by a *Conference*, whose members are elected by the congregations of certain districts. The Methodists are noted for their participation in the various charitable and moral agencies carried on by society, and they have devoted at times as much as £160,000 to their foreign missions in a single year.

More or less connected with the Methodists in doctrine and practice there is a considerable group of congregations which confine themselves to claiming for their adherents the belief in the supernatural Christ of the Evangelists, and whose members refuse to accept the brand of any sect whatever. Some of these are simply registered as "Unsectarians," or as "Christians owning no name but that of the Lord Jesus," or again as "Christians who object to be otherwise

---

1. In consequence of the measure passed in 1869 for the disestablishment of the Episcopal Church in Ireland, the State has resumed possession of all the property and revenue which it had conceded to that Church; but it left to it all the endowments which had been the result of private generosity since 1660. And further, it guaranteed to the actual holders of ecclesiastical preferments an annual sum for life, equal to the income previously derived from their office. Almost all the recipients capitalized this annuity on behalf of the Church, which thus found itself in possession of a part of its old resources.

designated." The same spirit prevails in the numerous revivals which at times end in the creation of new sects, but which, as a rule, respect the denominational connections of those who temporarily take part in their proceedings. Such is also equally the case with the Salvation Army, which draws its adherents from among the least educated in the sects which are possessed of an evangelical tendency, and from among a similar class who, as "unbelievers," are beyond the pale of all the sects.[1]

The English Baptists are neither less popular nor less active than the Methodists. They claim to number a million of adherents in the denomination, about 298,900 of whom have submitted to the rite of baptism. This rite they restrict to adults and administer by immersion, as the reader may be aware. They are the historical representatives of the Anabaptists of the sixteenth century, and they even claim a direct connection with the Apostolic churches by means of the Vaudois, the Cathari, the Paulicians, the Donatists, the Novatians, the Montanists, and the Euchites of the second century. Still their principal development dates merely from the last century. They boast that they are the only sect which has been persecuted everywhere, but has itself persecuted nowhere. Their churches, which number over 3,500 in Great Britain, are independent of each other. They have in their Sunday schools 401,517 children, and spend on an average £200,000 per annum in missionary and benevolent efforts. It is from their body that the first Foreign Protestant Missions sprang. This was in 1792. In theological opinions they are less rigid than the Methodists; Arminianism prevails in a great number of their churches, Calvinism in perhaps a still larger number, while a few border on Socinian and Unitarian doctrines.

The Presbyterians and the Independents, who are the representatives of the old Calvinistic Puritanism, have not increased in the same proportion as several of the other communions. In Scotland, Presbyterianism is the Established form of religion,[2] but in England the

---

1. At the annual meeting of the Salvation Army held in London during the month of May, 1883, "General" Booth stated that the Army comprised about a million-and-a-half of members, divided into 491 different corps. The annual revenue of the organization amounted to more than £120,000. During the meeting in question, a sum of £10,000 was subscribed.

2. A secession from the official Church (the Kirk of Scotland) took place in 1843, which led to the formation of a Free Church (the Free Kirk). This latter

denomination possesses only 275 congregations, with 56,099 members. In Ireland, on the other hand, it forms one of the most extended Protestant sects, for it possesses there 485,503 adherents.

Presbyterianism is essentially Calvinistic in its organization and in its doctrines. Each of its congregations is under the charge of a minister, who is assisted by elders. The congregations of certain defined districts are governed by *Presbyteries*, which are assemblies formed of the ministers of the district, and of a layman for each parish. The Presbyteries in turn, are united into Provincial Synods; and these latter again are subordinate to a General Assembly, composed on the same principle, that is partly of ecclesiastics and partly of laymen. Presbyterian worship is distinguished, especially in Scotland by its baldness: there is no organ, no liturgy, no altar, no ecclesiastical robes and no religious emblems. The churches, which are devoid of all architectural and artistic adornment, look like mere assembly rooms. In England, however, the Presbyterians tend more and more to deviate from the old rigidity, both as regards the form and the substance of worship.

The Congregationalists, who are the historical descendants of the old Independents, differ from the Presbyterians in but little more than the absolute autonomy of their churches. Their ministers have no need of special ordination; any person who is invited by a congregation secures through this choice the right of preaching and administering the sacraments. The overwhelming majority of the Congregational churches are connected by an organization, consisting of delegates, and known as the *Congregational Union;* but this association exercises no authority over the individual congregations. It has no other object, indeed, than to facilitate an interchange of opinion and to organize common action among the churches for philanthropical and kindred purposes. The Congregationalists possess in Great Britain 14 colleges for the education of their ministers and 4,158 places of worship.

---

holds the same principles and adopts the same organization as the official Church; it merely rejects the right of *patronage*, which at the time of the secession still existed in the Church of Scotland to the advantage of certain feudal proprietors. To-day, in both Churches alike, every congregation possesses the right of choosing its own ministers from among regularly ordained candidates. It may be worth noting that the secession just mentioned has greatly weakened the principle of union between the Church and the State; it is quite possible, indeed, that the disestablishment of the Church of Scotland is not far distant.

Passing over the Unitarians, of whom we shall speak further on, we come to the Quakers, or Society of Friends, with 17,977 members; the Swedenborgians, or New Jerusalem Church, with 64 congregations and 4,987 registered adherents; the Moravian Brethren, with 32 Chapels and about 5,000 members; the Irvingites, with 19 Churches; the Adventists, who are looking for the second coming of Christ; the Universalists, who believe in the final salvation of all men; the Plymouth Brethren, who claim to form the sole Church of God; the Christadelphians, who deny the doctrine of the Trinity as well as the immortality of the soul, and who look for an early re-establishment of a divine kingdom at Jerusalem; the Sandemanians, or Glassites, who give each other the holy kiss in their worship; the Peculiar People, who have gained a notoriety by refusing to take precautionary measures for the prevention of epidemics, and even to call in the aid of a doctor when their children are ill; the Mormons, or Latter-Day Saints, who, according to *Whitaker's Almanack*, possess 82 places of worship in Great Britain; and, finally, to make use of the official terms of the Census, " the believers in the divine visitation of Johanna Southcote, the Prophetess of Exeter," without reckoning the not less eccentric, but more ephemeral, sects which are born and die almost every day.

But though all these denominations look upon themselves as Protestant Dissenters, they play for the most part but a very subordinate rôle in the bosom of Nonconformity. This must be studied in the Calvinistic and Evangelical communions, which represent the Puritan tradition. It will then be seen to possess both the merits and the defects which I have already spoken of as the characteristics of the Low Church party: great strictness of life, philanthropy of the most developed kind, an extreme distrust of sacerdotal intrusion, with a keen sense of personal independence and of religious equality; but at the same time, a narrow view of life, a studied aversion of all scientific progress opposed to the claims of orthodoxy, slavery to the letter of the Bible, an exaggerated sense of sin and a tendency to look at the gloomy side of religion. It may be remarked that the Nonconformists constitute in politics the great bulk of Liberal electors, and that this suffices to explain the opposition which has been offered, even under the most progressive Government, to every attempt to encroach upon the legal observation of the Sunday, even when it is merely a question of opening picture galleries and museums.

Still even the most rigidly orthodox of the sects have not been able to remain absolutely uninfluenced by the progressive thought of the age. Here is Dr. Martineau's testimony to this fact, as expressed in 1876:—[1] "Without any loss of the fervour and spiritual depth of an earlier age and with unabated resort to scriptural imagery and expression, their foremost ministers no longer speak in the sense of the seventeenth century. They have put new wine into the old bottles and the bursting has yet to come. There have been occasionally instances of avowed theological change . . . and occasional explosions of frightened conservatism . . . . But these conspicuous examples afford no measure of the silent movement which is shifting the whole body into a different stratum of the theological atmosphere, and lessening the interval between the Puritan and the Rationalist modes of religious thought." We have ourselves stated above in the language of the *Christian Standard* that the organs of orthodoxy recognise the same fact, while deploring its existence.

There is not a denomination with whom belief in the miraculous is not declining. Even the Presbyterians of Scotland form no exception, as shown, of late, by the notorious trials for heresy, which were instituted against both ministers and professors of theology in that Church. The Scotch correspondent of the British and Foreign Unitarian Association stated in 1882 that the rights of Biblical criticism were beginning to be admitted in the Churches in Scotland. "It is hard," he adds, "to resist the conviction that it cannot be a very distant date, when by the consent of the people, the 'standards' will be abandoned and a decided step be taken in our direction, if not altogether into our own position."[2]

A more recent circumstance shows that this opinion was well founded. On the 14th of January, 1883, the Unitarian Church, at Aberdeen, held its anniversary services. Among the ministers present on the occasion, in addition to those of the Unitarian body, were a Congregationalist and the Rev. — Macdonald, a minister of the

---

1. Introduction to the Rev. J. J. Tayler's work: *A Retrospect of the Religious Life of England*, p. 26.

2. *British and Foreign Unitarian Association's Report for 1882.*

Established Presbyterian Church. After an address by the Rev. Frank Walters, on the progress of Rationalism in the Church of Scotland, the Presbyterian minister addressed the meeting and declared that his Church owed much to the Unitarians for having drawn their attention to the practical side of religion. "They had compelled Presbyterians," he added, "to remember that whatever they might ultimately make out in the supernatural direction, there lay much nearer to them what was more useful, interesting and perhaps, in the long run, more influential in determining the moral character and elevating the spiritual nature, than the supernatural, and that was the natural." These are noble and significant words which his Congregationalist colleague supported by saying that "as year after year went by he thought less of theology and more of religion."[1]

This tendency of the Churches to approach each other upon common ground has of necessity aided in softening down the old sectarian antagonisms, and has allowed the various religious bodies to unite their efforts in matters of general progress, in which they are pursuing the same end. The exchange of pulpits, formerly limited to ministers of the same denomination, has now, in many cases, crossed the barriers of sect. Hence, Dean Stanley was seen to place his Cathedral at the disposition of ministers beyond the pale of the Anglican communion, while he himself preached in Presbyterian Churches in Scotland. On the occasion of the Congress of Congregational Churches, held at Bristol in 1882, a deputation of Anglican ministers attended to publicly testify, as they said, to the good work which the Congregationalists were doing in the spread of the fundamental truths of the Divine law, and to bear witness to their piety and zeal, as well as to the ability and eloquence of their ministers. The address concluded by an appeal on behalf of the fraternal union of all those who are aiming at the establishment of the reign of Christian justice on the earth.

Not only when it is a question of obtaining funds to aid in the alleviation of some great public misfortune, or to organize a crusade against intemperance and misery, are the leaders of the different Churches to be seen exercising their influence in common efforts; but even in matters relating exclusively to forms of faith they none of

---

1. *The Inquirer*, of January 27th, 1883.

them hold, as in the recent persecution of the Jews in Russia, when they did not hesitate to unite in promoting a charitable manifestation, which was a genuine protest of the public conscience against the religious intolerance of a past age.[1] Even some years earlier than this, on the initiation of the Evangelical Alliance, a large number of Nonconformist ministers signed an address conjointly with the Archbishop of Canterbury, to protest, in the name of the principles of the Reformation, against the persecutions which the Swedish Government was inflicting upon the Roman Catholics of that country.

Would it be safe to conclude from all this that the various sects of British Protestantism are on the eve of uniting on a common religious platform, as they have already done in the domain of philanthropic and moral effort? This is very doubtful. For it must not be forgotten that in Nonconformist Churches, as much, or perhaps even more than in the Established Church, creeds remain an obstacle to the complete emancipation of conscience and thought. There is, indeed, especially among the Independents and the Presbyterians, a few congregations whose trust deed simply states its object to be "the worship of God after the manner of Dissenters." Still, speaking generally of the Protestant denominations, the Unitarian Church, as will be seen in the following chapter, is the only religious body which has fully and officially broken down all the barriers to theological freedom.

---

1. The requisition presented to the Lord Mayor asking him to convene a meeting to consider what means could be taken to aid the persecuted Jews, was signed by one archbishop and three bishops of the Anglican Church, by several well-known Nonconformist ministers, and also by Cardinal Newman, Mr. Darwin, Professor Tyndall, &c.

CHAPTER IV.

ENGLISH UNITARIANISM.

Correlation between the history of Unitarianism and the progress of free inquiry—Origin of English Unitarianism—Socinianism—Its spread in England—First Unitarian Conventicles under Cromwell—John Biddle: his life and apostolate—More or less open adhesion of Milton, Locke, and Newton to Unitarianism—Commencement of Unitarian worship in London in 1774—Doctrine and influence of Priestley—Reaction against the Sensational theology—Parallel between Coleridge and Channing—Increasing diversity of theological opinions among leading Unitarians—Opposition to the idea of a direct Revelation—Dr. Martineau and his influence on contemporary Unitarianism—The point of contact between advanced Unitarians and pure Theists—The Rev. Peter Dean's confession of faith—Unitarian Pantheists and evolutionists—Organization of Unitarian worship—Divergences in its Liturgy—Text of this borrowed from all kinds of devotional literature—Unitarian chapels—Ritualistic Unitarianism—Nonconformist congregations that have reached Unitarianism—Congregations in a state of transition—The attempt to substitute the term *Free Christian* in place of Unitarian: resistance of the two extreme sections of Unitarianism—Present statistics of English Unitarianism—The British and Foreign Unitarian Association—Constant intervention of this society in favour of religious liberty and equality—How extreme variety of belief and organization among Unitarians excludes neither unity of action nor the sentiment of spiritual fellowship.

The history of Unitarianism is closely connected in England with the development of free inquiry. Not that there are none to be found, beyond its pale, who have powerfully aided in the emancipation of thought, or that it is necessary in its growth more than elsewhere to identify the progress of reason with the varying phases of Christology. Still, the divinity of Jesus, whatever form the doctrine may have assumed, constitutes, none the less, the corner-stone of supernatural Christianity, the central dogma of the theology founded on a special revelation.

Besides, to reduce Unitarianism to a simple revolt against the dogma of the Trinity, or, indeed, against all the other dogmas which have arisen subsequently to the appearance of the Gospels, would be to take a very inadequate view of its scope and claims. From its origin it naturally became a centre of attraction for minds in search of the most advanced Christian communion of their epoch, and these, in turn, have re-acted upon its theology, modifying it according to the nature of the ideas at the heart of each successive generation. Thus the internal history of Unitarianism has been but a continued effort to bring Christian tradition into harmony with the requirements of science and philosophy. Even to-day its essential characteristic is that it forms a Church open to all who wish to pursue the progressive evolution of Christianity without let or hindrance.

Successive attempts have been made to connect modern Unitarianism with the Lollards, who were in existence as a scattered band at the time of the Reformation; with the Anabaptists, whom the persecutions of the sixteenth century caused to flee from the Low Countries into England; with the Italian and Spanish Protestants, who received the hospitality of Edward VI. and Elizabeth;[1] and, lastly, with the Socinian publications which were imported from Holland and circulated through the country during the reigns of the two first Stuarts. It is certain that, as early as the time of Henry VIII., Arianism showed itself in England, in a sporadic state, occurring here and there, as evidenced by the Unitarian martyrology, published by Mr. Spears,[2] and that, at or about the commencement of the Parliamentary Wars, there was an increase in the English translations of the works directed against the doctrine of the Trinity by the Socinians of Poland. But it was not till 1648, during the Long Parliament, that anti-Trinitarian conventicles were first held in London, under the presidency of a heretic, by the name of Welchman. The doctrine taught in them was to the effect that Christ had been a prophet who worked miracles but was not God.[3] These views were soon adopted by John Biddle, a Master of Arts of the University of Oxford, and a man so well versed in the knowledge of the Bible that he could recite from memory almost the entire text of the New Testament.[4] According to the Rev. J. J. Tayler, Biddle would seem to have been unacquainted with any Socinian works, and to have drawn the germs of his teaching from the study of the Bible itself. Expelled, in 1645, from St. Mary's pulpit in the city of Gloucester, he was subsequently imprisoned in Newgate as a common criminal, for the boldness with

---

1. J. Bonet-Maury, *Des Origines du Christianisme Unitaire chez les Anglais*.
2. R. Spears, *Rise and Progress of Unitarianism in Modern Times*, p. 7.
3. Bonet-Maury, p. 232.
4. J. J. Tayler, *A Retrospect of the Religious Life of England*, 2nd Edit., p. 221.

which he defended his opinions before the ecclesiastical commission appointed to examine into the charge of heresy preferred against him. But even from his prison cell he found the means to publish two treatises against the Divinity of Christ and of the Holy Ghost. The Parliament, then under the influence of the Presbyterians, condemned these works to the flames, and passed a statute which, among other pains and penalties directed against blasphemy, made the denial of the Trinity a capital offence.

Still, even then, the last word was not uttered in the struggle between a single modest thinker and the allied forces of Church and State. No sooner had the amnesty, granted by Cromwell in 1652, with the support of the Independents, opened the doors of Newgate to Biddle, than he hastened to hold private meetings every Sunday, in which, Bible in hand, he taught his doctrine. Hence Cromwell had him banished to the Scilly Isles; but it should be added, in justice to the Protector, that he caused means to be secretly forwarded to him, and that at last he allowed him to return into England. Biddle, however, simply made use of this toleration to resume the work of his apostolate. Arrested a third time, after the Restoration, for an illegal act of worship, he died in prison during the year 1662, at the age of 47.

In common with all martyrs of a just cause, Biddle left behind him numerous followers, among whom was his successor at Gloucester, the Rev. J. Cooper. Driven in turn from his office, and shut out from the English Church by the Act of Uniformity, Cooper organized, the very year after Biddle's death, a congregation at Cheltenham, to which he ministered for twenty years.[1] In London, thanks to the efforts of Thomas Firman, a rich merchant, who was entirely devoted to Socinian ideas, although he had not broken with the Established Church, the Unitarians maintained a centre of action which was kept up without any serious persecution through the latter years of the reigns of the Stuarts.[2]

The general toleration which James the Second sought to establish in the interest of the Catholics, naturally proved beneficial to all the proscribed sects, the Unitarians included. Still, it was necessary that a long time should pass before their doctrines could be openly proclaimed. Even the Revolution of 1688, which granted liberty of

---

1. Spears, *Op. Cit*, p. 21.
2. Tayler, *Op. Cit.*, p. 229.

conscience to Nonconformists, by an Act that Mr. Lecky does not hesitate to speak of as the *Magna Charta* of religious liberty, made a formal exception of all who recognised the authority of the Pope, and those who did not accept the doctrine of the Trinity.

So great was the strength of prejudice in this matter, that men like Milton, Locke, and Newton left the avowal of their Unitarian convictions to posterity.[1] The manuscript of the *Doctrina Christiana*, in which Milton demonstrates that, according to the Scriptures, "the father of Our Saviour Jesus Christ is the only God," remained buried in the archives of England till 1823. Locke again refrained from publishing his *Adversaria Theologica* during his own lifetime, and when accused of Socinianism by Dr. Edwards, he did not hesitate to say that "the Apostles Creed is no more Socinian than I am." As to Newton, at the moment when his *Exposition of Two Notable Alterations of Scripture* was about to be printed in Holland, he suddenly countermanded it, for fear that his authorship should be discovered, in spite of the veil of anonymity he had intended to throw around it.

This, however, was the epoch in which the writings of the Deist Woolston against the miracles of Christ sold to the extent of 30,000 copies. It is true that Woolston lost his position as a Fellow of the University of Cambridge, that he was condemned by the Court of Queen's Bench, and thrown into prison, as he had not wherewith to pay the fine. But speaking generally, it was a more dangerous thing to preach the Christianity of Socinianism than to spread the doctrines of the Deists or even of the Atheists, for this excellent reason that the latter were published simply as philosophical opinions, whilst Unitarianism aimed directly at the transformation of the current religious beliefs. In short, the Unitarians owed, if not official recognition, at least the public toleration of their worship, to the indirect action of the development of Latitudinarian and Arminian tendencies, in the bosom of the English Church.

The second chapel in which worship was oganized with a Unitarian liturgy, was opened in London in 1774, in spite of the penal enactments which still threatened the promulgation of anti-trinitarian doctrines, and which remained on the statute book till 1813. This congregation was originated by the Rev. Theophilus Lindsey, who had voluntarily given up his clerical position in the Established Church.

---

1. J. Bonet-Maury, *Op. Cit.*, pp. 245, &c.

Then again, the end of the seventeenth century was characterized by a considerable extension of Unitarianism, under the leadership of Dr. Priestley, who wrote numerous works to prove, on the authority of the Bible, the exclusively human nature of Jesus. Unhappily, his sympathy for the French Revolution marked him out as an object of popular hatred, and in 1794 he was driven to seek a place of exile in America, without foreseeing that the time would come when a statue would be raised to his memory, in that very town of Birmingham where the crowd had pillaged his house and scattered his congregation.

There is to be observed in the ideas of Protestantism respecting the nature of Christ, an evolution analogous to the one I have pointed out in the efforts of the Puritans to reach the primitive constitution of the Church. On the morrow of the Reformation, the dogma of the Divinity of Christ began to move, in an opposite direction, along the lines it had followed in its formation. Calvin, indeed, as M. Albert Reville has shown, by insisting upon the humanity of Jesus, had in a certain sense paved the way for a denial of his divinity.[1]

Christ soon becomes for Servetus, what he had previously been for Arius, exclusively the Divine Word, a sort of Demiurgus, the first-born of the creation. The Socinians make of him no more than a man, but a man miraculously conceived and ultimately associated in the Divine Majesty. Even Biddle admits that a sort of subordinate worship may be rendered to Christ, while at the same time he denies his right to divine honours. In the eyes of Priestley, Jesus is simply the Messiah, a special messenger of God, with supernatural power; and it is this interpretation which he seeks to establish by an appeal to the text of Scripture. Meanwhile, the day was to ultimately dawn in which more advanced reformers would take from the founder of the Christian religion the privilege of a supernatural origin, and even the special office of mediator between God and man, in order to leave him simply the glory of his moral and religious influence.

Priestley was profoundly convinced that the testimony of history established the validity of Revelation, and it is on this belief, as a faithful disciple of Locke and Hartley, that he bases his entire religious system. "If there be any truth in history," he wrote in his *Essay on the Inspiration of Christ*, "Christ wrought unquestionable miracles,

---

1. Albert Reville, *Histoire du Dogme de la Divinité de Jesus Christ*, p. 133.

as a proof of his mission from God; he preached the great doctrine of the Resurrection from the dead, he raised several persons from a state of death, and, what was more, he himself died and rose again in confirmation of his doctrine. The belief of these facts I call the belief of Christianity." This reasoning was in perfect conformity with the Rationalism of the period; but its adoption by the majority of Unitarian theologians contributed not a little to establish that reputation for coldness and lack of religious fervour, which was so long true of English Unitarianism.

The reaction came from America, where the writings of Channing had played in the Unitarian Church the same part which those of Coleridge performed in Anglican theology. Both, in short, the one guided by his veneration of conscience and the other by the tendencies of German philosophy, set the religious importance of the human soul in a new light, and awoke in their fellows the sentiment of moral responsibility with the idea of free will, then more or less compromised by the requirements of the theology of the Sensational school. But while the latter applied all the resources of the new method to repair the breaches of orthodoxy, the former used them to establish that distinction between religion and theology, which could alone enable liberal Christianity to bear the blows of modern criticism with impunity, and which has assured the future of Unitarianism by giving it the character of an indefinitely progressive doctrine.[1] Both admitted the infallibility of the Bible, with the consequences which flow from this, as to the nature and the office of Jesus. But whilst the English theologian tried to diminish, by a subtle interpretation, the difficulties which this admission presented to the most advanced minds of his Church, the American divine made them a matter of individual judgment, and sought the basis of religious communion beyond the pale of all creeds. From Channing, indeed, dates that increasing diversity of theological convictions in the Unitarian body which might scandalize those in love with doctrinal uniformity, but which none the less forms the peculiar characteristic and the strength of the Unitarian Church of to-day.

As early as the first third of the nineteenth century, in face of the school which adhered to the theology of Priestley, and which persisted in seeing in the miraculous elements of the Bible the keystone to the

---

[1]. James Martineau, *The Three Stages of Unitarian Theology*. London, 1882.

whole Christian edifice, there gradually sprang up a generation of Unitarians who preferred seeking the source of the religious sentiment, and even the claims of Christianity itself, in the moral commands of conscience and in the native aspirations of the soul. Regarding the Bible as a special depository of religious truth, and Jesus as the chosen of God for the spiritual salvation of humanity, this new school soon began to attach but a secondary importance to the external proofs of Revelation; and, consequently, it was able to sacrifice the letter of the Biblical narrative, without any unreasonable opposition, when this began to receive a formal rejection, either on the part of science or historical criticism. Up to this time its adherents had declined to deny, in general and *a priori*, the occurrence of miracles. But in proportion as the double critical and scientific current of modern ideas became distinct, views were seen to develop themselves, among the principal interpreters of Unitarianism, which excluded the possibility of a Divine intervention in violation of the laws of nature, and subjected Christianity itself to the general laws of religious evolution.

To-day, the Priestley school has almost disappeared. The moderate position which Dr. Martineau occupied thirty years ago,[1] has become the extreme right of the Unitarian Church; he himself, although maintaining the unique character of the Christian Revelation, and the absolute superiority of its Founder, has long since adopted the opinion that the Divine Action must be exclusively sought in the regular course of natural law, the progressive development of history and the native aspirations of the soul.[2] For the left wing of Unitarianism, Jesus is only a product of his age and country, greatly superior to his contemporaries by the elevation of his sentiments, and admirably inspired by a love of humanity, but, at the same time, subject to all the limitations of our nature and a member, in short, of the same family to which all the celebrated reformers of history belong.

This point of view is absolutely identical with that of the "Theists" who, long isolated in religious society, have thus found themselves occupying common ground with the advanced lines of Unitarianism. Professor F. W. Newman, for instance, who, for more than thirty

---

1. Ch. de Remusat, *Les Controverses religieuses en Angleterre* in the *Revue des Deux Mondes* of 1st of January, 1859.

2. James Martineau, *Loss and Gain in Recent Theology* (London, 1881), and *The Three Stages of Unitarian Theology*.

years was in opposition to every sect of Christianity, the Unitarians included, owing to his persistent denial of the revealed character of the Bible and the necessity of a Mediator, naturally found a place marked out for him in the ranks of Unitarianism, as soon as that communion no longer refused to identify itself with confessions of faith similar to the following, which the Rev. Peter Dean formulated before the Unitarian congregation, at Clerkenwell, in 1875:—"Faith in an infinitely perfect God is all our Theology. The Universe is our Divine Revelation. The Manifestations of Nature and the Devotional Literature of all Times and Peoples, are our Bible. . . The goodness incarnated in humanity is our Christ. Every guide and helper is our Saviour. Increasing personal holiness is our salvation. The normal wonders of Nature are our Miracles. . . Love to God and love to man—piety and morality—are our only sacraments."[1]

What Freethinker, however feeble his belief in God and his faith in progress, could refuse to sign such a declaration of principles as this, if he found himself in consequence placed in a better position to aid in the reconciliation of the religious sentiment with reason? There is no room for surprise that it was by a sermon delivered in the Clerkenwell Chapel, in 1875, that Professor Newman explained the reasons for his entrance into the Unitarian body. He was received, as a matter of course, with open arms and, since 1878, his name has figured in the list of the Vice-Presidents of the British and Foreign Unitarian Association.

Still more advanced, there exists a group of young ministers of ability who profess a sort of idealistic Pantheism, borrowed either from the ideas of Strauss or from the writings of Herbert Spencer. Their attitude towards the Christian tradition is almost identical with that of the Theists. But they prefer to simply see in God a mysterious and indefinable Power, who is working for the realization of order and justice in the world. Some of them go so far as to state that the object of religion, as they conceive of it, is the realization of the human ideal, and that it is this ideal they render divine in order to bow before it in adoration. Thus the gamut of the philosophical opinions represented in Unitarian theology is complete,

---

[1] Clerkenwell Unitarian Church. *The Minister's Religious Principles*, an appendix to a Sermon by Professor F. W. Newman, *Sin Against God*. London: Trübner, 1875.

extending, as it does, from a semi-orthodox Socinianism to the confines of the religion of humanity according to the Gospel of Comte.

It may be asked whether the progress of this evolution has not developed signs of declining fervour or of lassitude, which began to reveal themselves in the religious attitude of Unitarianism a third of a century ago: that is to say, at the time when the mass of Unitarians still shared the belief in the infallibility of the Bible and the miraculous power of Christ. In reply to this question, I shall quote a passage from a sermon, delivered on the 14th of June, 1883, by the Rev. R. A. Armstrong, before the members of the Western Christian Union.[1] After having admitted that the progress of Biblical criticism in England during the last twenty-five years had stripped Christianity of all its old supernatural claims, he remarked that, at first sight, this critical work could not fail to seem calculated to destroy the importance still accorded by Unitarians to the Biblical narrative and to the person of Christ. Still, he continued, "The result has wholly falsified all such gloomy anticipations. Not destruction, but reconstruction, has been the upshot of all this ferment. The Bible had ceased to interest. There was not the ring of truth in the way it was interpreted. We have faced the facts now. We have seen the true upgrowth of the marvellous literature which we did not understand before. . . . And so the Bible has come to be the most interesting of all histories, and we feel the movement of God through it all; and understand how, through error and folly and sin, He trains the nations up in the great school of our common humanity. We no longer call the Bible a supernatural Revelation, or give it any official or miraculously authoritative position; but we like it, some of us love it; we do not any longer find it dull, and we find that there is a well of pure waters in it, refreshing us to eternal life.

"And the Christ, he had lost touch of us; and then came the critics, and we thought he was going to dissolve into air, and be no more to us than the fancy-wrought figure of a myth. How is it now? Why, it is thus:—It is true we have dropped many an old phrase as too artificial and technical for our use now. It is true we no way put Christ between ourselves and the Father whom he preached: nothing,

---

1. R. A. Armstrong, *Hopes and Dangers of English Unitarianism*, a Sermon reproduced in the *Inquirer* of the 30th of June, 1883.

it seems to us, save sin, would have grieved him more. There are numbers of us now who do not believe that he had any other entrance into the world than other sons of honourable and loving parents; who do not believe that Herod in Palestine or the Magi of the East troubled themselves one whit about that baby boy; who do not believe one ripple on the Sea of Galilee was ever smoothed by magic word of his, or that any waters bore him as a ghost over their pathless face; who do not believe that the poor lacerated body, once dead, thrilled ever again with the currents of fleshly life; who do not believe that his spirit found its way to the bosom of God otherwise than those of others who have loved and served and perished bravely at their post. No; he is human to us altogether; and we see how it was that all those legends gathered to his fame out of the love and wonder of the men who followed in his steps. But for that very reason this Jesus has become to us real, vivid, bright, strong, beautiful. He is so utterly a brother of our own. We can see the happy boyish home, the young man wistful at the stern, strange, awakening word that came borne on the air from Jordan, the man in all the thick and press of ministry gasping ever and anon for a breath of lonely prayer on the mountain-side, the joy in the help and comfort he found he could give poor men and women, the sorrow at the perversity of understanding manifested by so many, the marvellous union of strength and tenderness, of indomitable purpose and winning courtesy, of passionate yearning and untroubled calm; and then by-and-by the closing in of the darkness above and around, and the lonely, heroic, consecrated death. And we can take this man for our type and model of the loveliest and noblest humanity has ever been; and we can love him with all our heart and soul.

"And if it had not been for the criticism, the microscopic examination of the life-nature, the ruthless scientific analysis, which seemed so destructive and so deadly, we should have been severed more and more from Christ; the historical and philosophical difficulties unsolved would have been driven as a solid wedge in between him and us; we should have had no Christ; and ere this, Christianity might have been to us a vain and foolish name."[1]

---

[1] This is substantially the position taken up recently by M. Renan, in his remarkable lecture delivered before the *Societé des Etudes juives* (v. *la Revue Politique et Litteraire* of the 2nd of June, 1883).

It will be readily understood that, under these circumstances, the Unitarians, like the members of the Broad Church party and the liberal Protestants of the Continent, have taken a considerable share in promoting the progress of Biblical criticism. This is exceptionally true of the Rev. P. H. Wicksteed, who has translated into English the principal works of the so-called school of modern Protestantism, which is represented with so much *éclat* by Professor Kuenen and his colleagues of the University of Leyden.

The forms of worship among Unitarians present the same diversity as their theological opinions. Each congregation determines its own mode of worship as it thinks best, or according to the preferences of its minister. The *Unitarian Almanack* for 1883 mentions the existence of twenty-five different liturgies in use in the denomination, without taking into account the innovations of separate congregations. Several of these devotional compilations speak the language of pure Theism; others continue to employ the old supernatural phraseology. The one most largely used is the *Book of Common Prayer for Christian Worship*, compiled by Dr. Martineau. It consists of ten forms of worship or "services"—it is commonly spoken of as the "Ten Services"—with special forms for Baptism, Confirmation, and Ordination, as well as prayers for the Queen, the Royal Family, the Church, Parliament, &c. These latter are but seldom used in the Unitarian body; but their retention in this manual of devotion is explicable from the principle on which it was drawn up—the author having simply confined himself to excluding from the Anglican liturgy all that possessed a Trinitarian or dogmatic significance—and perhaps also from the further idea that, in this form, it might be acceptable to orthodox congregations in a state of transition.

The "Ten Services" are at present used in more than two hundred Unitarian congregations whose ministers do not, however, hesitate to modify them to suit their own requirements. Besides, in a recent edition, the author or compiler—who has always kept abreast of his age and who, in this respect, admirably personifies the Unitarian evolution of modern times—has cut out all the passages which relate to what he characterises as the Messianic Mythology, that is to say the direct invocation of Christ as Messiah and Mediator. He explains, in the preface, that these ideas are not in harmony with the increasing tendency of our age, which leaves the soul more and more face to face with God.

In many Unitarian Churches, either because an antipathy has been maintained to formularies, from the Presbyterian origin of the congregation, or because the minister prefers having recourse to extemporaneous utterance, there is no form whatever, except the order and distribution of the service. This service, moreover, consists in all cases of an alternation of hymns, prayers and readings, with a sermon towards the close. Some of the ministers of an advanced type, such as the Revs. Frank Walters of Glasgow, and J. Taylor of Preston, no longer select their reading lessons exclusively from the Old and New Testament, but also from what the Rev. Peter Dean calls the sacred literature of all ages and peoples. In some cases the worshippers join in the singing of the hymns; at other times they allow them to be wholly sung by the choir, which, though an advantage from a musical point of view, robs the service of much of its fervour. There are some ministers who make use of a gown; others officiate in a frock coat with or without a white tie. The Communion Service is still administered in the majority of the congregations, not, as will be supposed, with a sacramental significance, but simply as a fraternal symbol in commemoration of Jesus. Some congregations, however, have formally suppressed it, or at least allowed it to fall into disuse.

In some few instances[1] discussion is invited at the close of the service, the minister giving over the subject of his sermon to the criticism of anyone who wishes to speak upon it. The effect controversies of this sort must have upon the traditions and even upon the principles of Christianity, will be readily conceived; but there is nothing in them which is not conformable to the eminently theological temperament of English society.[1]

Some of the buildings used for worship are so absolutely destitute of everything possessed of religious significance, that anyone might readily suppose himself in a lecture or concert hall, which, indeed, is frequently the case, Protestants having no prejudices in this matter. Such edifices, in short, with their bare walls and no fittings but a gallery for the choir, with seats for the worshippers and a pulpit for the minister, form what may be called the traditional type of Nonconformist chapels. There are congregations, however, on the other

---

[1]. This is true merely of certain new congregations formed, some time since, under exceptional circumstances; the practice is falling into disuse, if it has not entirely ceased.—*Translator.*

hand, who worship in churches which bear no trace of Puritan simplicity, either in their internal fittings or in their architecture. So far as London is concerned, I may mention Unity Church, in the Islington district, and the Free Christian Church in Clarence Road, Kentish Town, in illustration of this statement. Both are built in the Gothic style, and possess a happy arrangement of stained windows, as well as considerable refinement of internal decoration. More fortunate than their High Church brethren, the Unitarians can indulge in æsthetic effect as much as they please, without being liable to the reproach that they are on the road to Canossa in consequence of their ritualism.

This extreme independence of the individual churches, has facilitated the entrance into the Unitarian body of various congregations which originally belonged to other denominations—Baptists, Presbyterians, Independents—and which, either because they have gradually rejected their former confessions of faith, or because they never possessed any, have thus coalesced with the descendants of the old Socinians, in the acceptance of a Christianity stripped of all dogmatic elements. According to the Rev. R. Spears, half the existing Unitarian churches are the historic representatives of old Presbyterian congregations which have passed through Arminianism during their transition. With the great majority of them, even where they have retained their former name, as for instance in the term "Unitarian Baptists," the evolution has been long since completed; with a few others it is to be actually seen in progress. As examples of this I may mention the congregation worshipping at the Church of the Saviour, Birmingham, which was originally formed by Mr. George Dawson, on broadly evangelical lines, and is to-day ministered to by the Rev. G. St. Clair; and also the congregation of Bedford Chapel, London, the minister of which is the Rev. Stopford Brooke, formerly one of the most distinguished members of the Broad Church party.[1] In both

---

[1] Possessed of distinguished abilities, great learning, and a sympathetic mode of address, Mr. Stopford Brooke has carried with him the greater part of his old congregation, and what is very rare in the annals of secessions from the Establishment, he has been able to retain the building he used when in Anglican orders—the important Bedford Chapel, which is the private property of the Duke of that name. Mr. Brooke has, also, partly adhered to the form of the Anglican Service, and as he figured, long previously to the change, among the most heterodox preachers of the Broad Church party, there would scarcely be anything to mark the transition, were it not for that increase of boldness and even of power, which always results from the absence of compromise.

these instances the ministers hold views which assimilate them to moderate Unitarians, and their congregations are unquestionably composed of liberal Christian elements. Still they have not yet adopted the Unitarian name; nor have they taken their place in the denomination.[1]

A somewhat curious illustration of this once came under my own experience at the Unitarian Church in Clarence Road, Kentish Town. The preacher having taken as his text a passage from the writings of St. Paul relative to the dissensions of the early Christians, devoted his sermon to a defence of the attitude adopted by Unitarians, in refusing to consider belief in the miracles of the Bible and the divinity of Christ as essential elements of the Christian religion. To my surprise I learnt afterwards that the preacher was not a Unitarian, but a minister of the Independent Church. My informant added that the first time the minister in question exchanged pulpits with one of his Unitarian brethren—an act which is very common in the Nonconformist denominations—he astonished his hearers by the boldness of his language, whilst his friend, on the other hand, surprised the Independents by the cautious tone of his theological utterances. The circumstance is explicable from the fact that the Unitarian considered it wise to select the most orthodox of his sermons for the occasion, and the Independent the most liberal. But the possibility of such an occurrence shows clearly enough the difficulty there is in circumscribing the sphere of liberal Protestantism, as well as in drawing a clear line of demarcation between the most closely related elements of the different Churches which extend, in England, from Semi-Catholic Ritualism to the extreme limits of religious Rationalism.

With a view to bring into closer union the various Churches which have successively rejected their former creeds, a section of the Unitarian body, in 1872, proposed the abandonment of the old descriptive name "Unitarian," and the substitution of the more comprehensive term "Free Christian" in place of it. Under this latter designation, therefore, they founded a religious association with a view to embrace "all who deem men responsible, not for the attainment of Divine truth,

---

1. Mr. Brooke's connection with Unitarianism has become much closer of late, as shown by his having allowed his name to appear in the *Unitarian Almanack*, and above all by his having preached the annual sermons for the British and Foreign Unitarian Association in 1884.—*Translator*.

but only for the serious search of it, and who rely for the religious improvement of human life on filial piety and brotherly charity, with or without more particular agreement in matters of doctrinal theology."

A year later the Free Christians duly celebrated their first anniversary in the fine Masonic Hall, which is situate in Great Queen Street. Among the ministers present on that occasion were, side by side with Dr. Martineau and the well-known French pastor, Athanase Coquerel, an Independent minister, the Rev. W. Miall, and a member of the Anglican clergy, the Rev. C. Kegan Paul, who is now at the head of a great publishing firm in London. The "Free Christians" could hardly have taken a wiser course in order to emphasise their claim to comprehend all the sections of Christianity in a universal Church, founded no longer on what Channing calls "a degrading conformity to dogma," but on that community of sentiment which admits of independent thought within the bonds of religious association. They did not succeed, however, in bringing over to their views more than a somewhat restricted portion of the Unitarian congregations. The fact is they ran counter to the feelings of the conservative section who cling to their historic name, and also to the views of the more advanced minds who, taking the word *Unitarian* as the synonym of Monotheist, regard it as more comprehensive than the appellation "Free Christian," which cannot be extended beyond the bounds of Christianity.

The various Unitarian, Presbyterian, General Baptist and Free Christian congregations, which constitute the Unitarian denomination in Great Britain, are 374 in number, with 382 ministers, according to the *Unitarian Pocket Almanack* for 1883. The denomination possesses six monthly periodicals, a publication of some importance which appears every three months, the *Modern Review*,[1] a quarterly magazine devoted to Sunday school work: *Teachers' Notes*,[1] and finally three weekly journals: the *Inquirer*, which treats of social and political as well as religious questions, and in a like liberal manner; the *Christian Life*, the representative of the conservative tendencies of the body; and the *Unitarian Herald*, which occupies a moderate position between the other two.[1]

---

[1] The *Modern Review* has since been discontinued, but a new publication of the kind, though of more general scope, is contemplated. *Teacher's Notes*, too, has given place to a successor, *The Sunday School Helper.—Translator.*

As already intimated the Unitarian Churches are not bound together by any administrative or doctrinal authority. Still there has grown up among them a large number of special associations which aim at the spread of liberal principles in religion, and the promotion of educational and philanthropic efforts. The principal of these societies is the British and Foreign Unitarian Association which, founded in 1825 by the fusion of several pre-existing societies, concentrates, to-day, all the active forces of Unitarianism. Its programme comprises the following objects: The spread of the principles of Unitarianism at home and abroad; the maintenance of its worship; the diffusion of critical, theological and literary knowledge bearing on its doctrines; and the protection of the civil rights and interests of its adherents. The sum which the Association devotes to these different objects varies considerably, amounting in some cases to nearly £4,600 per annum. Constituting as it does the most authoritative permanent organization of Unitarianism, its voice is frequently raised in the name of the entire body, not only when the interests of the denomination are at stake, but also in relation to all those public questions which appear to its members to concern, in any way, the general interests of liberal Protestantism. Hence it rarely holds its annual meeting without having some petition to Parliament submitted for consideration by its committee.

It was not till 1844, for instance, that it succeeded in getting the State to recognize the rights of Unitarians in the ownership of their chapels. But in illustration of what has been just stated and in opposition to what takes place in the majority of Churches—and, unhappily, beyond the pale of Churches too—the Unitarians, I may add, have not been content with demanding justice for themselves. The Association, indeed, has been seen to successively interpose, in the most active manner, on behalf of the various movements organized for the emancipation of the Roman Catholics, the admission of Jews to Parliament, the institution of civil marriage, the acquisition of religious equality in the parish church-yards, and the promotion of secular education in the public schools.[1] As early as 1880, it petitioned Parliament for such a modification of the Oath as would no longer make the exercise of legislative functions dependent upon religious

---

1. See A summary of the History of the British and Foreign Unitarian Association, from its formation, in its 50th Annual Report. London, 1875.

or anti-religious opinions; and at the Annual Meeting of 1882, reverting to the question in more precise terms after the Bradlaugh incidents in the House, it passed the following resolution:—" That this meeting desires to place on record its affirmation of the principle that the profession of Atheism should not deprive any citizen of his civil rights, including that of representing his fellow-citizens in Parliament if duly elected; and directs the Executive Committee to take every fitting opportunity of petitioning both Houses of Legislature in this sense." Again, at the meetings of 1883, it adopted resolutions condemnatory of all trials for blasphemy, and for the release of the men just previously sentenced to long terms of imprisonment in connection with the *Freethinker* prosecution.

In addition to their Annual Meetings held in London, at Whitsuntide, and their autumnal meetings in the provinces, the Unitarians hold, from time to time, General Conferences, which are attended by ministers and delegates, as well as by many of the members of the various congregations. The last of these Conferences, which took place at Liverpool in April, 1882, was a brilliant success, and is regarded as having re-kindled the zeal of the denomination, which had somewhat declined during the previous years.[1] Seven hundred delegates, and nearly two

---

[1]. An equally successful Conference has been held in Birmingham this year—1885. It may be remarked, however, that it was not exclusively Unitarian, and that Mr. J. Allanson Picton, M.A., M.P.,—formerly a Congregational minister—who disavows Unitarianism, read a paper there on:—" The Influence upon Religion of the Modern Development of the Critical and Rational Spirit." This paper describes in a forcible and suggestive manner the condition of religious thought in many of the so-called orthodox Churches, and denotes in this way, at least indirectly, the great difficulty which Unitarianism has to encounter, as a special system of faith and worship. It has in short so full and direct a bearing on the question discussed in these pages, that the reader will be interested in the following extract from it, lengthy as it is:—

"Thirty years ago there was a strong line of demarcation between secular and religious periodical literature. The one for the most part carefully eschewed theology, or only took cognisance of it when applause could be won by vindicating the worldly wisdom of the Anglican *via media*. As to religious magazines and newspapers, the reputation they most coveted was that of defenders of the faith. The struggles of the *Westminster Review* and other humbler ventures of the same kind only go to confirm these remarks. But now how different is the state of things! Not only do the three chief monthlies find it practically safe and even profitable to dabble in heresy, but the most widely-circulated religious newspaper of the day is distinguished by the frankness with which it treats every question affecting the relation of theological dogma to scientific discovery or historic research. As to the popular magazines, one case speaks volumes, and the mere mention of it

thousand other friends of the movement responded to the appeal of the organizers. Hence the tone of the subsequent Annual Meetings has been one of great confidence in the future. It might be affirmed, indeed, that Unitarianism is on the eve of a new development; for some time past it has been attempting to reach the masses by the organization of popular services, the success of which has exceeded all expectation.[2]

---

will save the accumulation of instances. In the current number of the *Contemporary Review*, a magazine specially guaranteed *virginibus puerisque* by the well known character both of editor and proprietors, we find the most distinguished satirist of religious schism quietly appealing to the good sense of his readers to abandon the miracles of the Incarnation and the Resurrection, together with the prospect of a Day of Judgment, on the ground that they are hindrances rather than helps to religion. Now this and similar magazines are not addressed specially to readers of a negative and faithless temper. On the contrary, the vast majority of their readers are not only regular attendants on public worship, but more or less devout and active members of Churches. Unless the critical and rational spirit had spread very considerably amongst them, we may be sure that the appearance of articles like 'A Comment on Christmas' in their favourite magazine would not be as welcome to them as it evidently is. I think, therefore, I need say no more in illustration of what I mean by the 'modern development of a critical and rational spirit.'

"It is natural that even the most candid and courageous advocates of devoutness and faith should feel a little anxiety in view of this remarkable movement in opinion. And to the question, What is likely to be its influence on religion? no satisfactory answer can be given which does not allow for a much farther advance and wider spread of the same spirit. We cannot, with any sense of permanence, content ourselves with showing the harmlessness of the very moderate Rationalism prevalent just now. The time at my disposal does not allow me to give reasons, and I must limit myself to the observation that the same influences which have led to a very general abandonment of the six days of creation, and of the Legend of Eden, are quite capable of eliminating all miracle whatever, and all supernatural revelation from popular belief. Whether that will universally happen or not, is not now the question. It is pretty certain to occur very widely, and we are asking ourselves what will be the influence on religion. Suppose a whole generation regarding Christianity as a purely natural incident in human evolution, will they on that account be wholly without saving faith? It may be said that it is impossible to judge until the time comes. But I venture to think that we are not wholly without the means of forming an opinion now.

"It is notorious that there are in almost all Churches at the present day a considerable number of members who have abandoned every shred of belief in miracle or supernatural revelation in the ordinary sense, but who still worship with their old associates, and do not feel it necessary even to turn Unitarian. Observe, I am not speaking of ministers or clergymen, but only of ordinary attendants on religious worship. Unitarians always expect to get hold of these people. They even think they have a natural right to them, and are disposed to make charges of disingenuousness or cowardice because their expectations are not fulfilled. But there is no reason for such complaints. The change that has come over these people is not a conversion to Unitarianism, but the development of a spiritual agnosticism to

As we have seen, variety of belief, and even diversity of organization, does not exclude from among Unitarians either the feeling of denomination, unity, or the sentiment of a true spiritual communion. It is this which the Rev. R. R. Suffield, who has been the minister at the Unitarian Church, at Reading, in Berkshire, for several years past, and was formerly a Roman Catholic priest, shows in the following terms, in a sermon preached in 1881, with the title, *Why I became a Unitarian:*—" Amongst them there were, I perceived, various opinions as

which all creed-framed theologies are equally meaningless, and all real worship equally inspiring. I knew very well one of these people, who so far from being attracted to Unitarianism by his critical and rational development, was only drawn away from his own sect by a preference for Methodist fervour. The reason is very plain. These spiritual agnostics have so entirely abandoned all hope of enlightenment about the ultimate ontological mysteries of the Universe that they feel a resentment against preachers who bother them with an abandoned puzzle. But, on the other hand, there are none more grateful for a word that touches the heart with a human sympathy, or deepens reverence, or humbles pride, or inspires with the temper of Christ.

" If I may speak from a tolerably intimate knowledge of some typical cases of the kind, the people who have passed through this experience are singularly unconscious of any moral or spiritual change at all commensurate with the intellectual difference between their earlier and their later beliefs. In fact, even the intellectual difference does not appear to themselves so great as it does to unsympathising critics. But of that I may say a word presently. At any rate, their religious affections are very much what they were when first awakened in early years. If they then betook themselves to St. Thomas à Kempis they find his pages no less refreshing now. If they then found some of Wesley's hymns fit music for the Holy of Holies within them, it is only a few needlessly coarse notes that strike any discord now. If their hearts then glowed at the fervent though ungrammatical aspirations of an unlettered brother after a better life, they do not find the least decay of such susceptibility now. And if they are compelled to keep themselves at a distance, it is only out of respect for the painful suspicions entertained by the unlettered brother concerning them. Of course they have come to regard faith as a spiritual affection of loyalty to the best ideal known, and not in the least degree as a belief of facts or assertions. But they maintain that this was the essence of faith even in the teaching of St. Paul, though they allow that in his epistles intellectual processes and moral affections are not always kept distinct. But holding to the moral significance of faith as the only effective part of its confused connotation in old times, they find that in regard to the essentials of religion, Faith, Hope, and Charity, they are very much where they were in the days of their evangelical fervour.

" I am well aware of all the objections that may be made, first against the soundness of the position occupied by this admittedly exceptional class, and next against the probability of any wide extension of their experience in coming generations. As far as the narrow limits imposed on me will allow, I will try to sum up in a few concluding words the considerations which appear to me to outweigh those objections. These people say that their practical and regulative ideas of God, Christ, and the Bible are proved in their experience to be quite sufficient for the needs of life. Now if this is so, *solvitur ambulando*, and such experience, when

to the person and office of Christ, as to the supernatural or natural position of Christ, of Christianity, of the Bible; but I found them for the most part loyally and gratefully pursuing the central truth of their origin and co-operation, as worshippers of God, free to follow their reason, their consciences, and the holy law of Cosmic growth.

"Lastly, though I saw many Unitarians accorded to the Bible and to Christ a position I deemed exaggerated and erroneous, yet even with them I perceived an essential bond of unity and agreement, inasmuch as they always claimed for conscience and reason the mental and moral supremacy over life and action. So I was not forced to

---

real, generally proves to be catching. It is not a sufficient objection to show that the practical and regulative ideas left us do not solve the mysteries of human destiny. Of course they do not. But these spiritual agnostics say that such a solution of mysteries is no part of the work of religion. It is for philosophy to do that—if it can. The business of religion is not to give intellectual light, but moral strength and purity; not to enable us to understand the working of the universe, but to make us consciously, by unreserved loyalty of soul, contented cogs in the infinite machine. Spiritual agnostics, therefore, do not care in the least for the taunt that they explain nothing. They carry much farther than the old evangelicals their *protest* against the pride of intellect. In fact, what they chiefly find fault with in these old evangelicals is the spurious rationalism which pretends to declare 'the whole counsel of God.'

"What, then, it may be asked, are those practical and regulative ideas of God, and Christ, and the Bible, that are left to us? The author of 'Natural Religion' has well said that no man can be without a theology, though he may not call it by that name. We are so constituted that temporary existence is unthinkable without eternal being as a background; for we cannot imagine anything arising out of nothing. Whether we choose to call the everlasting by the name of God or not, we cannot think it away. And if we identify it with the universe, there remains that transcendent attribute of unity to which science bears increasing testimony, and which, when we try to realise it, sways the soul with an overwhelming awe. Many sufficient reasons have been given why we should give up this God or that; and with reverence be it spoken, the God of the earliest Christian congregations is not in all points the God of Christian congregations now. But no reason of any avail has ever been given why we should sever ourselves from the innermost life of humanity by wholly surrendering a name which amidst ten thousand variations always keeps a central significance of eternal being, authority and power. As Mr. Herbert Spencer has shown, the evolution of the idea of God exhibits a continuity from the beginning to the end in its retention of an indestructible instinct of kinship between the bottomless mystery within and the measureless mystery without. Aratus conceived of God in one way, and St. Paul in another, and our ideas are necessarily different from both; but there is a meaning for us all in the words that 'we are His offspring.' Before we were, He is. Of Him we are, as are all created things. He is that unity of power which co-ordinates innumerable forces to make the laws of nature and of life. The thought of Him stimulates the reverence which makes loyalty to universal law a holy obedience and a joy. Whatever has been said of God and His ways that science or historic criticism can disprove, we readily surrender. To do otherwise would be disloyalty to Him. We cannot picture Him

suffer the spiritual disadvantages of religious isolation, for I could honestly and happily find amongst Unitarian worshippers a religious home, and the benefits of religious sympathy, and the consolations of collective religious worship. And during eleven years I have never regretted my choice. Religious fellowship is always a blessing to oneself, but it is moreover a benefit to others, to be enabled to invite their attention to communities of worshippers wherein the most

---

as He is. But we picture Him as we can; for the visible universe is the skirt of His garment, and the experience of mankind is His partial revelation, the growing interpretation of the for-ever unknowable. And His worship draws us out of self into the better life of sympathy and loyalty.

"I have spoken of the experience of mankind as His partial revelation. I cannot pursue the subject, but can only speak of the one conspicuous illustration which makes us Christians. How shall a man best live in the thought of God? Christ is the answer. But it is said the picture of Christ is unhistorical. How far that is the case I cannot argue now. We have very good ground for believing that the loveliest features are historical enough for all practical purposes. But however that may be, the picture is there. It is the reflection of a life where self is dissolved in two strong, holy passions, loyalty to God and love to man. And that life expresses itself in words and deeds that are an immortal inspiration. I am told that many of the deeds are evidently distorted by imagination, for they are miracles, and miracles never occurred. Be it so. I am rather glad of it; for it removes one difficulty in the way of imitation. But the thought will arise that this very distortion suggests the transcendent mastery of a spirit whose deeds straightway transformed themselves into miracles in the memory of survivors. At any rate, the luminous simplicity, the strange, searching power of the words recorded, the far-reaching ideal they suggest, and the large-hearted love manifested in the deeds described, together form a picture which represents a very incarnation of that vague dream of a kinship or unity between God and man, which, according to Mr. Herbert Spencer, has haunted all human thought. This is a vision which the critical and rational spirit can as little mar as the theory of optics can degrade a rainbow."

This "spiritual agnosticism," of which Mr. Picton speaks, not only hinders the extension of the Unitarian Church from without; it tends, moreover, to check its development from within. For no sooner do its ministers and members get to feel that dogma is infinitely subordinate to worship, than they lose that *denominational* zeal which characterised their fathers. Besides, the growth of spiritual insight, the conviction that spiritual life clothes itself with a garment of belief adapted to the culture of the individual is another hindrance to the extension of the Unitarian Church, as a separate organization, to say nothing of the indifference that so often creeps in with the change or rationalistic growth of a creed.—*Translator.*

2. This is specially true of Leicester, where immense congregations have been drawn together in the Floral Hall, by the Rev. J. P. Hopps. But it should be added that these particular services are not continued throughout the year, and that no attempt has been made to crystallize the people who attend them into a permanent congregation, or to do more, indeed, than awaken religious reverence and a sense of human brotherhood, as far as possible, apart from any dogmatic creed.— *Translator.*

philosophic and independent thinker can co-operate without an hypocrisy and without an equivocation—to chapels wherein children are taught moral and sacred lessons, but always in harmony with the highest attained truth—to chapels wherein the various epochs of life and of its close, are sanctified by acts of devotion not founded on the mythological or interwoven with the superstitious."

CHAPTER V.

RATIONALISTIC CONGREGATIONS BEYOND THE PALE OF CHRISTIANITY.

The *Theistic Church* at Langham Hall—The Rev. C. Voysey and his expulsion from the Established Church—His use of an Anglican liturgy stripped entirely of its Christian character—His principles and aims—History of his congregation—Condition and future prospects of the movement—The society of *Independent Religious Reformers*—The "Free Church" in Newman Street—Rules of the Society—Causes of its failure—The *Humanitarians*—Their services at Claremont Hall—The "Fifteen points of the religion of God"—The philosophy of Peter Leroux in its bearing on worship—"Humanitarianism" in Castle Street—Growth of a new faith—Reformed Judaism—Origin of this movement tending to strip Judaism of its ceremonial, hygienic and national prescriptions—Gradual rejection of the belief in direct Revelation—Final barriers between the Reformed Jews and the Theists of Christian origin—*Idealistic Agnosticism*—The South Place religious society—Mr. Moncure D. Conway, the successor of W. J. Fox—Anti-dogmatic basis of the organization over which he presides—Religious worship at South Place chapel—Mr. Conway's opinion of the nature of religion and the identity of God with the human ideal—His affinity to the extreme left of Unitarianism—Literary merit of his productions—Parallel between Mr. Conway's and Mr. Voysey's congregations.

Men of a logical order of mind have reproached the Unitarians with not making their attempts at a religious synthesis sufficiently comprehensive. To keep the name of Christian and at the same time to reject the supernatural origin of Christianity is, they think, to take pleasure in the equivocal and to needlessly exclude from religious communion Jews, Mahommedans, Buddhists, and even Theists, who refuse to recognise the divine authority or the infallibility of the Bible. Besides, it is urged, why build up purely moral principles into a dogma when there is a declared purpose to found a religious association, not upon identity of belief, but upon simple uniformity to the needs of the religious sentiment. The universal church is not a Free Christian Church, but a Free Church, and therefore open to all who believe in the existence of God, and feel the need of approaching Him in an act of worship with their fellows.

An attempt was made in France, as the reader may be aware, at the end of last century by the Society of Theophilanthropes, to establish a system of worship on the basis of what were considered the truths of Natural Religion, or the principles believed to be held and accepted by all nations, which should be capable of uniting the adherents of every form of faith in a common aspiration to the Deity. It is on reasoning analogous to this, that the important congregation, to which the Rev. C. Voysey ministers in London, bases its claims for existence.

Mr. Voysey was a distinguished clergyman of the Established Church, who from the time he took Orders, manifested an extreme independence of religious opinions. He at length commenced the publication of a small periodical entitled—*The Sling and the Stone*, in which he called in question the Divinity of Christ, the Fall of Man, the Atonement, Original sin, and other orthodox beliefs. This excited such a storm of indignation in the ranks of both the High and the Low Church parties, that the *English Church Union* and the *Church Defence Association*, each offered £500 to cover the expenses of a trial of the offender for heresy, before a competent tribunal. As the result, Mr. Voysey was deprived of his position in the Church, when, without even passing through the Unitarian stage of development, on the 1st of October, 1871, he founded an independent congregation to which he still ministers.

St. George's Hall, where I heard Mr. Voysey, for the first time, in 1874, is a small structure, the interior and fitting up of which are an exact counterpart of our (the Brussels) Café Concert Halls. The stage was shut off by a curtain of red cloth. As a matter of course there was neither altar nor pulpit; but simply a kind of platform also draped in red cloth and raised somewhat above the footlights. The congregation, at the time of my visit, was composed of from two to three hundred persons, who bore the stamp of the intellectual, if not of the upper classes.

A circular, distributed in profusion over the seats, apprised me that the congregation had begun to raise funds for the erection of a Church, which was not to be commenced till the contributions had attained a sufficient amount to complete it. At the beginning of April, 1874, the sum reached was £613 16s. 0d.; to-day it amounts to £2000. A single person figures among the contributors for £500. Several anonymous donors have given as much as £100 each. I noticed among the contributors the names of officers and baronets, and many eminent scientists, such as the late Sir Charles Lyell, Sir John Bowring, &c.

The Rev. C. Voysey conforms to a type of clergymen which is somewhat common in England: small in statue, a slight tendency to corpulence, black and smooth hair and a carefully shaved face. I found on the seat where I was placed, as I had done in Unitarian Churches, a form of service specially drawn up for the use of the congregation. And just as Dr. Martineau's *Ten Services*, or the earlier of them, present a *résumé* of the Anglican Liturgy, in which all Trinitarian formularies are suppressed, so the Rev. C. Voysey's *Revised Prayer Book* appears to be a condensed form of it, stripped of every Christian formulary, with this exception, that several of the services have been composed by the compiler himself. I saw for the first time rites destined for the cremation of the dead, embodied in a liturgy; up to the present, however, the law has not permitted that method of disposing of the dead to come into general use.

When at the commencement of the voluntary Mr. Voysey ascended the platform, which serves him as reading-desk and pulpit, I noticed that he had retained the surplice and stole of the Anglican clergy. At first, a visitor cannot help feeling a certain surprise when he hears the most energetic attacks made not only upon the principles of certain sects, but even upon the doctrines and traditions of Christ himself, by a man who wears the vestments of the Christian priest, makes use of a service based upon those of the Churches, and draws a part of his devotional readings from the Bible. In his published sermon, *Christianity versus Universal Brotherhood*, for instance, after denying to Unitarians the right to make a distinction between the dogmatic and moral parts of their beliefs, Mr. Voysey reproaches Christianity with having accepted, only against its will, the great principles of charity and toleration, so often called into requisition by those who reject and oppose it.

This apparent anomaly disappears, however, when it is considered in relation to Mr. Voysey's conviction that above all things, in the matter of worship, we should try to introduce new ideas in the old forms. "As some form must be used," he says, in the Preface of his *Revised Prayer Book*, "the form most likely to find acceptance would be one which was already partly familiar to English ears, and yet stripped of all that has become obsolete and out of harmony with a pure Theism."[1]

The sermon I heard on the day to which I have alluded, was in refutation of the doctrine of the Atonement: that is to say, the expiation attributed to Christ for the redemption of humanity. That sermon, which might have been preached in any Unitarian pulpit, afforded me no insight whatever into the special doctrines of a Church which claims to be unique in its kind. Fortunately, I procured at the door the sermon preached by Mr. Voysey at the inaugural ceremony, on the 1st of October, 1871. "Our first work," says he, in this genuine manifesto, "is to undermine, assail, and, if possible, to destroy that part of the prevailing religious belief which we deem to be false"; that is, as he explains in detail, almost all the doctrines of Christianity. "But our work," he adds, "does not rest here. We should be both distressed and ashamed if all our energies were to be exhausted in putting down even false belief. So far from that, we only desire to eradicate false beliefs, that we may be able to plant true beliefs in their place." Hence, as he goes on to explain, it will be his duty, in the first place, to affirm his belief in the existence of a Supreme Being, infinitely good and just, whom, for want of a better name, he will call God. Then will come the affirmation of a future life, which he considers inseparably connected with the belief in God. "The two," he contends, "must stand or fall together." And, lastly, he will seek to develop truth, justice, purity, and brotherhood, which represent, in his opinion, the true marks of the religious character.

In 1880, the "Congregation of the Rev. C. Voysey" abandoned, at the suggestion of their minister, their decidedly personal designation and replaced it by the title "Theistic Church." In connection with this change of name, they adopted the following manifesto, in which some few rather high-flown expressions are to be found, as is often the case in the most rationalistic English theology; but these must not cause us to forget its elevation of thought and its breadth of sentiment. Speaking of the Church, its principles, beliefs, and practical aims, they say:—

"ITS MAIN OBJECTS ARE—

1. To promote the adoption of Theistic principles and beliefs.

---

[1]. The *Revised Prayer Book*, compiled by the Rev. C. Voysey, 2nd Edition. London, 1875.

2. To furnish a reasonable method of satisfying the religious emotions of those persons who can no longer believe the orthodox dogmas.

"THE LEADING PRINCIPLES of Theism are—

1. That it is the right and duty of every man to think for himself in matters of religion.
2. That there is no finality in religious beliefs; that higher and higher views of God and of His dealings are always possible: and therefore it is to be expected and wished that future generations will improve upon the creed now held by Theists.
3. That it is our duty to obtain the highest and purest truth discoverable; and when it is discovered, to proclaim it honestly and courageously. In like manner to denounce all detected error.
4. That personal excellence of character is necessary to a right knowledge of the goodness of God. Religion is thus based upon morality, and not morality upon religion.
5. That Theism is not aggressive against persons, but only against erroneous opinions.
6. That Theism recognises the value of all moral and religious truth, wheresoever it may be found.

"THE BELIEFS OF THEISM may be thus briefly expressed—

1. That there is one living and true God, and there is no other God beside Him.
2. That He is perfect in power, wisdom, and goodness, and therefore every one is safe in His everlasting care.
3. Therefore that none can ever perish or remain eternally in suffering or in sin; but all shall reach at last a home of goodness and blessedness in Him.
4. That as we have been created for this goodness, it is our wisdom and duty to be as good as we can, and to shun and to forsake all evil.

"THESE BELIEFS ARE FOUNDED UPON—

The Religious sense acting in harmony with the Reason, the Conscience, and the Affections.

"THEISM INCULCATES—

1. A filial trust in God, which may be strengthened and enlarged by prayer and communion.
2. Worship of God in public and in private.
3. A life of joy and thankfulness expressing itself in good deeds."

Now, careful as Mr. Voysey was to distinguish between *dogmas* which from their nature are necessarily immutable and *beliefs* which are open to change from all kinds of influences, this official adoption of Theism, pledging as it did the congregation to opinions which up to that time had remained personal on the part of the minister, could not fail to detach the secular and agnostic supporters who had rallied round him in his struggle with the Anglican Church, but who were by no means ready to accept his religious opinions. And to this must be added the fact that Mr. Voysey does not hesitate to strike right and left, since in opposition to the practices of Unitarians, among whom doctrinal controversy is for the most part avoided, he devotes a large number of his sermons to the refutation of the errors of orthodoxy or the negations of scepticism. Still the losses he sustained from among his original adherents in consequence of this change, were, it would seem, rapidly made good by the accession of new elements, and I may remark that on the occasion of my visit in 1882, I noticed far more attention and devotional fervour, on the part of the congregation, than was observable eight years previously.

Nor is this the only crisis that the Theistic congregation has had to pass through. For on a certain occasion its members found the doors of St. George's Hall, in which they had been accustomed to worship, unexpectedly closed against them. An Evangelical congregation had surreptitiously come to an understanding with the proprietors of the hall, on the principle that business takes no account of creeds, in order to devote to the God of Calvin and Wesley that den of unbelief, which was a scandal to the pious world. Happily, Mr. Voysey succeeded in finding another hall in the neighbourhood—Langham Hall—which he still occupies. According to the information with which he was good enough to furnish me, the congregation numbers from five to six hundred subscribing members or adherents. During the first eleven years the contributions of the congregation, over and above those relating to the building fund, amounted to more than £13,000. This sum does not include £1,100 devoted to charitable purposes.[1] The congregation possesses no special organ in the press

---

[1]. The sum total contributed to the movement up to the present time (1885) amounts to £21,000, with £1,200 more collected for charities alone. It appears, too, that there have been nine marriages, twelve burials, and thirty-three children brought for dedication and benediction during the thirteen-and-a-half years the congregation has been in existence.—*Translator*.

for spreading its views, but it has Mr. Voysey's sermons printed weekly, and circulates them widely among the educated classes. The total number of sermons thus distributed amounted some time since, to 450,000.[1]

It may be affirmed indeed by way of summarizing its condition and prospects, that Mr. Voysey's congregation has successfully passed through the chief difficulties incidental to the establishment of every New Church, and it is probable that even the disappearance of its founder now would not lead to the dispersion of its members. If, as there is every reason to hope, it succeeds in securing the funds required for building a Church in the heart of London, the movement will form a decisive answer to those who in these days contest the possibility of establishing a permanent Church on the principles of pure Theism.[2]

---

1. *Vide Our Aims, principles and Beliefs*, the eleventh anniversary sermon, preached at Langham Hall, Oct. 1st, 1882, by the Rev. Charles Voysey.

2. It may be stated here that at the end of 1884, the "Theistic Congregation" were able to purchase the lease of the Scots' Church, Swallow Street, Piccadilly, and that they began to worship in the new building on Easter Sunday of the present year—1885. In relation to this change of domicile, Mr. Voysey preached two special sermons, the former in the old and the latter in the new building, from each of which an extract or two will be of interest to the reader. In his last sermon, for instance, at Langham Hall, which was preached on the 29th of March, he speaks as follows of the difficulties passed through, of the fidelity of his people, of the acknowledged value of his work, and of the need of personal consecration in order to ensure future prosperity:—

"Almost from the very day when we lost our tenure of St. George's Hall, and took up our quarters here in Langham Hall, our prosperity began to decline, and—there is nothing to be gained by disguising the fact—the cause has been going down steadily, annual subscriptions diminished, the number of seat-holders diminished, the visits of strangers from the highest ranks in society became fewer, the building fund was almost forgotten, and the general fund in a chronic state bordering on collapse. The gaps caused by death among the influential, the wealthy and the aristocratic were not refilled. Whole families were separated from our congregation by emigration to the provinces and to the colonies. Some persons left us because they were offended at what they heard; the sermons were not sufficiently Atheistic, or not sufficiently Christian, were too controversial, or not controversial enough, to please them. Others left us because we would not use our pulpit or our bookstall in the interests of party politics or of some scheme or crotchet to which they were primarily devoted. Others stayed away, and alas, there were many of them, because the surroundings were so poor and mean and the congregation so scanty. Some also departed because they had what the Apostle called so scornfully 'itching ears' and cared only for novelties, startling assertions or bitter outbursts against beliefs which they discredited.

"Now, this fire of adversity has not been all evil, not all against the cause, but

Some years ago, I visited another Theistic congregation in London, which has since disappeared—the Free Church—organized, in Newman Street, by the Society of Independent Religious Reformers. Here, again, however, the somewhat imposing title, Free Church, referred, as regards the building, to a mere Music Hall, of rectangular shape, with a stage, and a circular gallery at each end of it. A leaflet, placed in my hands as I entered the building, contained, on the one side, a list of the sermons announced for each Sunday of the month, and, on the other, the fundamental rules of the Independent Religious

very much good, very much for its advancement. It has tried our work, of what sort it is. It has tried and tested too our workers, of what sort they are. The 'wood, hay, stubble' and paper supporters it has burnt up, and the wind has carried their ashes afar. The iron the silver and the gold the fire has cleansed, refined and made to glow with greater brilliance. The fire has strengthened and toughened the sincere and the true of heart. It has given them courage in the face of the world's anger or scorn. It has welded together souls that would have neither cared for each other nor for truth in easier and more prosperous times. It has brought out the pure metal purged of its dross and burnt away any lingering regard for the world's smile, and every lurking motive that was not highest and best. And I know how all this terrible adversity has acted on my work. The darker the clouds, the more threatening the aspect of the adverse sky, the greater has been my effort to do my best—my poor best if you will—but I have felt more anxious to do my best and have devoted more time and energy to make my work good and true, because I saw it needed far higher work than mine to save the cause from extinction. I became more bold, more daring, in my open avowal of what I believed to be the needful truth, the more I saw that some did not like it and were offended at it. The fire of their blame only burnt away the little lingering cowardice which lay hidden in my heart. And when I think of the constancy, devotion and fidelity which most of you have shown and which have alone made the work to endure so long and under such frightful drawbacks, again I must thank our adversity for testing these qualities and for calling out these energies and that zeal and those magnificent sacrifices which you have so generously and heroically given without the slightest hope or prospect of any earthly reward. You must feel, because you *are*, more noble for having overcome personal prejudices, dislikes, love of ease and social regard in order to do what you believed to be right, and what was demanded of *you* because there was no one else who would do it."

"Time would utterly fail me if I were to try to give you any adequate idea of the testimony which I have been receiving all along to the spiritual benefit of our religion and to the spread of our beliefs. I have hundreds and thousands of letters from men and women in various parts of the world full of joy and thankfulness at the proclamation of such blessed truths. Some are delighted to find openly expressed what they had so long privately believed. Others and many more have been helped by our Theism out of confusion of thought, out of lingering prejudice and superstition, out of morbid fear and doubt of God, and are never weary of thanking God for their deliverance and praying God to help and prosper our Church. Others again, once wholly Agnostic and the religious sense all but extinguished, have come round into a higher and more reasonable state of mind; they have shaken off the incubus of pessimism; they no longer believe that in Materialism is to be found the

Reformers. They stated their object to be—" First, to secure the association of such persons as are desirous of cultivating the religious sentiment in a manner which shall be free from the evil spirit of creed, the intolerance of sectarianism and the leaven of priest-craft, and of such persons as respect the authority of reason, and who reverently accept the decrees of conscience; secondly, to discover and methodize truth, connected with either the laws of nature, the progress of thought, or the lives of good men of all ages and countries, so that they may

full solution of human life, much less the solution of the still grander problem of the universe and its eternal cause. They have learnt not to contemn the idea and the practice of prayer and many of them have even learnt to pray. And—what is more encouraging—those who have been able to gain clearer insight and to have some true faith in God, have strongly prophesied that if religion is to survive, it must be, like ours, one that is in harmony with reason and common sense and yet not a mere cold philosophy destitute of power to kindle the emotions. In all that God has hitherto helped us and in this also,—that our faithful discharge of our duty in coming here to worship has resulted in a greater clearing of our own minds in looking at truth and its counterfeits, in a greater plainness of speech arising therefrom, better still, in stronger faith in God and His loving purposes, in wider hope for universal bliss, and in more ardent love to our Father and to our brethren. Our devotion to this work has had a manifest influence in improving our lives and our character."

"I have had to live with God and to hold more firmly by His hand, and to cling closer to his bosom the more I felt estranged, isolated and exiled from the approval and encouragement and sympathy of the world, sometimes of my dearest friends. The harder and more painful my task, the greater strength and peace have I had through trusting in Him. But do not mistake my purpose in referring thus so very personally to my own experience. I do so only because I know that one of the best ways, if not the best way, to impress others is to wield a bare fact, to state the simple and exact truth as we know it and have felt it, aye, and tested it a thousand times. A Church, so-called, composed of men and women who never pray, who never hold any kind of communion with God, if it could last a week, would be the most empty and contemptible of all the shams with which demented humanity has ever amused itself. It would be composed of 'souls which had been put to silence,' souls, for the time being, as dead as a corpse. And if I desire, as I do so deeply and fervently, that the Theistic Church shall *live* and *prosper*, shall live as life is measured by its Divine Author and Giver, and shall prosper as prosperity is measured by the Divine standard, I cannot put that desire into plainer words or give it deeper meaning than by saying this :—I would that every one of you would pray without ceasing, would live a life of prayer, would cling close to God and hold by His hand and be guided by His will and trust Him, trust Him utterly, with every breath you breathe."

Turning to the first sermon preached in his New Church, we find Mr. Voysey speaking in these words of gratitude and rejoicing :—

" This Easter-day may be taken by us as a symbol, not of the resurrection to life of a dead Saviour, but of the rising out of the ground of adversity and obscurity, of wintry cold and torpidity, of those living germs of truth which we prize so

be rendered of practical value as guides to a healthful, moral, and manly life; thirdly, to assist, as a religious duty, in the regeneration of Society, by co-operating with every organized body whose aim is to abolish superstition, ignorance, intemperance, political injustice, or any other of the numerous evils which now afflict Society." Every person, "male or female," desirous of aiding in the promotion of these various objects, might join the Society without signing any confession of faith, provided such person undertook to pay an annual contribution of not less than a pound sterling.

The services consisted, as, indeed, everywhere else, of an alternation of hymns and prayers, together with devotional readings and a

---

dearly, into a happy and hopeful spring. Of the vicissitudes of our society it is not needful to say much. But one cannot mention those days without recalling the dear names of many who are gone to their heavenly rest and are not here to-day to witness the fruit of their pious exertions. Among our committee were to be found Dr. Patrick Black, Sir John Bowring, Samuel Courtauld, Charles Darwin, Erasmus Darwin, Sir Charles Lyell, Andrew Pritchard, Judge Stansfield, and our chairman, the Right Rev. Samuel Hinds, formerly Bishop of Norwich, and many others, amounting to 254, whose deaths we still deeply deplore.

"In 1875, we were compelled to leave St. George's Hall and go to Langham Hall, much to our disadvantage in every way. But in 1880 a very important change was made, and I claim the full credit or discredit of having urged it and finally brought it about. The work had suffered from ignorant or wilful misrepresentation and we were not sufficiently known to be a really religious body, working from religious motives for a religious end. Hence it became needful to drop the unpleasant and personal title of the *Voysey Establishment Fund* and to re-organize the society and give it a distinctive and religious name. In this measure I was supported by the counsel and sanction of the late Dean Stanley. I, on my part, also wished that the property of the Church should be so vested on a new Trust that the work could be carried on in the event of my death or retirement, and this could not have been done under the old Trust, which was 'to establish me in a Church of my own in London.' So we re-organized ourselves and adopted the title of THE THEISTIC CHURCH. This day, then, after fourteen years, is fulfilled the purpose for which the *Voysey Establishment Fund* was set on foot, and I need hardly say what must be in the heart of every true Theist amongst us:—That we rejoice and are exceeding glad—yea, unspeakably thankful.

"'This is the Lord's doing, and it is marvellous in our eyes.' 'This is the day which the Lord hath made: we will rejoice and be glad in it. Help us now, O Lord, send us now prosperity.'

"The emotions which these words express are too deep in your hearts and mine to bear reiteration. Instead of dwelling on our thankfulness in words, it is far better that I should follow the natural current of thought and feeling which is always set flowing by heartfelt gratitude. From time immemorial, as our dear Book of Psalms shows, the sense of God's bounty and loving-kindness always begets a deeper sense of our responsibilities and a longing to give some practical proof of our thankfulness, ' to show forth Thy praise O Lord, not only with our lips but in

sermon. The sermon which I heard was entitled, "The Means and the Glory of Spreading the Knowledge of Religion." The preacher said a little about everything in it; and he specially insisted upon the mistake made by Christian missionaries who treat as idolaters, if not as savages, peoples greatly advanced in the knowledge of God, instead of presenting themselves, as St. Paul did to the Athenians, with the simple claim to complete the ideas of their hearers respecting the Supreme Being and the immortality of the soul. Unfortunately, his tone was somewhat monotonous and magisterial, apart from the fact that the address rose but little above historical criticism. In spite of the intervention of the singing, I could have believed myself present at a critical exposition or lecture on the history of religions, rather than at a religious service, though one of a purely Theistic order. I may add that the congregation took no part in the service; that they remained seated the whole time, and did not join in the hymns, even in the faintest manner; nor was there any liturgy used to indicate the changes of the service. These circumstances, taken together, afford an explanation of the failure of this movement, which, as regards principles, was so closely connected with Mr. Voysey's Theistic Church. It is worthy of remark also that Mr. Voysey has arrived at

---

our lives, by giving up ourselves to Thy service and by walking before Thee in holiness and righteousness all our days to Thy honour and glory.' . . . . We rejoice most because, as we hope, the Truth which is so dear to us will become more widely known. We take a legitimate pleasure in thinking of the greater publicity and prominence of our Church, of the many who will become acquainted with the fact of our work and be able easily to learn for themselves what it is we believe and hope and wish to impart. For this only do we rejoice in our greater publicity, because we hope and expect to bring more people of our own way of thinking to come here and worship with us and also to bring into the fold many who are dissatisfied with the old Churches and creeds and may be induced to embrace our religious beliefs and to join with us in worship. It is our hope also to bring under the influence of our religion many out of the vast masses of those who never go to worship at all. I must add here also, though I am half ashamed of it, that we rejoice in having become possessed of this Church because it will remove a prejudice common to so many minds against worshipping in a Hall or other place of secular entertainment. No longer can the excuse be made that we assemble in an unworthy or an unsuitable place. . . . . This Theistic Church of ours has only lived till now through faithful attendance, marked as it has been in some cases by persons travelling 10, 20, 30 and even 50 miles to be present at the service and in all weathers. You will say, and say most truly, that the outer world will judge of your love for the cause, of your attachment to the creed you profess, by your actions and not by your profession, and therefore if you desire others to come into our fold and worship with us and catch our enthusiasm, we must at least be here to receive them, must show that we do value the reasonable worship, and are ready to

I

the present form of worship by the continued and logical development of his spiritual vocation, while the Free Church of the Independent Religious Reformers bears incontestable witness to the stiffness and lifelessness of a religious service which is purely the outcome of rational principles.

Among the Theistic organizations of London I must not omit to mention the Humanitarians, were it only by way of keeping my recollection fresh and green. As I was walking up the Pentonville slope, on a certain Sunday in 1875, in order to attend Unity Church, the charming Unitarian place of worship, at Islington, I passed in front of a building called Claremont Hall, where there was a bill posted up, which announced a series of lectures to be given by the Humanitarian Society. Among the names of the lecturers there were several indicative of a Jewish, a German, and even a Sclavonic origin. The subjects for treatment were of the most varied description, from "The religion of God" to "The Social Condition of the Blind." My curiosity having been aroused, I plunged into a dark passage, following two young men who were conversing in German. I soon found myself in a large hall provided with seats, where some score or so of persons were sitting at their ease. Near to a platform intended for the preacher stood the inevitable piano, which was already trembling beneath the touch of a young person dressed in black. The time passed on. A second air succeeded the first, then a third, and yet there

---

make sacrifices of comfort in our zeal for the cause. . . . . God help us all to walk in that path and uphold us when our feet would slip and guide us lest we go astray! O Thou Eternal Righteous Father, who hast been our refuge and strength in every time of trouble, and hast mercifully brought us to this House of Prayer, pour upon us the riches of thy grace that we may faithfully and godly serve Thee; that this Church which we this day consecrate anew to Thy service may be to all our hearts a means of grace, a comfort in all our sorrow and a strength against all temptation. Keep far from us vanity and lies, compromise and cowardice, indifference and insincerity; and graciously bestow upon us the spirit of humility and truth, of honesty and courage, of earnest faith and true religion, of fervent love to Thee and to all men. And if our work be good in thy sight, 'Help us now, O Lord, O Lord, send us now prosperity.'"

These passages indicate the deep religious spirit which permeates Mr. Voysey's teaching in spite of his theological antagonism to Christian dogmas. Had that teaching been almost exclusively negative the movement would have died out long ago. Nor need we wonder at the religious fervour which is displayed here. Historical considerations and influences apart, there is not the slightest reason why pure Theism should not create the most beautiful piety; for was not this Theism the creed of the grand old Prophets and even of Jesus himself, if he is to be regarded as truly human?—*Translator.*

was no sign of the preacher or lecturer's appearance. Wearied by this waiting, I at length lost all patience and beat a quiet retreat; but not without attracting the attention of a respectable elderly man standing near the door, who slipped into my hands a pamphlet with these attractive headings:—"The Age of Light," "The God of Nature," "Humanitarian Marriages," "Fifteen Points of the Religion of God," &c.

Imagine my astonishment at finding in the theories preached at the Pentonville Music Hall, the system of Pierre Leroux, who claimed to find in pagan philosophy, and even in Christianity, grounds for a belief in the transmigration of souls within the limits of human life here on earth. The Humanitarians tend more to Pantheism perhaps, since they define God as an eternal and indivisible Being, whose essence pervades the whole universe in the double form of matter and spirit; but their theory of the soul is an exact reproduction of the doctrine of the French writer in question.

Over and above an exposition of the "religion of God," the pamphlet contained several curious dissertations and controversial statements,—a confession of faith which only needed to be signed "conscientiously," in order to give any person the right to use the name and enjoy the privileges of the Humanitarians; a few words of gratitude to the "God of Nature," entitled the *Prayer of the Humanitarians*; certain extracts from discourses delivered in the open air, "superior to and superseding the first four chapters of the New Testament, as well as the Sermon on the Mount"; and, finally, the rites for the "Humanitarian solemnization of marriage." These rites, it appears, were made use of for the first time in 1873, on the occasion of the marriage of Mr. Joachim Kaspary, the chief apostle of the movement, with the daughter of the originator. But as the civil legislation of England, which is not as yet "humanitarianized," would not have recognized the marriage had it taken place in Claremont Hall, the bride and bridegroom, with their friends, were driven, per force, to use, for the ceremony, a chapel, whose minister, Mr. Conway, had complied with the requirements of the law by having it duly licensed.

On my visit to London in the summer of 1882, I expected to find that the Humanitarians had long since disappeared; but, instead of this, I found them established in the heart of London, in a house in

Castle Street, where Mr. Kaspary, then become the head of the sect by right of succession, had constructed, in his back premises, a small wooden chapel capable of seating some sixty persons. As regards the service, it seemed to me simplified by the absence of the piano, and it was also commenced at the appointed hour. It consisted of an apologetic kind of discourse and an extemporaneous prayer by Mr. Kaspary, with a sort of interlude from Mrs. Kaspary, who ascended the platform to read the "Fifteen Precepts of the Religion of the Humanitarians." The congregation, a by no means numerous one, was formed exclusively of members of the male sex.

Still, the Humanitarians continue their mission with an energy which testifies to their sincerity; for they connect with their weekly Sunday services preaching in the open air—during the summer in Regent's Park, and under the arches of Chelsea Bridge in the winter. They also advertise their Castle Street meetings in the Saturday's *Daily News*, and they distribute an immense number of tracts, either gratuitously or at a reduced price.

The strangest aspect of this movement is not that an individual should have invented or formulated such a vague and questionable system as Humanitarianism, but that people should have been found to believe, follow, and support it. As yet, in truth, save and except the marriage of its adherents, preaching has constituted the only manifestation of the Humanitarian faith; but they will doubtless develop their ritual as fast as the need for this makes itself felt. It cannot be denied, indeed, that we see, in what I have described, the infancy of a new religion. If the movement does not succumb during this embryonic period, which may be called its metaphysical phase, we may foresee, from its tendency to dogmatic assertion, that it will not be slow to transform itself into a positive system of worship, with its necessary train of spontaneous or reflective practices, if not with a whole system of theology, based upon some pretended revelation. At present, however, Humanitarianism constitutes a tolerably harmless doctrine, which is perfectly moral in its precepts as well as in its practices, and is wholly confined to that super-sensible sphere where all sorts of religious speculations are permissible, so far as they are sincerely advanced, from the very fact that the processes of the scientific method can demonstrate neither their truth nor their falseness.

It should be clearly understood that, in mentioning the Humanitarian Society in this enumeration of the Theistic congregations, I do so because it forms a sort of religious curiosity, and not from any illusive ideas as to its real importance. It is only Mr. Voysey's congregation which offers to Theism a rallying point or centre of action capable of assuming a great development, if it should succeed in uniting all who accept its doctrines. Unhappily, it has to struggle against that absence of enthusiasm, or rather spirit of proselytism, which generally characterizes Theists, and leads them, as I have already intimated, either to remain in the churches which they have really outgrown or to shut themselves up in a sort of religious individualism when they have left them.

It is perhaps here that I should describe the doctrine of the Reformed Jews, who, rejecting the infallibility of their sacred books, have made common cause with a rationalistic Monotheism. The Jewish Reformation, which was set on foot, at the beginning of this century, by the German Jews, with certain simplifications of ritual, and which gradually extended to the Jews of all civilized countries, is at present seeking to denationalize the Jewish religion, or rather to transform it into a universal religion, by stripping off all the rites, practices, and ceremonies which possess a national, as distinguished from a purely religious, character. "Its realization," wrote, a short time since, one of the most distinguished representatives of the new school in England, Mr. Claude Montefiore, "would put Judaism on the same footing as Christianity, and would involve the removal of the present preliminary obstacles in the way of the diffusion, not yet desired by all reformers, of the old Jewish religion beyond the limits of the Jewish race." In this way, the reproach so frequently urged against Judaism, that it is only a tribal religion, would disappear, and the true Chinese wall, which separates its adherents from the people among whom they live, would fall to the ground. But the change cannot be made, as events have shown, unless Judaism also abandons those positive beliefs which are irreconcilable with modern science.[1]

The Jewish religion has always consisted of two distinct elements: a collection of doctrines, in which the belief in the unity of God is

---

1. *Vide* an article, by Mr. Montefiore, entitled "Is Judaism a Tribal Religion?" in the *Contemporary Review*, of November, 1882.

as a key-stone to the arch; and the ceremonial practices peculiar to it as a special system. Regarded from a doctrinal point of view, reformed Judaism, according to Mr. Montefiore, affirms, in common with orthodox Judaism, "the unity of God, His just government, the free relation of every man to God, the continual progress of humanity as a whole, the immortality of the soul, the Divine election of Israel, and that the Jews, under the will of God, possess a specific religious mission, not yet entirely fulfilled." On the other hand, the reforming party reject the authority of the Talmud, the literal infallibility of the Bible, comprising the Pentateuch, the belief in the advent of the Messiah, and the restoration of the Jewish kingdom in Palestine. While they hold, moreover, that the Bible contains the essential spirit of Judaism, they contend that it no longer contains this in its entirety; and they do not hesitate to accept the most advanced conclusions of contemporary criticism. As to ceremonial practices, they openly reject—with the exception of circumcision, which they make optional for converts—all the ritualistic, sanitary, and social prescriptions which are not possessed of an exclusively religious significance, as well as the Jewish laws relative to marriage and the regulations respecting the Levites. Finally, they have introduced into the synagogue the common or current speech of the worshippers, and suppressed the greater part of the festivals which possessed a purely national significance.

Under these circumstances, it may be asked whether Judaism is not in a condition to offer to Theists of Christian origin that historical rallying-point which, according to Miss F. Power Cobbe, they stand in need of. It is to be borne in mind, indeed, that the Jewish Reformation is still in progress, if not as regards dogma, at least in relation to its ceremonial practices. That prescription of the ancient law which is most repugnant to modern ideas, circumcision, is precisely the institution they seem to find the greatest difficulty in completely abolishing. Nor has the use of Hebrew entirely disappeared from their ritual, while the Old Testament remains the book of devotion *par excellence*, and the only one used in the services of the synagogue. In short, Mr. Montefiore himself declares that the reformed faith, while desirous of becoming a universal religion in form as well as in substance, intends to remain a historical development of ancient Judaism.

It appears, therefore, that Reformed Judaism simply maintains, with respect to Ancient Judaism, the position occupied by Unitarianism, or even by the Broad Church party, in relation to those Protestant Churches which have remained faithful to orthodox theology. Still, as Miss Cobbe observes, if the reforming movement continues to extend—and such an extension seems to be a question of life or death for Judaism—it will undoubtedly become a powerful auxiliary of Christian Theism, or Theism of Christian origin, while it will even be capable of exercising an important influence on the religious future of contemporary Society.[1]

Now, the simple belief in God is still a dogma, however little we define the attributes of the Divine Being and make of this definition the creed of any church. But if we admit that worship is merely a question of feeling, belonging neither to reason nor faith, we must free it from every positive formula, no matter how simple and comprehensive this may be. Setting out from this principle, Mr. Moncure D. Conway, a gentleman of American origin, who is favourably known in English literature, has, for the last twenty years, presided over a Church which is open to all those who desire to satisfy their religious aspirations, regardless of theological and metaphysical differences of belief, with the sole condition that they do not raise to a dogma the non-existence of the Deity. Such a conception embraces not only Theists of every school, but also Pantheists and the Positivists of the school of John Stuart Mill, with all the sceptics who refuse to express an opinion with regard to the reality of a Supreme Being. I should hesitate to say, indeed, that Materialists might not find a place in such a scheme of thought, since it excludes none but professed Atheists.

Mr. Conway, who assumes neither the title of reverend nor doctor, is a tall, thin man, about fifty years old, of robust aspect, greyish beard and keen changeful glance, whose whole physiognomy reveals his transatlantic origin. Born in Virginia and descended from a family of planters which has played a part in the history of the United States, he was brought up in that branch of the Methodist body

---

1. Miss Cobbe relates the curious fact that, at Manchester, some twenty young girls, belonging to Unitarian families, have married Jews, adopted Judaism, and even taken an active part in the affairs of the synagogue. *Vide* her article, "Progressive Judaism," in the *Contemporary Review*, of November, 1882.

whose members go forth from home every spring, in order to form those religious encampments so well described by Bret Harte in his stories of American life. Mr. Conway himself, indeed, in a sermon on *Revivalism*, draws a touching picture of the religious associations of his childhood, and of the vain attempts he made to share in the mental exaltation of his early surroundings. Having remained faithful to the Union at the time of the Civil War, he withdrew, with his young wife, into the State of Ohio, where he organised, into a free community, his father's slaves who had fled from Virginia. He then crossed the Atlantic in order to defend before the English public, by both tongue and pen, the Federal cause, which seemed to be daily meeting with increased hostility on the part of the British Government. In the course of this campaign, he had occasion to make his voice heard several times at South Place Chapel, where W. J. Fox had long been the minister. Mr. Fox was a Unitarian minister who had played a brilliant part, during the second generation of this century, in the Parliamentary struggles in which Bright and Cobden were such conspicuous figures. M. Guizot characterised his speeches as models of political eloquence. Nor was he less advanced in his religious than in his political opinions; he was in reality one of the first Unitarian ministers who openly broke with the supernatural, and though he retained the name of Christian, he afterwards remained isolated from the Unitarian body. Unfortunately for his congregation, when age had compelled him to retire, they could not find a preacher possessed of the same shade of opinions, and they were possibly on the eve of corporate dissolution, when at the commencement of 1864, they made choice of Mr. Conway for their minister.

Under the guidance of the young American, the congregation was not slow to regain the cohesion and the brilliant position of previous years; but this was not done without following that course of evolution which, with Fox, had caused it to advance beyond Unitarianism, and which, with Mr. Conway, was to carry it first from Christian Theism to pure Theism, and then to a form of faith with still fewer limitations: Mr. Conway contends, in short, that the religious sentiment may and must be separated from everything of the nature of dogma, belief or hypothesis.

South Place Chapel is but a few minutes' walk from Moorgate Street Station which, on the occasion of my visit, I reached by the undergound railway. In common with a large number of Nonconformist Chapels, its frontage is in the Greek style. The interior possesses a certain air of comfort and is capable of seating from four to five hundred persons. The organ is over the entrance. On each side there is a gallery supported by slender pillars. A large platform, with a sort of desk ornamented by two brass brackets, serves as a pulpit. Seats furnished with red cushions and well supplied with books fill all the available space. When I entered at a little past eleven the chapel was almost empty, but scarcely had the old lady, who acts as sacristan, assigned me a place under one of the side galleries, before the seats began to fill rapidly. A large number of ladies, some of them dressed in an elegant style, agreeably diversified the earnest and intelligent aspect of the audience. I learnt afterwards, that the congregation is chiefly drawn from the ranks of scientists and professional men, with a sprinkling from a few wealthy city families. It may be remarked here that South Place Chapel represents the extreme left in its political as well as in its religious tendencies, while at Langham Hall, on the other hand, Mr. Voysey has retained in his liturgy the Prayers for the Church, the Queen, the Prince of Wales, the two Houses of Parliament, &c.

Shortly after the entrance of the congregation, Mr. Conway ascended the platform in non clerical costume, turned on the gas in order to get more light, and, having opened a large book, gave out the number of the hymn by which the service was to be commenced. The singing was almost entirely confined to a well-trained choir, and the readings were chosen by the minister from one of his own works, the *Sacred Anthology*, in which he has collected with great discrimination more than 700 passages drawn from various ancient authors. The Bible figures there side by side with the Koran and the Védas, and Confucius is hand and hand with St. Paul. This work, Mr. Conway told me, is used in about a dozen congregations—probably among those Unitarians who have reached the confines of Theism. As to the hymns, they are contained in a small and very elegantly bound volume, *Hymns and Anthems*, and amount to more than 500 in number. The first 150 were compiled by Mr. W. J. Fox; the rest have been added by Mr. Conway. The latter told me he had chosen from preference such compositions as avoid all mention of a personal and conscious God. He rejects prayer, first because it so easily degenerates into an illogical appeal for change in the order of nature, and secondly because by invoking the Divinity, we seem to attribute to him sentiments, if not organs, analogous to our own. He has therefore replaced it in his order of service by "Meditations" or moral and religious monologues, which tend to elevate the soul without making a direct appeal to the Deity.

When Mr. Conway had finished his second "meditation," the organ was played for a short time in a subdued tone, to give the congregation an opportunity of entering into themselves and reflecting upon the words of their minister; then the choir suddenly burst forth into a well executed anthem by a composer with whose name I am not acquainted. Then came the turn for the sermon or discourse. Mr. Conway had chosen for the occasion a text of the most secular kind: public health. Still, while remaining wholly on practical ground, he took care to skilfully describe the relations which subsist between health of body and health of soul, in conformity with the Protestant adage, that cleanliness is next to godliness. Besides, it is one of his fundamental principles that to advance science is to promote the cause of religion.

Mr. Conway sometimes lends his pulpit to noted foreigners. Among those who have thus delivered addresses there, to say nothing of Unitarian ministers and University professors, we may mention an American, Colonel Wentworth Higginson, and an Indian Theist, a member of the Royal Council in the island of Ceylon. One evening a week, the members of the congregation meet in the chapel, which is transformed into a debating hall, in order to discuss some moral or political question. In common with the majority of Nonconformist congregations drawn from similar classes, the South Place congregation organize periodical *Soirées* for music and conversation, with picnics into the country and water parties on the Thames at the right season. In this way the Chapel is not only a religious home, but a centre or rallying point for the cultivation of social relations among its members. Meetings of this kind are generally announced from the pulpit, and tickets for them sold in the vestry.

Some years ago, Mr. Conway devoted his Sunday evenings to a second congregation, located in a small iron Church, situate in St. Paul's Road, Camden Town, which, from the simplicity of its architecture, reminded me of the wooden churches of the Scandinavian Peninsula. This congregation was formed by a colony of Free Christians, who had migrated, so to speak, from Clarence Road, in consequence of a disagreement on the choice of a minister. Mr. Conway, whom they had invited to take charge of the movement, succeeded so well in gradually bringing them over to his ideas that, at the time of my visit, in 1875, they had abandoned the name "Free Christian" and adopted the same kind of service as that in use at South Place Chapel.

This circumstance affords a striking illustration of the facilities which Protestantism affords for advancing, by a gradual and almost insensible transition, to forms of worship more in harmony with the continued development of the reason of the individual. The Roman Church, on the other hand, has its limits clearly circumscribed, and if anyone passes beyond these, it is at the expense of an abrupt and often painful process, in order to reach at a bound the utmost limits of scepticism, or at least to become the prey of religious indifference. But among Protestants, in spite of the dogmatic bonds in which they, in some cases, attempt to embody their doctrines, the churches of to-day are as landmarks, destined to indicate the stages traversed by religious thought in its evolution towards a larger and freer ideal. Hence it is possible for every one to halt at the precise point of this evolution, which corresponds with his own measure of moral and intellectual culture.

I attended two services in the St. Paul's Road Chapel. The form of worship was identical with that in Mr. Conway's other Chapel, except in so far as the absence of an organ led to the omission of the anthem. The singing, thus without an accompaniment, seemed to me of a less excellent order, but, on the other hand, the congregation joined heartily in the hymns. On each occasion, I found a congregation of from 200 to 250 persons, who, judging from their appearance, were probably drawn from lower strata of Society than those at South Place, though still belonging to the middle classes. The service struck me as being possessed of more interest and fervour than in the older congregation, almost all the people having service-books, and no one remaining seated during the singing.

I must add, however, that the St. Paul's Road congregation is no longer in existence, and that even its Chapel has disappeared. It is probable, indeed, that after being sold and taken down, the little edifice was re-erected elsewhere, and may perhaps serve to-day as the quarters of some regiment of the forces of "General" Booth, in his campaign against the army of Satan.

Mr. Conway lays it down as an axiomatic truth, that an instinct compels us to render homage to the superior principle, generally embodied in the idea of God; but, at the same time, he thinks we should not press this notion too far, for fear of identifying it with a dogmatic formula which may be found on the morrow in antagonism with some recent verification of science. For him God is not to be distinguished from the human ideal. This ideal, men are but too ready to project outside of themselves, as a concrete existence, and to clothe with attributes which crystallize into dogmas. Now, however valuable a doctrine may be as an individual conviction, it is no sooner embodied in a dogma, he contends, than it ceases to be true and fruitful—were it even the belief in the existence of God or the immortality of the soul: "If the idea of God have value," says he, "'tis as the supreme expression of an individual development of thought. If immortality be a noble idea it is as the flower of a soul's experience. Prescribe them, dictate them, impose them by bribe or threat, however refined, they become mere phrases, lifeless traditions, transmitted from crumbled systems of antiquity, not only choking the well of spiritual life, but heaping rubbish in the Jacob's Well of opinion itself."[1]

It is, however, in a sermon preached by Mr. Conway in May, 1880, on the *Religion of Humanity*, that I have found perhaps the most complete exposition of his religious beliefs, and in which the trace of Hegelian ideas is easy of recognition. He remarks there that history as a whole may be summed up as the struggle of humanity against external nature, but that our sentiments have always been on the side of our adversary. After transforming the forces of nature into Gods, we assigned to them, as their kingdom, all that transcended our own control, so much so that the true domain of humanity has always been in opposition to, and in conflict with that of Nature. At a later time the divinities, which were the personifications of inorganic forces, gave place to abstract dogmas; but these dogmas themselves merely translated into the language of theology the relentless activities of

---

1. *Jacob's Well.* A Sermon, 1882.

nature. Is it not a great misfortune to see men thus offering their adoration to what genuine religion commands them to combat and to subjugate? "We can little dream what a reinforcement of the human work it would be if all the devotion and wealth lavished on deities and dogmas were directed to aid and animate man in his tremendous task of humanising his world."[1] It is therefore high time for us to transfer our veneration and our worship to those moral and intellectual forces which aid us in our struggle with the blind forces of the world, and which constitute as a whole the essence of humanity.

Does it follow that there is no God, either of or in nature—that there is neither above nor beyond us any Power that tends to the realization of the Good? The religion of humanity answers: "Yes, there is a God in nature—a God and Ruler of nature; but that Divine Parent is nowhere discoverable, except in the spirit of humanity. You may cry for help to glowing suns and circling stars, to gravitation and electricity, to ocean and sky, or to all of them together, but no help or ray of pity will you get until you have turned to lean on the heart and arm of human love and strength; for these are the answers of the universe to your cry. The proof of love in nature outside you is a loving heart inside you. But we must credit nature with what has come out of it. . . . Out of it, all was evolved: the thinker to warn us; the man of science to show us the safe path; the physician to heal us; the artist to beguile us on the way; the poet to cheer us; the friend, the lover, the father, the mother, who try to guard us, or, if we are wounded, seek to heal our wounds. All these were evolved out of nature. They show us nature pointing us to humanity, the crown and hope of nature's own self, the power which nature has created for its own deliverance—in distrusting which we distrust the only God in nature, the God manifest within us and in the sweet humanities around us."[1]

I may add that as a speaker, Mr. Conway, though he does not aim at eloquence, possesses a very clear and above all a very moving voice. Hence he exercises an ascendency which extends beyond his immediate religious surroundings. He has, without doubt, contributed, for instance, to the formation in the Unitarian Church, of that group which I have already mentioned, as identifying the conception of God with the ideal of humanity. There is to be seen among its members,

---

1. *What is the Religion of Humanity?*

indeed, the same tendency to reject every dogmatic formula in favour of an exclusive appeal to the manifestations of sentiment and imagination, the same claim that religious services should possess a practical character, and the same optimist confidence in the future of humanity.

In his estimate of the person and work of Christ, Mr. Conway follows in some measure the methods of Unitarianism. Among the illustrious names inscribed in gilt letters on the walls of his chapel, that of Jesus occupies the place of honour above the reading desk, and by the side of it are the names of Shakespeare, Socrates, Voltaire and Moses. In several of his sermons, he speaks of the founder of Christianity as a "representative man," and he neglects no opportunity of characterising him as the religious reformer *par excellence*. All, he thinks, that is most elevated or comprehensive in the New Testament, all that is best calculated to strengthen the mind and heart, all, in a word, that is conformable to the views held at South Place Chapel, is really the authentic work of Jesus. On the contrary, whatever is to be found there of a narrow and irrational character and therefore opposed to the tendencies of our epoch, must have been introduced by the Evangelists, who were unable or unwilling to understand the Master.[1] Here Mr. Conway speaks more like a Christian than some among the Unitarians.

Now, in opposition to this, those Unitarians who seem nearest to an avowal of the "Religion of Humanity" do not hesitate to retain the name of God for that ideal which Mr. Conway treats as an impersonal and nameless Power, or even as purely subjective. Hence there is, with certain of the younger ministers belonging to the advanced

---

1. Thus in his *Jacob's Well*, in reproducing the conversation of the Master with the Samaritan woman, he describes, in excellent language, the sublime beauty of the words which John puts into the mouth of Jesus: "The hour cometh when ye shall neither in this mountain nor yet at Jerusalem, worship the Father. . . . But the hour cometh and now is when the true worshippers shall worship the Father in spirit and in truth." Now these two sentences are separated by the verse which affirms that "salvation is of Jesus." Mr. Conway does not hesitate to say that this verse must have been interpolated by the narrator, and he adds that this interposition of bigotry and superstition proves how far even the evangelist, most comprehensive in his tendencies, was from being able after the lapse of three or four generations, to rise to the level of Jesus. Further, the fact that the three synoptical evangelists have omitted the entire episode, although they were nearer to Jesus in point of time, probably arose from their being too Jewish to appreciate this abandonment of the religious monoply of Jerusalem. With this system of critical thought it is easy for Mr. Conway to justify his statement "that the real issue is between Christ and Christianity."

section of Unitarianism—as, for instance, with the Rev. Frank Walters, of Glasgow—a combination of religious elements, which enables them to unite, in their preaching, all the results of modern inquiry with the spiritual power comprised in the idea of a Supreme Being.

To sum up my remarks, the religious organization over which Mr. Conway presides bears the same relation to the Rev. C. Voysey's "Theistic Church" that Unitarianism does to Liberal Anglicanism. In vain will Mr. Voysey urge that his Church retains no dogmas, but merely perfectible beliefs; for his programme will none the less result in the exclusion of those who believe in Revelation, on the one hand, and those who decline to affirm the existence of a personal God, on the other—in a word, the orthodox, together with Pantheists and Agnostics. South Place congregation, however, forms an open Church to the full extent of the term. Not that the minister is destitute of all beliefs, or even dogmas, as to the nature of the universe, the indefinite perfectability of human society, and the like. But he does not seek to establish between the members of his flock any other bond than that of spiritual communion, founded on the identity of the moral, religious, and humanitarian sentiments, and this he does regardless of all theoretical divergence. His congregation has a further advantage over that at Langham Hall, in the possession of a historic past, a flourishing budget, and a building adapted to the purpose for which it is used. And yet, if I ventured to give an opinion of its future, I should hesitate to affirm that its existence is not bound up with the life of its present minister.[2]

It is not every day, indeed, that a Moncure Conway is to be found to succeed a W. J. Fox, for the drawback which attaches to brilliant personalities is that when they adopt neither a definite doctrine nor a collective organization, they at last absorb the groups of which they assume the direction. Mr. Conway seems to have felt this himself when, in a recent letter to the Boston *Index*,[1] in relation, it is true, to Positivism and Theism, he showed that the religious development of England is rather along the lines of existing Unitarianism than in any other direction.

---

1. Since the text of this work was written, Mr. Conway has resigned the South Place pulpit, but as yet (October, 1884) no successor has been appointed, though a gentleman is spoken of as likely to prove the elect of the congregation.—*Translator*.

2. The *Index*, of June the 8th, 1882.

CHAPTER VI.

COMTISM AND SECULARISM.

The philosophical and religious system of Auguste Comte—Worship of the Grand-Etre, Humanity—Organization of the Positivist priesthood—The new calendar—Comtism in England—Dr. Congreve and the Positivist liturgy of Chapel Street—The secession of 1878—Professor Beesley, Dr. Bridges, Mr. Frederic Harrison, and the worship of Humanity at Fleur-de-Lis—The London Positivist Society—Sincere faith and mental discipline of the Comptists—The attempt to unite in a common conception the Grand-Etre of Comte with the Unknowable of Herbert Spencer—A religion which proscribes the religious sentiment—Meaning of Secularism—Its self-satisfied ignorance of the super-sensible—Utilitarian character of its morality—The National Secular Society and Mr. Bradlaugh's aggressive attitude—Mr. G. J. Holyoake's secession and the establishment of the British Secular Union—Associations for the free use of the Sunday—The Secular Liturgy, with a Preface by Mr. Bradlaugh—Secular religious services a proof of the religiousness of the English mind—Conclusions suggested by the oscillations between faith and scepticism in England—Increasing purification of the religious sentiment and the gradual emancipation of Thought.

It may have been supposed by the reader that with Mr. Conway's congregation we had reached the extreme limits of religious organizations, and that beyond it there could be no possibility of worship, since there is no longer a recognition of the Divine existence. Still, if by religion we are to understand a theory of life which adopts as its central fact man's sense of dependence upon a Superior Being, this word may certainly be applied to the Worship of Humanity which has been established in England by Comtism, or to speak more definitely, by that fraction of Positivism which has remained faithful to the religious as well as to the philosophical doctrines of Auguste Comte.

It was the opinion of Comte that religion alone is capable of leading to the predominance of altruism over egoism in the life of the individual: that is to say, of making social considerations more powerful than personal interests. To accomplish this mission, however, it was necessary, he held, that religion should become independent, not only of all supernatural beliefs, but also of all theological ideas, so that it

K

might simply represent that condition of spiritual unity resulting from the convergence of all our thoughts and of all our actions towards the service of Humanity.[1]

Every form of religion, he remarks, comprises three essential elements: dogma which addresses itself to reason, worship which makes an appeal to sentiment, and ethical precepts which govern the action of the individual. In the Religion of Humanity, dogma is made identical with the positive philosophy, that is to say, with science considered as the study of law in nature, to the exclusion of first and final causes. As to worship or sociolatry, it is made to consist of homage rendered to the Grand-Etre, Humanity, in other words to the totality of human beings, past, present and future, with the exception of the mere parasites of life who have not co-operated usefully in the world's common work, but inclusive of the useful animals, the worthy helpers of human life. Lastly, the ethical precepts of the Comtist creed constitute a collection of hygienic, moral, social and political prescriptions, in which its originator seems to have thrown together, pell-mell, ideas borrowed from all the socialist systems of the day. An extreme tendency to authoritative prescription pervades these rules of life, and the whole are cemented together by a sense of duty to Humanity on the one side, and by the absolute authority of the Positivist priesthood on the other.

Worship is made to possess three forms: personal, domestic and public. Personal worship *(le culte intime)* is to be rendered to those who are related to us by blood or affection. It consists of three daily acts of prayer—one on rising in the morning, a second in the midst of our ordinary occupations, whether they are practical or theoretical, and the last at the approach of sleep. The first two are to take place before the domestic altar, instituted according to our richest memories, and in the attitude of veneration; the last should be performed after we retire to rest and continued as far as possible till the coming on of sleep. To prayer there may be added the use of various accessories "borrowed from the æsthetic treasures of humanity," such as songs, pictures and the like.

---

[1]. Comte's religious views are to be found in his *Systeme de Politique Positive* or *Treatise on Sociology*, which institutes the Religion of Humanity (Paris, 1851-54), as well as in his *Catéchisme Positiviste* or *Summarized Exposition of the Universal Religion* (Paris, 1852).

Domestic worship consists of nine "social sacraments:" 1st, *Presentation*, in which the child receives the name of a "theoretical" and also the name of a "practical" model or pattern saint—he will choose the "artistic" himself as he grows up; 2nd, *Initiation*, at 14; 3rd, *Admission*, at 21; 4th, *Destination* or the final choice of an avocation, at 28; 5th, *Marriage*, beginning at 29 with men, and at 21 for women—neither widows nor widowers can re-marry; 6th, *Maturity*, at 42, the age of complete cerebral development; 7th, *Retirement* from active life, at 63; 8th, *Transformation*, a sort of extreme unction in which the priest mingling the regrets of society with the tears of the family, worthily commemorates the life which is about to close; and 9th, *Incorporation*, seven years after death, when judgment is pronounced on the deceased, in conformity with the custom of ancient Egypt. According to the sentence thus pronounced, the remains are to be cast into an obscure place designed for reprobates, with the bodies of criminals, suicides, and duellists, or on the other hand, deposited "in a sacred wood," where a simple inscription is to be placed on the tomb, with a bust or statue, in harmony with the degree of honour attained.

Public worship is to be celebrated in churches placed among the tombs of the *élite*, and so built that the worshippers may have their gaze directed towards the metropolis of the world, which "the common voice of the past has long identified with Paris." A woman of 30, holding her son in her arms is to symbolize the Grand-Etre, or Humanity. The same emblem figures upon a white and green banner, which is to be used in processions, and to bear on the other side the sacred formula of Positivism: *Vivre pour autrui, l'amour pour principle, l'ordre pour base, le progrés pour but.*[1] The reader will judge for himself how far Professor Huxley was justified in saying that the Positivist faith was Catholicism minus Christianity; to which remark an adherent of Comtism replied that it was Catholicism plus science.

In addition to its religious addresses, Positivism has its various festivals, which bear a direct relation to its reformed calendar. This calendar, which is much more logical than that in common use, contains thirteen months of twenty-eight days, with a complementary day each year, and a second of such days in the Leap Year. Each month

---

[1] "We live for others: love is our principle, order our method, progress our aim."

is divided into four weeks of seven days, and the months themselves are dedicated respectively to Moses, Homer, Aristotle, Archimedes, Cæsar, St. Paul, Charlemagne, Dante, Gutenberg, Shakespeare, Descartes, Frederick the Second, and Bichat. The days of the week (*Maridi, Patridi, Filidi, Fratridi, Domidi, Matridi, Humanidi*) have also names of "saints" borrowed from the list of illustrious persons who have rendered service to humanity. Comte modestly declined to inscribe his own name on the roll of the world's illustrious sons, but the omission has been made good by his followers, who have instituted festivals commemorative of his birth and death, in his old apartments, Rue Mons. le Prince, at Paris. It is worthy of note that though he has placed the names of Hercules, Haroun-al-Raschid, St. Theresa, Innocent the Third, and Joseph de Maistre on the roll in question, he has omitted the name of Christ.

The complementary day of the calendar is designed as a universal festival of the dead, and the additional day of the Leap Year forms the festival of Reprobates, which has been specially instituted for the reprobation of the three principal traitors to progress, Julian the Apostate, Philip the Second, and Bonaparte. The Positivist era dates from the destruction of the Bastille in 1789, and its calendar is intended for use in the organization of the concrete worship of Humanity; that is to say, in the worship of the Grand-Etre, adored in the person of a few individuals who are worthy of being regarded as typical of the best in humanity. But, in addition to this, an abstract form of worship is instituted, in which the worshipper no longer bows before this or that historical personage, but before some form of human relationship, such as marriage, paternity, woman's character and influence, the priesthood, and the like.

The most original and perhaps the most severely criticised feature of the Comtist system, is its conception of a priesthood which forms a true theocracy without a *Theos*. No order of society, says Comte, can be maintained and developed without some kind of priesthood. Hence he advocates the desirability of three orders of clergy, at the rate of one "spiritual functionary" for every 6000 persons. This priesthood, sovereignly directed by a High-Priest of Humanity resident at Paris, would have the exclusive charge of education, of developing "the higher branches of theoretical science, of cultivating poetry and practicing medicine, and lastly of giving a moral tone to the government of the Western Republic, which will be concentrated in the hands of some few bankers!

Anyone who knew Comte simply by this exposition of his social and religious system, would be tempted to see in it, either a Utopia deliberately devised by some wit, or else a scheme which originated among the lunatics at Charenton. And yet, to-day, some twenty-five years after the death of its author, the Comtist system is fully accepted by groups of intelligent and sincere men in France, England, Ireland, Sweden, the United States, Brazil, &c. Among its adherents, in England more especially, there are men who occupy the front rank in the intellectual aristocracy of the country. Certainly Comte himself was anything but a visionary or an impostor; and no one can study his modest and laborious life without feeling a genuine esteem for him as a thinker of the first order, who in spite of his caprices and oddities was capable of exercising a complete fascination upon those who surrounded him. Besides, if the philosophical principles of Positivism are accepted, its religious doctrines appear far less arbitrary and strange than at first sight one is apt to suppose them.

England early showed a willingness to accept the religious as well as the philosophical doctrines of Positivism. It is true, Stuart Mill rejected the former, and that he slightly modified even the latter in order to adapt them to English ideas. Still others accepted the system of the French philosopher in its entirety, and among them were Dr. Richard Congreve, an Oxford Professor, and Dr. Bridges, the Inspector-General of Manufactures. On the death of Comte, in 1857, when his executors had accepted Mons. P. Lafitte as their leader *ad interim*, Dr. Congreve, who was placed at the head of the English branch of the Positivist Church, drew together its London adherents into a building in Chapel Street, where he gradually organised the Worship of Humanity. This "Church," which I visited in 1875, resembles an ordinary Dissenting place of worship, and the visitor might take it for such, were it not for the presence on its walls of thirteen plaster casts of those who have given their names to the months of the calendar. The service, which at present takes place every Sunday, consists of hymns, pieces of music, readings, and a sermon or lecture, with prayers to the Grand-Etre, as well as thanksgivings addressed to the most meritorious types of humanity.

Here is a summary of the curious liturgy which Dr. Congreve has composed for the celebration of the festival of Humanity, which is fixed for the first of January by the Comtist Calendar. The ceremony begins by an invocation: that is to say, by the reading of the sacred formulary I have already mentioned. Then follows a reading from the *Imitation*, after which comes a collect, in which the officiating minister addresses himself directly to humanity in these terms:— "Thou Power Supreme, who hast hitherto guided thy children under other names, but in this generation hast come to thy own in thy own proper person, revealed for all ages to come by thy servant Auguste Comte, we praise thee," &c. (*The Religion of Humanity*, page 2.)

After this collect, the following dialogue in relation to humanity takes place between minister and congregation:—

Priest—We bow before thee in thankfulness,

People—As children of thy past.

Priest—We adore thee in hope,

People—As thy ministers and stewards for the future.

Priest—We would commune with thee humbly in prayer,

People—As thy servants in the present.

All—May our worship, as our lives, grow more and more worthy of thy great name.

The sermon being over and another prayer having been said, the service is brought to a close by the following benediction: "The Faith of Humanity, the Hope of Humanity, the Love of Humanity, bring you comfort and teach you sympathy, give you peace in yourselves and peace with others now and for ever.—*Amen*." This liturgy, as the reader will have seen, draws largely upon the spirit and even the text of the *Imitation*.[1]

Here again is the text, from the same manual, of a collect for St.

---

[1] Thomas à Kempis is in great favour among the orthodox disciples of Comte, who have strongly recommended the use of the *Imitation* as a manual of piety and holiness of universal acceptance, on condition, of course, that Humanity be substituted for God, the social type for the personal type in Jesus, our spiritual progress for the rewards of a future life, our social instincts for grace, and our selfish instincts for nature. "So used," says Dr. Congreve, in his little manual, *The Religion of Humanity*, "its lessons of devotion and humility, of intimate communion with the type we adore, of unceasing moral culture, of self-denying service, of the service not of ourselves, but of others, are not the less available because they are clothed in the language of an older faith and sanctioned by the experience of many generations of faithful and devout men."

Francis of Assisi, whose festival or day of commemoration occurs on the twentieth of Charlemagne in the Comtist calendar (7th of July):—
"In another time and with another belief, we, who on this day reverently honour the memory of this eminent saint of the older dispensation, St. Francis of Assisi, pray that his example may not be lost upon us, but that his seraphic love for the object of his devotion may teach us a like love for the suffering and wounded Humanity whom we preach and serve, that in the force of that love we may catch some portion of this saint's great humility, of the richness of his spirit of renunciation, of his unbounded simple affection for all his fellow men, for all living beings, for all outward objects; lastly of his patient and loving resignation—So by our lives glorifying our service as he glorified his; so spreading, as he spread his faith; the nobler and more enduring faith into which that of Mediæval Europe has in our times been transfigured."

I shall close these extracts by the reproduction of the prayer which Dr. Congreve has drawn up for the sacrament of the presentation of children:—

"Grand Power whom we adore as the source of all good to men, Humanity; we thy servants, met for the consecration of a new life to thy service, humbly and earnestly pray that the child by this sacrament presented and consecrated may be lovingly, faithfully, and wisely trained; that under all wholesome influences of affection, and submission, and reverence *he* may grow up to be in his turn rich in such influences for others, taking his part in thy continuous work. We pray, moreover for ourselves, that whatever our share in this celebration, we may all alike use it rightly to re-kindle our devotion, and as an occasion for renewing our dedication of ourselves to thee; that it may leave us at once humbler and better—humbler from the sense of our great shortcomings, better by the resolve to use more carefully the opportunity still left us for improvement, self-sacrifice for others, zeal and activity in thy cause—so glorifying thee for thy past and preparing for thy more glorious future.—*Amen.*"

The early stages of the Positivist church were attended with considerable difficulty. Some dozen years ago an able writer, Mr. Mark Pattison, being questioned as to what he had seen on a certain occasion at the Comtist chapel, replied that he had found there three persons, but no God. Positivism, it is true, has always forbidden all inconsiderate proselytism, which explains both the smallness of its numbers and the distinguished character of its adherents. To speak merely of London, we may mention as among its principal champions to-day, one of the most brilliant essayists in England, Mr. Frederic Harrison, whose name is familiar to the readers of the great English reviews; Professor Beesley, of University Hall; Mr. James Cotter Morrison, one of the staff of the *Fortnightly Review*, and Mr. Henry Crompton, a barrister of ability and an energetic champion of the interests of working men,—not to speak of others, whose names may be found on the list of weekly lectures arranged for by the Positivists in their chapels. In addition to the London centres of the Positivist faith, others have been established during recent years at Dublin, Liverpool, Birmingham, Manchester, and Newcastle.

It is to be remarked that a secession took place in the Church of Humanity in 1878, which threatened for a moment the unity of Comtism, but which was at last reduced, at least as regards England, to a simple personal difference. Dr. Congreve having at this time, together with several of his French co-religionists, rejected the authority of M. Lafitte, whom he charged with making too much of teaching and too little of preaching,[1] the most eminent English Positivists refused to follow their compatriot in this matter; and hence they formed at Newton Hall, an old Scottish Chapel in Fetter Lane, a new branch of the Church of Humanity, which M. Lafitte came over to solemnly consecrate in 1881. Weekly meetings are held there, the festivals of Humanity being observed and the sacraments administered exactly as at Chapel Street. The only difference consists in a greater simplicity of ritual. But it is probable that this will become more elaborate with the lapse of time. We shall perhaps have to wait for—said Mr. Harrison on the 1st of January, 1880, on the occasion of the fete of Humanity—"the due commemoration of this day; the full embodiment of all those thoughts, feelings, resolves that come to us at the opening of one year more, may not be yet. Our meagre expressions are such as belong to the difficulties of a small beginning. We believe, as much as the adherents of any faith, that

---

1. Comte himself distinguished between the functions of the apostle and those of the priest. The latter should address himself exclusively to minds imbued with Positive teaching, the former ought to make a direct appeal to the sentiments of the masses.

a truly religious sense of duty in men and women gathered together in common convictions and with joint purpose, will ere long issue in enthusiastic appeals to the noblest of all the human feelings, with all the resources of art and poetry.[1]

The Positivists of Newton Hall have organised an entire system of instruction, which they have gratuitously placed at the disposal of the public, and which has been wholly arranged according to the scheme of education devised by Comte. The meetings of the " London Positivist Society" are held in the same hall. This society is under the presidency of Mr. Harrison, and it aims at influencing public opinion, with a view to promote the moral and social doctrines enjoined by Positivism. It is this organization which has given utterance during recent years to the most vehement protestations against the war in Afghanistan, the annexation of the Transvaal, the policy of coercion in Ireland and the Egyptian expedition.

At a period in which the great majority of men are in doubt about everything and often of themselves too, the orthodox Positivists possess a faith whose comprehensiveness and ardour, are a source of moral restfulness and intellectual pleasure. In their opinion Auguste Comte truly revealed to the world the last word of method, if not of truth, and there is not perhaps a single Comtist who has ever allowed himself to criticise the least important assertion of his master, except to interpret or complete its significance. In all this, there is doubtless evidence of a re-action against the intellectual anarchy through which modern society is struggling; but this rare instance of mental discipline is none the less strange when we bear in mind the superiority of the men by whom it has been freely adopted.

It is to be noted that the Comtists profess the most unswerving confidence in the full and final triumph of their faith; the only question of which they are in doubt is whether this triumph will take place early enough to save European civilization from the destruction which, as they think, the Religion of Humanity can alone prevent. "There is a great and terrible uncertainty hanging over the immediate destinies of the West," said Professor Beesley, at the festival of Humanity, on the 1st of January, 1881. Will the diffusion of Positivist ideas among a sufficient number of good people be accom-

---

1. Frederic Harrison, *The Present and the Future; a Positivist Address.* London, 1880.

plished in time to arrest the forces which are hurrying Europe towards anarchy, or will the disorganization be upon us before the only reorganizing doctrine has been able to make itself sufficiently known, or has leavened the mass outside of a few scattered groups?" It is thus that the early Christians were constrained to speak when they saw the approaching ruin of the Roman world, which is symbolized by the visions of the Apocalypse.

Positivists of the Stuart Mill type are at present rare in England, and the school of Littré is perhaps still less represented there. All those who have not accepted Comte's system in its entirety appear to have been drawn into the vortex of evolution. Hence orthodox Positivists are not sparing in their condemnation of the writings of Herbert Spencer, whom they charge, not only with mistaking the value of the scientific classification established by Comte, but also with exceeding the limits of observation by affirming the reality of the Unknowable, as well as with promoting moral anarchy by disregarding the necessity of an appeal to sentiment in order to ensure the predominance of the Altruistic over the selfish impulses in the individual. It is notorious, indeed, that Spencer in his system of ethics, claims that the happiness of the community flows out of the happiness of the individual, and that he sees in the latter the direct or indirect source of all our actions; whence the conclusion that duty is an illusion and the spirit of sacrifice a mere phantom of the imagination. The Positivists, on the other hand, regard the happiness of others as the first consideration, while the happiness of the individual is, in their opinion, only a consequence or corollary of this. No one has, perhaps, seen more clearly than Mr. Harrison has done the weakness of the evolutionary philosophy, regarded in its ethical bearings. "A Power," says he,[1] "which is to comfort us, control us, unite us, and a Power that is to have any religious effect on us, must comfort, control,

---

[1] *Pantheism* and *Cosmic Emotion*, in the *XIX. Century*, of August, 1881.— Among the Positivists of the Continent and specially those of the school of Littré, Mr. Spencer's Philosophy is treated still more severely. Ten years after the publication of the article in which M. Laugel said of Spencer in the *Revue des Deux Mondes*, that he was condemning himself to poverty and obscurity from his devotion to speculations of an unpopular kind, the *Revue Positive*, of Paris, charged him "with having turned his back on the immortal Stuart Mill to sacrifice to the golden calf, the source of all popularity, in company with Darwin, Lubbock, Tyndall and Huxley." (*Le Transformisme devant le Positivisme*, in the *Revue Positive* for January and February, 1875).

unite,—must be a Power that we conceive as akin to our human souls; a moral power, not a physical Power; a sympathetic, active, living Power, not a group of phenomena or a law of matter. You might as well tell a mother to bring up her child on the binomial theorem."[1]

---

[1]. Some reference to the controversy on this subject, which was carried on in the pages of the *XIX. Century* during 1884, between Mr. Spencer and Mr. Harrison, will not be deemed out of place here. It originated in an Article which the former published in the January number of the Review, with the title,—"Religion: A Retrospect and a Prospect." He begins this article by stating that, "Unlike the ordinary consciousness, the religious consciousness is concerned with that which lies beyond the sphere of sense." He then shows, or attempts to show, that the "ghost-theory," with its "other self, supposed to wander in dreams," illustrates and explains the origin of this consciousness. And he adds,—"Thus, recognising the fact that in the primitive human mind there exists neither religious idea nor religious sentiment, we find that in the course of social evolution and the evolution of intelligence accompanying it, there are generated both the ideas and sentiments which we distinguish as religious; and that through a process of causation, clearly traceable, they traverse those stages which have brought them, among civilized races, to their present form." But, continues Mr. Spencer, it may be objected "The ghost-theory of the savage is baseless. The material double of a dead man, in which he believes, never had any existence. And if by a gradual de-materialisation of this double was produced the conception of the supernatural agent in general—if the conception of a Deity, formed by the dropping of some human attributes and transfiguration of others, resulted from continuance of this process, is not the developed and purified conception, reached by pushing the process to its limit, a fiction also? Surely if the primitive belief was absolutely false, all derived beliefs must be absolutely false. This objection looks fatal, and it would be fatal were its premiss valid. Unexpected as it will be to most readers, the answer here to be made is that at the outset a germ of truth was contained in the primitive conception—the truth, namely, that the power which manifests itself in consciousness is but a differently-conditioned form of the power which manifests itself beyond consciousness." . . . See now the implications. That internal energy which in the experiences of the primitive man was always the immediate antecedent of changes wrought by him—that energy which, when interpreting external changes, he thought of along with those attributes of a human personality connected with it in himself, is the same energy which, freed from anthropomorphic accompaniments, is now figured as the cause of all external phenomena. The last stage reached is recognition of the truth that force as it exists beyond consciousness cannot be like what we know as force within consciousness; and that yet, as either is capable of generating the other, they must be different modes of the same. Consequently, the final outcome of that speculation commenced by the primitive man, is that the Power manifested throughout the Universe distinguished as material, is the same power which in ourselves wells up under the form of consciousness."

It will seem to most readers that these thoughts are not only sublime in their suggestiveness, but that they disclose the most solid of all foundations for the religious sentiment—nature itself. Anyhow, Mr. Spencer goes on to say as to the result of science in its bearing on religion,—"Those who think that science is dissipating religious beliefs and sentiments seem unaware that whatever of mystery is

I must not omit to mention an attempt which has been made to unite the Unknowable of Herbert Spencer with the Grand-Être of Comte, in a common religious conception. For although it is Mr. William Frey, an American Positivist, to whom this attempt is due, I consider it desirable to give an exposition of his views in this chapter, because no better conclusion could be found for what I have advanced respecting the general character of Positivism and its special development as a system of faith and worship.

In a paper published in the *Index*, of the 3rd of August, 1882, Mr. Frey showed, with great power of reasoning and a truly compre-

---

taken from the old interpretation is added to the new. . . . Under one of its aspects scientific progress is a gradual transfiguration of Nature. Where ordinary perception saw perfect simplicity it reveals great complexity; where there seemed absolute inertness it discloses intense activity; and in what appears mere vacancy it finds a marvellous play of forces. . . . When the explorer of Nature sees that, quiescent as they appear, surrounding solid bodies are sensitive to forces which are infinitesimal in their amounts—when the spectroscope proves to him that molecules on the earth pulsate in harmony with molecules in the stars—when there is forced on him the inference that every point in space thrills with an infinity of vibrations passing through it in all directions; the conception to which he tends is much less that of a Universe of dead matter than that of a Universe everwhere alive—alive if not in the restricted sense still in a general sense. This transfiguration, which the inquiries of physicists continually increase, is aided by that other transfiguration resulting from metaphysical inquiries. Subjective analysis compels us to admit that our scientific interpretations of the phenomena which objects present are expressed in terms of our own variously-combined sensations and ideas— are expressed, that is, in elements belonging to consciousness, which are but symbols of the something beyond consciousness. Though analysis afterwards reinstates our primitive beliefs, to the extent of showing that behind every group of phenomenal manifestations there is always a *nexus*, which is the reality that remains fixed amid appearances which are variable, yet we are shown that this *nexus* of reality is for ever inaccessible to consciousness. And when once more we remember that the activities constituting consciousness, being rigorously bounded, cannot bring in among themselves the activities beyond the bounds, which therefore seem unconscious, though production of either by the other seems to imply that they are of the same essential nature; this necessity we are under to think of the external energy in terms of the internal energy gives rather a spiritualistic than a materialistic aspect to the Universe: further thought, however, obliging us to recognise the truth that a conception given in phenomenal manifestations of this ultimate energy can in no wise show us what it is. . . . Amid the mysteries which become the more mysterious the more they are thought about, there will remain the one absolute certainty that he (the thinker of the future) is ever in presence of an Infinite and Eternal Energy, from which all things proceed."

Now there is much in the foregoing passages, to say nothing of other parts of the Article, which could not fail to rouse the hostility of an orthodox Positivist, and no one acquainted with Mr. Frederic Harrison's brilliant controversial talents, can have been surprised when two months later he joined issue "with the acknowledged

hensive range of thought, that the principal source of our religious sentiments is to be traced to a sense of dependence upon the universe. But man has always sought to represent, under concrete and tangible *human* forms, the mysterious Power upon which he feels dependent. And although the idea of the Infinite, as Mr. Spencer shows, has been gradually freed from all its anthropomorphic attributes and transformed into the indeterminate conception of the Unknowable, it is to be borne in mind that the importance of the human element in the object of worship has not only suffered no diminution, but has even been increased in proportion as the conception of the Divinity has become

head of the Evolution philosophy," to use his own words. And in order to make his attack all the more formidable, as it would seem, he began by praising his opponent who had uttered "the last word of the Agnostic philosophy in its long controversy with theology," and in so conclusive a manner that it was "hard to conceive" how theology could "rally for another bout." But the essay, he said, which was "packed with thought to a degree unusual even with Mr. Herbert Spencer," dealt rather with the "Ghost of Religion" than with "Religion" itself. It was divisible, he added, into three parts, the third of which "deals with the evolution of religion in the future, and formulates, more precisely than has ever yet been effected, the positive creed of Agnostic philosophy."

"Has, then, the Agnostic a positive creed, he asks? It would seem so; for Mr. Spencer brings us at last 'to the one absolute certainty, the presence of an Infinite and Eternal Energy, from which all things proceed.' But let no one suppose that this is merely a new name for the Great First Cause of so many theologies and metaphysics. In spite of the capital letters, and the use of theological terms as old as Isaiah or Athanasius, Mr. Spencer's Energy has no analogy with God. It is Eternal, Infinite and Incomprehensible; but still it is not He, but It. It remains always Energy, Force, nothing anthropomorphic; such as electricity, or anything else that we might conceive as the ultimate basis of all the physical forces. None of the positive attributes which have ever been predicated of God, can be used of this Energy. . . . . It shares some of the negative attributes of God and First Cause, but no positive one. It is, in fact, only the Unknowable a little more defined; though I do not remember that Mr. Spencer, or any Evolution philosopher, has ever formulated the Unknowable in terms with so deep a theological ring as we hear in the phrase 'Infinite and Eternal Energy, from which all things proceed.'"

Clearly the sting of Mr. Spencer's article lay in these words—in the differentiation of the Ultimate "Energy" from the "all things" proceeding from it, which they imply. But Mr. Harrison continues: "Agnosticism, perfectly legitimate as the true answer of science to an effete question, has shown us that religion is not to be found anywhere within the realm of Cause. Having brought us to the answer, 'no cause that we know of,' it is laughable to call that negation religion. Mr. Mark Pattison, one of the acutest minds of modern Oxford, rather oddly says that the idea of Deity has been 'defecated to a pure transparency.' The evolution philosophy goes a step further and defecates the idea of Cause to a pure transparency. Theology and ontology alike end in the everlasting No, with which science confronts all their assertions. But how whimsical is it to tell us that religion, which cannot find any resting place in theology or ontology, is to find its true home in the

more vague; men have simply endowed their fellows with the attributes stripped from the Unknowable, as the formation and development of the most recent great religions attest.

Mr. Spencer admits the necessity of representing the Infinite by some concrete symbolism; all that he asks is that the symbols made use of shall be regarded as possessed of no resemblance whatever to the Reality for which they stand. "But," asks Mr. Frey, "what symbol of this nature is susceptible of awakening in us the sympathies which play so preponderating a part in the complex character of the religious sentiment? This inscrutable Power, stern, inflexible in its mysterious way, requiring a complete submission to its will, punishing

---

Everlasting No. That which is defecated to a pure transparency can never supply a religion to any human being but a philosopher constructing a system. It is quite conceivable that religion is to end with theology, and both might in the course of evolution become an anachronism. But if religion there is still to be, it cannot be found in this No-man's-land and Know-nothing creed. Better bury religion at once than let its ghost walk uneasy in our dreams. . . . . Mr. Spencer has unwittingly conceded to the divines that which they assume so confidently—that theology is the same thing as religion, and that there was no religion at all until there was a belief in superhuman spirits within and behind nature. This is obviously an oversight. We have to go very much further back for the genesis of religion. There were countless centuries of Time, and there were and there are countless millions of men for whom no doctrine of superhuman spirits ever took coherent form. In all these ages and races, probably by far the most numerous that our planet has witnessed, there was religion in all kinds of definite form. Comte calls it Fetichism—terms are not important : roughly we may call it Nature-worship. The religion in all these types was the belief and worship not of spirits of any kind, not of any immaterial, imagined being *inside* things, but of the actual visible things themselves—trees, stones, rivers, mountains, earth, fire, stars, sun and sky."

Then again as to the "Unknowable," Mr. Harrison says: "As the universal substratum it has some analogy with other superhuman objects of worship. But Force, Gravitation, Atom, Undulation, Vibration and other abstract notions have much the same kind of analogy, but nobody ever dreamed of a religion of gravitation or the worship of molecules. . . . . It would be hardly sane to make a religion of the Equator or the Binomial theorem. . . . . But to make a religion out of the Unknowable is far more extravagant than to make it out of the Equator. . . . . I suppose Dean Mansel's Bampton Lectures touched the low-water mark of vitality as predecated of the Divine Being. Of all modern theologians the Dean came the nearest to the Evolution negation. But there is a gulf which separates even his all-negative Deity from Mr. Spencer's impersonal, unconscious, unthinking and unthinkable Energy. . . . . One would like to know how much of the Evolutionist's day is consecrated to seeking the Unknowable in a devout way, and what the religious exercises might be. How does the man of science approach the All-Nothingness? . . . . Imagine a religion which excludes the idea of worship, because its sole dogma is the infinity of Nothingness. Although the Unknowable is logically said to be something, yet the something of which we neither know nor conceive anything is practically nothing.

every transgression of its laws, may be compared with an autocrat who shows no partiality, puts everybody on the same footing, and inflicts the same punishment on his best subject as on the meanest. Such a Power may enforce humility, terror, and awe—the very same feelings which were so prominent among primitive men—but never excite the sympathetic feeling. Children may love the parent only when conscious of being loved and protected by him during their helplessness and in time of trouble. The cold, stony-hearted, immovable Power of Agnostics cannot excite in man the feelings of love, self-sacrifice, and devotion." It is not sufficient, adds Mr. Frey, to possess an acquaintance with the laws of nature; we need also a stimulus, which shall impel us to act in conformity with their requirements and serve as a guide just where science ceases to do this. The most selfish man, for instance, may unhesitatingly accept all the deductions of Herbert Spencer without becoming the better for it. Even more, he

. . . . There is one symbol of the infinite Unknowable, and it is perhaps the most definite and ultimate word that can be said about it. The precise and yet inexhaustible language of mathematics enables us to express, in a common algebraic formula, the exact combination of the Unknown raised to its highest power of infinity. That formula is (x^n), and here we have the beginning and perhaps the end of a symbolism of the religion of the infinite Unknowable. Schools, academies, temples of the Unknowable, there cannot be. But where two or three are gathered together to worship the Unknowable, there the algebraic formula may suffice to give form to their emotions: they may be heard to profess their unwearying belief in (x^n), even if no weak brother with ritualistic tendencies be heard to cry, 'O (x^n), love us, help us, make us one with thee!'"

Now it need hardly be said, by way of concluding this long note, that Mr. Harrison in speaking of the "Unknowable" as the "All-Nothingness," completely misunderstands or perverts his opponent's teaching, and this the latter had no difficulty in showing, while in his first reply he dealt, moreover, a rude thrust at the so-called "Religion of Humanity," and completely negatived the assertion that the earliest form of worship was directed to natural objects *per se* "without trace of ghost, spirit or god." Suffice it to add that the controversy consisted of three articles from Mr. Spencer and two from Mr. Harrison, while the Rev. Canon Curteis and Sir James Stephen also took part in it from their respective standpoints. The author of this work too published an excellent article on the controversy in the *Revue de l'Histoire des Religions*, in which he shows that "the conditions indispensible to becoming the object of a religion are found in the Unknowable, as well as in the Eternal, the Absolute, the Self-Existent, the Most High, the Only Pure or whatever other qualifications men may have made the equivalent of the divine," and that "before becoming the scientific faith of Spencer, Huxley, and even Haeckel, this religious conception has sufficed for men of the highest order of mind and of the most religious susceptibilities, such as Giordano, Bruno, Spinoza, Kant, Goethe, Shelley, Wordsworth, Carlyle, Emerson, and even M. Renan."—*Translator*.

will possibly find in the ultimate axioms of science, relative to the struggle for life and the survival of the fittest, an excuse for acts most at variance with the claims of justice and humanity.

Happily, whatever incompleteness or even pernicious tendency there may be in this conception, it is capable of being supplemented or corrected by the great discovery of Comte, that, between man and the universe there exists humanity. "We see in humanity a source of all our blessings, because from her we obtain our knowledge and inspirations; only by and with her can we live and perfect ourselves. And as our material bodies which are fed upon the earth, do not perish, but return to the earth and live for ever with it, so our achievements, activities, and influences which are obtained from humanity do not perish, but return back to humanity, and live for ever with her, having their share in her future development. Viewed in such a light, humanity ceases to be our master only; it becomes our protector and comforter also. And the sense of gratitude, combined with the sense of duty, compels us to pledge our life to its improvement and perfection."

The conception of humanity as a living organism, continues Mr. Frey, gives us a key for the most difficult moral problems. It explains why man cannot attain to true happiness if he does not live for others. It lays the foundations of morality, moreover, neither in the freedom of the Will, nor in a fatalistic conception, but in the instinct of preservation, which belongs to Humanity as well as to every individual organism. From a religious point of view it cannot fail to call forth, in the highest degree, all the good effects which were brought about by the human element in the old religions.—" If more than a third of the human race prostrates itself, if millions of Christians worship a good man hanged as a criminal, if a still greater number of Mussulmans get their inspiration from Mohammed, well may we bow in admiration and love before Humanity as a galaxy of all great men and all noble thought and actions which ever stirred the human soul."

Does it follow that in imitation of certain Positivists who are dazzled by the grandeur of this discovery, we should try to put Humanity in the place of God? In relation to this question, Herbert Spencer has justly said—" No such thing as humanity can ever do more than temporarily shut out the thought of a Power of which Humanity is but a small and fugitive product—a Power which was in course of ever-changing manifestations long before humanity, and will continue through other manifestations when humanity has ceased to be." (*Study of Sociology*, p. 312.) Mr. Frey yields therefore to the necessity of admitting both the existence of the Unknowable and our dependence upon that mysterious Power, as well as our inability to fathom its inscrutable nature.—" We differ from the pure Agnostics of Herbert Spencer's stamp, only when we come to the solution of a burning question which always was pre-eminent in every religion: Who will reveal to us the laws of nature, who will be our Saviour?"—Science, answer the Agnostics, who thus restrict religion to its element of mystery.—No, says Mr. Frey, it must be a concrete, living, superior being which represents the human element of religion in the purest and loftiest manner: "The blank left in our souls by the omission of a personal God is filled now by the image of Humanity as our protecting and guiding father. We worship humanity as the mediator between man and the Infinite for all ages to come, and, in serving humanity, we have all that is needed to unite persons of the most diversified taste, temperaments, and dispositions into one religious brotherhood."

It is clear the Agnostic can feel no scruple in accepting a form of faith thus understood, since humanity is not a product of the imagination, but a fact verifiable by science. On the other hand, what objection could be urged against this conception, by Positivists, who address their worship to humanity, without taking into account the element of mystery in religion? "The intense feeling of gratitude and adoration which they feel toward humanity will become only deeper and stronger if humanity be regarded as mediator between man and the Infinite, because then will come into play the strongest chord of religious sentiment—*i.e.*, man's yearning for the Infinite. In humanity, then, we shall see not only a being imposing in itself, but, for us, the only conceivable image of the Infinite, and the laws of morality, which we derive from our relation to humanity, become a reflection of the supreme laws of the universe, which all must obey who wish to escape punishment."

In these views, it is urged, there will be found a point of contact between the schools of both Herbert Spencer and Auguste Comte, and the group of thinkers who claim that a philosophy of life is to be found in the guidance of the individual conscience. "That which these Moralists regard as philosophy is but the promptings of their

L

noble souls. They mistake in the supposition that every man can obey the dictates of inner nature just as easily as they do, or that he will follow the same direction of activity which they choose. They forget that the moral nature of every man is tinged by one or another of evil propensities which he inherits together with the good ones; and when he attempts to arrive at some definite conclusion by the dictates of his soul, he unconsciously becomes the victim of his inclination. It is not enough to awake a man from spiritual slumber: it is necessary to keep before him a certain standard of morality, so as to enable him to educate his conscience before he will consult it." Doubtless, many men unconsciously perform their duty towards the Grand-Etre by doing good, instead of merely preaching it. The acceptance of the views which Mr. Frey advocates will make no change in the conduct of such persons; it will simply give them a new impelling motive, and secure for them an irresistible ascendancy, by adding the attraction of a solid, rational and ennobling philosophy to the charm of natural goodness.

"In conclusion," says Mr. Frey, "the Religion of Humanity is the only form of Agnosticism which can stand the severest tests of sceptics and is able to continue the mission performed by the past religions. Let us not be afraid to indorse it. It will for ever remain an embodiment of progress, because, being based on science, it has no stationary dogmas which may be outgrown in the future. The Religion of Humanity is the only safe anchorage for those who are tired both of the metaphysical rambles of idealists and of the sophistical arguments of the selfish. Under its banner will come all who are in search of true religion, all who are craving for spiritual food, all who find in their experiences how futile are the best planned reforms if not illuminated and sanctified by the religious sentiment."

It simply remains to express the opinion that if the Religion of Humanity is destined to extend, it will be in the form indicated by Mr. Frey. Even now, indeed—except as regards the Comtist ritual—it is the form of faith, at once practical and elevated, which is taught by Mr. Conway and by a certain number of Unitarian ministers. As presented by the American Positivist, it answers to a double tendency of the modern mind: An aspiration, on the one hand, towards some certainty able to close the era of metaphysical controversy; and, on the other, a desire to direct religious activity into channels where it will tend to the individual and social amelioration of the human race.

Having previously considered a form of worship which makes belief in God optional, we have just discussed the claims of another system of religion, which suppresses it in the most formal manner. Here we come to a third,—if religion it may be called—which goes so far as to proscribe even religious sentiment itself. I refer to Secularism, which has, it is true, provided itself with a liturgy for use in all the solemn circumstances of life, but which abstains from seeking its support or leverage in sentiment, that is to say, in those emotional faculties to which the Positivists themselves turn as the essential element of religion.

The aim of Secularism is to concentrate the activity of man upon the concerns of the present life, which are under the control of experience. It starts from the principle that we can know nothing about the existence of God and the reality of a future life; and it refuses, therefore, to concern itself with such questions either by way of affirmation or denial. The purpose which it assigns to life is the realization of individual happiness, which it does not, however, separate from the happiness of all. But this double result can only be attained by human efforts, based upon science and experience. Hence it claims, in the first place, the most absolute freedom of thought, and in the second, the right to use this freedom in the search for truth, within the sphere of sensible observation. Every speculation which tends to draw the mind from this ground, it deems idle and therefore mischievous.[1]

---

[1] It may be readily conceded that Secularism possesses a noble aim, and this aim is, in some cases, a purifying fire and a source of divinest strength. Here, for instance, is a fine passage from a work entitled, *Secularism in its Various Relations*, which, though published anonymously in the *Secular Review*, was written by the late James Thomson, a poet of no mean gifts—at least in the opinion of George Eliot. Speaking of the happiness Secularism aims at, the writer says:—"This happiness implies, firstly, material well-being, sufficiency of food, clothing and house-room, with good air, good water, and good sanitary conditions; for these things are necessary to bodily health, and this is essential to the health of the mind: and only in health is real happiness possible. Again, it implies mental well-being, sufficiency of instruction and education for every one, so that his intellect may be nourished and developed to the full extent of its capabilities. Given the sound mind in the sound body, it further implies free exercise of these—absolutely free in every respect, so long as it does not trench on the equal rights of others or impede the common good. In this full development of mind as well as body, it need

This essentially utilitarian doctrine is found, above all as a tendency, in the majority of contemporary nations. But it is only in England, so far as I know, that there has been any attempt to make a religion of it. It was the two brothers Austin and G. J. Holyoake who gave an organized form to Secularism about the year 1846, by founding the National Secular Society, which was intended to become a centre of activity and propagandism. But this Association became at last so mixed up with the anti-theological, political, and social struggles of the noted agitator Mr. Bradlaugh, the editor of its organ, *The National Reformer*, that after the death of Mr. Austin Holyoake in 1874, the foremost leaders of the Secular movement set about the formation of a rival society, the *British Secular Union*, on the following basis:—

"I.—PRINCIPLES.

"1. That the present life being the only one of which we have certain knowledge, its concerns claim our primary attention.

"2. That the promotion of our individual and of the general well-being in this world is at once our highest wisdom and duty.

"3. That the only means upon which we can rely for the accomplishment of this object is human effort, based upon knowledge and experience.

"4. We judge conduct by its issues in this world only. What conduces to the general well-being is right; what has the opposite tendency is wrong.

---

scarcely be said that true happiness brings into its service all the noblest and most beautiful arts of life. Some persons seem to fancy that Utilitarians have nothing to do with music, painting, sculpture: care nothing for the glories and grandeurs of the world; have no part in the treasures of the imagination,—as if there were no utility in any of these. But we recognize in them the very high utility of touching to rapture some of the finest chords in our nature; we know and feel just as well as others—and perhaps better than most, since we give ourselves more to scientific study of man—that there are different kinds and degrees of enjoyment, and that some kinds are far superior to others, and we know how to value the superior as compared with the inferior. But yet more, this social happiness implies all the great virtues in those who can attain and keep it :—Wisdom, for without this, transitory and selfish pleasures will be continually mistaken for happiness, and even with a desire for the common good, this good will be misconceived, and the wrong means taken to secure it; Fortitude, to bear when necessary—and the necessity in the present state of the world is as frequent as it is stern—deprivation of personal comfort, rather than stifle our aspirations and relax our efforts for the general interest; Temperance, for with excess no permanent happiness is possible; Magnanimity, for only by aid of this virtue can we keep steadily in view, as the sole aim of all our striving, the sole aim worthy of true men and women, the greatest good of the greatest number: all little-mindedness ever turns to selfishness; Justice, and above all else Justice, for it is the profound and unchangeable convic-

"5. On all questions outside these positive principles of Secularism, members are free to hold any opinions, and to promulgate such on their own responsibility.

"II.—OBJECTS.

"1. The disseminating, promoting, and popularizing of the above principles by all legitimate means.

"2. The increasing of Secular Halls and Institutes in the cities and towns of Great Britain.

"3. The advocacy of Secular principles by lecturers, and the establishment of Secular lectureships in populous districts.

"4. The dissemination of cheap literature expository or defensive of the Society's principles.

"5. The removal of all civil disabilities grounded on belief and the abolition of all public grants for sectarian purposes.

"6. The promotion of a purely Secular system of national education.

"7. The promotion of political, social, or religious reform in anywise tending to increase the secular happiness of the people."

Such, then, are the principles and aims of the *British Secular Union*, which justly claims to be the most numerous, influential, and "respectable" of all the free thinking Associations in England.[2] Its

---

tion of the equal rights of all which alone can inspire and impel us to seek the freedom and happiness of all: oppression since the world began having been based on injustice, the oppressors exaggerating their own rights at the expense of those of the oppressed. And to these great virtues of the mind we must add, as essential to true happiness, what are commonly called the virtues of the heart, the fervour of Zeal or Enthusiasm, and the finer fervour of Benevolence, Sympathy, or, to use the best name, Love. For if Wisdom gives the requisite light, Love alone can give the requisite vital heat: Wisdom, climbing the arduous mountain solitudes, must often let the lamp slip from her benumbed fingers, must often be near fainting in fatal lethargy amidst ice and snow-drifts, if Love be not there to cheer and revive her with the glow and the flames of the heart's quenchless fires."

Now these words breathe the spirit of a noble piety; and they might be ascribed to a devout Theist of any age—to a man capable of looking through the ever-changing forms of religious life and of recognising that reverence for God must end in blessedness for man. But the great defect of Secularism is its blindness with regard to the true significance of religious beliefs and their practical value in life. Hence the Secularist contemptuously casts aside what the philosophical Theist looks upon as a most marvellous natural provision for the spiritual needs of human life. Nature cares for her productions in a thousand ways, and even the grossest forms of religious belief, and the superstitions of the lowest types of civilization are evidences of such care in relation to the human soul. For as Emerson says, it takes a whole bundle of principles to make a girdle as strong as one superstition in the conduct of life; while no one who watches with an unprejudiced eye the calm and happy days which simple and perchance very superstitious piety brings to unawakened minds, can doubt its consolatory influence in life. But Mr. Thomson

president is the Marquis of Queensberry; Pasteur and Renan are among its vice-presidents; while Victor Hugo figures in the Society as an honorary member. The moral theories of its principal supporters are absolutely irreproachable, and they never lose a fitting opportunity for showing that Secularism is not to be confounded with Atheism, or the entire negation of religion. Mr. G. J. Holyoake, indeed, has preached more than once in Unitarian pulpits, both in England and America—a fact which speaks as well for the toleration of the Unitarians as it does for his own. The *Inquirer* having once expressed some surprise at this fact, Mr. Holyoake stated, in reply, that Unitarian ministers had often been invited to speak at Secular meetings, and that between Unitarianism and Secularism there was the common ground of practical morality.

The desire to make Secularism a substitute for the old forms of faith in all the circumstances of life, has induced the Secularists to provide themselves with a ritual, which is entitled, *The Secularist's Manual of Songs and Ceremonies*.[3] Drawn up by Austin Holyoake and Charles Watts, it constitutes a true Secular liturgy for the naming of children, for marriage, for funerals, &c. The preface, which is written by Mr. Bradlaugh, explains that this ritual answers to a pressing

---

seems to see nothing of all this; the wisdom of which he speaks has brought him no spiritual insight. In common with a very large number of Secularists his attitude to religion is hostile and negative; he is influenced by a sort of chronic phase of that fever of Scepticism which, as Schiller tells us, has to be passed through by all the best minds in their transition from the religion of dogmatic authority to that of consciousness or personal choice. Hence he says of God: "The true Secularist loves and reveres his fellow men whom he knows, not a phantasmal God-Fiend of whom he knows nothing." Then again of Christianity his words are: "It is ignoble in what it deems its noblest emotions, its love and reverence and adoration of the Deity, its eestacies of Divine influx and communion. For these emotions are irrational, the object of the love is a dream and a delusion, the God revered and worshipped is pourtrayed in its own Bible as capricious, unjust, vindictive, merciless; and these orgies of religious excitement which overstrain, rend, and often ruin the moral fibre, are as harmful as any other drunken revels. . . . . It (Christianity) is thus essentially stagnant and inert; it does but little useful work in the world; it is perishing of atrophy, brain and heart and limbs irretrievably wasting away. In this life it has no future; its future is in the life to come (or not to come!); its ideal is in the past, to which its vacant eyes are ever reverted in the dense gloom of its prison-cell."—These extracts speak for themselves; and they will show the reader that though Secularism professes to be neutral with regard to religion, it is not seldom blindly and bitterly hostile to all that the vast majority of mankind have hitherto looked upon as divine.—*Translator*.

2. See the *Secular Review* for the 19th of August, 1882.
3. London: Austin & Co.

and frequently-expressed need of the English Freethinkers.—" As to the Marriage Service," it adds, "the Socialists formerly, and the Comtists recently, set us an example: the legal ceremony must be gone through before the Registrar, but the marriage can be celebrated in the usual place of meeting. The Naming of Infants is a frequent matter at our meetings, and a set form saves the possibility of the introduction of ridiculous or objectionable words. For the Burial Service, the last funeral I attended—in which emotion prevented me from completing my address at the grave—convinced me of the need to have some form of words always at hand for such occasions."

It would require too much space to reproduce this manual in its entirety; I will merely quote the first and last paragraphs of the address prepared for the naming of children :—

"In publicly naming the infant now before us, we recognise the parents' desire to identify their offspring with the Secular Party, which proclaims the necessity of unfettered thought during the formation of character. Diversity of organization precludes uniformity of belief. We do not, therefore, guarantee that in after-life a child shall profess any class of opinions. But by keeping its mind free from theological creeds, we enable it the better to acquire a more liberal education than is permitted by the conventional faith of the Church." . . .
"We sincerely hope that in after-life *(here name the child)* he *(if the child be a girl, substitute the feminine gender)* may have reason to rejoice in his fellowship with us. May the principles of Freethought enable him to brave successfully the battle of life. And as he sails o'er the billows of time, may experience increase his guiding power, that when arriving at maturity, he shall have acquired sufficient knowledge to enable him to regulate aright his further career. And when the evening of his existence has arrived, may he obtain consolation from the reflection that his conduct has won the approval of the wise and the good, and that to the best of his ability he has been faithful to the mission of life."

This extract shows how completely the Secularists have succeeded in excluding every element of sentiment and imagination from their solemn ceremonies. Their manual certainly embodies a considerable number of hymns, but apart from a few which are pretty freely suffused with the breath of Pantheism, these utilitarian lyrics are of so commonplace a character that in some cases they border on parody, not to say more in disparagement of them.[1]

Now, however foreign these productions may appear to the religious sentiment, they are none the less fitted to show that the fundamental religiousness of the English character persists, even under the guise of modern scepticism. Thus the claim of the Secularists to find a substitute for religion and their attempts to imitate its forms, and to paraphrase its language, are, in a sense, the counter-proof of the same tendencies which are revealed under other circumstances by the doings of the Salvation Army, and in the persistent growth of the strangest sects. To-day, we are certainly far enough from the state of things which justified Montesquieu in saying, on his return from London: "*La religion est morte en Angleterre. Si quelqu'un parle de religion, tout le monde se met à rire.*"

It is true the religious re-action which swept away, during the first half of this century, the indifference of the preceding period, seems to have passed its culminating point, and it is quite possible that in the presence of the difficulty of adjusting ancient beliefs to modern ideas, a new wave of scepticism may roll over English society. But what conclusion should be drawn from these oscillations of the religious sentiment, other than a lesson of more cautious judgment on the part of those who, yielding to the feeling of the moment or the whim of the hour, delight to proclaim, in turn, the final triumph of a definite faith, or the fading twilight of the last day of the gods? The most we can clearly deduce from these phases of belief is the law which, through all the oscillations of the English spirit, reveals to us the steady progress of religious thought towards a more rational view of man's relation to the universe.

---

1. Here, for instance, are the verses intended to replace the *Ite Missa est*, in Secular meetings:—

"DISMISSION."

"Farewell, dear friends! adieu, adieu;
In social ways delight;
Then happiness will dwell with you:
Farewell, dear friends! good-night.

"Farewell, dear friends! adieu, adieu;
Remember us this night;
We claim to do the same for you:
Farewell, dear friends! good-night.

"Farewell, dear friends! adieu, adieu;
Till we again unite;
The social system keep in view:
Farewell, dear friends! good-night."

PART II.

CHAPTER VII.

THE GENESIS OF UNITARIANISM IN THE UNITED STATES.

Puritan origin of New England—John Robinson exhorting the pilgrims of the *May Flower* not to confine themselves to the theology of Luther and Calvin—What the *Pilgrim Fathers* sought in America—The Democratic and Autonomous organization of the Calvinistic congregations—Their intolerance—The causes which were destined to gradually lead Puritan society to the admission of religious liberty—Arminian re-action against the dogma of Predestination—Early controversies between religious liberals and Calvinists—Liberal tendencies of the Harvard University—Channing in 1815—His Baltimore sermon—Rapid development of Unitarianism—Divisions in the old Calvinistic congregations—Foundation of the American Unitarian Association at Boston—The liberal side and the rationalistic side of the Unitarian development; their relative importance—Weak points in the theology of Channing.

As every one is aware, the religious sentiment played an important part in the colonization of Anglo-Saxon America. Three out of the four great settlements which the English founded on the western shores of the Atlantic, in the seventeenth century, owed their origin to those who had been proscribed on account of their religious opinions: the Puritans in New England, the Catholics in Maryland, and the Quakers in Pennsylvania. It was above all the first of these three elements which became an all-important factor in the development of American society. For it is its impress, modified by the spirit of the age, which even to-day, in spite of the incessant influence of emigration, is still to be everywhere found beneath the existing beliefs, customs and institutions of the United States.

We have already seen how the Puritan movement began in England as early as the reign of Elizabeth, in the shape of protestations against the Liturgy and the official hierarchy. Spreading chiefly among the populace, it carried to extremes the democratic and religious principles of Calvinism. It will be readily understood, therefore, that its adherents soon came into collision with the established authority. But the persecutions they underwent in the reigns of Elizabeth and

James I. merely served to increase their numbers.[1] In 1608, when the great majority of them were resigned to passively endure fines or imprisonment and even death itself on their native soil—awaiting the terrible revenge which, with the assistance of the Presbyterians, they were soon to inflict upon their persecutors—the most ardent and energetic, under the leadership of John Robinson, the former pastor of a congregation at Scrooby, fled to Leyden, in Holland.

In this retreat they lived quietly for several years. Still their small community became more and more reduced, and it was not difficult to foresee that it would be ultimately absorbed by the Protestantism of Holland. They conceived, therefore, the bold project of founding a sort of religious colony in America, which should admit of their remaining connected with England and even receiving recruits from the mother country, by assuring them an asylum against new persecution. Had they at that time any vision of the future that would open up before them? Be this as it may, their boldest dreams must assuredly have fallen far short of the great things their descendants have realized.

The British Government, which simply desired to free the country of sectarians, alike troublesome to the Church and the State, did not long hesitate to grant them the distant concession in Virginia for which they asked; and the first body of emigrants, numbering a hundred men, women and children, embarked on board the *May Flower* on the 27th of July, 1620—a date and a name of classic import in the United States. Our readers are doubtless aware how the chances of the voyage led the emigrants to land on the shores of New England, and how they availed themselves of this circumstance to organize in their own fashion an authority on this free soil, which was centred in themselves alone, and was not due in any way to the concession of a King or a company.

John Robinson had remained in Europe, where he was making preparations to embark with the remainder of the community. Like a new Moses, however, death was to strike him down before he could reach the promised Canaan. In his farewell address to the pioneers of the Puritan emigration, on the Leyden quay, he uttered these

---

1. It was stated in Parliament, in 1593, that more than twenty thousand persons frequented conventicles, and a proposition was advanced that they should be banished from the country, as the Moors had been from Spain.—Bancroft's *History of the United States.*

words, which may well be regarded as prophetic, whatever the sense he attached to them : "The Lord has more truth to break forth from his Holy Word. I cannot sufficiently bewail the condition of the reformed churches who are come to a period in religion and will go at present no further than the instruments of their reformation. Luther and Calvin were great and shining lights in their times; yet they penetrated not into the whole counsel of God." (Bancroft's *History of the United States*).

This language was not to fall upon barren soil. Still it was too much in advance of its time to be immediately applied and understood by those to whom it was addressed, or indeed by him who uttered it. What the pilgrims of the *May Flower*, fleeing from the persecutions of the Established Church, demanded of the New World, was not religious liberty as a general principle but *their* religious liberty, that is the right to form a Church after their own fashion, without the concurrence of the English hierarchy or the use of the English Liturgy. The government which they formed was a true democracy; but it was emphatically a theocratic democracy, and we should seek in vain for anything in its constitution conformable to modern ideas, either in relation to Church and State, or even in regard to the rights of conscience and the liberty of worship.

The Bible was their supreme law; it was to inspire and supplement written laws. Their first care, when they founded any settlement, was to build a church, which soon became the centre of their individual and social life. The first election was that of a Minister and Elders. The expenses of worship were charged upon all the inhabitants; but the rights of citizenship belonged to "communicants" only, and the religious society reserved to itself the power to excommunicate infidels, sinners, or even the lukewarm whose only crime was that they did not consider themselves "in a state of grace." The first dissenters from the Puritan faith who wished to settle in the infant colony—two members of the English Church—were sent back to England by the ship which brought them. A series of Draconian laws closed the entrance into New England to Anabaptists, Antinomians, Quakers and Catholics. In case of infraction, heretics were exposed to whipping and mutilation, and also to forced labour, "till they could be sent back at their own expense." The blasphemer and the Sabbath-breaker were liable to punishment which might even extend to death itself. This ferocious legislation did not remain a dead letter. New England had, in the seventeenth century, its Calas, its Labarre and its Urbain Grandier: in Massachusetts witches were executed down to the year 1692.

It would, however, be unjust to forget that notwithstanding its intolerence, its austerity, and its narrowness of horizon, Calvinism, of all the current faiths of the epoch, was best fitted to make of a handful of emigrants the founders of a great and free nation. It is impossible not to observe its influence in the qualities which distinguished the first emigrants, and which are still prevalent among their descendants: confidence in the power of individual organization, determined persistence of labour, a taste for learning, with respect for women and a sentiment of the seriousness of life. We may smile at the minute and often vexatious rules in which the Puritan genius thought to find a barrier to the corruption of manners; but American Puritanism has none the less given, to the society, marked with its impress, two centuries of a morality more sincere and more general, if not indeed higher, than any other people has known.

In short, the world is indebted to it for having made men equal and free. Constitutions drawn up with a great reinforcement of Biblical texts, in the first years of colonization, were so impregnated with the idea of self-government, that, except in those features which were contrary to liberty of conscience, they have remained nearly intact, down to the present day, in the New England States, and have served as models for the Federal Constitution, as well as for the particular constitutions of the States subsequently formed in the Union.

The religious organization of Calvinism was itself only an application of popular sovereignty. With Calvinists, the priest is no longer a being of superior virtue, invested with supernatural authority by the fact of his ordination, but simply a representative of his fellow-believers, the first among equals. It is universal suffrage, "the universal vote of the congregation of Christ," as Milton said, which forms the basis of association, appoints the officers, the pastor included, fixes the contribution of each member, tests the receipts and expenditure and decides all pending questions, without appeal. Indeed, among the Puritans, as at present among the Congregationalists —their direct descendents—the body of the faithful constituted, not a Church, but a collection of Churches absolutely independent and autonomous. It is easy to understand how greatly this organization which, notwithstanding the parallel development of the Anglican and CalthoIic communions, may be considered even to-day as the national type *par excellence* of the American Church, must have favoured the establishment of democracy and thus prepared the way for the republic. But it must equally have led, by gradual extension, to the legal equality of other Churches, which, by the same principle claimed to interpret the Bible in their own way; and this breach being once opened to the multiplicity of the Protestant sects, the civil tolerance of all opinions in religious matters was only a question of time.

It is true the old world outran the new in this respect, since we find that as late as 1838 a citizen of Boston was condemned to a term of imprisonment for the crime of Atheism. But—while it is to the adversaries of the Church that we owe liberty of worship in Europe— in the United States, it is the natural product of an evolution which began in the religious origin of the nation. The pastor, Roger Williams, when he founded in 1636 the colony of Providence (now the State of Rhode-Island) upon the principle of absolute liberty and equal advantage for all forms of worship;[1] William Penn inserting, in 1681, in the Charter of the State which bears his name, the prohibition of defraying the expense of any worship whatever from the public treasury, "in order to prevent the ascendancy of any one sect above another;" the members of the first Congress who forbade imposing a religious oath on the federal officers as well as the imposition of laws "relating to the establishment or to the prohibition of a religion;"

---

[1]. The colonization of Rhode-Island is certainly the starting-point of religious liberty in the United States. It has often been asserted that the Catholics, who founded, with Lord Baltimore, the colony of Maryland in 1649, established there the principle of religious liberty. It is true the Charter of this colony states that, in order to better assure the maintenance of reciprocal charity and friendship among the inhabitants, no one, provided that he professes to believe in Jesus Christ, shall be troubled, disturbed, or molested in his opinions or in the public worship connected with them. But in another passage of the same Act, it is said that any one who blasphemes the name of God, or denies the Holy Trinity or one of the Persons composing it, shall be punished with death (Ed. Laboulaye, *Histoire des Etas Unis*. Paris, 1855). On the other hand, the Charter of Rhode-Island, which was drawn up in 1643, conformably to the liberal views of Roger Williams, and was confirmed in 1663 by the British Government, proclaims the most absolute liberty of conscience. "This colony," wrote the fanatic Colton Mather, in 1649 (quoted by Ed. Laboulaye), "is a hive of Antinomians, Anti-Sabbatarians, Socinians, Quakers, Convulsionaries— in a word, of all creeds but those of true Christians. If a man lost his belief, he would be sure to find it in some village of Rhode-Island. *Bona terra, mala gens.*"

and finally, the local legislators who established these principles, in the special constitutions of their States, were, speaking generally, anything but sceptics or rationalists: they were believers convinced of the infallibility of the Bible and of the excellence of their worship. MM. Laboulaye, De Laveleye and the other apologists of American democracy are right in claiming that the political and the religious liberty of the United States are both daughters of the Reformation; only, it should not be forgotten that the second is much the younger.

But there is a liberty of another order which, though much younger, may claim the same descent: this is intellectual liberty, the rejection of dogmatic prejudices, in a word, Rationalism. In this case again Europe was in advance of America. Still, here, too, an important distinction is to be noted. It is that, among the peoples of our Continent standing at the head of modern culture, science has developed in an inverse ratio to religion; while in the United States the most complete free inquiry appeared as the final outcome of religious evolution. From John Robinson to Theodore Parker, the line of descent is unbroken.

The first immigrants professed Calvin's doctrines of Original Sin, Grace, and Predestination in all their integrity. But this gloomy fatalism by which man, incapable of attaining to any good by his own efforts, finds himself elected beforehand, by the arbitrary decree of his Creator, to salvation or damnation, shocked too much the most elementary principles of justice and humanity not to speedily provoke a reaction in conformity with the requirements of human liberty and responsibility. The third generation of the Puritans had not disappeared indeed before the dogma of predestination was found to clash with its old enemy Arminianism, which is the last stage before Deism, according to the remark of Wilberforce. In 1737, several New England ministers began to teach that though human nature had doubtless been rendered essentially corrupt by original sin, still, owing to the Expiation on the Cross, man had been made to a certain extent the master of his own destiny. And though it was readily admitted that salvation must be regarded as the work of divine grace, it was nevertheless held that this grace was accorded to those most worthy of it.

Arminianism having once secured a footing, Socinianism was not long in making its appearance. President Adams said at the end of his career that, from 1750, a number of pastors and of the laity were more or less drawn over to Unitarianism. But still, the progress of this evolution was at first apparent only by the guarded silence respecting contested dogmas. Perhaps the Liberals were frightened at their own audacity, or did not exactly realize their beliefs. Even at the end of the century, when other recently created sects (the Universalists, the "Christians") had openly repudiated the dogma of the Trinity, the advanced Calvinists still rejected the qualification of Unitarians, and even maintained the necessity of remaining in doubt upon all points of doctrine, —such as predestination, eternal punishment, the divinity of Christ,— when the Bible did not express itself in clear and formal terms. "The expressions of the Bible are only qualified to formulate Biblical mysteries." Such was the answer they invariably opposed to their adversaries, when the latter summoned them to define their belief. Thus, by a strange inversion of parts, it was the Rationalists who wished to hold strictly to the letter of revelation, while the orthodox cried up the right and the duty of penetrating into its sense and developing its consequences. But this position was not long tenable for the Liberals; and the true ground of conflict was delineated when, driven to the wall, they brought into the controversy the authority of natural religion and historical criticism.

In 1805, Harvard University, which dated almost from the beginning of the colonization, but which had always shown itself hospitable to the most advanced tendencies, confided its Chair of Theology to a liberal minister, Dr. Ware. "They who came under Dr. Ware's influence," wrote one of his pupils—Ezra Stiles Gannett—at a later period, "can never forget the calm dignity, the practical wisdom, the judicial fairness, or the friendly interest which secured for him more than respect. It was veneration that we felt. That clear, strong mind abhorred double dealing with truth or with men."[1] Such was

[1] Ezra Stiles Gannett, Unitarian minister in Boston; *A Memoir*, by his son, W. C. Gannett. Boston, 1875.—Ezra Stiles Gannett, the disciple and co-worker with Channing, exercised ministerial functions at Boston from 1824 to 1871, with a devotedness which was characterized by a modesty equal to its intensity. His biography, written with pious care by his son, Mr. W. C. Gannett, embodies information on the religious life of New England which is all the more instructive because the author has skilfully grouped around the sympathetic figure of his hero the events and personages of the whole period. The work has been reprinted in a popular edition by the British and Foreign Unitarian Association. It is surprising that no liberal Protestant writer has been as yet tempted to translate it into French, since it would be difficult to find a more striking description of Unitarianism and its teachers.

the theologian who was about to mould the future ministers of the national church. The orthodox cried out against the scandal, and established at Andover a school of theology, which was never to attain the celebrity of its rival. At the same time, they began to build churches for the voluntary exiles from the liberal congregations; and, where they were in the majority, as in Connecticut and New Hampshire, they improvised ecclesiastical jurisdictions which expelled liberal ministers from the pulpit. An attempt was even made to introduce this procedure into Massachusetts, where Liberalism had its headquarters, but it failed, and served only to precipitate the development of the schism.

This was in 1815. W. E. Channing was then thirty-five years old. He had already officiated for more than twelve years in one of the most liberal and, at the same time, one of the most fashionable churches in Boston. His antecedents, his mental temperament, and even the amplitude of his religious conceptions predisposed him to great caution in order to preserve the historic unity of the old Puritan congregations. But an accusation of hypocrisy, which Dr. Morse had openly thrown out against liberal ministers, led him boldly to vindicate the Unitarian name, and soon to take the head of the reformatory movement. It was only four years later that he pronounced at Baltimore the famous sermon, considered the definitive manifesto of American Unitarianism. "It made a sensation," says one of the best historians of this period, Mr. W. C. Gannett, "greater probably than any other sermon ever preached in America, before or since."[1]

After having declared that he accepted, "without reserve or exception," all the doctrines *clearly* taught by the Scriptures, Channing claimed that "the meaning [of the Scriptures] is to be sought in the same manner as that of other books;" that is to say, by the constant exercise of reason. "It is to the tribunal of reason," said he, formally, "that God leaves the care of deciding the truth of revelation." Starting from this principle, he repudiated the favourite dogmas of Calvinism, in order to reduce the essential teachings of Scripture to the unity of God, to the immortality of the soul, to the regenerative mission of Jesus, to the moral perfection and the paternal government of the Creator. In fine, after an eloquent picture of the Christian virtues, he maintained that true Christianity consisted much more

---

1. W. C. Gannett, *Op. Cit.*, p. 55.

in the practice of these virtues than in adhesion to any *credo* whatever.

"To all who hear me," concluded he, "I would say with the apostle, 'Prove all things, hold fast that which is good.' Do not, brethren, shrink from the duty of searching God's Word for yourselves, through fear of human censure and denunciation. Do not think that you may innocently follow the opinions which prevail around you, without investigation, on the ground that Christianity is now so purified from errors as to need no laborious research. . . . Much stubble is yet to be burned; much rubbish to be removed; many gaudy decorations, which a false taste has hung around Christianity, must be swept away; and the earth-born fogs, which have long shrouded it, must be scattered before this divine fabric will rise before us in its native and awful majesty, in its harmonious proportions, in its mild and celestial splendours. This glorious reformation in the Church, we hope—under God's blessing—from the progress of the human intellect, from the moral progress of society, from the consequent decline of prejudice and of bigotry, and, though last, not least, from the subversion of human authority in religion, from the fall of those hierarchies and other human institutions by which the minds of individuals are oppressed under the weight of numbers and a papal dominion is perpetuated in the Protestant Church."

It has been said, with reason, that this discourse marked an epoch in the religious history of modern society. Undoubtedly, there had been seen elsewhere Christians proclaiming the necessity of bringing faith into accord with the progress of reason; but never, since the foundation of Christianity, had the head of a church repudiated thus boldly all sectarian intolerance, and so openly declared war against every form of Orthodoxy. Calvin put, or replaced, democracy into Christianity : Channing introduced liberty.

In her previous history, New England had generally had but one church and one pastor in a town. But, from this time, old congregations were divided. Boston, which for a long time had proved itself the intellectual capital of the United States, was almost entirely conquered by the new ideas. In Massachusetts, one hundred and twenty-five congregations broke away from Calvinism, and, among them, the first three churches which the Pilgrim Fathers founded upon the shores of America. To this number may be added the numerous liberal churches which, in imitation of the Calvinists, the Unitarians founded wherever they withdrew from the existing church. In the neighbouring States, the movement made less sensible progress; but congregations, which became centres of propagandism, were established successively in Baltimore, New York, Charleston, Philadelphia, Washington, and even in cities of the West.

Notwithstanding the reluctance of those who feared lest in creating an ecclesiastical organization they should follow too closely the steps of Orthodoxy, the American Unitarian Association for "diffusing the knowledge and promoting the interests of pure Christianity," was founded at Boston in 1825. It was not, however, a federation of Churches, but an association of individuals, who, in creating a valuable agency for the spread of Unitarian opinions, never aimed at a system of denominational discipline.

In fine, the Unitarian reformation represented a double effort: on one side, to give to Christianity a form more humane, more rational, and better adapted to the exigencies of the age; on the other, to substitute, in the formation of churches, sympathy of religious sentiment for agreement in dogmatic belief. Of these two features, the first, which seemed to contemporaries the more audacious, was, in reality, the less important for the future of Unitarianism. In suppressing the theological basis of the Church, Unitarians gave to religion the elasticity necessary to accommodate it to all the transformations which the ulterior development of scientific knowledge could require. They made it a religion indefinitely progressive, like the human mind itself. Their doctrinal innovations, on the contrary, —radical as they were for the epoch,—represented only a transitory state, a *moment* in the religious evolution of the mind.

Channing doubtless proclaims the sovereignty of reason in the most absolute manner: "The truth is," said he, "and it ought not to be denied, that our ultimate reliance is and must be on our own reason. . . . . I am surer that my rational nature is from God than that any book is the expression of his will." Would he have expressed himself with so much assurance if he had not possessed the conviction that his personal views on the pre-existence of Christ and the validity of the Biblical Revelation, had nothing to fear from free inquiry? This is a question which it is neither possible to answer nor even fair to ask. Channing, like all the American Unitarians of the first generation, remained faithful to the theology of Locke, which, as we have seen, sought in miracles the proof, if not the credentials, of Revelation, while they left its interpretation and significance to the ordinary processes of reason.

It must be remembered that, at the commencement of this century, Biblical exegesis had as yet to be entirely created; and, besides, the first Unitarians of the New World, absorbed in their struggle against Calvinism, had enough to do in extirpating the parasitic excrescences of the primitive revelation. It was at the hour when this controversy began to subside, in consequence of reciprocal weariness, that there arrived simultaneously from Germany the first results of a religious criticism henceforth emancipated from dogma, and the idealistic theories of the school of Kant, then in all the splendour of its popularity. The movement of ideas which this double leaven excited among the Unitarians of the second generation tended to nothing less than the founding of a new religion under the cover of Christianity. I refer to the doctrine to which Americans gave the name of Transcendentalism.

CHAPTER VIII.

THE TRANSCENDENTAL MOVEMENT—EMERSON AND PARKER.

Transcendentalism; origin and signification of the word—German Idealism in the United States—Circumstances favourable to the substitution of a mystic Rationalism for the Sensational supernaturalism of the old Unitarian theology—Ralph Waldo Emerson, "the prince of the Transcendentalists"—His opinions on the unity of Nature, the continuity of progress, the identity of substance with mind, and of the Moral Law with the purpose of the universe—Sensation created by his discourse at the Harvard University in 1838—The Transcendental Club and the leaders of the Transcendental movement—Attitude of the conservative Unitarians—Theodore Parker, the prophet of Transcendentalism—His sermon in 1841, on the transitory and the permanent elements in Christianity—His isolation in the midst of the Unitarian Churches—Growing success of his preaching at Boston—His work in the anti-slavery agitation—His double method: observation and intuition—His theology: the immanence of God in Conscience and in Nature—Application of his doctrine to morals and to politics—The golden age of Boston—The connection between the reign of Transcendentalism and the richest intellectual life of New England.

The old Sensational school made of the soul a *tabula rasa*, a mirror, limited to reflecting the impressions transmitted by the senses. Kant combatted this negative psychology in his *Critique of Pure Reason* by showing that the human mind possesses an innate organization of its own, independent of experience, and necessary for the formation of thought. Yet, from what reason thus apprehended, under the form of Transcendental conceptions,—that is, above the sphere of experience,—namely, ideas of the absolute, the infinite, the ideal, he did not deduce, necessarily, the real existence of corresponding entities. Fichte, his disciple, advanced farther still in the way of subjective idealism, since he affirmed our inability to know anything with certainty outside of our own mind and its laws. Jacobi, on the contrary, and especially Schelling, inferred from the fact of our inward conceptions the objective reality, as much of the spiritual world as of the sensible. Later, Schleiermacher, placing the origin of religion in the feeling of our dependence upon the Absolute, endeavoured to trace to individual revelation the dogmas of Christianity, without seeing that he sapped them at their base by his doctrine of the direct communication between the soul and God.

After conquering the university lecture-room, renovating theology, and illuminating German literature, Transcendental idealism passed into France, where Cousin enchased it in his brilliant mosaic, under the name of *impersonal reason;* and into England, where Coleridge became its apostle, Carlyle its historian, and Wordsworth its poet. But, considerable as was its action upon the development of European thought during the most fruitful and enthusiastic literary period of our century, nothing here is comparable to the influence which it exercised in New England in all the spheres of activity, intellectual, religious, and even social.

It was by the works of Coleridge and Carlyle that it penetrated into the United States in the first-third of this century. The interest which it excited led the most distinguished writers of Boston to study German and French, that they might read at first hand Jacobi, Fichte, Schelling, Herder, Schleiermacher, and De Wette, and also Cousin, Jouffroy, and Benjamin Constant. Philosophic at first, the movement was not tardy in becoming exclusively religious. In 1835, James Walker, Professor of Ethics in Harvard University, assailed the sensational method of the dominant theology, and extolled recourse to a philosophy which constantly recalls our relations 'to the spiritual world.

The new method was especially attractive to minds which had carried farthest the work of demolition, undertaken by modern exegesis, upon the dogmas of Christianity. The only traditions which the Unitarians had left as the basis of their religious system, the preexistence of Christ and the authenticity of miracles, began to be shaken by the incessant progress of free inquiry. How natural, then, that those who were desirous of preserving the foundations of their faith, in this general shipwreck of dogmas, should have welcomed with eagerness a doctrine which, in extending to all men the privilege of a direct communication with the Divine Being, allowed them to reduce to human proportions the person of Jesus, without taking from him the prestige of inspiration! How could they have been other than attracted by the ingenious hypothesis of a sixth sense, which, open to the spiritual world, rendered useless the intervention of miracles to establish the existence of God and the immortality of the soul!

It may be said that Transcendentalism presented at the same time the complement and the corrective of the Unitarian reform. This latter was, pre-eminently, a religion of the head, the product of a critical and negative tendency. Its theology, as far as it had any, came by the process of subtraction, or by taking away successively from the Christian traditions the dogmas condemned by free scholarship. Transcendentalism proceeded by the way of clear and positive affirmation. It took for its point of departure the existence of a special faculty which permitted the human mind to seize directly spiritual truths. Regarding as facts of consciousness the three great axioms of Theism,—God, immortality, duty,—it placed them upon foundations which reason itself proclaimed independent of all experience and of all demonstration. Thus entrenched in the depths of consciousness and in the realm of the ideal, it easily found access to the sources of mysticism, which, by a singular phenomenon among a people so practical, never seem exhausted in the American mind. In short, by its doctrine of impersonal reason, it embraced the profoundly Aryan conception of the neo-Platonic Word, which the Unitarians had suppressed from Christianity, in order to adhere to the strict Monotheism of the first evangelists. It thereby allied itself to the mystic sects founded in Protestantism upon the principle of interior illumination, except that it extended to all men the privilege of inspiration, which these sects wished to reserve to the adepts of a distinctive faith.

"Transcendentalism," says its principal historian in New Zealand, Mr. O. B. Frothingham,[1] "possessed all the chief qualifications for a gospel. Its cardinal facts were few and manageable. Its data were secluded in the recesses of consciousness, out of reach of scientific investigation, remote from the gaze of vulgar scepticism—esoteric, having about them the charm of a sacred privacy, on which common sense and the critical understanding might not intrude. . . .

---

1. O. B. Frothingham, *Transcendentalism in New England a History.* New York: Putnam, 1880. I. Vol.—The author himself, although really belonging to a later generation, took an active part in the religious movement he has described; but, since the failure of the Rationalistic Church which he had founded in New York, he has devoted himself to letters, in which he occupies, above all as a critic, a distinguished rank. Much was said, about a year ago, respecting his conversion to Orthodoxy; but he took care to deny this report in a letter to the New York *Evening Post,* on the 13th of November, 1881, in which he stated that, while recognizing that his old opinions did not embody the whole truth, he saw no reason to change them.

It possessed the character of indefiniteness and mystery, full of sentiment and suggestion, that fascinates the imagination and lends itself so easily to acts of contemplation and worship. . . . Piety was a feature of Transcendentalism; it loved devout hymns, music, the glowing language of aspiration, the word of awe and humility, emblems, symbols, expressions of inarticulate emotion, silence, contemplation, breathings after communion with the Infinite."

Unitarianism, as a whole, was, however, far from casting itself into the arms of German idealism. The Unitarians of the first generation who wished to adhere to the positions conquered from Orthodoxy, and, in general, all who were not troubled in their belief in the supernaturalness of the Bible, regarded the progress of the new method with more distrust than enthusiasm. Some predicted that it would lead to fatal divisions in the bosom of Unitarianism; others, that this invasion of idealism would bring, as usual, a sceptical re-action. Channing himself, who had so much insisted upon the authority, the grandeur, the divinity of the human soul, wrote, nevertheless, in the last years of his life, to Dr. Martineau, that the Transcendentalists appeared to him to be advancing toward the substitution of individual inspiration for Christianity.

There was then in Boston a young minister who had just quitted his congregation through a scruple of conscience, because he was no longer willing to administer the sacrament of the communion. This was Ralph Waldo Emerson, the essayist, who, with the poet, Henry W. Longfellow, held, during a third of the century, the sceptre of American literature. In his first work, *Nature*, published in 1836, he revealed that vigorous idealism which has caused him to be surnamed, in the United States, the Prince of Transcendentalists. Notwithstanding the fact that the blood of eight generations of clergymen flowed in his veins, he was anything but a theologian and a controversialist. Imagination and feeling were his leading characteristics; he might almost be called an *illuminé* of Rationalism. Some of his poetical productions and indeed of his prose dissertations on the eternal One, on the universal Spirit, of which Nature is simply the product and the symbol, and on the ineffable union of the individual soul with the universal or over-soul, suggest the latest philosophers of the Alexandrian school and even certain mystics of India : "All goes to show," says he, " that the soul is not an organ, but animates and exercises all organs, is not a function like the power of memory, of calculation, of comparison, but uses these as hands and feet; it is not a faculty but a light, it is not the intellect or the will but the master of the intellect and the will; it is the back ground of our being in which they lie, an immensity, not possessed and that cannot be possessed. From within or behind, a light shines through us on things and makes us aware that we are nothing, but the light is all. A man is the façade of a temple wherein all wisdom and all good abide."

This is certainly Pantheism, but a subjective Pantheism which tends to absorb God and nature into man, rather than man and nature into God. Besides, it is in the human mind that Emerson sees a solution of the problem of nature, together with the secret of history: " Let man learn the revelation of all nature and of all thought to his heart; this, namely: that the Highest dwells with him, that the sources of nature are in his own mind, if the sentiment of duty is there." "This human mind wrote history, and this must read it. The Sphinx must solve her own riddle. If the whole of history is in one man, it is all to be explained from individual experiences. . . . . We are always coming up with the emphatic facts of history, in our private experience, and verifying them here. All history becomes subjective, in other words there is properly no history only biography."

It is from this respect and reverence for the human individuality that Emerson escapes the rock upon which mysticism is ordinarily wrecked, and that he keeps his feet on the earth though he lifts himself up to the heavens: "As soon as every man is apprised of the divine presence within his own mind, is apprised that the perfect law of duty corresponds with the laws of chemistry, of vegetation, of astronomy, as face to face in a glass; that the basis of duty, the order of society, the power of character, the wealth of culture, the perfection of taste all draw their essence from this moral sentiment, then we have a religion that exalts, that commands all the social and all the private action. . . . . Pure doctrine always bears fruit in pure benefits. It is only by good works, it is only on the basis of active duty that worship finds its expression."

Another question in which he shows himself to be entirely a child of the present age, is his extreme deference to scientific truth, which he regards as a revelation of God. Twenty years before the publication of the *Origin of Species* he wrote thus in *Nature*—

> "A subtle chain of countless rings,
> The next unto the furthest brings.
> The eye reads omens where it goes,
> And speaks all languages the rose.
> And striving to be man, the worm,
> Mounts through all the spires of form."

This led Tyndall to say: "In him we have a poet and a profoundly religious man who is really and entirely undaunted by the discoveries of science, past, present and prospective. In his case poetry, with the joy of a bacchanal, takes her graver brother science by the hand and cheers him with immortal laughter."

It has been contended that in Emerson the poet obscures the philosopher, and that no one could affirm to what system of philosophy he belonged. In truth—as the Rev. Heber Newton showed, shortly after his death, in a funeral oration, which made a sensation in New York—Emerson professed the philosophy and the religion of Nature, but of a Nature idealized, and it is to this that the secret of his influence on contemporary society is to be traced.

Not only does he admit the continuity of the universal development as well as the unity of Nature, of which he makes the Sphinx say,

> "Who telleth one of my meanings
> Is master of all that I am,"

but, even more, passing beyond the sphere of scientific observation, he glances at the essence of things as a spiritual force: "Nature is the incarnation of a word . . . the world is mind precipitated," and he proclaims the identity of this force with the moral law revealed in the human conscience: "This ethical character so penetrates the bone and marrow of Nature as to seem the end for which it is made."

Moral progress, moreover, is to him only a mirror of universal progress: "The moral sentiment speaks to every man the law after which the universe was made. We find parity, identity of design through Nature, and benefit to be the uniform aim; there is force always at work to make the best better and the worst good." Finally, he considers love to be an undeniable attribute of the Universal Power:

> "Wilt thou freeze Love's tidal flow,
> Whose streams through Nature circling go?"

Such is the doctrine which shines through all his works, but which he abstains from developing systematically and from discussing with those who deny it, so fully does it embody for him an order of truth that lies beyond the range of controversy. He deemed it worthy, moreover, of furnishing the plan of that harmonious temple to which he likened, in the following terms, the religion of the future: "There will be a new Church, founded on moral science, at first cold and naked, a babe in the manger again, the algebra and mathematics of ethical law, the Church of men to come, without shawns or psaltery or sackbut, but it will have heaven and earth for its beams and rafters, science for symbol and illustration; it will fast enough gather beauty, music, picture, poetry."

Emerson was at the beginning of his renown when, in 1838, he pronounced before the Theological School of Harvard the celebrated discourse in which Transcendentalism avowed itself, for the first time, in open hostility with all Christian Churches, not excepting the Unitarian. The orator reproached them, without distinction, with having looked for miracles—that is, the intervention of God—elsewhere than in the normal functions of natural laws; with having disfigured, by their compromising exaggerations, the personality of Jesus, "the only soul in history who has appreciated the worth of a man;" in short, with having neglected the exploration of the human soul and its relations with the divine mind. . . . . "It is time," said he, "that the ill-suppressed murmur of all thoughtful men against the famine of our Churches should be heard through the sleep of indolence and over the din of routine. . . . The prayers and even the dogmas of our Churches are like the Zodiac of Dendérah and the astronomical monuments of the Hindus, wholly isolated from anything now extant in the life and business of the people. . . . With whatever exceptions, tradition characterizes the preaching of this country; it comes out of the memory and not out of the soul."

The remedy for these defects was "first, soul, and second, soul, and evermore soul."—"I look for the teacher," added he, "that shall see the world to be the mirror of the soul, shall see the identity of the Law of Gravitation with purity of heart, and shall show that the Ought, that Duty, is one thing with Science, with Beauty and with Joy."

This appeal was understood by all who were affected by the idealistic ferment. They soon had their centre of propagandism, the Transcendental Club, and their organ, *The Dial*. In the first ranks of the young phalanx was seen another mystic, Bronson Alcott, a fervent admirer of Pythagoras and Plato, whom he regarded as the direct ancestors of Kant and of the whole Transcendental school; George Ripley and James Freeman Clarke, who had been the first to carry into the pulpit the teachings of German idealism; Samuel Longfellow, who, without attaining to the renown of his brother, has a collection of hymns and of poetry highly esteemed by his compatriots; Orestes Brownson, an ardent propagandist, but of an unstable mind, who, at first a minister of a Presbyterian congregation, passed over to Rationalism, then to Universalism, and who, not content with pursuing his transformations into the most extreme Transcendentalism, finished by seeking mental repose in the bosom of the Romish Church; William Henry Channing, a nephew of the founder of Unitarianism, who became a missionary of the new gospel; the future colonel of a national negro regiment in the War of the Secession, T. W. Higginson, who represented the practical tendencies of the movement, as Samuel Johnson personified its extreme individualism; and, finally, C. A. Bartol, W. H. Furness, John Weiss, John Pierpont, Professor Francis, and, above all, Theodore Parker, the apostle and prophet of Transcendentalism.

On the other hand, the conservative section of Unitarianism had taken the alarm; and there were Unitarians who questioned whether Emerson ought still to be regarded as a Christian, precisely as twenty years before the question had been agitated whether they themselves belonged to Christianity or to "the religion of Boston." It was worse still when, in 1841, Theodore Parker, at an ordination in the Unitarian church of South Boston, delivered his sermon upon "The Transient and the Permanent Elements in Christianity." The permanent element was the great religious and moral virtues which Jesus, "that perfect type of the religious man," had manifested in himself, and had vivified in his love of humanity. The transient element was the rites and doctrines of Christianity, comprising the belief that the Bible contained a special revelation, and that the nature of Christ was unique in history.

According to Mr. W. C. Gannett, this discourse made as much noise as the famous sermon of Dr. Channing, preached at Baltimore twenty-two years before. This time, it was no longer a question whether the author was a Christian: he was treated as an infidel, a blasphemer, an atheist. The Boston Association of Ministers debated whether they should not expel him from their ranks. As their rules were opposed to this, they took the official step of requesting him to resign. "I am sorry for the Association," he answered, "but I cannot help it. I cannot take upon my shoulders the *onus damnandi*. This would be to avow that there is good cause for my withdrawal. . . . . They have, in a measure, identified me with freedom in religious matters."

Certain members thought of a dissolution of the society, which would have allowed them to reorganize without the author of all this scandal. But the voice of moderation prevailed,—thanks to the sympathy, more or less acknowledged, felt for Parker among the younger ministers; and perhaps also to the intervention of Dr. Ezra Stiles Gannett, who, although belonging to the conservative party, had a high esteem for the frank and loyal character of his fellow-minister. "It is not our way," he reminded his brethren, "to pass ecclesiastical censure. We are willing—at least we have said we were willing—to take the principle of free inquiry, with all its consequences." The Association, therefore, passed no resolution against the audacious reformer; but all the pulpits in Boston were henceforth closed against him. This situation continued until 1845. The adherents of the proscribed man then had a meeting, at which they resolved that "Theodore Parker shall have a chance to be heard in Boston." They hired for him the Melodeon, a concert hall, in the hope that there would soon be gathered the elements of a congregation. The success of the movement surpassed all expectation, and the lapse of years merely served to increase it. In 1852, Parker had to be installed in a larger edifice where, until 1859, he announced Sunday after Sunday, the good news of Transcendentalism before thousands of auditors. His activity during this period, was truly immense:—When he could write and preach but one sermon a week, says one of his biographers, he fancied he had done nothing, and when he gave only twenty-four lectures a year he found that but a small matter. He was equally at home in all subjects, and whether it was a question of religion or politics, of the mischievous tendencies of public opinion or the evil of private scandal, nothing intimidated him when his conscience commanded him to speak. In this respect, M. Albert Reville has characterized him justly in speaking of him as a "prophet" in the old Biblical sense of the word.

One day as he was denouncing, at a public meeting, the injustice of the war which the United States had declared against Mexico, some armed volunteers who were in the room tried to silence him by the threat of death. You wish to kill me, he cried. Well, I declare that in such case I will return alone and unarmed, and not one of you will be able to touch a hair of my head. Thus he went on with his speech, and no one dared to stop him.

Slavery had not a more determined adversary, and he played a preponderating part in the abolitionist movement, whose final triumph he predicted. When the Party in favour of slavery were in power and passed the *Fugitive Slave Bill*, in 1851, which enacted that fugitive slaves should be everywhere arrested, Parker declared that he would open his house to them, and that he would defend them even with arms in his hand. He kept his word, and, when reproached in consequence, for having put himself above the laws, he stated, in one of his sermons, that, on a certain occasion in Palestine, a no less legal decree of the High Priest, had ordered the pursuit and arrest of a certain stirrer up of sedition, named Jesus of Nazareth, and that Judas Iscariot was the only man who had had the courage to fulfil his constitutional obligation. And yet, added he, Judas Iscariot has anything but a good reputation in the Christian world. He is called the Son of Perdition. His conduct is declared to be criminal, and even the New Testament assumes that the Devil must have entered into him to inspire his odious crime. Ah! continued he, what error has blinded us all! Judas Iscariot a traitor! Indeed! Why he simply conquered his *prejudices*. He merely knew how to perform a disagreeable duty. He maintained the law and the Constitution. He did all in his power to save the Union. Judas thou art a saint: the law of God never commands us to disobey human laws. "*Sancte Iscariote, ora pro nobis.*" This sermon, which caused an immense stir, brought upon its author a criminal prosecution. But it merely ended in his triumphant acquittal, and he only continued his propagandism with increased energy.

We may regard Parker as the clearest and most logical interpreter of Transcendental principles. "A Transcendental religion needs," he said, "a Transcendental theology." His posthumous essay,

Transcendentalism, and also his first work, *A Discourse on Matters Pertaining to Religion*, admirably sum up the doctrines which inspired his whole life, and which he believed destined to become the religion of enlightened minds during the next thousand years. There must not be sought in them a rigorous analysis of the psychological phenomena which serve as the basis of the philosophy of intuition. Parker had adopted as a starting-point the method of the followers of Kant. Henceforth, therefore, he declines to discuss its underlying principles, and contents himself with the application of it, to the search for and the development of religious truth. To be sure, he rejects neither the control nor the support of external observation; but it is above all to internal phenomena that he turns in order to obtain decisive evidence for the existence of God and the doctrine of immortality.

He begins by showing that there is in human nature a religious faculty or tendency side-by-side with our moral, emotional, and intellectual faculties. This faculty furnishes us with the first conception of the Infinite and the Absolute, just as our senses afford us a knowledge of the qualities of matter. This primordial notion, fact of consciousness, or necessary truth, is afterwards laid hold of by Reason, which deduces from it the idea of a God infinite in power, in intelligence, in justice and in love. It is no longer the God of Deism or Sensationalism, external to the world and of doubtful utility. But rather it is a God universally and eternally active, who is immanent alike in mind and in matter. The laws of nature are his modes of action and miracles are therefore impossible, since they would form a violation of the divine laws. But God is not only immanent, he is also transcendent, that is, without limitations of any kind, infinite and absolute. The universe, as the manifestation of his activity, participates in his perfection, but only in relation to the purpose for which it was created. As to the immortality of the soul, the best evidence of this is to be found in the longing for continued existence which is in the heart of man.

Since God is immanent in human nature, "it follows that man is capable of inspiration from God, communion with God, not in raptures, not by miracles, but by the sober use of all his faculties, moral, intellectual, affectionate, religious. . . In this way Transcendentalism can legitimate the highest inspiration and explain the genesis of God's noblest son, not as monstrous, but natural. In religion as in all things else there has been a progressive development of mankind. The world is a school; prophets, saints, saviours, men more eminently gifted and faithful, and so most eminently inspired—they are the schoolmasters to lead men up to God."

Here are the terms in which Parker shows that science being a form of religion cannot possibly be in antagonism to it :—

"Men of science, as a class, do not war on the truths, the goodness and the piety that are taught as religion, only on the errors, the evil, the impiety which bear its name. Science is the natural ally of religion. Shall we try and separate what God has joined? We injure both by the attempt. The philosophers of this age have a profound love of truth, and show great industry and boldness in search thereof. In the name of truth they pluck down the strongholds of error, venerable and old. All the attacks made on religion itself by men of science from Celsus to Feuerbach, have not done so much to bring religion into contempt as a single persecution for witchcraft, or a Bartholomew massacre made in the name of God."[1]

---

[1]. It is much to be regretted that Parker is not better known here in England. Many of those who are familiar with his name look upon him mainly as an advanced religious thinker, who was more at home in opposing the claims of orthodoxy than in teaching spiritual religion. But as a matter of fact he spoke at times with the voice of an inspired poet, whose words glowed with holy fire. Take in illustration of this, the following fine passage on the Joy of Faith, from his *Discourse on Matters Pertaining to Religion*, where he says—"No doubt there is joy in the success of earthly schemes. There is joy to the miser as he satiates his prurient palm with gold : there is joy to the fool of fortune when his gaming brings a prize. But what is it? His request is granted, but leanness enters his soul. There is delight in feasting on the bounties of Earth, the garment in which God veils the brightness of his face ; in being filled with the fragrant loveliness of flowers; the song of birds ; the hum of bees ; the sounds of ocean; the rustle of the summer wind, heard at evening in the pine tops; in the cool running brooks ; in the majestic sweep of undulating hills ; the grandeur of untamed forests; the majesty of the mountain : in the morning's virgin beauty ; in the maternal grace of evening, and the sublime and mystic pomp of night. Nature's silent sympathy—how beautiful it is!

"There is joy, no doubt there is joy, to the mind of Genius, when thought bursts on him as the tropic sun rending a cloud ; when long trains of ideas sweep through his soul, like constellated orbs before an angel's eye ; when sublime thoughts and burning words rush to the heart; when Nature unveils her secret truth, and some great Law breaks, all at once, upon a Newton's mind, and chaos ends in light; when the hour of his inspiration and the joy of his genius is on him, 'tis then that this child of heaven feels a God-like delight. 'Tis sympathy with Truth.

"There is a higher and more tranquil bliss when heart communes with heart ; when two souls unite in one, like mingling dew-drops on a rose, that scarcely touch the flower, but mirror the heavens in their little orbs; when perfect love transforms

It is in the individual conscience that the Transcendentalists exclusively sought the basis and sanction of morality. Some confined themselves to seeing in conscience a perfectible organ, demanding rational cultivation in order to reach its full development. But the majority held that man possesses within himself an absolute criterion of good and evil. Such, too, was the opinion of Parker—

"While experience shows what has been or is, conscience shows what should be and shall. Transcendental ethics look not at the consequences of virtue in this life or in the next as motive, therefore, to lead men to virtue. That is itself a good, an absolute good—to be loved not for what it brings, but is."

Applied to politics, the Transcendental method led to the search for rules of government in conscience: "It does not so much quote precedents, contingent facts of experience as ideas, necessary facts of consciousness; it only quotes the precedent to obtain or illustrate the idea. . . . Conscience, in politics and in ethics, transcends experience, and, *a priori*, tells us of the just, the right, the good, the fair; not the relatively right alone, but the absolute right also." In his

---

two souls, either man's or woman's, each to the other's image; when one heart beats in two bosoms; one spirit speaks with a divided tongue; when the same soul is eloquent in mutual eyes—there is a rapture deep, serene, heart-felt, and abiding in this mysterious fellow-feeling with a congenial soul, which puts to shame the cold sympathy of Nature, and the ecstatic but short-lived bliss of Genius in his high and burning hour.

"But the welfare of Religion is more than each or all of these. The glad reliance that comes upon the man; the sense of trust; a rest with God; the soul's exceeding peace; the universal harmony; the infinite within; sympathy with the Soul of All—is bliss that words cannot pourtray. He only knows, who feels. The speech of a prophet cannot tell the tale. No: not if a seraph touched his lips with fire. In the high hour of religious visitation from the living God, there seems to be no separate thought; the tide of universal life sets through the soul. The thought of self is gone. It is a little accident to be a king or a clown, a parent or a child. Man is at one with God, and He is All in All. Neither the loveliness of Nature, neither the joy of Genius, nor the sweet breathing of congenial hearts, that make delicious music as they beat—neither one nor all of these can equal the joy of the religious soul that is at one with God, so full of peace that prayer is needless. Nature undergoes a new transformation.—A story tells that when the rising sun fell on Memnon's statue, it wakened music in that breast of stone. Religion does the same with Nature. From the shining snake to the waterfall, it is all eloquent of God. As to John in the Apocalypse, there stands an angel in the sun; the seraphim hang over every flower; God speaks in each little grass that fringes a mountain rock. Then even Genius is wedded to greater bliss. His thoughts shine more brilliant when set in the light of Religion. Friendship and love it renders infinite. This is the joy Religion gives; its perennial rest; its everlasting life."—*Translator.*

respect, indeed, for the claims of the right, revealed by intuition, Parker goes so far as to maintain that no one owes obedience to a law which clashes with the requirements of absolute morality and right. "By birth," says he, "man is a citizen of the universe, subject to God. No oath of allegiance, no king, no parliament, no congress, no people can absolve him from his natural fealty thereto and alienate a man born to the rights, born to the duties of a citizen of God's universe. Over all human law, God alone has eminent domain."

Parker does not fail to show the Transcendental character of the Declaration of Independence, which founded a Republican Government in the United States, or, to employ his happy definition, "the government of all, for all, and by all." In the same way he does not hesitate to recognize the idealistic character of the French Revolution:

"In France men have an idea yet more Transcendental: to the intellectual idea of liberty and the moral idea of equality, they add the religious idea of fraternity, and so put politics and all legislation on a basis, divine and incontestable as the truths of mathematics. They say that rights and duties are before all human laws. America says: 'The Constitution of the United States is above the President, the Supreme Court above Congress.' France says: 'The Constitution of the Universe is above the Constitution of France.' Forty million people say that. It transcends experience; it is the grandest thing a nation ever said in history."

It is not customary to regard the French Revolution as the realization of a religious idea; but there is nothing surprising in Parker's views, for those who know what he understood by religion.

His preaching, which extends from 1841 to 1859, corresponds to the principal development of Transcendentalism. It was equally the golden age of Boston, and it may be added of American literature. The middle of this century has seen, indeed, within the narrow territory of Massachusetts, one of those marvellous out-blossomings which are rarely reproduced in the moral culture of a people. Channing died in 1842; but it may be said that Parker worthily replaced him in the vanguard of religious Rationalism. By the side of Emerson, who was equally pre-eminent as philosopher and poet, Bancroft carried the principles of Transcendentalism into history; Sumner, into international law; Alcott, into pedagogy; Whittier, into poetry; Margaret Fuller, into criticism; Oliver Wendall Holmes revealed himself as a humourist; Prescott published his *History of the Spanish Conquest of Mexico ;* Hawthorne put into romance his power of psychological analysis; H. W. Longfellow attained the meridian of his glory; and finally, Massachusetts furnished for the National Senate, Daniel Webster, the ablest orator the United States has produced. I merely cite those names whose echo has reached Europe. But by the side of these illustrious leaders, a whole army of writers, lecturers and orators did their part either in the literary and philosophical publications which multiplied in Boston, or in the different associations which were organized for the promotion of temperance, for the emancipation of woman, for the instruction of the people, for the suppression of war, for prison reform, and, above all, for the abolition of slavery.

It is not difficult to discover the influence of Transcendentalism in these numerous "agitations;" not only because the exponents of this philosophy were found in the first rank, but also because these movements were the direct and logical consequence of a doctrine attributing to every human being the same faculties and the same rights. To this influence, moreover, belong other more or less successful experiments, which aimed at radically reforming the principles of social organization. At one time it was George Ripley, who spent his fortune in organizing a free community upon the principle of co-operation; at another, it was A. B. Alcott, who, claiming the right to renounce the burdens as well as the advantages of actual society, allowed himself to be imprisoned for refusing to pay his taxes. This fever of reform was not confined to Rationalism. Revivals, exciting even to delirium the fervour of the various sects, passed like a billow over the whole of Protestant America, and New England furnished its quota to the eccentricities of Spiritualism and "free love."

Yet what gives to this period a character very rare in times of religious and social fermentation, is that laxness of morals did not coincide with excessive mental excitement. Calvinism, in losing its dogmatic authority, had left with the people its strong moral discipline. Unitarianism had introduced free inquiry into matters of belief, and Transcendentalism had limited itself to adding thereto an enthusiasm for noble ideas.

CHAPTER IX.

FREE RELIGION AND THE RELIGION OF ETHICS.

Death of Parker; his last significant words—Decline of Transcendentalism in its struggle with the New Scientific Philosophy—The two schools of Unitarianism in 1864—Establishment of the *National Unitarian Conference*—Mr. Francis E. Adams and "the battle of Syracuse"—Formation of the Free Religious Association in 1867—Principles and objects of the Free Religious Movement—Congregations which have adopted its programme at Dorchester, Providence, Florence, &c.—The first congregation of New Bedford—The Religion of Ethics—Mr. Felix Adler—The Philosophy of the categorical imperative—Distinction between Theism and its doctrinal basis—The Religion of Duty—The *Society for Ethical Culture* at New York and at Chicago—Its philanthropical works—Recent mutual approach of Unitarianism and Free Religion—Rejection of every obligatory *Credo* by the National Unitarian Conference—Emancipation of the Unitarian Churches in the West—Free Religion among the Progressive Quakers and Spiritualists—The *Freie-Religiöse-Gemeinde*—Reformed Judaism in America—Increasing Practical Character of religion in the United States—Progressive tendencies among the Episcopalians, the Methodists, the Baptists, the Presbyterians, the Congregationalists, &c.—The Rev. H. Ward Beecher and the Brooklyn Association of Congregational Ministers—The Catholics of the United States.

Parker died in Italy, May 10, 1860, on the eve of that War of Secession which he had perhaps hastened by the energy of his denunciations against slavery. It is related that, at the moment of dying, he murmured: "There are two Theodore Parkers now. One is dying here in Italy: the other I have planted in America. He will live there, and finish my work." The prediction of the dying man is realized, but perhaps not in the sense he attached to it. Parker lives more than ever in the United States, through the power exercised over imagination and character by the example of his inflexible fidelity to conviction, of his passionate love for truth and justice, and of his unshaken faith in the reconciliation of religion and progress. But, as to his favourite doctrine,—not admitting, with certain of his most recent biographers, that he would to-day with the same ardour extol the exclusive use of the experimental method,—it must be recognized that the philosophy of intuition has not answered the highest expectations of its prophet.

The emancipation of the slaves was the great triumph of Transcendentalism, but it was also the beginning of its decline. The movement owed a great part of its popularity to the indifference which almost all the established churches had shown in opposing the scourge of slavery. When this odious institution was consumed in the flames of civil war, Transcendentalism lost its principal motive power over one portion of its adherents. On the other hand, individualism, which was at the bottom of its aspirations, was always a serious obstacle to its efforts at propagandism and to the grouping of its forces. Its essential aim, according to an expression of Samuel Johnson, was to lead each individual to become a church by himself, — which was to condemn the very principle of all permanent organization upon religious grounds.

The majority of its interpreters did not break away completely from Unitarianism, which had served as a cradle to the Transcendental doctrine; and, of the independent congregations which some of them endeavoured to establish in imitation of Parker, few had a long duration. Indeed, Transcendentalism represented a reaction against the exaggerations of the Sensational method of philosophy; and, like all reactions, it went beyond its mark. Not content with affirming the importance of psychology, the necessity of recurring to internal observation to explain the origin of our knowledge, the aptitude of the mind to conceive certain notions which cannot be the exclusive product of sensible experience, the existence of moral liberty, and the imperative character of duty, it professed to find in the human soul a complete and infallible perception of religious and moral truth.

This was to prepare the way for an aggressive return of Sensationalism, at the time when this philosophy, strengthened by the prodigious discoveries made by the natural sciences, claimed to furnish the synthesis of the universe. The weapon which had assured the victory to the school of Kant over the partisans of Locke was the verification in the human mind of ideas which are not introduced there by experience. The neo-Sensationalism of our epoch has displaced the ground of controversy, by explaining the presence of notions *a priori* in the individual by hereditary transmission of accumulated experiences in the past of the race, and under this rejuvenated form it spread so much the more rapidly in the United States, because it was directly introduced there in the works of the scientific school at present predominant in England.

It will be clear, however, that this return blow of contemporary Sensationalism, though calculated to weaken the authority of the

Transcendentalists in the bosom of the Unitarian Church, could hardly profit the partizans of the Sensational theology of Locke and Priestley. The Transcendentalists were still attached in a certain degree to the Christian tradition. Emerson, whose Christianity was contested by the conservatives, made of Jesus the principal educator of humanity; and Parker, who was treated as an atheist, identified the moral teaching of Christ with absolute religion. The new school, on the contrary, pursuing to the end its work of critical destruction, has stripped of his aureole the founder of Christianity, whom it places on a footing of equality with Buddha, Zoroaster, Moses, and Mohammed. At the end of the civil war, therefore, Unitarianism found itself more than ever divided into two factions: on the left, the Liberals who began to accept the name of Radicals; on the right, the Conservatives of the old school (old-fashioned Unitarians). These, perhaps, did not insist with so much energy as formerly upon the Socinian theories of the pre-existence of Christ; but they continued to make belief in the authenticity of Revelation the corner-stone of Christianity. The former, on the contrary, maintained that difference of opinion upon the infallibility and even upon the moral value of the Bible was not an obstacle to religious fraternity, and that the essence of Christianity was the practice of Christian virtues.

On this last ground, indeed, agreement was easy, and there was an equal amount of enthusiasm in the two parties, when, after the Civil War, in 1864, Dr. Bellows proposed to unite the delegates from all the Unitarian Churches in a permanent confederation, in order to give more unity to their works of charity, of instruction, and of propagandism. The provisional assembly, composed of three delegates from each church and each local association, met at New York the first day of April, 1865. But differences appeared as soon as they came to settle the principles and even the title of the new association. Finally, after rejecting a long profession of faith drawn up in the name of the extreme right wing by Mr. A. Low, and adopting a declaration stating that the decisions of the majority should not be binding upon the minority, the delegates voted, perhaps in the spirit of compromise, a preamble expressing the "obligation of all the disciples of the Lord Jesus Christ to prove their faith by self-denial, and by the devotion of their lives and possessions to the service of God and the building up of the kingdom of his Son." This phraseology gave umbrage to the

Radicals, who saw in it a declaration of allegiance to Christ; and, in the following meeting, which opened at Syracuse, Oct. 10, 1866, one of their most distinguished representatives, Mr. Francis Ellingwood Abbot, proposed to substitute for this preamble a declaration that "the object of Christianity is the universal diffusion of love, righteousness, and truth; that perfect freedom of thought is the right and the duty of every human being;" and that the basis of religious organization should be "unity of spirit rather than uniformity of belief." At the same time, Mr. Abbot proposed to substitute the words "Independent Churches" for "Christian Churches," which figured in the title of the Conference.[1]

Perhaps, in the preceding year, the propositions of Mr. Abbot would have had some chance of being adopted; for they served, chiefly, only to maintain in Unitarianism a *statu quo* consecrated by the experience of half a century. But, after the Conference had officially hoisted its colours, this change of name and programme would not have failed to be represented as a repudiation of Christ and of all Christian traditions. The only concession which it showed itself ready to grant was to add to its title, "The National Conference of Unitarian Churches," the words, "and other Christian Churches." This was a tender to Universalists and to all liberal congregations whose internal development had, by degrees, brought them near to Unitarian doctrines. But Mr. Abbot, seeing his propositions rejected, withdrew from Unitarianism; and the following year he, with many of his liberal colleagues,—who, however, did not think it necessary to follow him in his withdrawal,—formed at Boston the Free Religious Association, which had for its object to realize, outside of every Christian communion, the programme rejected by the Conference of Syracuse.

It is certain that the Unitarians were wanting in logic, when, on one side, they proclaimed the absolute sovereignty of reason, and, on the other, sought to identify themselves with the belief in the religious and moral superiority of Christianity. There was, therefore, a place for a broader organization, which should accept, in its most remote consequences, the principle of free inquiry, and which should remain open not only to "all the disciples of Christ," but also to "all the disciples

---

[1]. James Freeman Clarke and Francis Ellingwood Abbot, *The Battle of Syracuse*, Two Essays: Boston, 1875.

of truth,"—Christians, Jews, Buddhists, Mohammedans, Positivists, and even Atheists,—provided they should have in common the love of truth and the desire for goodness. The organizers of "Free Religion" did not impose upon them the sacrifice of their particular beliefs, nor even of their connections with other religious associations: all that they asked of them was to unite upon the ground of spiritual unity detached from all dogmatic intolerance.

The first article of their constitution states it to be the object of the Association "to promote the practical interests of pure religion, to increase fellowship in the spirit, and to encourage the scientific study of man's religious nature and history." The second article adds: "Membership in this Association shall leave each individual responsible for his own opinions alone, and affect in no degree his relations to other Associations; and nothing in the name or constitution of the Association shall ever be construed as limiting membership by any test of speculative opinion or belief, or as defining the position of the Association, collectively considered, with reference to any such opinion or belief, or as interfering in any other way with that absolute freedom of thought and expression which is the natural right of every rational being."

The first public meeting, which was held in Boston, May 30, 1867, was a great success for the promoters of this movement. Not only a large number of the ministers and laity belonging to Unitarian congregations responded to their appeal, but also a considerable number of well-known persons from the liberal elements of the most diverse sects—Universalists, Progressive Quakers, Jews, and even Spiritualists. The Association chose for its president a Unitarian minister—who, later, transformed his society at New York into an independent organization—Mr. O. B. Frothingham, and for secretary, one of his colleagues at New Bedford, Mr. William J. Potter, whose name was soon erased from the official list of Unitarian ministers for his refusal to retain the name of Christian.

Besides its annual meetings, devoted to discussions and papers, the Free Religious Association instituted a series of lectures in different cities of the country, and published a large number of pamphlets to disseminate its views. It has for its organ *The Index* of Boston, a weekly paper—edited first by Mr. Abbot, and now by Messrs. Potter and Underwood—which deserves to be presented as a model for all free-thought publications in both hemispheres, as well for the attractiveness of its articles as for the breadth of its ideas, and more especially for the elevation of its moral tone.

During the fifteen years since "Free Religion" thus took form, it has accomplished a work at once positive and negative—negative, by its Rationalistic utterances, which undermine more and more the bases of dogmatic sects, as well as the privileges still accorded to the Churches,[1] and positive, by its efforts to assign a common purpose to the religious activity of its members.

At its annual meeting in 1882, the Free Religious Association resolved to undertake a more active propagandism, with a view to bring about the establishment of local associations to put in practice the principles of Free Religion. Up to the present, however, the congregations based upon the programme of the Association remain but few in number. I have seen no reference to any but those at Boston, Florence, Dorchester, East Dennis in Massachusetts, and Providence in Rhode-Island. A somewhat curious characteristic of the Free Religious Congregation, established at Dorchester by some fifty families, is the fact of its being under the supervision of a lady, Mrs. Clara Bisbee. Some idea will be gained of the activity of the "ministress" when it is borne in mind that Mrs. Bisbee conducts the service, presides at the organ, preaches the sermon, superintends a Sunday school, and gives lessons on the historic growth of religion to a class of adults.[2]

---

[1]. The separation of the Church from the State is not so complete among the Americans, as we are often led to suppose. It is true, the religious communities manage their own affairs as they please, and that on the other hand they receive no kind of subsidy from the Civil Authority. But the public institutions are still strongly impregnated with Christianity. Congress and the State Legislatures have their chaplains as well as the fleet, army and prisons. The Bible continues to be read in a great number of schools. The invocation to the Deity is, speaking generally, obligatory in the judicial and even in administrative oaths. In Pennsylvania the Constitution demands that he who occupies a public office, must believe in God and the sanctions of a future life. The Constitution of Maryland does not accord liberty of conscience to any but Theists. Elsewhere the laws relating to blasphemy have never been formally abrogated. In certain States the tribunals lend their influence more or less indirectly to enforce the observation of the Sunday. In 1880, a court of law declined to recognise, even as a natural obligation, a debt contracted on the Sunday; and a traveller injured in a railway accident has seen himself deprived of compensation, on the ground that he had no right to take the train on the Lord's Day. And lastly, the landed property devoted to the maintenance of worship is, to a large extent, freed from all kinds of taxation.

[2]. *Index* of the 29th of June, 1882.

Another Free Religious congregation at Providence, R.I., in 1881, obtained for its minister the right of performing legal marriages,—a privilege till then reserved to ministers regularly ordained by a religious denomination and to justices of the peace. In connection with this there occurred, between the minister of the Free Religious congregation, Mr. F. A. Hinckley, and the committee appointed by the local legislature to decide whether "Free Religion" was really a religion, a dialogue which throws a very curious light upon the attitude adopted by the adherents of the new worship, in regard to theological questions, properly so called. As the constitution of the society assigned to it "the practice of virtue, the study of truth, and the brotherhood of man," the chairman of the committee remarked that he could not discover to whom the petitioners addressed themselves in worship.

Rev. F. A. Hinckley—"As individuals, we represent all shades of liberal opinion; but, as a society, we have a distinct element of worship. All sane minds recognize a Power over and above us. We claim that the one great essential principle is recognized when we recognize this Power, though we do not recognize it in the same manner as do other denominations."

A Member—"What do you worship?"

Rev. Mr. Hinckley—"I am perfectly willing to tell you; but I do not think it is within the province of the State to define what men shall or may worship."

Member—"I understood that you said the other day that you did not recognize God, Christ, or the Bible."

Rev. Mr. Hinckley—"What I said was that we could not recognize them as the creeds do. We do recognize a Power over and above the human."

Member—"What you call a Power is what other people call God?"

Rev. Mr. Hinckley—"Now, you begin to define. The moment you do that, you find irreconcilable differences in the Churches as well as out of them."

It should be said that the petitioners obtained the support of several ministers belonging to the Episcopal, Congregational, and Unitarian Churches of the city. We see thus that the spirit of religious toleration has not degenerated in the old colony of Roger Williams.

To the congregations directly founded upon the principles of "Free Religion" may be added certain independent societies of every religious denomination, as the First Congregation of New Bedford, which continued to sustain its minister, Mr. William J. Potter, when his name was erased from the Unitarian *Year-Book*. This Church, having its origin among the Puritans in the beginning of the eighteenth century, is reckoned as one of the first societies of Calvinistic descent which openly raised the Unitarian standard; for this rupture with Orthodoxy dates from 1810,—that is, nine years before the discourse of Channing, which was the distinctive signal of the schism. It would be very interesting to follow the movements of ideas which thus led from the strictest Calvinism to the most absolute Liberalism, a congregation standing in the ordinary conditions of American Churches. The different stages of this evolution would appear only in successive modifications of the ritual; the widening of the profession of faith imposed upon communicants; the disappearance of all distinction between communicants and non-communicants, between the members of the church and the members of the society; the transformation of the sacrament of the communion into a ceremony commemorative of the foundation of Christianity; the displacement of Christian symbolism by a service in honour of all the great religious and social reformers. It is this which Mr. Potter set forth as follows in a sermon preached before his congregation in 1874 :—

"The Society has been in your day, as in the days of our ecclesiastical ancestors, under the law of evolution. It has progressed by natural growth. . . . There has been no break, no violence, no revolution, no *coup d'état*. Your present has grown out of your past, and whatever it be, is the logical consequence of your past. You have come in your historical career,—and that not so much by the special design of the Society, at any particular moment, as by the force of the natural logic of your course,—to the point where the use of creeds and covenants and even of names as representing theological distinctions, having naturally dropped away, you have opened the door to anyone of whatever faith, who may be drawn to seek fellowship among you. . . . No one stands there to question any comer's present belief, or religious antecedents. Should any of those who have been called 'infidels' for any reason, secret or open, be attracted to these services, and desire regularly to associate with you, there is nothing in your rules of membership, and I know of nothing in your spirit, that would shut the door against them. Or should any of the Progressive Jews, who are becoming prominent in the Judaism of this country, or any of the liberal adherents of the Asiatic faiths, Hindu, Buddhist, Mohammedan, chance to come to our city, as temporary or permanent residents, as is possible in this era of migration and travel, and should they find anything helpful in these Sunday services, and be drawn to seek religious fellowship among you, again I know of nothing in your spirit, and there is certainly nothing in your rules of membership, that would exclude them. Though organized and progressing historically as a Christian Society, yet by the logical force of the Protestant principle of the right of private judgment, and of free inquiry, you have gradually widened your conditions of fellowship, until you recognize no conditions less broad than the human aspiration after truth and virtue and spiritual peace. Consistently with this record, the only opinion you could call heresy would be the opinion that should put creed before character, and subordinate the reality of a religious life to the wearing of a religious name."[1]

Though independent of the Free Religious Association, the Society for Ethical Culture in New York equally deserves a place in the first rank among the associations which have set up the standard of "Free Religion." Its minister, or rather its director, Mr. Felix Adler, from 1878 to 1882 was president of the Free Religious Association, whose ethical and humanitarian tendencies he especially represents—that is, the part of the constitution above cited which relates to "the practical interests of pure religion." It cannot be disguised that one of the most threatening issues for the future of modern society is that the weakening of positive religion weakens the power of morality, which has been so long linked to religious dogmas. Rationalists have seen this peril in the United States as in Europe; but, while here they have endeavoured to establish morality upon principles independent of religion, there they seek to subordinate religion to it. Such is at least the tendency of which Professor Felix Adler is to-day the most brilliant interpreter. Mr. Adler is a young man whose mystic physiognomy recalls certain heads of the apostles. His father filled

---

[1] W. J. Potter. *Two Discourses delivered before the First Congregational Society.* New Bedford, 1874.

the office of rabbi in the principal Jewish synagogue in New York. He himself was destined for the priesthood; but, having been sent to Germany to complete his education, he there acquired Rationalistic convictions, which barred him from following his father's career. On his return to the United States, in 1873, he accepted a professorship in Cornell University, which he quitted three years afterwards to establish at New York a new religious association, under the title of "The Society for Ethical Culture."

In philosophy, Mr. Adler belongs to the intuitive school, since he believes in the existence, in the human mind, of certain elements anterior and superior to all individual or even hereditary experience. But, in metaphysics, he holds strictly to the postulates of Kant, without attributing objective reality to the notions of God and immortality. "I do not accept Theism," he says, in one of his lectures, "but the foundation can exist very well without a particular structure, and others may be raised upon it when the ancient one has crumbled into ruins. I cling with all my soul to the foundation on which Theism has been built: first, the denial of chance, the conviction that there is order in the world; secondly, the conviction that this order is a good order, that there is progress in the world." According to this, it is not God, but moral law, which should be the object of religion. This religion, moreover, would be eminently practical. "Since divergency of beliefs will continue to be emphasized, it is necessary to place the moral law where it cannot be discussed—in practice. Men have so long disputed about the author of the law that the law itself has remained in shadow. Our movement is an appeal to conscience, a cry for more justice, an exhortation to more duty."[1]

The first condition of success in such an undertaking, is to preach by example, and in this respect Ethical Culture is not less rigid than the old religious morality; only its field of action is much more extended.

The associations for moral culture, says Mr. Adler, exercise an influence which is the more efficacious because they are founded on the personal regeneration of their members, and he mentions the

---

[1] *Index* of the 15th of September, 1881. This Agnosticism does not prevent Mr. Adler from recognizing the existence of an "Ultimate Reality which lies behind all phenomena and from which the harmony of the world arises." (*Index* of the 22nd of September, 1881).

Temperance societies as an instance of this. But these pursue only one special aim, whilst Ethical Culture, being a religious reform, must be extended to every sphere of human activity. Thus, to borrow an illustration from the domain of Political Economy, he continues, suppose you believed in the justice of a tax to be fixed progressively according to a person's income: then you would not rest content with waiting for such an arrangement to become law; but, if you wished to fulfil your religious duty, you would hasten to cast into the Public Treasury the sum which the general and obligatory application of your system would demand from you.

It is upon these principles that Mr. Adler has organized his society in New York, with the concurrence of the most advanced minds of American Judaism. By degrees, some "Gentiles" have joined it, attracted as much by the growing reputation of the young reformer as by the largeness of his ideas; and, since 1880, the society has been obliged to occupy a more spacious hall. It has, indeed, one of the largest congregations in New York. Its "services," which take place on Sunday mornings, consist only of a lecture, between two pieces of music. But, after the public have left, the members come together in a private meeting for considering the different social works which they have established. These institutions are: (1) a Sunday School for the teaching of morals, as well as for instruction in the history of the principal faiths and even in the philosophy of religion; (2) a public kinder-garten organized after the method of Froebel; (3) an industrial school, which was opened in 1878, with but one teacher and eight pupils, and possesses to-day a principal, eight assistant masters, and 250 scholars between the ages of three and nine: its instruction is free and in certain necessitous cases food and clothing are given to the children gratuitously; (4) a technical museum attached to the school; and (5) a service of visitors or rather district nurses, who daily carry on their labour of love among the sick poor in the most wretched district of New York.

The success of these undertakings has been a new means of propagandism for the Society for Ethical Culture, which has thus won the esteem of even those who are hostile to its principles. It leaves, moreover, complete freedom to its members in the choice of their individual religious beliefs. All that it asks from them is, that they shall place the duties of religion exclusively in the individual and social regeneration of humanity.

A branch of the Society for Ethical Culture has been recently organized at Chicago, under the direction of Mr. W. Salter, and it has already begun to surround itself with philanthropical institutions based upon the model of the parent association.[1]

The Religion of Ethics is sometimes called by its adepts the Religion of Humanity. And assuredly it possesses as strong a claim to this appellation as Comtism, and a still stronger one than Secularism. It might be defined, indeed, as Comtism without dogmatism, and as Secularism with the addition of the religious spirit.

The influence of "Free Religion" is not limited to those societies which have accepted its name or its patronage. The Free Religious Association has become for Unitarianism what Unitarianism itself has been for other communions—a leaven of intellectual liberty. The Unitarians reckon, in the United States, according to their Annual Report of 1880, three hundred and forty-four congregations, three hundred and ninety-nine ministers (of whom three are women),[2] two colleges, one at Harvard and the other at Meadville, one monthly review and several weekly journals, together with numerous charitable and philanthropical institutions.

It might have been feared that after the secession of Messrs. Abbot, Potter, &c., their National Conference would incline more to the right wing. As a matter of fact, it did not hesitate to introduce into its rules, on the motion of the Rev. George Hepworth, a new paragraph in which, while re-affirming "allegiance to the Gospel," it solicited the co-operation of all "who wish to be followers of Christ." But shortly afterwards the author of this proposition went over to orthodoxy, and with this disappearance of extreme elements, disappeared also the principal vitality of the controversy which had been carried on from the foundation of the Conference; and Unitarianism was thus able to concentrate its activity upon practical measures calculated

---

1. Another branch from the parent society was established in Boston last year (1884).—*Translator.*

2. It was one of these ministresses, Mary A. Safford, who preached the anniversary sermon of the Western Unitarian Conference, on the occasion of its meeting at Chicago, in 1883. The subject was: "Religion, its nature and development."— See *Unity*, of the 16th of May, 1883.

to bring it nearer to the position chosen by the Free Religious Association. Hence to figure in future on the roll of Unitarianism it will suffice to style oneself a Christian after the manner of the Rev. — Chadwick, of Brooklyn, who extends this term to all who have formed their religious beliefs within the line of development of Christian civilization. The National Conference has even resolved to inscribe on its official list of ministers the names of all who might desire this, and who, in consequence, would consider themselves in their place there. At the session of 1882, indeed, it introduced into its constitution a new article, drawn up as follows, by the Rev. Minot J. Savage :—

"While we believe that the preamble of the articles of our Constitution fairly represent the opinions of the majority of our Churches, yet we wish distinctly to put on record our declaration that they are no authoritative test of Unitarianism, and are not intended to exclude from our fellowship any who, while differing from us in belief, are in general sympathy with our purposes and practical aims."

On several occasions within recent years Unitarian ministers have been seen to place their pulpits at the disposal of Agnostics such as Messrs. Adler and Underwood, while Mr. Holyoake, as a Secularist, and even Mr. Gottheil, of New York, a liberal Rabbi, have not been excluded.

The United States have remained the head quarters of Unitarianism. A proof of the influence it still possesses there is to be seen in the fact that in the autumn of 1882, it collected by private subscription, in a few days, the sum of a hundred thousand pounds, to found a new theological institution. Still it cannot be said to have extended in proportion to the growth of population. Even in Boston, where it possesses about thirty congregations, it has scarcely penetrated to the lower classes, in which the predominance of Irish emigrants has developed to a considerable extent the power of Catholicism; and among the superior classes it is opposed by the Episcopal Church, which is becoming more and more the fashionable Church of the United States. Besides, Boston itself has ceased to be the exclusive centre of intellectual culture, "the hub of the universe," as the neighbouring towns less favoured in the domain of intelligence, have ironically called it. On the one hand, the invasion of luxury and of social frivolity, has somewhat broke in upon the simplicity of manners and the thirst for moral enjoyment which had survived the severity of

Calvinistic theology; on the other, St. Louis, Chicago and other towns of recent growth, are disputing with it the monopoly of letters and the direction of American thought.

Happily for its numerical development, Unitarianism has found a fertile field for exploration in the states of the interior, where it responds at once to the double need of intellectual liberty and of religious culture. It is not surprising, that it has taken a more independent position there than in the Eastern States. The Western Unitarian Conference has omitted in its constitution the preamble which provoked such regrettable dissensions in the National Conference of 1865.[1] Its principal organ, *Unity*, edited with great breadth

---

[1] The following particulars respecting the constitution and principles of the various Unitarian Churches and organization of the West will be of interest to the reader :—

I.—BASES OF THE GENERAL UNITARIAN ASSOCIATIONS OF THE WEST.

(1) *The Western Unitarian Conference.*

"*Resolved*, that the Western Unitarian Conference conditions its fellowship on no dogmatic tests, but welcomes all thereto who desire to work with it in advancing the Kingdom of God."—*Resolution adopted unanimously at Chicago, May 7, 1875.*

Its object: "The transaction of business pertaining to the general interests of the Societies connected with the Conference.—*Articles of Incorporation, May 20, 1882.*

Motto on its Seal: "Freedom, Fellowship and Character in Religion."

(2) *The Women's Western Unitarian Conference.*

Its object: "The advancement of freedom, fellowship and character in religion."—*Articles of Incorporation, May 3, 1882.*

(3) *The Western Unitarian Sunday School Society.*

Its object: "To improve the quality of Sunday School publications, and to aid in making Sunday Schools effective nurseries of progressive, reverent and helpful Churches."—*Articles of Incorporation, May 22, 1882.*

II.—BASES OF THE UNITARIAN STATE CONFERENCES OF THE WEST.

(1) *Wisconsin Conference of Unitarian and Independent Societies.*

"*Resolved*, that charity being the central truth of all, and Unitarianism's grandest mission being to unite men in "the unity of the spirit in the bond of peace," we will welcome and fraternize with all men of whatever denomination, who are trying to advance in religious life."—*Adopted, 1872.*

"*Resolved*, that the Conference re-affirms its broad platform of faith in God and man ; that we will work for the advance of truth rather than the defence of dogma ; for humanity rather than for any sect ; for charity against churchism; and that we hold the name Unitarian in no narrower sense than that of effort to unite the best methods and spirit in all denominations under a peace that may become universal."—*Adopted, 1873.*

(2) *Michigan Conference of Unitarian and other Christian Churches.*

"*Whereas*, we are persuaded that the truth on all subjects, as fast as it becomes known to us, is the sole and sufficient authority for all human belief; that justice is

of view by the Rev. Jenkins L. Jones, has taken for its watchword the motto of Free Religion: freedom, character and fellowship in religion. Numerous churches and even entire groups of congregations, such as the Conferences of Michigan and of Kansas, the Fraternity of the Liberal Religious Societies of Illinois, are declared open to all who can work with them, or derive any good from them. Thus the committee of the Free Religious Association said in their report for 1881, that "in the broadening and liberalizing of Unitarianism in the West, perhaps, can be found the most tangible evidence that one of the missions of the Association, in its fourteen years of existence, has not been in vain; and evidence too that its work is not yet completed."

---

the certain and practicable law of all human conduct: that love is the highest and most effective temper of the human spirit: and

Whereas, we desire to rally the liberal minds of Michigan around this common centre, therefore, *resolved*, that the Michigan Unitarian Conference conditions its fellowship on no dogmatic tests, but welcomes all thereto who desire to work with it in advancing the kingdom of truth, righteousness and love."—*Adopted, October, 1878.*

(3) *Illinois Fraternity of Liberal Religious Societies.*

"We associate together as a religious fraternity in the interest of liberal and advanced thought. . . . We cordially invite to our fraternity all who would assist us in the advancement of truth and righteousness."—*Constitution.*

Purpose: "We associate together as a religious fraternity in the interest of liberal and advanced thought; our meetings to be so conducted as shall most directly conduce to our fraternal fellowship, our spiritual welfare and usefulness. We cordially invite to our fraternity all who would assist us in the advancement of truth and righteousness."—*Adopted, 1875.*

(4) *Iowa Association of Unitarian and other Independent Churches.*

"The object of this Incorporation shall be the promotion of the interests of religion, of righteousness, freedom, and fellowship."—*Articles of Incorporation, 1879.*

(5) *Kansas Unitarian Conference.*

Its object: "To advance the cause of freedom, fellowship, and character in religion throughout the State of Kansas.

"This Conference conditions its membership on no dogmatic tests, but invites the co-operation of all those willing to work with it for the advancement of truth and righteousness."—*Constitution, adopted, 1880.*

(6) *Nebraska Unitarian Association.*

Object: "To be the advancement of freedom, fellowship and character in religion in the State of Nebraska."—*Articles of Incorporation, 1882.*

III.—RECENT UNITARIAN CHURCH COVENANTS IN THE WEST.

(1) *The Church at Ann Arbour, Michigan.*

"Believing in that Religion of Nature and the Human Soul, which existed before all Bibles, which has uttered itself with greater or less clearness through the religious teachers of all lands and ages, but which was taught and impressed

The course of ideas which has thus emancipated Unitarianism has been equally felt by many other sects. The Universalists, for instance, who claim to have a thousand congregations, possesses an advanced section who fraternize with the Free Religious movement. In the same way, the Progressive Friends of Longwood, in Pennsylvania, have absolutely adopted the programme of " Free Religion," if we are to judge from this manifesto put forward by their General Assembly in 1881 :—" The object of this meeting is to promote religion construed broadly as embracing all good, physical, moral and spiritual. Untrammelled by dogma, we paternally invite to meet with us all those who desire to make the world purer and better, and who hold the truth in higher honour than any creed or sect. We would meet

upon the world with unequalled power by Jesus of Nazareth, the great prophet of God, from whose words and life came Christianity, we (the undersigned), do hereby associate ourselves together as a Christian Church, for the purpose of promoting that religion in ourselves and in society around us, by cultivating among ourselves a spirit of sincere and loving brotherhood, and by endeavouring in every way in our power to do good in the world. Imposing no creed upon the consciences of any, we cordially welcome all to a place among us who sympathize with us in these our general aims."— *Adopted, 1880.*

(2) *The Church at Des Moines, Iowa.*

Bond of Union : " Recognizing the Fatherhood of God, the Brotherhood of Mankind, receiving Jesus as Teacher, seeking the 'Spirit of Truth' as the guide of our lives, and in the hope of immortal life, we associate ourselves together to maintain the public worship of God and to promote the welfare of humanity."— *Adopted, 1877.*

(3) *The Church at Cincinnati, Ohio.*

Bond of Union : "We, whose names are here recorded, join ourselves together, heart and hand, as members of the First Congregational Church of Cincinnati, for the maintenance of a free, rational and liberal worship, the study and practice of the religious life, and to promote truth, righteousness, reverence and charity among men ; and we cordially invite to our fellowship all who sympathize in these purposes and will co-operate with us in working for the Kingdom of God."— *Adopted, 1879.*

(4) *The Church at St. Paul, Minn.*

The Bond of Fellowship : " As those who believe in Religion ;

"As those who believe in Freedom, Fellowship and Character in Religion ;

"As those who believe that the Religious Life means the thankful, trustful, loyal and helpful life ;

" And as those who believe that a Church is a brotherhood of helpers, wherein it is made easier to lead such a life,—

"We join ourselves together, name, hand and heart, as members of Unity Church.

" To sign this Bond of Fellowship is a solemn act of faith, of brotherhood, and of consecration. Of *faith* in certain high ideals of life, which we revere as more important than any intellectual beliefs whatever ; of *brotherhood* to the men on common ground as brethren to consider by what means we may labour most effectually to lift humanity to higher levels. In a reverent spirit, we would examine the religious institutions which have grown out of the wants and convictions of the past, accepting them so far as they commend themselves to our conscientious judgment, and rejecting them freely when we must. Our supreme allegiance is due, not to the decrees of men, but to truth itself."

With regard to Reformed Judaism, there is an important section who,—while entirely refusing to renounce their historic position, in order to avoid all suspicion of giving up their ancestral faith, in consequence of the social prejudices which persist even in the New World—have nevertheless seized the occasion for allying themselves,

---

and women who here join themselves together, name, hand and heart; of *consecration*, because one cannot take a pledge like this, of religious faith and fellowship, save in a reverent, earnest and unselfish spirit. To join our Church, then, is to enter into a covenant of love and service and right endeavour with each other, and to do this thoughtfully and reverently, as before One whom most of us rejoice to think of as 'our Father.'

"All who in this reverent and earnest spirit believe that our Church-home is truly their Church-home, and who feel that that which our Church stands for in religion is what they mean their life to stand for—all such, provided none show good reason for objection, are welcomed heartily within our Fellowship."—*Adopted, 1879.*

(5) *The Church at Quincy, Illinois.*

The Covenant: "We believe—

"That *Religion* is *natural* and *needful* to the human soul;

"That the *many* things of the universe have their being in *One* Life, Power, Mystery, Righteousness, Mercy and Love;

"That the *universe* is beautiful and beneficent *Order*, in which 'is no variableness, neither shadow of turning;'

"That '*all things work together for good;*' that the Infinite Life in which we have our being is Power in the world to destroy the wrong, to establish the right; that no good thing is failure and no evil thing is success;

"That we ought to reverence all *holy saints, seers* and *prophets* who 'have wrought righteousness,' and bless them for the light of their wisdom and goodness;

"That we ought to *work* to make the *world better;*

"That *character* is the supreme matter—not the beliefs we hold, but *what we are in the heart;*

"That in the search for truth, we ought to hold fast to *freedom* for ourselves and for all men;

"That we ought to welcome to our *Fellowship* all who are of earnest and sincere spirit and humble lovers of the truth; that we should set the bond of *human brotherhood* high above that of creed or church; and that we ought not to hold theological beliefs as conditions of our membership.

"In these principles, and that we may help, comfort and cheer each other, we join our hearts and hands in this Church, and hereto set our names."—*Adopted, 1883.*

on the practical ground of religious fraternity, with the intellectual and moral forces of a civilization to which they will be for the future completely assimilated. The Reform of Judaism has perhaps been carried further in the United States than anywhere else. Not only have the party of Reform freed themselves from all the ritualistic, hygienic and social prescriptions which constitute the old law; but there are also Rabbis who, not content with rejecting the infallibility of the Bible, go so far as to question the Divine Personality, that corner-stone of Semitic beliefs. Thus Rabbi S. W. Sonnesheim did not hesitate to declare at the seventh meeting of the Free Religious Association, that Reformed Judaism corresponded with the "Free Religious movement of the day."

As much might doubtless be said of the numerous *Freie-Religiöse-Gemeinde* which the Germans have imported into the United States. By being brought over the Atlantic the greater part of these institutions have certainly assumed a more Radical character, as may be seen by the programme which was adopted by their delegates at the Convention of Milwaukee, in 1870. They there virtually declared in Article 2, their exclusion of all idea of a God, personal or impersonal," without seeing that they re-introduced the conception of the Deity in the following Article: "In Nature we recognise Justice, the continual development towards perfection and towards that fulness of the Beautiful which suffuses our existence with joy."

And lastly we must not forget in this enumeration, the Spiritualists, who claim to possess three million adherents in the United States and who, according to Mr. O. B. Frothingham, certainly amount to at least one million. In the United States even more than in England Spiritualism tends to become an actual religion. Here is what Mr. W. Hepworth Dixon stated, fifteen years ago, in his curious work, *New America:*—"These millions, more or less, of Spiritualists announce their personal conviction that the old religious gospels are exhausted, that the churches founded on them are dead; that new revelations are required by men. They proclaim that the phenomena, now being produced in a hundred American cities—signs of mysterious origin, rappings by unknown agents, drawings by unseen hands—offer an acceptable ground-plan for a new, a true and a final faith in things unseen. They have already their progressive lyceums, their catechisms, their newspapers, their male and female prophets, mediums and clairvoyants; their Sunday services, their festivals, their pic-nic parties, their camp-meetings, their local societies, their State organizations, their general conventions; in short, all the machinery of our most active, most aggressive societies.[1] . . . When we essay to judge a system so repugnant to our feelings, so hostile to our institutions, as this school of Spiritualism, it is needful, if we would be fair in censure, to remember that, strange as it may seem to onlookers, it has been embraced by hundreds of learned men and pious women."

The Legislature of Illinois recently imposed on every medium a license costing three hundred dollars; immediately the Spiritualists cried out against it as an act of religious oppression, on the ground that the mediums fulfil with their co-religionists the functions of the priest in the Protestant, Catholic, and Jewish religions. On the other hand, Spiritualism seems to fraternize everywhere, not only with the adherents of Free Religion, but also with Agnostics, Atheists, and even Materialists, lending them its buildings, the aid of its journals, and even its lecturers.[2] "Every Spiritualist is of necessity a Free Religionist,—said one of its partisans, Mr. Giles B. Stebbins, at the fourteenth meeting of the Free Religious Association—because the Spiritual philosophy, broad, eclectic and inclusive, knows no prejudices, no limitations, no barriers, recognises no authority for truth, but only the truth of the soul for authority, and accepts the instructions of the human spirit, the testimony of human reason, the truth of human experience, and the results of scientific experiment as its basis of education."[3]

---

1. *The Index* of October 23rd, 1884, announces the completion of the First Spiritual Temple in Boston. The building, whose cost is about 250,000 dollars, or £52,000, includes a main hall for 500 people, besides small halls for lectures, schools and other purposes.

2. See the Proceedings of the Congress of Free-Thinkers, held at Brussels in 1880: Mr. L. Rawson's Report.

3. Here is the first article of the constitution of the *American Spiritualist Association*: "The objects and aims of this association are to study Spiritualism in its scientific, philosophical and religious aspects, and to teach its truths as we learn them; to maintain high and pure principles on all vital questions of practical life and duty; to seek for the best spiritual culture and the most harmonious character." The same document proclaims the indestructibility of the soul, the possibility of entering into communication with Spirits, by the intervention of privileged but not infallible individuals, the universality and immutability of the laws of Nature, the necessity of placing morality before faith and conduct before belief, and finally, the continuity of progress in the Universe.

All these advanced-guards of American religious life have been represented, simultaneously or in turn, on the Committee of the Free Religious Association: the Unitarians by the Rev. M. J. Savage, W. C. Gannett, John Weiss, John J. Sargent, &c.; the Transcendentalists by Emerson and Colonel Higginson; the Quakers by Lucretia Mott, who died in 1882, at the age of eighty; the Spiritualists by Robert Dale Owen; the German Materialists by Mr. Schunemann-Pott; and the Reformed Jews by the Rabbi Isaac Wise, &c. It will be seen, by this genuine mosaic of religious opinions, how widely the action of that Society extends. We may add that on several occasions it has received messages of sympathy and encouragement from the Brahmoists of India by the intervention of Keshub Chunder Sen and Protab Chunder Mozoumdar.

Doubtless, practical minds that have neither the leisure nor the taste to investigate religious questions; Conservatives who, through distrust of the unknown, remain faithful to the beliefs of their fathers; sceptics who see in worship only an element of social life necessary for the education of the young and for the celebration of domestic solemnities—in a word, the great majority of the nation, remain, and will for a long time remain, attached to the different forms of positive Christianity. Without being held in such high esteem as in former ages, ecclesiastical functions still figure in the first rank of the liberal professions. According to the Census of 1870, there existed in the United States 72,000 congregations, or one for every 529 inhabitants. The value of the property belonging to them was estimated at upwards of forty millions sterling, irrespective of annual contributions. In the rich congregations of large towns, it is not rare to find ministers in receipt of a salary ranging from two to three thousand pounds a year.[1] The proportion of persons attending public worship has continued to increase, if we may rely upon the statistics furnished by the Rev. R. Spears, according to which the aggregate of American Churches constituted in 1775 but one member in sixteen of the inhabitants; in 1792, one in eighteen; in 1825, one in fourteen; in 1853, one in seven; in 1860, one in five; and, finally, in 1875, nearly one to every

---

1. At New York the Revs. Dix and Potter (Episcopalians) each receive 12,000 dollars per annum; the Rev. John Hall (Presbyterian) 15,000 (*Index*, 21st April, 1881). The Rev. Ward Beecher (Congregationalist), of Brooklyn, receives 20,000 or upwards of four thousand pounds (*Inquirer* of Feb. 3rd, 1883).

two.[1] I must add, however, that an article, published by *The Nation*, of the 29th of November, 1883, makes certain reserves with respect to these figures. Since, 1850, according to this article, the increase of population has been 116 per cent., whilst the number of persons belonging to the Churches has increased at the rate of 185 per cent. It is true that many congregations, as *The Nation* observes, reckon to-day the children in the statistics of their members.

However this may be, even among the most orthodox sects, the Utilitarian tendency, which has created Free Religion, is becoming more and more observable. Tocqueville remarked some time since, that instead of insisting upon the other life, American preachers turned constantly to the earth, and had so to speak great difficulty in detaching their gaze therefrom. If one reads to-day the American journals of Monday the report of the principal sermons preached the preceding day by the ministers of the different sects, he will be surprised to see the small place which theology occupies compared with morals. The old Calvinistic theology is nowhere taught in its integrity. Even the flames of hell have become an argument in bad taste, which is willingly left to Revival preachers and missionaries of the Far West. "A heathen, desirous to learn the doctrines of Christianity," recently wrote a contributor to the *North American Review*, in an article on *The Religion of the day*, "might attend the best of our churches for a whole year and not hear one word of the torments of Hell or the anger of an offended Deity; and not enough of the Fall of man or the sacrificial sufferings of Christ to offend the most bigotted disciple of Evolution. Listening and observing for himself, he would infer that the way of salvation consisted in declaring his faith in a few abstract doctrines, which both preacher and hearer seem quite ready to explain away as far as possible; become a regular attendant at church and church sociables; put something into the contribution-box every Sunday, and in every way behave as much as possible like his neighbours."

---

1. It would be interesting to ascertain in what proportion these gains are shared by the different sects. According to an article "Religion in America," published in the *North American Review* of January, 1876, the Churches stood as follows in the order of importance about the year 1780: 1st, Congregationalists; 2nd, Baptists; 3rd, Episcopalians; 4th, Presbyterians; 5th, Reformed Germans; 6th, Reformed Church of Holland; 7th, Catholics. According to the Census of 1870, however, they stand thus: 1st, Methodists; 2nd, Baptists; 3rd, Presbyterians; 4th, Catholics; 5th, Christians; 6th, Lutherans; 7th, Congregationalists; 8th, Episcopalians.

Some three or four years ago, Colonel Ingersol[1] having uttered a violent philippic against the American Churches, one of the most respected chiefs of the Republican party, Thurlow Tweed, replied to the attacks by saying, "Our clergymen no longer emphasize the gloomy sides of theology as formerly. At the present day their ministry is a ministry of peace, charity, and benevolence. This generation is learning to love and serve rather than to dread our Creator and Lord."

There is at present a party in all the Protestant denominations whose object is to enlarge, interpret and extend the field of their

---

1. Colonel Ingersoll speaks or writes in a "smart," flippant and sometimes coarse style ; and unfortunately he does not possess the dimmest conception of the origin and true significance of the legendary and other Biblical stories which he ridicules. This is strikingly shown in his lecture entitled "*Mistakes of Moses.*" What, as landmarks of the long ago, is full of interest to the scholar and thinker, by the mere negation of orthodox literalism, he treats with contempt. His method is that of Voltaire, and though he puts certain inconsistencies of the orthodox world in a striking and forcible manner, it may be doubted whether he really advances serious religious thought. In the lecture in question, for instance, he introduces the following imaginary dialogue in illustration of the importance religious people attach to mere belief. The scene is the Day of Judgment, and the recording angel or "secretary" says to the soul of a man :—"Where are you from?" "I am from the world." "Yes, sir. What kind of a man were you?" "Well, I don't like to talk about myself." "But you have to. What kind of a man were you?" "Well, I was a good fellow ; I loved my wife, I loved my children. My home was my heaven ; my fireside was my paradise, and to sit there and see the lights and shadows falling on the faces of those I love, that to me was a perpetual joy. I never gave one of them a solitary moment of pain. I don't owe a dollar in the world, and I left enough to pay my funeral expenses and keep the wolf of want from the door of the house I loved. That is the kind of a man I am." "Did you belong to any church?" "I did not. They were too narrow for me. They were always expecting to be happy simply because somebody else was to be damned." "Well, did you believe that rib story?" "What rib story? Do you mean that Adam and Eve business? No, I did not. To tell you the God's truth, that was a little more than I could swallow." "To hell with him! Next. Where are you from?" "I'm from the world too." "Do you belong to any church?" "Yes, sir, and to the Young Men's Christian Association." "What is your business?" "Cashier in a bank." "Did you ever run off with any of the money?" "I don't like to tell, sir." "Well, but you have to?" "Yes, sir ; I did." "What kind of a bank did you have?" "A savings bank." "How much did you run off with?" "One hundred thousand dollars." "Did you take anything else along with you?" "Yes, sir." "What?" "I took my neighbour's wife." "Did you have a wife and children of your own?" "Yes, sir." "And you deserted them?" "Oh, yes ; but such was my confidence in God that I believed he would take care of them." "Have you heard of them since?" "No, sir." "Did you believe that rib story?" "Ah, bless your soul, yes ! I believed all of it, sir ; I often used to be sorry that there were not harder stories yet in the Bible, so that I could show what my faith could do." "You believed it, did you?" "Yes, with all my heart." "Give him a harp."—*Translator.*

operations. With the Episcopalians who long since rendered the use of the Athanasian Creed optional in their liturgy, this tendency has brought on the schism of the Episcopal Reformed Church, which is directed as much against the Broad Church party as against the ritualistic practices of the High Church section. Among the Methodists and Presbyterians the tendency is shown, as indeed among their co-religionists of the British Isles, by the numerous trials for heresy brought before their Conferences and Synods, in relation to both ministers and congregations. Even the popular Baptist body is not escaping the influence of this liberalizing movement, at least in its most advanced section: the Christians of the New Connection and the Campbellites, or Disciples, who have always been Liberals, or at least Arminians in theology. "We are glad to learn by a recent letter from America—wrote Mr. Spears in 1876—that the Disciples are becoming more and more liberal among themselves and towards others. It is not unlikely that the 'Christian' Connection and the Disciples may soon form one grand Christian organization of about 5,000 churches, called by the Christian name and based on nothing but the Christian scriptures."[1]

But the progress of ideas is most perceptible among the Congregationalists, who have no central authority to maintain doctrine and discipline in their Churches. The most celebrated and popular of their preachers, the Rev. Henry Ward Beecher, said in a sermon on *Religious Doubt*, preached in 1881: "let no man count himself an infidel who believes that righteousness is the great end of human life, and who longs for a more perfect reduction of his will to the moral sense." Might we not suppose these to be the words of Mr. Potter or Mr. Adler or even of the convention of Milwaukee?

So great is the present popularity of Mr. Beecher that several policemen are required to keep order in the crowd which collects round the doors of his vast "Tabernacle" twice every Sunday. With a view to hear one of his sermons I have myself been obliged to wait half-an-hour in the open air during a pelting rain, and even then only succeeded in getting a seat at the extreme end of the building. The interior of his Church, which will contain several thousand persons,

---

[1] *Rise and Progress of Unitarian Doctrines in Modern Times*, p. 33. Among the American sects which have renounced the Trinity, Mr. Spears mentions also the Christadelphians, the Adventists, and the Followers of John Winnebrenner, who, some thirty years ago, gathered together fifty thousand adherents into a communion called the Church of God, &c.

is extremely simple in common with all Congregational Churches. There is no religious symbolism, not even a cross; the only ornamentation being the flowers round the pulpit. The back of the building is occupied by an immense organ whose roll and swell accompany the voices of an admirably composed choir. The congregation join in the singing of the hymns with a fervour which no one would expect in such a vast gathering. The mere letting of the front seats brings in, I was told, from seven to eight thousand pounds a year.

Mr. Beecher is an old man with long white hair, of middle height and a tendency to corpulence; but in spite of his seventy years, he displays activity and vigour, whilst he is possessed of a powerful and singularly pathetic voice.[1] He long since freed himself from dogmatic Calvinism; recently, however, he seems to have assumed a more aggressive attitude towards the theology still literally accepted by a certain number of congregations. Thus, in a recent article in *The North American Review*, on the "Progress of Ideas in the Church," he develops this threefold thesis: that religious activity, so far from diminishing, is increasing every day in America, as may be seen by the multiplication of new Churches; that this activity embraces a world of influences unknown to the Puritans; and, finally, that the lines of demarcation between the various Christian sects are everywhere disappearing. He then makes a direct attack upon the theology of the Middle Ages, more particularly with regard to the doctrines of the Fall and Predestination, which he treats thus: "The present generation can remember the time when these hideous doctrines were widely and vigorously preached. The explosions of indignation which they called forth were looked upon as a proof that the heart of man was in a state of revolt against God. They may be preached still, but it is in apologetic terms, and no longer with that tone of authority which carries conviction: they rather defend

---

[1]. The second time I saw him was in the autumn of 1880, at a political meeting, where he spoke on behalf of the candidature of Mr. Garfield, who was seeking the Presidential chair. Being on a balcony of the Fifth Avenue, a few days after this meeting, in order to witness a grand review of the Volunteers of New York, I suddenly saw the eager masses on the pavement below salute with their applause one of the principal regiments of Brooklyn. On horseback, by the side of the colonel, there was a gentleman dressed in black, with his sword at his side, who was saluting right and left in response to the hurrahs of the crowd. It was Mr. Beecher, who was fulfilling the duties, or rather was present officially, as the chaplain of the regiment of his district.

than affirm themselves. Speaking generally, they lie at the bottom of the pulpit like a corpse in the sepulchre."

The criticism which this rejection of the old theology called forth from certain of his colleagues, led Mr. Beecher to tender his resignation as a member of the Congregational body in the autumn of 1882. But the Brooklyn Association of Congregational Ministers unanimously refused to accept it by passing a resolution stating that "the full and proffered exposition of doctrinal views which he has made at this meeting, indicates the propriety of his continued membership in this or any other Congregational Association." This incident, which made a great noise, is not only a striking sign of the progress realized in the ideas of American Protestantism, but it is also calculated to promote the spirit of freedom among preachers and congregations in the sects which remain nominally faithful to orthodoxy.

Even Catholicism, which, though unable to change its dogmas, seeks to enlarge its influence, above all by its good works, by the extent of its charities, by the excellence of its day and boarding schools, and by co-operating, as occasion requires, with the clergy of the Protestant Churches in the common work of some moral or philanthropic undertaking.[1]

---

1. The Roman Church, which is placed in the United States on a footing of absolute equality with the other sects, has not been able to wholly disregard the bonds of spiritual confraternity, which are superior to all dogmatic divergences. For instance, we see from the biography of Ezra Stiles Gannett, that at the time of his ordination in 1830, in the Federal Street Unitarian Church at Boston, the ceremony, presided over by Channing, was honoured by the presence of ministers belonging to the Congregational, Evangelical, Baptist, Universalist, Presbyterian and *Catholic* communions.

CHAPTER X.

COSMISM AND THE RELIGION OF EVOLUTION.

Persistence of Metaphysical Speculations in the United States—Importance given to religious questions in the press and in literature—Clubs and Philosophical Associations—The Hegelian Academy at Concord—Religious Fermentation in the West—Symptoms Characteristic of Changing Beliefs—Aspirations for a New Religious Synthesis extending even to the ranks of the Free Religionists—Eclipse of the Transcendental school—Progress of Evolution in the United States; the religious character it has assumed there—Professor J. Fiske's Cosmic Philosophy—Cosmism according to Mr. W. Potter: "Faith and Confidence in the Universe" —The Rev. Minot J. Savage and the Religion of Evolution—Cosmism regarded as the crowning result of Christianity—Tendency of the American mind to transform Philosophy into Religion—Quotations from the writings of O. B. Frothingham, F. A. Abbot, and W. Gannett—The Theology of Evolution in the orthodox congregations—Tocqueville's Prediction that American Democracy would end in Pantheism.

Are we to conclude from what has been just stated that America is on the eve of sacrificing theology and even metaphysics on the altar of Positivism, and instituting a religion like that dreamed of by Comte, having for its objects humanity and earthly life instead of God and a future life? This conclusion would be rash. There are, undoubtedly, in the United States a certain number of persons systematically hostile to every ontological conception, as well as to every religious idea, who proscribe even all mention of the Absolute and the Unknowable, because they see in such phrases an approach to theology. Some confine themselves to referring to the primordial properties of matter for the explanation of all phenomena. Others hold still to the criticisims of Voltaire and Hobbes, without suspecting that the progress of science has profoundly modified the conditions of the problem. It is this class which is represented by the *Truth Seeker* of New York and the *Investigator* of Boston. In the latter city, they have for their headquarters an edifice erected to the memory of an American member of the French Convention—Thomas Paine—whose philosophical writings, though completely forgotten in France, still play in the religious controversies of the United States a part equally exaggerated by reason of the indignation of their adversaries and the enthusiasm of their admirers. But Positivism, properly so called, whether in the sober and severe acceptation which Littré has given to the doctrine of Auguste Comte, or under the more embellished form of *Comtism*, which has obtained considerable success in England, has but few followers in the United States, notwithstanding the favour which the positive methods enjoy there. If, as a matter of fact, the "Religion of Humanity" predominates among the followers of Mr. Potter and Professor Adler, as well as among the Free Religionists, it is not associated with Comtist dogmatism, but is in the form which Mr. W. Frey has given to it—that is, without the exclusion of a belief in the mysterious Power of which the universe is a manifestation. The American shows no predilection for fasting, even in metaphysics. Never has speculation taken higher flights than in these later times in the United States. There are, outside of the religious press,—even in localities of secondary culture,—journals whose title alone is sufficiently significant, such as *The Platonist*, of Osceola, Mo.; *The Journal of Speculative Philosophy*, of St. Louis, devoted to the advocacy of the doctrines of Hegel; *The Religio-Philosophical Journal*, of Chicago, which printed lately, it is said, nine thousand copies.

After having shown in *The Index* of February 23rd, 1882, that the severest phase of the struggle is over for the advocates of Liberal ideas, Mrs. Sarah A. Underwood points out for instance that religious speculation has never been more free and active. "The newspaper most prompt to report any new departure in the religious world," she wrote, "is apt to be the newspaper with the largest daily circulation. Our magazines discuss more leisurely and with greater dignity the grave religious questions of the hour. Our reviews are mainly devoted to discussing religious issues. Our new evangelists are making religion, more than ever before in the history of the world, the leading topic in literature. Even the romance writers weave religious discussions into both warp and woof of their stories."

From New York to San Francisco, from Chicago to Cincinnati, every city of consequence has its metaphysical club or institute. The most celebrated is, unquestionably, the School of Philosophy, opened at Concord, Mass., in 1879, by Mr. Bronson Alcott, with a vigour that does honour to the eighty years of this venerable neo-Pythagorean, as well as to the vegetable diet of which he has, from principle, been a faithful adherent for more than forty years. The School at Concord seems an attempt to reproduce, in the midst of American society of the nineteenth century, the garden of the Academy where Plato and his disciples discoursed under the shade of the olive-trees. Every summer in the month of July, an intelligent company, drawn from all points of the Union to the little town of Concord, meet at Mr. Alcott's place,—the Orchard House,—where are given courses, or rather free lectures, upon philosophy. The principal difference from the Greek Academy—wholly to the advantage of Concord—is that the door is not closed against the fair sex, who largely profit by it, if the reports may be believed, which attribute to them two-thirds of the attendance, estimated in 1882 at nearly a hundred and fifty persons. There are two lectures a day, one at nine o'clock in the morning, the other at half-past seven in the evening. In the interval, the students, male and female, arrange their notes, take their meals at home, or walk in the pine woods, exchanging their ideas upon the grave problems of our destiny. Among the principal lecturers, besides Mr. Alcott, are Dr. Jones, the founder of the Platonic Clubs in Illinois; Professor Harris, editor of *The Journal of Speculative Philosophy;* Mrs. Howe; William Henry Channing; Professor Emory, etc. Emerson himself was heard there in 1880.

These names sufficiently show that the philosophy of Hegel prevails almost exclusively at Concord, although the founders of the school proclaimed the most absolute liberty of opinion. It is a strange phenomenon of the religious movement of the United States, this revival of the Hegelian doctrine, at the time when, in Germany, the death of Professor Rosenkranz has vacated the last chair devoted to pure Hegelianism. Such has been the increasing success of the institution founded by Mr. Alcott that the orthodox have felt obliged to establish a competitor by founding, two years ago, on the same basis, at Greenwood, near New York, an "Encampment of Christian Philosophy."

Among the less cultivated population of the West, the instability of belief has naturally taken a more violent and aggressive form. A member of the Free Religious Association reported, at the general meeting in 1881, that there were in Kansas, even in the smallest towns, groups of Liberals not only unchurched, but openly hostile to all existing forms of religious organization. At the same session another speaker (a Spiritualist) told of the existence of a hundred meetings in the open air in the Western States, independent of all sects, of people who came together "to say before God what they believed in their souls to be the truth,"—labourers from their farms, men of business forsaking their offices, women leaving their household cares, all "drawn by an inward hunger for spiritual nourishment." These two statements have nothing contradictory about them; they rather complement each other. They equally prove the thirst for a new faith among those who are no longer satisfied with the old religious forms. It is, in some sort, the last term of the disintegration, or of the breaking up, which, as its goal, the spirit of Protestantism has never ceased to pursue into the very heart of dogmatic Churches and confessions of faith. But it might also be the inevitable transition between two currents of belief.

Coming side by side with this intellectual fermentation, the tendency to relegate theology to the second place in religious activity, even in certain orthodox Churches, which has found its most complete expression in the platform of the Free Religious Association, may well be considered a symptom of the religious interregnum, long ago predicted by Emerson. It is probable, and we may rejoice at it, that religion will preserve in future the eminently practical and humanitarian character which has come to distinguish it, more and more, in the United States. But men will always have a tendency to group themselves according to their beliefs; and we already hear, even in the ranks of the Free Religious Association, the day predicted when a new religious synthesis shall present itself for acceptance, by the force of evidence alone, to all the adherents of "Free Religion."

"We do not contend," said the Executive Committee of the Free Religious Association, in its fourth annual report, "that the religious sentiment is historically exhausted, and that it has uttered the last word of absolute religion. On the contrary, we are of opinion that the organ of the religious consciousness is as full of life to-day as it has ever been, and we think that the approaching transformations in the religious condition of the world, whatever their nature, will be produced, not by mechanical combinations of the best elements of the religions of the past, but by a regular, organic and progressive development." Mr. F. E. Abbot, again, wrote, in 1872, in a small pamphlet, entitled *The God of Science:* "The world for half a century has been groping blindly to find this greatly-needed philosophy of science. . . . That philosophy has not yet come. But when it comes, as come it must and will, it will create, sooner or later, throughout the civilized world, a unity of intellectual convictions which has never yet been paralleled, even in the boasted "ages of faith,"—not, of course, a unity of all opinions, but a unity of fundamental principles and methods of thinking. And when it comes,— a philosophy of science whose basis shall be solid truth, and whose philosophy shall be unfettered reason,—then, I most profoundly believe, will the enlightened idea of God be so firmly fixed in the human mind that Christianity and Atheism shall become alike mere traditions of the past."

Is it possible now to foresee whence will be drawn the elements of this new theology? According to Mr. Potter, the existing rival schools of intuition and observation will both have a part to play in the formation of the philosophy destined to perfect the work of "Free Religion." We share with Mr. Potter the profound conviction that intuition will have its word to utter in the future development of psychology, and we are far from contesting the happy and durable influence which Transcendentalism has exercised upon the public mind of the American people. We cannot, however, repress the question whether, as a system of metaphysics and religion, the school of German Idealism may not have run its course in the United States as it has in Europe? Almost all its old champions have remained loyal to the faith of their youth. Emerson, Johnson, Margaret Fuller, Ripley, Lydia Child, died, as they had lived, in the Transcendental faith. Those who survive, Higginson, Wasson, Samuel Longfellow, and Henry Channing, use to-day the same language they did forty years ago, with a conviction and enthusiasm which neither age, nor the friction of life, nor even the progress of positive science has cooled. But their ranks are thinning more and more; and, notwithstanding the momentary fashion of Hegelianism at Concord, new recruits do not come to take the place of those who have gone to seek in another world the confirmation of their hopes.

Of a considerable number of congregations founded by the Transcendental movement, there remained, lately, only the Church of Samuel Johnson, at Lynn, Mass. Even this probably owed its longevity only to the personal influence of its minister, and it is to be feared that it may have disappeared with him. In Boston, the survivors of the Twenty-eighth Congregation meet every Sunday in the spacious edifice gratefully erected to the memory of Theodore Parker. But, in this pulpit,—from which their founder formerly denounced the method and doctrines of Sensationalism,—the fathers of the church whom they quote and comment upon to-day are Spencer and Huxley, Dalton and Tyndall, George Lewes and Claude Bernard. This is a sign of the times.

It is, indeed, the doctrine of evolution, in the form it has assumed from the recent generalizations of Herbert Spencer, which has rapidly become the dominant philosophy of Americans. Recently, one of the present editors of *The Index*, Mr. B. F. Underwood, stated that this doctrine was received by the majority of the Free Religious Association. In the United States, however, even more than in England, it has assumed the metaphysical form of Monism, which, while foreign to the old quarrel between the Materialists and the advocates of a spiritual philosophy, is as profoundly religious in its conclusions as it is faithful to the positive method in its premises.

Its introduction into America is attributed to Professor John Fiske, a personal friend of Herbert Spencer, who, under the name of "Cosmic Philosophy," set about developing the synthesis of evolution, by insisting upon the possibility of combinations of matter and force as much superior to humanity as humanity is to the crystal or the alga, and by emphasizing the existence of an indefinable Power "eternally and universally manifested in Nature." This doctrine rapidly formed a school as Cosmism, an appellation due to the happy blending of the positive method of Spencer with the naturalistic idealism of Dr. Strauss in its second phase, and one which is perhaps destined to become the name of a new faith. Already officially adopted by the free congregation at Florence, in Massachusetts, it is accepted by Mr. Potter, the minister of the New Bedford congregation, and the president of the Free Religious Association, as well as by the Rev. Minot J. Savage, the most advanced Unitarian minister of Boston.

Mr. Potter is never weary of asserting that religion is essentially the expression of our relation to the universe: "Of religion, as thought, the central idea is that of man's relation to the universe and to its vital forces ; of religion, as feeling, the central sentiment is that of obligation, imposed on man by this tie of vital relation ; of religion, as practice, the centre of action is man's effort to meet this obligation, and thus to put and keep himself in right relations with the universe and its vital powers. At the same time, the formula is only a statement of facts pertaining to man, which the strictest scientific thought must recognize. In whatever way the universe came into being and is sustained, man *is* in actual relation to it and its vital forces. Of all finite beings within the range of our knowledge, he is the culmination of its vital processes. It is also a fact that he feels himself under obligation to give service for what he has thus received, and that only that kind of conduct which shall put him in right and normal relations with the universe of persons and things, of which he is a part, can satisfy this inward sense of obligation."[1]

This is nearly identical with the definition of Fichte, who saw in religion "the synthesis of the Ego and the non-Ego." Mr. Potter, however, desires to remain faithful to the exclusive use of Positive methods, and though he admits there is in nature, as it reveals itself to us, the manifestation of an unknown and unknowable Power, he refuses to place this Power outside the universe, with all its possibilities and all its resources. On the other hand, he does not hesitate to invest the Power in question with a moral significance, or rather he identifies it with the moral law itself. Modern science, he says, has shown in vain that moral ideas are due to the reaction of the environment in which the human organism is placed; for since man, as the product of the universe, possesses the conception of morality and duty, these latter must certainly exist in the universe.

It is clear that the Cosmos thus understood may become an object of real worship, and it would ill become us to cavil with Mr. Potter, who, when questioned on the nature of his beliefs, summed them up in these words: "Belief and trust in the universe. This is the cornerstone of our faith. If a new name were wanted for those who hold a faith thus grounded, why not call them Cosmians."[2]

The Rev. Minot J. Savage, again, the minister of an important Unitarian congregation in Boston, has made himself an eloquent and

---

[1]. *The Index* of the 5th of January, 1882.

[2]. See *The Index* of the 30th of June, 1881. In the opinion of Mr. Hinckley, the minister of the Free Religious Congregation at Florence and the present secretary of the Free Religious Association, the new God is the unknown and universal Power, acting by and in all things with superhuman intelligence and love.— The General Meeting of the Free Religious Association, May the 27th, 1881.

indefatigable apostle of evolution in his works, *The Religion of Evolution* (1876), *The Morality of Evolution* (1880), and *Belief in God* (1881). And the members of the Free Religious Association who heard him, at their meeting in 1881, discourse upon the state of contemporary morals, witnessed the curious spectacle of this Christian minister maintaining against a so-called Atheist, Mr. Felix Adler, that morals have for their foundation social utility, and for their origin the experience acquired by the race. Still, if Mr. Savage rejects the idea of an absolute and transcendent morality, he none the less admits that, in the midst of human variations as to the rules of conduct, the principle of a distinction between good and evil as well as the significance of the idea of duty represent among men "something constant and immutable as a rock in the midst of the waves."

In his work on *The Religion of Evolution*, Mr. Savage begins by showing that the progress of science has given the death-blow to almost all the conceptions of traditional theology.[1] It is, as he thinks, the theory of evolution which will henceforth bear sovereign rule in philosophy as well as in science. He does not hesitate to affirm that the marvellous hypothesis of Herbert Spencer serves to explain almost all known facts, without being in antagonism with any, and he goes so far as to characterize it as the greatest work the mind of man has ever performed.

But if this philosophy be the last word of science, what does it leave us in the shape of religion? Mr. Savage examines successively the modifications of thought which the acceptance of evolution would produce in the current conceptions of Christian theology and in metaphysics in general. Now, though this method tends to destroy the Biblical traditions respecting the origin of the universe and the appearance of man, the anthropomorphic idea of the Deity, the belief in the Devil, the possibility of miracles, the acceptance of a special revelation, and the popular conception of heaven and hell, it leaves us, on the other hand, and even places on the most solid of foundations, our feelings of confidence and reverence in the presence of that mysterious Power which transcends all definition, but which reveals itself in all phenomena,—the consciousness of a close relationship

---

1. *The Religion of Evolution* (Boston: Lockwood, 1876). See also his other works, *The Morals of Evolution* (Boston: Ellis, 1880); *Belief in God* (Boston: Ellis, 1881); *Beliefs about Man* (Boston: Ellis, 1882).

with all the members of the human family and even with all the forms of life in nature,—the hope of a future life and the necessity of complete submission to the moral law.

From the fact that it excludes caprice and arbitrary intervention, the philosophy of evolution admits of the reconciliation of the principle of love with the reign of universal law in the manifestations of the universe. It is also the only doctrine which offers a satisfactory solution to the problem presented by the existence of evil. Evil, indeed, is shown to be merely a maladjustment in relation to the conditions of physical, moral and intellectual environment—that is, to the laws of the cosmic order. It may therefore be claimed that evil is an essential condition of progress, either as, when in nature it acts through the disappearance of the feeblest to the advantage of those best fitted to survive, or when, as with man, it presents itself as the corrective of ignorance and misconduct. "Even pain is only a signal marked danger, that is set up along the railways, at the switches and crossings of human life. . . . Pain is simply God saying: 'Get out of danger' or 'Get up higher.'"

But what becomes of Christianity in this scientific conception of religion? Mr. Savage points out that religion itself is subject to the law of evolution like all the other manifestations of our moral and intellectual activity. It matters not therefore that Christianity is the last and most perfect system of religion; since it is a product of evolution it will be set aside by evolution. But it is only the superannuated forms and the excrescences which will be thus cast off by evolution; this law or process does not effect what is in its nature permanent and universal. If the cosmogony, the dogmas, the ceremonies and the ecclesiastical organizations of Christianity are doomed to disappear, it is otherwise with the precepts in and through which Jesus identified religion with morality and the Supreme Being with universal life. Now, if these truths embody the essence of Christianity, whoever accepts them has a right to retain the name of Christian, and on this point the philosophy of evolution merely continues the work of Christ, which was misunderstood even by his first disciples.

In a sermon preached before his congregation in 1880,[1] Mr. Savage speaks still more explicitly:—

"All these religions may be grouped under three main classes.

---
1. See his work, *The Morals of Evolution*, p. 187.

Whatever their manifestation, however perfect or imperfect, they fall naturally into one of these three. In the first place there is Paganism, that is the worship of isolated, detached manifestations of the universe, whether of power, or beauty or what not. Then there is the Worship of Humanity. The highest specimen of this is Christianity; for Christianity, if you will think of it, is simply the highest type of the Worship of Humanity, because God himself in Christianity is conceived of in the image of the ideal and perfect man. Then there is another form of religion that may be called Scientific, or *Cosmic*. The object of its wonder, its awe, its admiration, is the universe considered as a universe; the unity, the mystery, the wonder, the power of this great Being of whom I have spoken, out of whom we have come, and on whom we depend. I believe that the religion of the future, the ideal religion will combine in itself all these. It will take up into itself, the admiration, the beauty, the might that manifested itself in Paganism. It will feel kindly towards art and towards all the manifestations of this mysterious life of nature, whether under our feet or over our heads. It will take up into itself all that is good and beautiful and perfect in Christianity, the worship of the ideal, loving, tender man. It will take up into itself that larger unity, of which both Christianity and Paganism are only parts,—this Cosmic worship of the universe."

It is but right to add, that the Theory of Evolution is not accepted merely by Cosmians and Unitarians, who are beginning to make of it an essential feature of religion, but that it has conquered with a high hand pulpits more or less orthodox, in which case an attempt is sometimes made to accommodate it to the demands of Revelation, while in other instances there is a loyal recognition of its incompatibility with the belief in an infallible Biblical record. Of the ministers who have not hesitated to accept it with this last corollary, may be mentioned, as the chief among the Episcopalians, the Rev. Heber Newton, of New York, and among the Congregationalists the Rev. Henry Ward Beecher. The latter does not hesitate to affirm that to admit the truth of Evolution is to renounce the reigning theology.[1]

---

1. See Mr. Beecher's article in *The North American Review* of August, 1882. Being present with several other Protestant ministers at the banquet given to Mr. Herbert Spencer, at New York, on the 9th of November, 1882, Mr. Beecher made use of the occasion to propose a toast to the illustrious philosopher, and, in doing so, he once more affirmed the impossibility of reconciling Spencer with Calvin, without concealing his preference for the former.

Here, however, appears a phenomenon characteristic of the American mind, which, when it adopts the philosophy of the old world, immediately transforms it into religion, as already seen in regard to German Idealism. Religious genius, indeed, consists precisely in the power to perceive, under a special angle, those philosophical and scientific theories which are in appearance the most refractory to all metaphysical manipulation. It is this process of spiritualization which Mr. O. B. Frothingham in some measure described, when he said, on opening the third session of the Free Religious Association: "Vogt and Büchner profess Materialism, and demonstrate intelligence; Huxley talks of protoplasm, and sets us wondering at thought; Moleschott tells us that light is the author of life, and bends our head before the uncreated Light." "And what wonder," wrote Mr. W. C. Gannett, in 1875, "that religious *awe* is deepening as science looks and speaks? . . . Science to-day is making everything reverent to us by increasing its mystery. . . . If science claims to be religion, tell her No; but from wise lips she makes no such claims. If she only claims to be the giver of the known, tell her that you value her for that, but as much for the Unknown, that vision of the *more-to-know* which she everywhere suggests. To hint this latter is as distinctly her function as is discovery of fact. And the best of all—I love to repeat it—is that this vision of the Unknown is not in the heights, not in the depths, but in the common and the near, and in each and all things. That brings God's life so close! The Power so absolute is here! I do nothing without it. I am speaking, you are listening, by it; we shall fall asleep and rise, or *not* rise, by it. The atoms and the instants are packed with heights and depths, bringing to everywhere the Presence which is Law and Right and Love."[1]

It may be objected that this is all pure mysticism. But the thoughts which such language reveals are none the less important factors in the existing life and activities of what may be spoken of as American Rationalism. If the reader were to peruse the lectures and essays, summarized or reproduced every week in *The Index*, he would be surprised, not only at the number and zeal of those who have adopted the synthetic side of evolution, but also at the resources they find in

---

[1]. *Proceedings at the Eighth Meeting of the Free Religious Association.* Boston: 1875.

it for opening up new horizons to the religious sentiment, and for the satisfaction of it, even in its most exalted aspirations. It is true many of these works possess little, if, indeed, any value except as landmarks of the tendency of thought. But here a page by Abbot, Wasson, Gannett, or Savage, and there a lecture or sermon by Potter, Frothingham, or Chadwick might be pointed out which are as much marked by rigour of demonstration as by elevation of thought and poetical language. These latter, indeed, deserve the attention of all who are afraid that the progress of modern thought will lead to the destruction or even the weakening of those sentiments which give power and greatness to the human mind.

It is worthy of remark that this movement corresponds with the views of Mr. Herbert Spencer himself, if we are to judge by the following letter, which he wrote on the 9th of January, 1883, to the first and most enthusiastic of his religious interpreters in America, Mr. Savage:—

"I have read with much interest your clearly reasoned and eloquent exposition of the religious and ethical bearings of the evolution doctrines. I rejoice very much to see that those doctrines are coming to the front. It is high time that something should be done towards making the people see that there remains for them, not a mere negation of their previous ethical and religious beliefs, which, as you say, have a definite scientific and unshakeable foundation. I hope that your teachings will initiate something like a body of definite adherents who will become the germ of an organization. I have been long looking forward to the time when something of this kind might be done, and it seems to me you are the man to do it."[1]

This letter, whose publication was authorized by Mr. Spencer, is all the more significant from the fact that Mr. Savage, in common with Mr. Graham and Matthew Arnold, sees in the Unknowable an ordain-

---

[1] See *The Christian Register* of the 29th of March, 1883. By a singular co-incidence, it was only a few weeks later that Dr. Putnam, one of the most authoritative representatives of the Conservative school of Unitarians in America, spoke of Mr. Savage as the ablest and most influential of their Radical preachers, adding that, however hostile his sermons and writings might be to much that many Unitarians regarded as essential, they seemed to him to reveal a more affirmative tone of thought and a more believing Christian temperament than those of Parker and the greater part of the Radical school.—(Dr. Putnam's address on *American Unitarianism*, at the meeting of ministers in connection with the annual meeting of the British and Foreign Unitarian Association. *The Inquirer* of June 9th, 1883.)

ing Power who follows, if not a definite and foreseen purpose, at least a progressive aim, and that, though he refuses to see in the soul a distinct entity, he pronounces in favour of personal immortality.

It only remains to add that, though it would be rash to predict that America will have the honour of giving the world a new faith, as some of its writers affirm, still, whether we take note of the Cosmians, the Transcendentalists, or those who occupy a position intermediate between these two schools, or stop at the last phases of the Rationalistic movement, which began, as we have seen, in the revolt of Unitarianism against the dogmas of Predestination and the Trinity, we find everywhere, as an affirmative element, side by side with free thought carried to its utmost limits, the perception of an absolute and unconditioned Being, who reveals Himself in nature under the infinite diversity of phenomena.

Whether the object of this common faith be named the "Eternal One" with Emerson, or the "Cosmos" with Professor Fiske; the "God of Science" with Mr. Abbot, or the "God of Evolution" with Mr. Savage; the "Universe in all its possibilities" according to the definition of Mr. Potter, or the "Power which slowly raises us towards perfection" with Mr. Gannett; or, indeed, "the Being behind all appearances," to use the definition of Mr. Adler,—it is, in a word, Pantheism which is flowing with full force through the advanced regions of religious thought in the United States. And thus the prediction made by Tocqueville, at a time when the Unitarian reform, then in full vigour, seemed rather to indicate a recrudescence of Monotheism, is being realized: "In democratic times the idea of unity besets the human mind; it seeks its realization on all sides, and when it believes this has been found, gladly lies down in its arms and rests there. Not only does it come to see in the world a single creation with one Creator, but even this dual conception becomes too burdensome, so that it sets about enlarging and simplifying its thought by regarding God and the universe as parts of a single whole."[1]

---

1. *De la Democratie en Amerique.* Paris: Lévy, 1864. Vol. III., p. 50.

PART III.

CHAPTER XI.

THEISM IN CONTEMPORARY INDIA.

A recollection of Calcutta—Brahmoism—The Hindu religion and free inquiry—Philosophy among the ancient Brahmans—The idealistic Pantheism of the Vêdânta—Intermediate Divinities—Syncretism and confusion of the Hindu faith—The Vishnuite Reformers and the doctrine of *Bhakti*—Attempts at reconciliation, on the ground of the Divine unity, between the Hindu and Mohammedan creeds—Kabir, Nânak, Akbar—Influence of European ideas upon the religious mind of India—Râm Mohun Roy : his eclectic doctrines and his preaching against idolatry—Organization of the Brahmo Somâj of Calcutta—Debendra Nâth Tâgore, the successor of Râm Mohun Roy—The controversy respecting the Monotheistic character of the Vêdas—Mission of the four Pandits to Benares—Rejection of Vêdic infallibility by the Brahmo Somâj—The drawing up of a Rationalistic confession of faith, the *Brahma Dharma*—Accession of Keshub Chunder Sen.

It has been contended that pure Theism might suit exceptional temperaments, cold enough to rest satisfied with a vague religiosity, and too idealistic to do without it, but that it could never satisfy the aspirations of the masses, nor furnish means for the organization of a durable system of faith and worship. Still, the world has witnessed, for more than half-a-century, the constant progress of a religious movement which, though based exclusively on the principles of natural religion, presents all the characteristics of a positive faith : churches, priests, and worshippers. But it is in India where we must look for this.

Having, on the last Sunday in August, 1876, walked along the Machoua-Bazar Street, in the native part of Calcutta, I entered a sort of neo-gothic chapel, which was already occupied by some three or four hundred natives, draped in those white and flowing shawls which form so striking a contrast with the bronzed complexion of the Bengalese and suggest the fine effect of the ancient toga. There were scarcely more than a dozen women to be seen, who were seated in one of the aisles, but certain rustlings behind the gauze veil which concealed the gallery rightly led me to suspect that the general audience was not so exclusively comprised of the stronger sex. Immediately in front of the entrance stood a *védi*,—a small marble platform, raised to a height of several steps and surrounded by a balustrade,—where the officiating minister, in a simple muslin surplice and squatting in Oriental fashion, was waiting for the hour to commence the service. I could have believed myself in some native Protestant congregation had it not been for the entire absence of all Christian symbolism. On the other hand, there was neither the perpetual fire of the Guébres nor the grinning idols of the Hindu Pagodas; and, though the building, as a whole, possessed the austere simplicity of a Mosque, its architecture presented none of the details which characterize the edifices devoted to the worship of Allah. In fact, the God worshipped here was neither the Divinity of the Christians nor the Guébres, neither the Deity of the Hindus nor the Mussulmans: it was the God of a new religion, which claims to be a fusion of all the faiths of India, and even of the entire world, in a religious synthesis based upon the universal revelation of reason and conscience—the God of Brahmoism.

The sect, or rather the religious school, of Brahmoism is of relatively recent origin, since it was only in 1880 that it celebrated the fiftieth anniversary of its foundation by the Rajah Râm Mohun Roy. Still, it already possesses more than 170 congregations, some thirty organs of the native press, many thousands of adherents,—among whom figure some of the most eminent men of the native society,—and, finally, a whole religious and philosophical literature, both in English and in the various local dialects. In spite of its opposition to the tendencies of orthodox Christianity, it has succeeded in securing the attention and sympathy of all religious parties, even among the English. These are no longer the days in which Victor Jacquemont thus described, in a letter from Calcutta, the sentiments of the Anglo-Indians towards the noble and worthy Râm Mohun Roy:— "The honest English execrate him because he is, they say, a frightful Deist."[1]

[1] The principal historian and most ardent champion of Brahmoism in Europe to-day is Miss Sophia Dobson Collet, who according to her own avowal, accepts Trinitarian Christianity, a circumstance which speaks as well for the breadth of her ideas as it does for the value of her testimony, in favour of a form of worship "combining Evangelical piety with Unitarian theology." In addition to several small treatises on the history of Brahmoism, *Indian Theism* (1870), *Brahmo Marriages* (1871), Miss S. D. Collet has published every year since 1876 an Annual, called *The Brahmo Year-Book*, which embodies the most complete and circumstantial details of the Theistic movement in India.

There is no need for astonishment that such a movement should have sprung out of Hinduism. The religion of the Brahmans has always been on good terms with free inquiry and intellectual progress. Even before the rise of Buddhism, philosophical speculation had attained to considerable eminence among the Aryans of the Punjaub and the Ganges. So far from opposing this tendency, the sacerdotal class gave it the right of citizenship in the Vedaic teaching, on condition that criticism, though perfectly free in the matter of dogma, should respect the nominal infallibility of the Vedas, the separation of caste, and the privileges of the Brahmans; and though, at a later time, they struggled against the doctrine of Buddha, it was not because this doctrine tended to Atheism, but because it proclaimed the equality of mankind, and denied the necessity of a priesthood.

Then were seen to develope, in the Brahmanic schools, the most diverse and even the most contradictory systems of thought. Some sought an explanation of the universe in an atomic theory which suggests the doctrines of Epicurus and Haeckel. Others taught a more or less disguised Evolutionary Atheism. The philosophy however, which at length gained the predominance was the system of the Vedânta, an idealistic Pantheism which had previously existed in outline in certain hymns of the Veda.[1] According to this doctrine, which is summed up in the word *advaita* (non-dualism), God is the sole real existence and the world exists only in him; all the phenomena which appear to us as real are only an illusion of our senses. It will be seen, therefore, that if the idea of the divine personality seems new in India, it is not the same with what concerns the belief in the unity of God.

This abstract conception of the divinity was but ill adapted to the worship of the masses who remained faithful to the most striking and living figures of the ancient gods. But the Pantheistic philosophy of the Vedânta lent itself completely, like its Western equivalent, neo-Platonism, to the maintenance of subordinate gods, regarded as intermediate between man and the Absolute. The Brahmans, therefore, succeeded easily enough in accommodating the objects of the popular faith within the frame-work of their theology; and this is true of those most removed from the Vedaic tradition, since they were regarded as the forms or personified energies, or indeed as the incarnations or

---

1. *Rig Veda* X. 90. See Monier Williams's *Indian Wisdom*, 3rd edit., p. 24.

Avatâras of the supreme Divinity. It was on this principle that the Brahmans made of Buddha an incarnation of Vishnu, in order to facilitate the absorption of Buddhism, and that even to-day certain Vishnuites accept Christ as the last incarnation of their god.[1]

This elasticity and eclecticism may be said to form the essential features of the Hindu religion. There has never, indeed, been a god really accepted by the people to which India has closed the doors of its pantheon; there is not a religious idea, coarse or sublime, which it has not accepted with equal readiness at some moment or other of history. And since, moreover, it has never been able to resolve upon the rejection of an acquired belief, but has confined itself to the superposition of its new conceptions,[2] there has resulted from this a confused and odd jumble, which shocks in the highest degree our European conceptions, but which none the less serves to explain the prodigious vitality of Hinduism. "Starting from the Vêdas," says Prof. Monier Williams, in the introduction to his *Indian Wisdom*, "it ends by appearing to embrace something from all religions and to present phases suited to all minds. It has its spiritual and its material aspect, its esoteric and its exoteric, its subjective and objective, its pure and its impure. It is at once vaguely Pantheistic, severely Monotheistic, grossly Polytheistic and coldly Atheistic. It has a side for the practical, another for the devotional and another for the speculative."

At the close of the Vêdaic period, the only way of salvation lay in the observance of minute rules and in the fulfilment of the more and more complicated rites which the Brahmans had established. The re-action against excesses of the sacerdotal spirit produced Buddhism on the one hand; while on the other, it led the very defenders of the old religion to admit the value of renunciation, contemplation and ecstacy as the supreme means of attaining to union with the Divinity, the absorption of the individual soul in the Divine Essence. But this concession did not prevent the momentary triumph of the Budd-

---

[1]. This fact is mentioned by Professor Monier Williams in his little treatise: *Hinduism*. London, 1880, p. 108.

[2]. Prof. Max Müller, who finds it difficult to speak with severity of the Hindus, has pleaded extenuating circumstances in relation to this process in his *Origin and Development of Religion studied in the light of the Religions of India*. The eminent Indianist specially insists on the lesson of practical toleration which Europe might learn from it.

hists who were, in this particular, more logical than their rivals. It was at this time that there arose a third school, better adapted to respond to the aspirations of the masses. Their doctrine was that of *Bhakti*, already present in outline in the poem of the Bhagavad-Gîtâ, and which has chiefly prevailed among the worshippers of Vishnu.

From the twelfth to the fifteenth century a series of reformers, such as Râmânuja, Mâdhava, Vallabhâcârya and Chaitanya, without contesting the value of sacrifices or of asceticism, placed, by the side of and above these two religious practices, faith and love *(bhakti)* towards the Divinity, considered in some one or other of his principal incarnations. According to this doctrine, the worshipper, in order to reach beatitude, must gradually realize the following states:—1st, the contemplation of God; 2nd, voluntary subjection; 3rd, sympathy; 4th, filial affection; and, 5th, passionate love. To facilitate this increasing exaltation, the reading of the old Vedaic *Mantras* was replaced by songs and dances and by the waving of lights and the sound of instruments before the images of the god; the prayers were henceforth to be in the language of the people, and the distinctions of caste were proscribed from the interior of the sanctuaries or even during the entire period of religious festivities. Chaitanya, above all, insisted upon the importance of these practices, in order to attain to communion with Krishna. Tradition relates, indeed, that he drowned himself when in one of his ecstacies and whilst he was bathing near Puri.

The greater part of these reformers admitted the personality of God, and attributed to him an existence distinct from physical nature, as well as from the individual or finite soul.[1] But the theory of incarnation, which they allowed to keep its place in their respective systems, was destined to re-open the door to all the abuses of idolatry which have continued to characterize the Vishnu sects down to the present day. It was not, therefore, from that direction that a purification of religion could arise.[1]

In the meantime, Brahmanism, while scarcely freed from the difficulties it had to encounter in Buddhism, found itself in antagonism with a new adversary, whose zeal for proselytizing could be abated neither by fire nor sword. Still it was in vain that the zealots of

---

[1]. Monier Williams, *Indian Theistic Reformers*, in the XIIIth Volume (2nd Series) of the Royal Asiatic Society.

Islamism massacred the priests, enslaved the worshippers, and despoiled and sacked the temples of Hinduism; they could not overthrow the religious and social edifice of native civilization,—it may even be asserted that they borrowed more from it than they gave to it.[1] The chief result of this contact of the rigid Monotheism of the conquerors with the elastic Pantheism of the conquered, was that there sprang up, in the minds of certain adherents of each of the two faiths, an idea of mutual approach towards reconciliation, if not of an actual fusion, on the ground of their common principle—the belief in one God.

Among those who sought to give practical effect to this idea, with a view to diminish idolatry, we find in the 15th century, a disciple of the philosopher Râmânanda, the weaver Kabir, who attacked at one and the same time the authority both of the Koran and the Vedas, in order to substitute for it a purely spiritual worship. He disavowed, moreover, all distinction of caste and said that all who loved God and did good were brethren, whether they were Hindus or Mussulmans. His preaching drew around him numerous followers attracted indifferently from the two faiths whose vital principles he claimed to teach, and the legend by which is memory is enshrined in the popular song of Bhakta-mâl, relates this characteristic detail, that at his death Mussulmans and Hindus disputed the possession of his body, the latter desiring to burn and the former to bury it, according to their respective rites; but that when the coffin was opened there was found nothing whatever in it but flowers. It appears, however, that a part of these was burnt at Benares and the ashes deposited in the Chapel of Kabir-Chaura, which still attracts the devotees of Hindustan; while the remainder was buried at Mogar, where the reformer died, and the monument raised above the spot is visited yearly by numerous pilgrims at the time of the annual fair. More than once in history contemporary religious systems have been seen to damn the same heretic; this is perhaps the only instance in which two hostile faiths have been seen to canonize the same apostle.

A disciple of Kabir, Nânak Shah, likewise sought to fuse the two great religions of his country into a single faith, with no other dogma

---

1. Monier Williams, *Modern India*, 2nd Edition (London: Trübner, 1878). Garcin de Tassy, *Mémoire sur les Particularités de la Religion Mussulmane dans l'Inde* (Paris, 2nd Edition, 1869).

than belief in the unity of God, in the necessity of moral purity and in toleration towards other forms of faith, together with an absence of all ceremonial rites except ablutions and prayers. Such was the origin of the Sikhs, who formed, at first, a purely religious association. Finally, the celebrated Akbar, Grand-Mogul as he was, conceived of the organization of a new faith, under the striking name of "Divine Monotheism," in which, while preserving certain forms of Islamism, he introduced practices borrowed from the Hindus, the Guébres, the Christians and even from the Jews.

Unfortunately the time was not ripe for such a magnificent synthesis. The sect of the Kabir-panthis which, moreover, never secured a wide extension, became identified with the worship of Râma, an incarnation of Vishnu, and to-day it has even added the worship of its *gourous* or spiritual chiefs. The Sikhs, after being transformed into a military confederation by the Mussulman persecutions, gradually reopened their temples to the idols and superstitions of Hinduism. Finally, the syncretism of Akbar was destined to scarcely extend beyond the walls of his palace, and the only vestige of it which has remained, is, perhaps, to be found in the eclectic architecture of the cruciform temple in the town of Brindaban, which was dedicated to Krishna by the rajah Man-Singh, the friend of Akbar. This edifice possesses a gothic nave lined with Hindu pillars, which are surmounted by Moorish arches.

The introduction of European civilization gave a new impulse to the speculative mind of the Hindus. It must not be forgotten that, side by side with Christianity, the English have carried into India the arts, sciences and methods, in short the whole literary and philosophical heritage of Europe. Hence, although Brahmoism seems to have sprung from Hindu traditions by a gradual and original evolution, it is easy to discover the traces of European influence in the three men who have, in a sense, personified the successive phases of the movement; Râm Mohun Roy, Debendra Nâth Tâgore and Keshub Chunder Sen.

Râm Mohun Roy was born in 1774,[1] at Râdhnagar, and belonged to a Brahmanic family specially devoted to the worship of Vishnu.

---

[1]. In 1780 according to Garcin de Tassy (*Histoire de la Littérature Hindouie et Hindoustanie.* Paris, 2nd Ed., Vol. II., p. 348).

From his infancy he was remarkable for his devotion to the idol of the paternal house. But being sent early to the Mussulman school at Patna to learn Arabic and Persian, it was not without effect that he found himself in contact with Semitic Monotheism, and he had scarcely returned to his family, when, at the age of sixteen, he drew up a protest against the practices of Hindu idolatry. His father, who occupied a distinguished position in the district of Burdwān, judged it prudent to send him from home again, in the hope, perhaps, that contact with the world would cool the glowing zeal of the young reformer. But the latter simply took advantage of his travels to devote himself exclusively to the study of comparative theology, at first in the principal temples of India and afterwards in those of Tibet, where the independence of his criticism brought him into collision with the adherents of Buddhism. When, after an absence of four years, he re-appeared in his native town, not only had he fully adopted the principle of the divine unity, but what is more, he had resolved that no obstacle should deter him from combatting the superstitions of his fellow-countrymen.

"After my father's death in 1803," he himself wrote in a letter subsequently published in the *Athenæum*, "I opposed the advocates of idolatry with still greater boldness. Availing myself of the art of printing, now established in India, I published various works and pamphlets against their errors, in the native and foreign languages. The ground which I took in all my controversies was not that of opposition to Brahminism, but to a perversion of it, and I endeavoured to show that the idolatry of the Brahmins was contrary to the practice of their ancestors, and the principles of ancient books and authorities which they profess to revere and obey."[1] He had courageously set himself to learn—in addition to Persian, Arabic, Sanscrit and English —Hebrew and Greek, in order that he might be able to obtain from original sources a knowledge of the principal religions which have played a part in history. Prof. Monier Williams speaks of him as the first really earnest investigator in the science of comparative theology, which the world has produced.[2]

These researches, by adding still greater amplitude to his religious

---

1. See *The Athenæum* of London, for October 5, 1833.

2. *Indian Theistic Reformers*, in the XIIIth Vol. (2nd Series) of the Royal Asiatic Society.

horizon, had inspired him with the project of founding a faith on the simple belief in the unity of God and of a future life. But, being disinherited by his father, he found himself reduced to an acceptance of the humble position of dîwân with the English collector of taxes at Rangpoor, and it was not till 1814 that he was able to settle at Calcutta in order to devote himself there to the spread of his doctrine. This doctrine was drawn directly from the Vêdânta. Still, of the two propositions which constitute the basis of the Vêdântine philosophy,— the unity of God and the illusion of individual existence,—he attached himself almost exclusively to the first, compiling the Vêdas in order to furnish himself with arms against the Polytheism of his contemporaries. He cannot, therefore, be called a Monotheist to the extent that this term is applied to the believers in a distinct and personal God, such as the Jehovah of Moses or the Allah of Mohammed. But, while remaining wholly faithful in this respect to the Vêdaic tradition, he seems to have made the essence of religion consist exclusively in the recognition of the Divine, as this principle is formulated either by the Pantheism of the Brahmanas or by the Monotheism of the Bible or the Koran. Hence he felt an equal veneration for all who had taught him—Moses and Jesus, Myaça and Mohammed. This eclectic tendency is specially noticeable in his work on *The Precepts of Jesus, the Guide to Peace and Happiness* (1823), in which he renders homage to the moral value of Christianity, while he at the same time rejects the divinity of its Founder.

It has been said that Râm Mohun Roy delighted to pass for a believer in the Vêdânta with the Hindus, for a Christian among the adherents of that creed, and for a disciple of the Koran with the champions of Islamism. The truth is that his eclecticism equalled his sincerity. As a curious illustration of his influence, it is said of him that he converted to Unitarianism a Baptist missionary who rendered great service to the cause of education in India, the Rev. W. Adams. In his turn, however, it was from the religious meetings held by Mr. Adams in Calcutta that he conceived the idea of organizing a Theistic form of worship for the use of the Hindus.

He had already grouped his adherents into an association entitled *Atmîya Sabhâ* (Spiritual Society). In 1829, he introduced into it the celebration of a divine service divided in four parts: the recital of Vêdic texts, the reading of an extract from the Upanishads, together with a sermon and hymns. The new sect was not slow to become known by the name of Brahma Sabhâ or Brahmo Somâj (the Society of God). As the reader is aware, according to the Hindu theology, Brahma is not only the first person of the Trinity but he is also, as the neuter of his name, Brahman, serves to indicate, the absolute and eternal Being whose creative, preserving and destructive agencies are respectively personified by Brahmâ, Vishnu and Siva.

In 1830, the Brahmo Somâj installed itself in a house which its founder had purchased for that purpose at Calcutta. The deed of gift says that "No sermon, preaching, discourse, prayer or hymn is to be delivered, made or used in such worship, but such as have a tendency to the promotion of the contemplation of the Author and Preserver of the universe, to the promotion of charity, morality, piety, benevolence, virtue and the strengthening of the bonds of union between men of all religious persuasions and creeds." One portion of this building was reserved for the use of the Brahmans in their reading of the esoteric texts, which in the Vêdas cannot be communicated to the other castes.

Unhappily, Râm Mohun Roy embarked shortly afterwards for England, where he was sent with the title of râjah in order to make certain demands on behalf of the Grand-Mogul at the Court of St. James. He had long cherished the idea of visiting Europe, where he was already known by reputation. The upper classes in England gave him the kind of reception which they know so well how to offer, altogether apart from political considerations, to eminent men of every country and race. He had no sooner disembarked than he became the lion of the season in London, and yet this flattering attention did not diminish in the slightest degree the ease and the natural modesty of his character. Miss S. D. Collet, who remembers having caught a glimpse of him at this time, states that he won the sympathy of every one by the affability of his manners, no less than by the cultivation of his mind; and Garcin de Tassy, who met him the following year at Paris, describes his personal appearance in these terms: "His physique answered to his fine moral qualities; he possessed a noble and expressive physiognomy; his complexion was extremely bronzed, almost black; but his regular nose, his brilliant and animated eyes, his broad forehead and the beauty of his features rendered his countenance remarkable. He was six feet in height and well proportioned. His dress was habitually blue; but he wore over it a white shawl, which was rolled upon his shoulders and reached down to his waist in front. He enclosed his hair with a turban after the manner of the Mussulmans of India."[1]

His mission being accomplished, he was preparing to return to India, in order to make use of the experience he had acquired in England for the advancement of the reform he was carrying out, when, exhausted by his exertions and perhaps a victim to the climate, he fell ill and died at Bristol on the 27th September, 1833. His remains rest in the cemetery of that town, beneath a monument built in the Oriental style by his disciple and friend, Dwarka Nâth Tâgore, who came himself to die in England some years later.

Deprived of its leader, the little Church of the Brahmo Somâj languished for about a dozen years, and seemed at last on the point of dying out, when it placed the young Debendra Nâth Tâgore at its head. This latter, who was born in 1818, was the son of Dwarka Nâth Tâgore, just mentioned as the friend of Râm Mohun Roy, and he belonged to the Brahmanic clan of Piralis. When scarcely twenty years of age, he had already founded an "Association for the Search of Truth" (*Tattva Bodhini Sabhâ*), which proposed to itself "to sustain the labours of Rajah Râm Mohun Roy, by introducing gradually among the natives of this country the Monotheistic system of Divine worship inculcated in the original Hindu Scriptures." The Association met weekly in the house of the elder Nâth Tâgore, to discuss religious questions; once a month it celebrated a Divine service, in which hymns were sung and passages read from the Uphanishads. It had even begun to train missionaries to preach, throughout India, the need of reform in the national worship, when, in 1843, it incorporated itself into the Brahmo Somâj, in imitation of Debendra. Together with its pecuniary resources, it brought also to this institution its habits of intellectual activity; so that—thanks to the new element— the work of Mohun Roy soon resumed a progressive course. Still, even in 1847, the avowed Brahmoists did not number a thousand. At that date, however, a crisis occurred which seemed to presage their dispersion, but which became, on the contrary, the chief cause of

---

1. Garcin de Tassy, *Histoire de la Littérature Hindouie et Hindoustanie*. Paris, 1870. 2nd Ed., Vol. II., p. 151.

their subsequent rapid success among the enlightened classes of the country.

Râm Mohun Roy had included in his organization all who admitted the unity of God, on the sole condition that they should keep up no connection whatever with Polytheistic doctrines and practices. Still, in point of fact, the Brahmo Somâj was a simple Hindu sect, since its members admitted the infallibility of the Vêdas. The prayers and hymns composing its entire liturgy were profoundly impressed with the Vêdântic spirit, which manifested itself in the guise of continual allusions to the dogmas of metempsychosis and those of identity with the divine essence. Now nothing was more opposed than this to the tendencies of Debendra Nâth Tâgore and his friends, who—possibly owing to the influence of a more complete European education—had reached the conception of a personal God distinct from nature.

The new comers who had rapidly attained to a position of pre-eminence in the Brahmo Somâj, sought at first the confirmation of their views in the Vêdas themselves. It has been said that anything and everything may be proved from the Bible, an assertion which would apply with still greater force to the Vêdas. The Vêdas—or more correctly *the* Veda, that is science—are, in the theology of the Brahmans, regarded as the direct breath of God, which was communicated to the *Richis*, the bards of the Aryan migration, and transmitted by them from mouth to mouth, down to the time when the Brahmans, their legitimate successors, judged it desirable to fix the truths of this divine revelation in writing. In reality, the Vêdas form a collection of innumerable liturgies and theological treatises composed, as a rule, by unknown authors, the most recent of whom lived at the dawn of our era, and the most ancient at the time of the first Aryan invasions of India. It will be easily understood that among literary fragments so varied in origin and date, traces are to be found of all the currents of thought which have successively or simultaneously contributed to the formation of Hindu beliefs. These range from the worship of the deified elements of nature by the naive genius of the Aryans, up to the most abstract connections of Pantheism or even of pessimistic Atheism, developed within the shadow of the temples by several ages of philosophical elaboration—from the gross superstitions with which the invaders were innoculated in their contact with Fetishism and foreign idolatries, up to the minute ceremonies introduced by the ritualism of the Brahmans, in order to give a sacred sanction to the religious and social subjection of the enslaved castes—the whole being intensified in its effect by the presence of a profound and sincere piety, revealing itself in mystic aspirations towards an ideal Being and suggesting at times, as Edgar Quinet remarks, the personal and living God of the Monotheistic religions.[1]

This tendency is so marked in certain hymns of the Rig-Vêda that the majority of Sanscrit scholars thought at first they had discovered in them, not the natural evolution of the Hindu mind towards the unity and simplicity of the First Cause, but the last trace, as a sort of feeble echo, of some primeval Monotheistic religion, which had existed anterior to the ancient Naturalism.

In the most recent portions of the Vêdaic literature, moreover, passages, possessed of a moral and philosophical elevation, that the loftiest metaphysical system of our epoch would not repudiate, are to be found side by side with the most absurd and degrading theories. Even when we include the Puranas—that supplementary Vêda styled the popular Bible of the Hindus—there is no part of this vast sacred literature which does not constantly recognize, behind the changing and transparent physiognomy of its gods, that Being whom one passage names "the powerful Lord, immutable, holy, eternal, and of a nature always true to itself, who reveals himself as Brahmâ, Vishnu or Siva, the creator, preserver or destroyer of the world."

At the time when Debendra Nâth Tâgore and his friends resolved to controvert even passages from the Vêdas themselves, they began by calling in question, not the infallibility of the sacred texts, but the fidelity of the partial versions in their own and their opponents' possession. And here it will be well to bear in mind that the Vêdas comprise thousands of isolated passages; that the knowledge of their most important parts had been the exclusive monopoly of the Brahmanic caste; that European science had not as yet made the true sense of the Hindu Scriptures common property, even in India itself; and that, finally, they were written in a dead language, Sanskrit, but

---

1. We may cite, as examples, the well-known hymn to Varuna (*Rig-Vêda*, II., 28), which bears the impress of so intense an aspiration after moral purity and so profound a sense of sin that M. Pillon has called it a Vêdic *Kyrie eleison* ; or, further, the hymn, "To what God shall we sacrifice?" (*Rig-Vêda*, X., 121); and the hymn on the origin of the universe (*Rig-Vêda*, X., 129).

little known even to native theologians, beyond the limits of a few centres specially devoted to the study of sacerdotal matters. Hence the Brahmo Somáj decided, at the suggestion of Akhai Kumar Datta, the editor of the *Tattvabodhini Patriká*, to commission four young pandits to copy, at Benares itself, the four Védas, of which the sacred town of Brahmanism alone possessed a copy claiming to be complete and authentic.

This undertaking lasted two years, and when its result was communicated to the Brahmo Somáj, no one could avoid the saddening conviction that, side by side with sublime precepts, the Védas embodied passages forming a justification for the grossest superstition,—in short, a collection of dogmas utterly irreconcileable with the principles of Monotheism.

The infallibility of the Scriptures was now courageously thrown overboard, and the Brahmo Somáj breaking with the tradition of Hinduism, as well as with the entire notion of any specially revealed religion, became a purely Theistic Church—the first, perhaps, except the Unitarian, which has ever acquired a serious importance in the world. Debendra Náth Tagore caused it to adopt under the name of *Brahma Dharma* "the rule of Theism," a confession of faith, which without falling into an exaggerated dogmatism, summed up the elementary principles of all worship within the bounds of natural religion: the unity and personality of God; the immortality of the soul; the moral efficacy of prayer; and the necessity of repentance to ensure restoration from the effects of evil-doing.[1] Up to this time, the most important part of their worship, that is to say, the recital of the sacred texts, had taken place among the Brahmans with closed doors, and the adherents of any other caste were only admitted to hear the sermon and join in the hymns. Henceforth, however, the Brahmo Somáj made no distinction between its members, and it was

---

[1]. See *The New Dispensation and the Sádhárán Brahmo Somáj*, by the pandit Sivanáth Sástri. Madras, 1881, p. 10.—The *covenant*, or constitution of Brahmoism, which the members were to sign, embodied the four following propositions:—
(1) In the beginning, God was alone, and he has created the universe. (2) God is intelligent, infinite, benevolent, and eternal; he governs the universe, he is omniscient, omnipresent, the refuge of all, without body, immutable, unique, without an equal, all-powerful, self-existent, and above all comparison. (3) It is by venerating him, and by this alone, that we can attain to supreme beatitude in this world and in the next. (4) To love him and do the things that please him constitute the worship we owe to him.

recompensed for this by the numerous accessions which it received, not merely in Calcutta but also in the provinces.

Still such is the persistence of social prejudices that the greater part of the Brahmoists remained faithful to the prescriptions of caste sanctioned by the ancient faith, and notably in relation to the important question of marriage. Even more, men of excellent parts—a state of things not peculiar to India and the Brahmo Somáj—continued to practice in their families, for the sake of appearance, ceremonies which they denounced as contrary to reason and the dignity of man, in the meetings of the Brahmo Somáj. All this happened because the convictions of the Brahmoists, as yet, lacked that fervour which is ready for every sacrifice and if badly directed too often ends in intolerance, but which is none the less indispensable to the success of every great religion or social reform. The *Brahma Dharma* was above all the formula of a philosophy; it was reserved for Keshub Chunder Sen to make of it the gospel of a religion.

CHAPTER XII.

THE SOCIAL REFORMS OF THE BRAHMO SOMÂJ.

Keshub Chunder Sen—His influence on the religious activity of the Somâj of Calcutta—Gradual abandonment of the distinctions of caste—Conservative and Liberal Brahmoists—Keshub's controversy with Debendra Nâth Tâgore on the social bearing of Brahmoist reform—Schism of the Brahmo Somâj into the Adi Somâj and the Somâj of India—Exuberance of religious life among the neo-Brahmoists—The Brahmostabs—Inauguration of the new Mandir, or Temple—Keshub's efforts to secure a recognition of the validity of Brahmoist marriages, the suppression of premature unions, the legal consent of the bride, &c.—Institution of civil marriage as optional by the Native Marriage Act of 1872—The foundation by Keshub of the Indian Reform Association—Participation of this Society in all the movements for the regeneration of India—Establishment of schools, emancipation of women, repression of drunkenness—Means of propagandism and rapid spread of Brahmoism in the provinces—Institutions characteristic of the different Somâjes.

Keshub Chunder Sen was born in 1838, and his family belonged to the Vaidya caste. His father who had filled important posts in the government of Bengal, was a votary of Vishnu, and was celebrated for the brilliancy of the festivals held in his house in honour of the god. It is from these surroundings, which were anything but favourable to Monotheistic tendencies, that the young Keshub sprang as Râm Mohun Roy had previously done; but attendance at the Anglo-Indian College of Calcutta had the same influence upon his convictions as the teaching of the Mohammedan College at Patna had produced upon the religious ideas of his predecessor. When hardly twenty years old, Keshub had grouped around him a certain number of young men who were eager, like himself, for instruction in Western literature and philosophy. It was then that one of the Brahmo Somâj pamphlets, falling by chance into his hands, revealed to him the existence, in his own country, of the ideal Church of his imagination. His adhesion to it was not delayed, and, like Debendra Nâth Tâgore, he was able to secure the allegiance of the small group who were already accustomed to look up to him as their spiritual guide.

"There are two sorts of Theism," says one of the most faithful disciples of Keshub, the Baboo Protâb Chunder Mozoumdar. "One of these is what is ordinarily termed Natural Religion—the faith that is formed in man's mind by the action of natural phenomena and laws upon its faculties and instincts. This may be termed Philosophical Theism and it is therefore assailable by Philosophy. The conception and principles of this kind of Theism are, to a certain extent, changeable, inasmuch as man's ideas on natural facts and laws are subject to change. The second division is Revealed Theism— the deep spiritual religion produced by the action of God's spirit within man's soul. This religion is unchangeable and unassailable; it is beyond the reach of science and ordinary philosophy. . . . The first Theism is man seeking God, the second Theism is God seeking man."[1] Now it is this second form which Keshub insisted upon in the Bramho Somâj, attaching himself to what Miss S. D. Collet names the Augustinian side of religion, that is to say "the passionate thirst for God, the strong sense of sin, the low estimate of the merit of actions and of mere morality, the yearning to sink self in the fathomless ocean of divine love."

Keshub possessed, moreover, the true temperament of a reformer. Energetic and swayed by conviction, endowed, too, with eloquence which, while clear and persuasive, was at the same time coloured and captivating, he joined to the prestige of talent and knowledge that innate ascendency which furnishes the key to all hearts and consciences. Equally versed in the native dialects and in the English language, he combined the gravity and sweetness of Oriental manners with a conventional simplicity and an activity of mind altogether European.

If I may refer to the impression which he made upon me a few years later, he was assuredly, of all the personages whom I had an opportunity of getting a glimpse of in India, the one who seemed to me to best personify his generation and the change wrought by the action of European ideas upon the tendencies of Hindu society. Even his adversaries never denied his being an exceptionally endowed man. His great defect, as will be seen further on, was perhaps that of believing and saying this himself.

As the result of his influence, there soon appeared, in this Rationalistic Church, an intensity of religious life which seems everywhere

---

1. *Indian Mirror* of the 25th of April, 1875.

else to have remained a monopoly of the sects and to be the outcome of their miraculous theology. The meetings of the Brahmo Somâj became more frequent and were better attended; a number of newcomers were attracted by the reputation of the young preacher and retained by the seductive charm of his words. A true revival took place, and, as a first consequence, it gave to the members of the Brahmoist Church the energy needed for a definitive break with the practices of Hinduism.

Debendra Nâth Tâgore preached by example in the month of July, 1861, when he allowed the marriage of his own daughter to be celebrated without any of the idolatrous rites required by the tradition of the Brahmans. In the following year he renounced the domestic idol which he had up to that time tolerated, under his roof, and, on the initiative of Keshub, he discontinued the use of the sacred cord symbolic of caste, during divine service.

But Keshub wished to go still further in this direction, and the very day on which he was chosen an assistant minister of the Somâj of Calcutta, he ignored the fact that he was a Vaidya by birth and went with his wife to dine at the table of Debendra Nâth Tâgore, who, in the Brahmanic hierarchy, was only a Pirali. Now, a Brahman may associate with persons of a lower clan, or even of an inferior caste, for the widest variety of objects, but he cannot share in their meals without incurring an excommunication, which makes an alien of him in his family, deprives him of his goods, and drives him from his home. In vain, too, would he seek to attach himself to the group from association with which his loss of rank had been occasioned:—birth alone can give caste. He would fall, therefore, beneath even the *soudras* into that degraded herd of outcasts who no longer figure in the minutely adjusted hierarchy of Hindu society.

Formerly, it was with difficulty that the least infraction of the etiquette of caste, even if involuntary, could be atoned for at the price of long penitence and enormous fines paid to the priests. But English rule has not existed in vain in India. The sympathy shown to the assistant minister of the Brahmo Somâj in his disgrace by the most enlightened of his fellow-citizens, soon made it evident that for the first time perhaps since the social insurrection of Buddha, revolt against the prescriptions of caste had become possible in Hindu society. Some time afterwards, when Keshub had fallen dangerously ill, his family repented of the course they had taken, and agreed to reinstate him in his patrimonial rights.

Scarcely restored to health, Keshub proposed to make the abandonment of the Brahmanic cord obligatory upon the ministers of the Brahmo Somâj. Debendra Nâth Tâgore, although he had personally set an example of this kind, refused to make it an indispensable condition for the exercise of the sacred office. Hence there resulted a lively controversy, in which the Brahmoists were to be seen divided into two camps under the respective generalship of the two ministers. Both parties seemed more or less agreed on questions of principle. But the Conservatives led by Debendra Nâth Tâgore, whom so many innovations were beginning to alarm, maintained that the Brahmo Somâj should confine itself, as far as possible, to reforms of a purely religious character, that it was necessary to take into account the existing customs and that the complete repudiation of social distinctions was contrary to the traditions as well as to the national spirit of the Hindus. To this agreement the progressive party replied with Keshub, that it was impossible to separate religious from social reforms, that before God all class distinctions should be put aside, and that a Church, feeling itself in possession of truth, should proclaim it in its entirety with neither scruple nor hesitation.

This controversy reached a climax, when Keshub undertook to officiate at the marriage of a Vaidya with a young widow of a different caste, after which the whole wedding party, including the minister, partook of the same repast. The scandal this caused assumed such proportions, even in the Brahmo Somâj, that Keshub, in despair of gaining a majority in favour of his ideas, voluntarily quitted the association with some hundreds of adherents, and in the following year completed the schism by founding a new Church under the title of *Bhâratbharsia* Somâj or Brahmo Somâj of India, in contradistinction to the Brahmo Somâj of Calcutta, which subsequently became known by the name of Adi (the old) Somâj.

This new society was not intended to be merely the rival of the Church of Debendra Nâth Tâgore in Calcutta itself; it aimed, moreover at the organization of all the Brahmo Somâjes of the country into a confederation, of which it was to be the centre. "We see around us," said Keshub in his inaugural address delivered on the 11th of November, 1866, "a large number of Brahmo Somâjes in different parts of the country for the congregational worship of the one true God, and hundreds upon hundreds of men professing the Brahmo Faith; we have besides, missionaries going about in all directions to preach the saving truths of Brahma Dharma; books and tracts inculcating these truths are also being published from time to time. To unite all such Brahmos and form them into a body, to reduce their individual and collective labours into a vast but well organized system of unity and co-operation—this is all that is thought to be accomplished. . . . We must endeavour to realize, so far as it is in our power, the true idea of the Church of God."

In common with Presbyterian Christians, the neo-Brahmos would accept no head but God himself; still Keshub was none the less their real chief, under the title of secretary of the Bháratbharsia Somáj and minister of the Calcutta Congregation.

Masters of their own actions the neo-Brahmos, as was to be expected from the leadership of Keshub, gave themselves up to an exuberance of religious life which their minister did not seek to moderate, but merely to regulate by the institution of a ritual in conformity with the spirit of the new organization.

The weekly service, which was fixed for the Sunday to correspond with the regular stoppage of business introduced by the English into the habits of India, was henceforth to consist of prayers, hymns, a sermon and readings, the latter being borrowed indifferently from the Védas, the Old and New Testament Scriptures, the Koran and the Zend Avestâ, according to the pleasure of the minister.[1] This was supplemented by a "family service," which each Brahmo could use daily in his own house. As to the ritual previously in use for the ceremonies of initiation, marriage, cremation, *játkarma* (thanksgiving after the birth of a child) and *námkaram* (the choice of a name), they were simply modified by the elimination of formulas not in harmony with the programme of the reforming party. The ceremony of *shrádha*, a funeral service closely allied to the theory of metempsychosis, was completely remodelled in keeping with the doctrines professed by the Brahmos on the future destiny of the soul. Finally

---

[1]. Here is the Bháratbharsia Somáj Order of Service:—1, Hymn; 2, Invocation; 3, Hymn; 4, Adoration; 5, Silent communion; 6, Prayer in common or with responses; 7, Prayer for universal good; 8, Hymn; 9, Reading from sacred books; 10, Sermon; 11, Prayer; 12, Benediction; 13, Hymn.

Keshub instituted a series of *brahmostabs* (festivals of the Lord) which recur at stated periods and last an entire day.[1]

These festivals appear to have exercised an influence which is only to be explained by the contagious nature of even the most rationalistic form of mysticism. "The change produced in certain persons who were present on the occasion of these Brahmostabs is truly astonishing," wrote Protâb Chunder Mozoumdar in 1868. "The humility, the hope, the prayerfulness, reverence, love, faith, and joy, that flow in celestial currents at such times, catch men's souls by a sort of holy contagion. . . . . Men and women are similarly affected; new converts are every time brought in, old converts are regenerated and refreshened. Those Brahmos who desire to know what it is to see and feel God (we speak with the humble reverence of sinners) should come and attend one of the Brahmostabs."[2] Sometimes, at the close of the ceremony, the worshippers formed into a procession, and, with the minister at their head, paraded the streets of the native quarter, singing hymns to the glory of the one and only God.

A part of these innovations, if we are to believe the pandit Sivanâth Sâstri, were due to the better understanding which was reached at the

---

[1]. The following is a description of one of these festivals, the Bhadrostab of 1871, taken from the *Indian Mirror* of the 22nd of August, 1871, and it at least proves the fervour of those who took part in it:—

Precisely at six o'clock a hymn was sung in the upper gallery of the *Mandir* to announce the solemnities of the day. Others followed with the harmonium accompaniment, and thus the singing continued from hymn to hymn till the commencement of the service which, including the sermon, lasted from 7 to 10 o'clock. A part of the congregation then withdrew for refreshment, but the remainder surrounded the *Vêdi* to ask the minister for an explanation of various points of his sermon. At noon, when the meeting was again full, four pandits came forward and recited Sanscrit texts in succession. At one o'clock, the minister gave an address on the following four points:—(1) The Vêda is inferior to the true Scripture, in which the eternal God reveals himself; (2) The sage must everywhere reject error and retain truth; (3) It is the spirit or essence of all Scriptures, great and small, which should be sought, for this is truth; (4) To find God, we must turn to the Scriptures, to the sages and to conscience. Then came several philosophical theses and religious expositions by their authors. Hymns, meditations and prayers in common brought the congregation to close upon 7 o'clock, when seven new Brahmos were to be initiated by a special ceremony. This, with a connected sermon, did not last less than two hours and the meeting, if we are to believe the chronicler, showed no signs of weariness after these fifteen hours of continuous devotion, but separated singing that it had not even then had enough: "The heart wishes not to return home."

[2]. *Indian Mirror* of the 1st of July, 1868.

commencement of the Bhâratbharsia Somâj between the party led by Keshub and the school of *Bhakti*, principally represented in Bengal by the followers of Chaitanya. The neo-Brahmos borrowed from the latter, for instance, the hymns which they sang in their *Sankirtans*, and though these lyrical compositions were doubtless freed from all Polytheistic allusion, they bore the impress of that sweet mysticism which is at once the charm and the peril of the Hindu genius. "The metres are peculiar and usually vary in the same hymn," says Miss S. D. Collet, "and the wild recitative-like tunes are such as sorely task a European ear to apprehend and retain; but however ineffective they may sound to us, a very great effect is produced by them in India, especially when sung in unison by hundreds of believers, all warmly moved by the sentiments expressed."[1]

The Mandir, or Church, which the Bhâratbharsia Somâj built for itself was not finished until 1869. The opening service took place on the 29th of August, in the presence of a very large and enthusiastic audience. Keshub read on that occasion the following declaration, which I reproduce in full, because it contains a clear exposition of his views at the time:—

"To-day, by Divine grace, the public worship of God is instituted in these premises, for the use of the Brahmo community. Every day, or at least every week, the one only God, without a second, the Perfect and the Infinite, the Creator of all, omnipresent, almighty, all-knowing, all-merciful, and all-holy, will be worshipped here.

"No man or inferior being or material object shall be worshipped here as identical with God or like unto God or as an incarnation of God, and no prayer or hymn shall be chanted unto or in the name of any except God. No carved or painted image, no external symbol which has been or may hereafter be used by any sect for the purpose of worship or the remembrance of a particular event, shall be preserved here. No creature shall be sacrificed here. Neither eating nor drinking nor any manner of mirth or amusement shall be allowed here. No created being or object that has been or may hereafter be worshipped by any sect shall be ridiculed or contemned in the course of the Divine service to be conducted here. No book shall be acknowledged or revered as the infallible word of God; yet no book that has

---

[1]. See some translations of these hymns in *The Brahmo Year Book* for 1877, page 50.

or may hereafter be acknowledged by any sect to be infallible shall be ridiculed or contemned. No sect shall be vilified, ridiculed or hated. No prayer, hymn, sermon or discourse, to be delivered or used here, shall countenance or encourage any manner of idolatry, sectarianism or sin. Divine service shall be conducted here in such spirit and manner as may enable all men and women, irrespective of distinctions of caste, colour and condition, to unite in one family, eschew all manner of error and sin, and advance in wisdom, faith and righteousness. The congregation of the Brahma Mandir of India shall worship God in these premises according to the rules and principles hereinbefore set forth. Peace! Peace! Peace!"

The Bhâratbharsia Somâj had soon made their organization the rallying-point of the great majority of the Somájes which already existed in the provinces, and the number of their adherents became in a short time greater than that of the original Association. There was, however, a legal obstacle which deterred many from the public adoption of Brahmoism, even after they had accepted its doctrines. The Indian law, for instance, sanctioned only religious marriages—that is, marriages regularly celebrated according to the rites of some recognized religious body. What was there binding, therefore, in unions celebrated without the formalities required by the traditional religion? The importance of this question was soon seen from a decision given by Mr. T. H. Cowie, the Attorney-General of India, to the effect that Brahmoist marriages were not valid and that the children born of such unions were illegitimate. The Brahmos immediately drew up a petition, praying the Government to place their new ritual on a common footing with the Hindu rites.

Nothing was more just than this, nothing simpler in appearance. Hence, in 1868, notwithstanding the reserve and the slowness with which the English Government ventures to interfere with the development of national traditions and customs, above all among its Asiatic subjects, Sir H. Sumner Maine, who presided over the department of justice in the Vice-regal Cabinet, introduced a Bill which exceeded even the request of the petitioners by making civil marriages optional among the natives of India—that is to say, the recognized religious bodies retained the right to celebrate legal marriages, but it was lawful for every one, Christians excepted, to marry, without any religious ceremony, before a civil functionary or registrar appointed by the Government.

The project naturally called forth from the orthodox of every creed protestations similar to those with which we have long been familiar in Europe. Parsees and Brahmans forgot their differences to denounce in common the danger to which religion, the family and society were about to be exposed if their co-religionists were authorized to do without priestly intervention in the most solemn act of life. In the presence of this agitation, the Government withdrew the Bill, and it was not till the commencement of 1871, after an interval of two years, that the successor of Sir H. Sumner Maine, Mr. Fitzjames Stephen, proposed a new measure, "The Brahmo Marriage Act," which was drawn up with the conditions demanded by the Brahmos. By thus seeking to give validity to the ritual of Keshub Chunder Sen, the Government was thereby sanctioning certain reforms of the greatest importance for India.

In spite, for instance, of the formal text of the Vêdas, which recognize a certain independence in women, these have fallen, in consequence of the Mussulman invasions, into a condition of subjection which leaves them no preference in the choice of a lord and master. Brahmoism, which has done so much for the emancipation of the Hindu woman, could not pass over such a disregard of the equality of the sexes, and, in the reform of its ritual, it at once introduced into the marriage service the condition, hitherto unheard of, that the consent of the woman had been "freely given before God, the All-powerful." Another innovation, contained in the proposed measure and made equally at the suggestion of Keshub Chunder Sen, who had long been preaching against the scourge of premature marriages, fixed a minimum of 18 years for young men and 14 for girls. Finally, the Bill introduced monogamy into the Hindu code, by making it obligatory upon all those who might avail themselves of the provisions of the new Act.

Although restricted to a special sect, the new Bill met with the same opposition as the preceding one, and it may be mentioned as a characteristic detail, that the members of the Adi Somáj were among its bitterest opponents. Two thousand persons professing to be Brahmos went so far as to petition the Legislative Council of India, praying that the measure might be rejected as useless, excessive, and dangerous. A middle course between the proposal of Mr. Stephen and that of Sir H. S. Maine was therefore adopted. The Legislative Council struck the name of the Brahmos from the Bill and made it applicable, under the title of "The Native Marriage Act," to "persons who do not profess the Christian, Jewish, Hindu, Mohammedan, Parsi, Buddhist, Sikh or Jaïna religion,"[1]—a negative enumeration calculated to re-assure the adherents of the different religious bodies against the abandonment of their altars by sceptical or impatient bridegrooms.[2]

The very vehemence of the opposition which the neo-Brahmos had been compelled to overcome in obtaining legal sanction for their marriages, could not fail to advance their cause, since it brought them under the notice of all who were seeking an agency for social and religious regeneration, as Keshub himself had formerly done. Immediately after his return from the journey he made to England, with four disciples at the end of 1870, the minister of the Bháratbharsia Somáj founded at Calcutta the Indian Reform Association, "with a view to promote the moral and social reform of the natives of India." Open to all the natives without distinction of race or creed, but composed chiefly of Brahmos, it was divided into five sections under the following heads: (1) The amelioration of the lot of women; (2) education; (3) cheap literature; (4) temperance; (5) philanthropical activities.

From its commencement, this society was to be found at the head of all the movements set on foot to secure the moral and material re-

---

1. A somewhat numerous sect in the East of India who profess doctrines bordering on those of Buddhism.

2. Here is the text of the declaration which the new law, promulgated on the 22nd of March, 1872, and requires to be signed by the contracting parties in the presence of the registrar and three witnesses:—"I, A. B., hereby declare as follows: (1) I am at the present time unmarried; (2) I do not profess the Christian, Jewish, Hindu, Mohammedan, Parsi, Buddhist, Sikh or Jaïna religion; (3) I have completed my age of eighteen (or fourteen) years; (4) I am not related to C. D. (the other contracting party) in any degree of consanguinity or affinity which would, according to the law to which I am subject or to which the said C. D. is subject, render a marriage between us illegal; (5) and (for cases where the legal age or majority is not attained) the consent of N. M., my father (or guardian as the case may be) has been given to the marriage between myself and C. D. and has not been revoked; (6) I am aware that if any statement in this declaration is false, and, if in making such statement, I either know or believe it to be false, or do not believe it to be true, I am liable to imprisonment and also to fine." (See *The Brahmo Year Book* for 1879).

generation of India. The education of women and the suppression of intemperance seem to have specially engaged its attention. In 1871, it founded on behalf of the native women, an adult school and also a training college, to which was attached a girls' elementary school, to serve as a means for the acquisition of experience. By 1875, the students of the normal college had formed among themselves a mutual instruction society, which arranged for periodical lectures under the direction of Keshub, and published its transactions in the organ of the Association, the *Bâmâbodhini Patrikâ*, which was widely circulated among the families of Bengal. Another educational institution, the Bengal Ladies' School, was opened at Calcutta in 1876, to prepare governesses for the examination, which had been organized by the Government; and among the students who at once gave in their names, were four widows. Together with these schools Keshub founded in 1882, the *Bhârat Assam*, a sort of boarding house to serve as a home for native women desirous of living in common under the protection of the Brahmo Somâj.

These institutions, which were imitated in many particulars by the local congregations, have had as their immediate result, not only the improved condition of women among the disciples of Brahmoism, but their existence has, moreover, indirectly provided the sex with a solid vantage ground in the struggles they have to carry on against the dominant religions of India. Miss Collet states in her *Year Book* for 1876, that the Brahmoist women rival the originators of the movement, in their activity and enthusiasm. Now, the more a reforming movement comes into collision with national customs and traditions, the more necessary is the co-operation of the feminine element, to enable it to overcome the resistance of the social environment. It is by woman's agency that new ideas take possession of the family, and it is through the family that the regeneration of society commences. The Brahmos have seized upon a truth here, which is too often overlooked in European countries.

Meanwhile the Indian Reform Association was also applying itself, with no less success, to a search for a remedy against the habit of intemperance, which is a recent vice in India. Before the arrival of the English, it is an undoubted fact that the Hindus and the Mohammedans vied with each other in sobriety, which is, moreover, enjoined by the nature of the climate. With European civilization the taste for fermented liquors unhappily introduced itself, and for the last third of a century drunkenness has been extending through India like a deadly leprosy.

The Association began its work by establishing a journal, *Mad na Garal?* (Wine or Poison?) and by organizing lectures for inculcating abstention from strong drinks. But these efforts not having produced sufficient results, Keshub, after making an inquiry himself in all parts of Bengal, presented a petition to the Governor-General, signed by 16,200 Bengalese, in which he requested the Government to place restrictions on the sale of fermented beverages. The prayer of the petitioners was granted, on the revision of the general tariff in 1876, when the duty on the importation of wines and spirits was considerably raised; besides this, in the following year, a special measure was passed by the Legislature, which restricted the number of wine shops, prohibited the clandestine sale of alcoholic drinks, declared public-house debts unrecoverable by legal means and forbade dealers in such beverages to accept goods as a pledge of payment. And finally the Lieutenant-Governor of Bengal was intrusted with the power to transfer to the justices of the peace, in any locality he might think fit, the right to withdraw the license from public-houses.[1]

These examples show how largely the Brahmos had become an embodiment of the reforming spirit of native society, in the eyes of the Anglo-Indian Government. The late Viceroy, Lord Northbrook, did them ample justice in this respect when on his departure from Calcutta in 1876,[2] he publicly expressed, to their secretary, the lively sympathy with which he regarded their moral and social labours, "though, of course, theologically he differed from them in opinion."

Meanwhile the religious proselytism of Brahmoism went on hand-in-hand with its social activities. People came from all parts to hear the fervent and inspired utterances of Keshub, who, on certain occasions, drew together audiences numbering from two to three thousand persons. At the same time, innumerable tracts, containing prayers, sermons, lectures, and moral or religious dissertations, were distributed all over the country with that indefatigable prodigality, the secret of which our reformers had borrowed from the Bible Societies of England.

---

1. *The Brahmo Year Book* for 1876.

2. The vice-regal sceptre of India changes hands every few years, and two viceroys—Lord Lytton and Lord Ripon—have completed their term of office since Lord Northbrook's rule came to an end.—*Translator.*

But it was above all by means of missionaries that Brahmoism extended its conquests in the interior of the peninsula. These missionaries, who are trained in a theological institute established for that purpose, aim at maintaining the faith of their own people and at extending their doctrines among others. Every year, towards the time of the principal Brahmostab, they meet in conference at Calcutta, and set out thence to the very extremities of India, following a route traced out beforehand. Visiting the congregations already in existence, they also seek everywhere to found new ones. Their families they leave behind, at the expense of the community, so that they may be free to devote themselves exclusively to the interests of the Church. Stopping wherever there is any hope of a sympathetic or even of an attentive hearing, they preach the good word in the public squares, beneath a tree, on the edge of a pond, in the midst of a fair or even on the roof of a house. In some instances, they request one of their co-religionists to assemble a few friends in his own house, where they worship with closed doors. As soon as they have in anyway brought together a nucleus of followers, they organize them into a regular congregation, which begins at once to collect funds for building a mandir.

It must not be supposed that the Brahmans, or, speaking generally, the orthodox Hindus, are slow to create every kind of embarrassment for them. More than once, especially in Bengal, the populace have been seen to interrupt and break up their meetings; they have even taken possession of and burnt the building after maltreating the congregation, as was the case at Cagmari in 1871. But these acts of violence, which are repugnant to Hindu manners, seldom occur and never happen a second time in the same place. The opposition shows itself more frequently in the shape of those social excommunications which the law is powerless to foresee and to repress. Some years ago, for instance, an Association was formed in Bengal, the members of which pledged themselves to maintain no social relations whatever with the adherents of Brahmoism, even though such persons should be their own nearest relatives. In some localities the shop-keepers, barbers and others refused to accept the Brahmos as customers. These facts, however, are not specially applicable to India alone, for they are to be seen manifesting themselves every day in the Catholic villages of Belgium, at the expense of the Free-thinkers domiciled there. Still, persecutions of this kind, whether direct or indirect, were powerless to arrest the progress of Brahmoism, and during the year 1876 alone the number of Somâjes increased from 108 to 128.[1]

All these congregations, scattered as they are throughout India, seek more or less to imitate the parent congregation. Speaking generally, the influence exercised by each Somâj depends less upon the number of its members than upon their zeal and activity. Small congregations, especially in remote districts, often become ardent centres of proselytism, sending missionaries in all directions and creating libraries and even schools for the use of the neighbouring populations.

Here is Miss Collet's description of the principal institutions which characterize a Somâj in its full development :—

A.—RELIGION. (1) Common worship at least once a week, but generally at shorter intervals; (2) Religious festivals on special occasions; (3) The use of an order of service in celebration of births, marriages and funerals; (4) A series of religious discussions; (5) A Theistic library; (6) An organization for spreading the principles of Brahmoism, carried on by means of missionaries, pamphlets and a journal.

B.—PHILANTHROPY. (1) Distribution of alms; (2) Dispensaries for the sick; (3) Associations for checking intemperance, early marriages, &c.

C.—EDUCATION. (1) Various agencies for the instruction of women, such as lectures, special publications, ladies' associations, &c.; (2) Schools for both sexes; (3) Night schools for the working classes.[2]

When I visited Calcutta at the end of 1876, the question of holding a general assembly was under consideration. It was proposed that the conference should consist of delegates from all the congregations affiliated to the Bhâratbharsia Somâj, and the proposition was carried into effect on the 23rd of the following September, under the presidency of Keshub. The basis of a representative organization for the

---

[1]. Of this number 61 were in Bengal, where some towns possessed two. At Bengalore, a few officers of the native camp had established a military Somâj with a school for the daughters of the soldiers. At Lahore, the wife of the minister had commenced a congregation consisting exclusively of women, in which she herself officiated.

[2]. Preface to *The Brahmo Year Book* for 1880.

regulation of the general interests of the neo-Brahmo Church was agreed upon by this assembly, and it was arranged to hold another meeting the following year to complete the work thus commenced.

But this arrangement was made without any knowledge of the circumstances which were about to endanger, if not the cause of Brahmoism, at least the unity of the Bhâratbharsia Somâj and the prestige of its founder. It is often in the hour of greatest prosperity that Churches, like States, find themselves shaken to their foundations, by an excessive application of the principles which have formed their strength and greatness.

CHAPTER XIII.

THE ECLECTICISM OF THE BRAHMA DHARMA IN ITS STRUGGLE WITH HINDU MYSTICISM.

Theodicy and Morals of Brahmoism—Its relation to the schools of Vêdântine Philosophy and German Idealism—Rationalistic Eclecticism of the Brahma Dharma—Mystical theories of Keshub Chunder Sen on the mission of great men and the nature of inspiration and prayer—Asceticism in the Bháratbharsia Somâj—Keshub's letter to Miss Collet—The Bairâgya movement—Keshub's sacerdotal tendencies—The opposition they called forth—Proposed marriage of Keshub's daughter to the young Mahârâjah of Couch-Behâr—Dissatisfaction caused among the Brahmos by the immature age of the young couple—Incidents of the wedding at the Court of Couch-Behâr—Keshub's concessions to the nuptial practices of Hinduism—Attempt of his Brahmo opponents to bring about his deposition at Calcutta—Founding of the Sâdhâran Somâj—Programme of the new Brahmoist Church—Its rapid development.

Both as theodicy and morals Brahmoism springs, at once, from the Vêdântine Idealism, which is still the dominant philosophy of the enlightened Hindus; from German Idealism, which the writings of Carlyle and Coleridge have popularized even in India; and, at a later date, from English Theism and American Transcendentalism. In imitation of this latter the Brahma Dharma declares that "intuition is the root of Brahmoism." It consequently admits of two methods for the attainment of truth. It asserts that the genuine scriptures given by God are two in number: the book of Nature and the ideas implanted in the mind of man. "The wisdom, the power, the goodness of God are written, it declares, in letters of gold upon the face of the universe: we know God by the study of his works. In the second place all fundamental truths are met with in the spiritual constitution of man, as primordial, self-evident convictions."

The God of Brahmoism is the Ultimate Being, infinite in Time and Space, the Creator and Preserver of all things, who is both just and merciful. Brahmoism formally rejects the doctrine of Incarnation. We read in the Brahma Dharma for instance: That God never makes himself man by assuming the human form. His divinity dwells in all men though it specially manifests itself in some. Thus Jesus Christ, Mohammed, Nânak, Chaitanya and all the great religious reformers of different epochs, have rendered eminent services to their fellows in the name of religion, and possess a claim upon the gratitude and love of all. They were neither absolutely holy nor infallible, they were only gifted men.

Brahmoism distinguishes between four kinds of duty: (1) Duty towards God: faith, love, worship, the practice of virtue, &c.; (2) duties to ourselves: the preservation of health, the pursuit of knowledge, holiness, &c.; (3) duties in relation to our fellows: truth, gratitude, the love of our neighbour, justice, the fulfilment of our engagements, benevolence in the most extended sense, &c.; (4) duties towards the inferior animals, such as kind and humane treatment.

Brahmoism is naturally an eclectic and universal religion. The Brahma Dharma proscribes the distinctions of caste and declares that all men are brethren. The Brahmos consider it distinct from all other religions and yet the essence of all. It is not hostile to other creeds; it accepts whatever truth they contain, and rejects only their errors. Being based upon the nature of man it is therefore permanent and universal. It is confined to no special epoch or race; so that men of every age and land who profess this natural form of religion are Brahmos.

As to the soul—and it is here above all that Brahmoism becomes radically separated from Pantheistic doctrines—God created it, as all other material or immaterial things, but though it has thus had a beginning it will have no end. God alone is eternal; the soul is only immortal. On the dissolution of the organism which it animates, it will quit the terrestrial regions, with its virtues and its vices, in order to indefinitely carry forward in other spheres the struggle for truth and perfection. It is in this sense we are to understand the teaching of the Brahma Dharma, that "the Paradise of the Brahmo consists in the society of God."

With a conception thus elevated of our relation to God, the "process of salvation," is necessarily the pursuit of the ideal by the search for the true and the practice of the good. Still Brahmoism would not be a religion, if it did not inculcate the necessity of some form of worship, with a view to bringing its adherents into communion with the Absolute—a form of worship which it makes to consist entirely of love, adoration and prayer, and not of ceremonial observances. It is above all to individual and spontaneous prayer that it assigns an important place in its liturgy, not with a view to obtain a miraculous modification of the laws of nature or even to render unnecessary the expiation of sins actually committed, but in order to procure for the sinner, thus purified by repentance, the moral strength needed to avoid falling back into his former evil ways.

To this scheme of theology, which is as simple as it is natural, Keshub attached theories that appear to be an unconscious re-action of Hindu mysticism against the rigidity of the Rationalistic tendencies developed in Brahmoism by its contact with European philosophy. As early as 1866, in a sermon on "Great Men," which excited no little attention in Calcutta, he sought to prove that, over and above conscience and external nature, there is a third channel through which God reveals Himself to the human mind : it is the influence of men providentially raised up, who thus specially represent "God in History." The benefactors and reformers of the human race may therefore be regarded, he urged, as incarnations of the Divine, not in the common acceptation of the term, which lends a human form to the Infinite Being, but in this sense : that God, who is present in all men, reveals Himself more fully in certain superior natures. Let the East and the West appreciate and honour each other's great teachers, he said, and "thus hostile Churches and the dismembered races of mankind shall be knit together into one family in the bonds of faith in the common Father and universal gratitude and esteem towards their elder brothers, the prophets." This was a very elevated conclusion, but from the development which he gave to his definition of providential men, Keshub made of them a special class, intermediate agents between the masses and God, who were supposed to be superior to the apparent laws of the moral universe and infallible in their opinions when under the influence of divine inspiration.

But by what signs are the chosen of Providence to be recognized ? Keshub gives us no clue whatever to this ; he merely explains that the prophetic office may become the mission of any one who, through fervency and continuance in prayer, knows how, in a sense, to lay hold of the Divine. In a discourse on "Inspiration," preached in 1873, for instance, on the occasion of the 43rd anniversary of the Brahmo Somâj, he said :—

"Prayer and inspiration are two sides of the same fact of spiritual life. Man asks and God gives. The spirit of man kneels and is quickened by the spirit of God. The cause and the effect seem hardly distinguishable, and in the reciprocal action of the human and the Divine spirits there is a mysterious unity. Hardly has man opened his heart in prayer when the tide of inspiration sets in. The moment you put your finger in contact with fire, you instantly feel a burning sensation. So with prayer and the consequent inspiration. The effect is immediate, necessary, inevitable. . . . Observe the process : God acts upon the soul and the soul re-acts upon God, and there is re-action again and again. That response stirs the deepest depths of the heart, and we pour forth our feelings and sentiments of love and gratitude, and consecrate our energies unto God. These are again sent down with greater blessings and increased power, so that the heart is more than ever quickened and sanctified. Thus we gradually ascend from the lowest point of communion to its higher stages, till we gradually attain that state of inspiration in which the human will is wholly lost in the divine. Blessed he who has realized this but once in his life-time. . . . Nay, the inspired soul goes further. It does not rest satisfied with having cast off the old and put on the new man; it aspires to put on divinity. With the profoundest reverence, be it said, that it is possible for man, when inspired, to put on God. For then self is completely lost in conscious godliness, and you feel that you can do nothing of yourself, and that all your holy thoughts, words and actions, are only the breathings of the Holy Spirit. So the great prophets of earlier times thought and felt. They felt strong in God's strength and pure in God's purity, and to Him they ascribed all honour and glory."[1]

It is easy to see in the author of this language, so interspersed with ecstatic pictures and ardent invocations recalling the visions of God among the mystics of the Middle Ages, a descendent of that contemplative and exalted race which deified prayer under the name of Brahma and subjected the will of the gods to the incantations of men. It is doubtless true that Keshub avoids falling into Pantheism, which he condemns for having "dishonoured God and ruined man," by sapping the foundations of morality and true religion in Hindu society : " In Pantheism man with all his impurity fancies he is God.

---

1. *Inspiration, a Lecture delivered on the occasion of the Forty-third Anniversary of the Brahmo Somáj*, Calcutta, 1873. The principal sermons and discourses of Keshub have been collected into a volume, which was published in English, at Calcutta, in 1882.

In Theism man is purified and so attuned to the divine will as to become one with it. The Theist's heaven is not absorption into the divine essence, but the Nirwana of *Ahankar* or the annihilation of egotism. In the highest state of inspiration, man's only creed is: 'Lord thy will be done!'" Still, it is none the less true that by thus making union with God, through renunciation and ecstacy, man's supreme aim, Keshub furnished a dangerous element to the spirit of asceticism and contemplation, which is so powerful among his fellow countrymen, while at the same time, by his theory of *Adesh*, that is to say direct and special inspiration, he placed the vargaries of the individual mind above the general laws of reason and morality.

The appeal to the sentiments of *bhakti* had unquestionably contributed to the rapid progress of the Bháratbharsia by means of the fervour and persistence with which it fired the adherents of Keshub after their secession from the Adi Somáj. Miss Collet even supposes that it was these sentiments which saved Brahmoism from final dissolution.[1] But confined, like every movement of the sort, within the domain of sentiment and imagination, it was exposed to the danger of over-shooting the mark and of encroaching upon other spheres of activity. In 1874, Keshub called forth the enthusiasm of his friends to such an extent that they remained six hours "in continual communion with God," and were sometimes led to withdraw into solitude, in order to chant the divine name there, with passionate fervour.[2] At the same period he organized a pilgrimage into the Himalaya Mountains with a small company of devotees. They all took up their abode at a romantic spot commanding a vast panorama of snowy peaks, and went out every morning, each in a different direction, to give themselves up to prayer and meditation in solitude; then they met to pray and sing in common, sometimes in a glade or on the slope of a valley, sometimes by the side of a stream or a waterfall.[3]

---

1. *Bramho Year Book* for 1877. One of the first things Keshub took care to do, when he organized the Bháratbharsia Somáj, was to establish, in addition to a theological school, a Sangat sabhá (an association for religious conversation), a Society of Theistic Friends, missionary conferences and other institutions for the cultivation and elevation of the religious sentiment in its various forms.

2. See his essays in the early numbers of the *Indian Mirror*. A part of these articles were republished in 1874, in a small volume entitled: *Essays, Theological and Ethical, from the Indian Mirror*, in which are to be found all the tendencies which subsequently developed themselves in the New Dispensation.

3. *Essays: Theological and Ethical*, p. 147.

Charged, and not unjustly, with fostering the development of asceticism, Keshub defended himself as follows, in a letter to Miss Collet, dated the 10th of December, 1875: "The amount of ascetic self-mortification actually existing among us, has been greatly exaggerated. If you come and see us as we are, you will be surprised to find how little we possess of that sort of asceticism, which has caused so much anxiety and fear in the hearts of English friends. If we were like the Roman Catholics or Indian Hermits, the sharp criticism called forth would have been deserved. But my asceticism is not what is generally accepted as such. . . . Energy, philanthropy, meditation, work, self-sacrifice, intellectual culture, domestic and social love, all these are united in my asceticism. Why, then, you may ask, this special outburst of ascetic zeal at this time? It is needed. That is my explanation. Providence has pointed out this remedy for many of the besetting evils of the Somáj in these days. A like asceticism is needed as an antedote. . . . Do regard it then as a remedy for the time most urgently needed."[1]

Meanwhile, at the commencement of 1876, the movement assumed a still more pronounced character, under the form of *bairágya* (renunciation), with a view, as it was said, to facilitate the removal of those obstacles which the carnal passions offer to moral and religious progress. Its members were divided into four sections or orders: *yoga* (communion with God); *bhakti* (love of God); *gyan* (researches for God); *shaba* (service of humanity).[2] Each of these four classes com-

---

1. *Brahmo Year Book* for 1877, page 22.

2. Here is a specimen of what was taught in the *yoga* section; it will be clear from this that what Keshub understood by asceticism is rather pure mysticism. "O you learner of *yoga*, know that true communion is not possible unless thou dost draw within thyself wholly. All thy senses, nay thy whole being must be absorbed in the profound contemplation of the object of thy yoga. Yet thou shalt not always tarry within thyself. There must be the reverse process of coming from within to the world outside. . . . True yoga is therefore like a circle. It is a wheel continually revolving from the inner to the outer. From the outer it goes to the inner again. As the yoga advances, the gyrations become more rapid and frequent, till the distance and difference between the inner and the outer become continually less. Forms grow formless, and formlessness shapes itself into forms. In matter the spirit is beheld; in spirit matter is transformed. In the glorious sun, the glory of glories is beheld. In the serene moon, the serenity of all serenities fills the soul. In the loud thunder, the might of the Lord is heard from afar. All things are full of Him. The yoga opens his eye, lo! He is without. The yoga closes his eye, lo! He is within. Thy yoga, O disciple, will then become complete. Do thou always strive after that completeness."—*Yoga Teachings*. (*Brahmo Year Book* for 1877.)

prised two grades of membership: the initiated or novice *(sadhac)*, and the advanced or superior *(sibha)*; this last position gave to those possessing it a special authority over their co-religionists: "There will henceforth be a difference between you and those who surround you," said Keshub to the superior order. "The divine light will come by your intervention, and they will have to receive it from you." This is an illustration of how, in forms of faith originally the least dogmatic and ritualistic, there arises that distinction between clergy and laity, which ultimately engenders sacerdotal theocracies, if nothing occurs to arrest its complete development.

A proof of the danger which now threatened the Brahmo Somáj of India, is to be found in the fact that the first two orders in which the contemplative prevailed, immediately absorbed all the activity of the congregation, to the detriment of philosophical or literary studies and of the institutions designed to promote social reform. In 1876, for instance, Keshub breaks off his jubilee lectures and passes the greater part of his time in a garden in the environs of Calcutta, giving himself up to contemplation and prayer with his principal disciples, all of them being seated for hours together in the shade of trees on mats or tigers' skins. In a number of the *Theistic Quarterly*, in 1877, Protâb Chunder Mozoumdar—who shared, it may be remarked, the tendencies of Keshub—complains of the neglect in which his coadjutors were beginning to leave the useful elements of life, thought and sentiment, introduced by Western influence. In his report of the following year, he mentions with regret that the schools of the Bháratbharsia Somáj were in a state of decay. In 1877, the Brahmo Niketan[1] had to be closed, and some months later the normal school for girls which Keshub had founded saw itself deprived of the Government grant on the ground of its inefficiency.

There were certainly some few sober spirits in the congregation at Calcutta, who raised a protest against this sad tendency; but all they gained by their opposition was a charge of lukewarmness and jealousy. Several years earlier, indeed, the enemies of Keshub taking note of his doctrine of great men, and also of the display of veneration which in Eastern fashion he received from a part of his followers, had accused him of wishing to resuscitate the theory of Avatars to his own advan-

---

1. A sort of model boarding house, organized by Keshub, in 1873, for the use of Brahmoistic students.

tage. But the very exaggeration of this reproach had contributed to strengthen his influence in Calcutta, as well as in the provinces, and he seemed to personify Brahmoism more than ever, when, at the end of 1877, the news that he was going to marry his daughter to the Mahârâjah of Couch-Behâr fell like a thunder-clap upon the Brahmo Somâj.

Couch-Behâr is a tributary state of the Anglo-Indian Empire, situated in the north of Bengal, at the foot of the Himalaya, with an area of 1292 square miles, and a population of 532,000 souls. Its ruler, who was still a minor, had received a liberal education, which had more or less freed him from the prejudices of religion and of caste. It was hoped, therefore, that this union, while it increased the moral power of Keshub, would at length gain over the young Prince to the doctrines of Brahmoism, if indeed it did not lead some day to his playing the part of a second Constantine in his dominions.

Still the news of this marriage was far from meeting with a favourable reception from all sections of the Brahmos. The Rajah was but fifteen years old and his bride only thirteen, that is to say neither of them had reached the age required by the "Native Marriage Act," and it was urged that Keshub had been one of the first to demand that Act with a view to prevent premature marriages. As a matter of fact, the law was applicable neither to Couch-Behâr nor to the person of its sovereign. Still, was this any reason for not respecting a legal arrangement, whose introduction into Anglo-Indian rule had been regarded as one of the most important social achievements of Brahmoism? Then again, if the marriage was not to be celebrated according to the requirements of the "Native Marriage Act," there remained but the use of the Hindu ritual, more or less freed from its Polytheistic formulas, or of that employed in the Adi Somâj, and it must not be forgotten that the latter ritual, besides containing several ceremonies opposed to the spirit of neo-Brahmoism, left the door open to polygamy and other abuses. If the young Rajah was a genuine Brahmo why did he not make the "Native Marriage Act" binding in his dominions, and why did he not wait a year longer in order to marry according to the principles of his co-religionists, after attaining the matrimonial majority prescribed by the new law?

Keshub Chunder Sen, who had entered into communication with the Deputy-Commissioner of Couch-Behâr, an English functionary, acting as guardian to the young prince, at first made his consent dependent upon the following conditions:—(1) That the Mahârâjah should adhere explicitly to Brahmoism; (2) That the marriage should be celebrated according to the rites of the Bhâratbharsia Somâj, with the simple addition of such local and traditional ceremonies as might be deemed necessary, provided that they did not imply any idolatrous practice; (3) that the solemnization of the marriage should be deferred till the bride and bridegroom had attained their matrimonial majority. On the first two points he obtained all the assurances he desired; but with regard to the third, he was told by the Anglo-Indian Government that as the Rajah had formed the project of an approaching journey to England, it was absolutely necessary that he should be married before carrying out this intention. At last, therefore, he yielded and, on the 9th of February, 1878, the *Indian Mirror* of Calcutta contained an official announcement that the marriage would be celebrated at Couch-Behâr in the early days of March.

Protestations immediately began to shower down upon Keshub. In the course of eight days, he received no less than forty-four; one was signed by twenty-three of his principal followers in the capital, another by the students of Calcutta, and a third by Brahmoist ladies, while at least thirty came from various provincial congregations. Meanwhile a committee was formed in the Calcutta congregation to watch over the interests of the Brahmo Somâj during the crisis. This committee at once called several meetings at the Town Hall, one of which, composed of at least 3000 persons, according to the *Indian Daily News*, formally condemned the marriage project, adding, by means of a resolution, carried by a large majority: "That the Secretary of the Brahmo Somâj of India by countenancing this marriage, and by the utter disregard he has shown of the strong expression of Brahmo public opinion on the subject, has forfeited his claims to the confidence of the Brahmo community." The day before this meeting, Keshub had set out for Couch-Behâr with his daughter and a large party of friends.

His position was even more delicate and difficult than it was thought to be at Calcutta. There existed at the Court of Couch-Behâr, as indeed in the majority of the native Principalities, two parties: a party of reform, more or less directly encouraged by the English Government which was carrying on the administration during the minority of the sovereign, and the orthodox party, openly supported by the Princesses of the Royal House, the Ranies. When the preliminary festivities had already lasted five days, the mother and grandmother of the young prince declared, at the instigation of their pandits, that Keshub having lost his caste, could not be present within the sacred enclosure at the nuptual ceremony; that only Brahmans wearing the symbolic cord would be allowed to take part in the service; that all the expressions introduced into the Marriage Service by the Brahmos, including the passage relative to the consent of the bride, would be cut out; and finally that the married couple would have to celebrate the Hom or Homa, the sacrifice of fire. These claims were communicated to Keshub during the evening of the 4th of March.

All the following day was spent in vainly attempting to bring about a compromise. In order not to interrupt the regular course of the arrangements, Keshub had already given over his daughter to the attendants whose duty it was to convey her to the Ranies; when driven, however, to extremities by the demands of the pandits, he declared he would rather break off the marriage than yield to such conditions, whatever scandal might be the result. But they told him this was too late, and that his daughter would not be given back to him, unless he consented to pay the expenses of all the preliminary festivities—a lac-and-a-half of rupees, or fifteen thousand pounds sterling. For a short time he adhered to his refusal, but his friends calmed him, and, thanks to the intervention of the Deputy-Commissioner, an arrangement was concluded on the following basis: The bride was to be led to the altar by her uncle, Krishna Bihari Sen, a Brahmo who had not lost his caste; the ceremony originally agreed upon in the stipulations for the marriage was to be followed; the young wife was then to retire, and the Homa to be celebrated in the presence of the young Rajah alone.

It was two o'clock in the morning before this compromise was settled and the negotiations had lasted from day-break the previous morning. Both parties betook themselves at once to the court of honour, which had been prepared for the ceremony. The Brahmos, however, who had been solemnly promised that no idolatrous symbol should be introduced, were disagreeably surprised to find there certain objects of an equivocal form, such as jars of water half covered over with banana leaves, and above all, two kinds of pillars about a yard-

and-a-half high, enveloped in red cloth covers. These were probably images of Hari and of Gouri, the patron or tutelary divinities of Hindu marriages, whom there had been found means of inviting *incognito* to the wedding. Meanwhile the Deputy-Commissioner calmed the suspicions of the Brahmos, as well as he could, and the ceremony proceeded without a hitch till the moment when the friends of Keshub began to recite the prayers of their liturgy. Then there arose a clamour which drowned their voices, and it was in the private apartments of the Prince that the exchange of vows had to be made, a feature of the ceremony specially disagreeable to the Hindus of the old traditional school.

A week later the young Mahârâjah set out for Calcutta, in order to embark there for Europe. This journey, which was about to compromise his caste privileges, caused the orthodox of Couch-Behâr a feeling of perhaps even greater pain than his marriage with the daughter of a Brahmo. A despatch published by the *Indian Mirror* of the 13th of March, states that on the announcement of his departure, the Ranies, maddened with grief, struck their heads against the walls till they bled profusely, and that the prince had to take refuge against their lamentations in the residence of the Deputy-Commissioner, without even venturing to bid them good-bye.

Here is a passage from a petition which these princesses addressed at that time to the Commissioner of Couch-Behâr: "We are helpless, weak women, you are wise and powerful. The honour and prestige of our family is entrusted to your hands. We, therefore, repeatedly pray that you will not, during the minority of the Mahârâja, and in opposition to the wishes of all, send him to England. The Mahârâja's servants have all fled; his Brahmin (cook) refuses to go and we cannot get another (to serve him). If you are not averse to a matter so destructive to our caste and religion, then we request that you will at once send this petition to His Honour, the Lieutenant-Governor. When our caste and religion are about to go and this life and future life are both in peril, we are prepared to send this petition of powerless and unsupported women to the bright throne of Srimati, the Empress of India." It should be added that the other relatives of the Rajah had even declined to be present at his marriage.[1]

---

1. *Brahmo Year Book* for 1878, pages 9—68.

All these incidents, however trivial and futile they may appear to us at a distance, will not astonish those who reflect upon the profoundly conventional nature of ancient Hindu society, and the dissolving influence exerted upon it by its sudden contract with European civilization. When we bear in mind, indeed, the obstacles, if not the ill-feeling, which mixed unions encounter, even in countries where civil marriage is a legal institution, we cannot be surprised at the importance attached to the least formality calculated to determine whether this princely union should be regarded as a Hindu or a Brahmoist marriage. Nor will anyone be astonished to learn that the Orthodox and the Reformers were alike disappointed by the result. The adherents of Hinduism complained that certain essential formulas of their liturgy had been omitted to satisfy the claims of a heretical creed; on the other hand the Brahmos were aggrieved that a premature marriage had been sanctioned, a compromise made with the spirit of caste, and idolatrous rites permitted at the ceremony.

Now in my opinion the conduct of Keshub should not be judged too severely in this matter; for he struggled as best he could, though unsuccessfully, to maintain the integrity of his Brahmoist principles. He even succeeded in his desire that the marriage should not be consummated before the return of the Maharajah from his trip to England, and when this took place the young couple were re-united at Calcutta according to the ritual of the Brahmos.[1] Still it cannot be denied that Keshub failed in loyalty to his own principles, and in cases where a simple follower might be excused for yielding to the pressure of circumstances, a leader is expected to adopt a more uncompromising position. He who would exercise a religious or political ascendency over his fellows must make it his first care to shape his private life to his public career, his acts to his teachings.

By violating in his own family the rules he had laid down for the use of others, the reformer who had separated himself from the Adi Somaj with so much *éclat*, because it was not sufficiently free from Hindu prejudices and traditions, had committed one of those incon-

---

1. *Brahmo Year Book* for 1881, page 76. The London *Truth*, of Dec. 22nd, 1883, states that "the young Rajah who has just attained his majority, is one of the most popular men in Calcutta, and his bright intelligent face is to be seen at social gatherings of every description. The Maharani is a charming little woman, who knows how to receive her guests with a grace and an ease of manners that might be envied by many an Eastern hostess."

sistent acts which even necessity does not suffice to justify; and the matter was made worse when, to defend himself from the attacks with which he was assailed, he entrenched himself behind the famous doctrine of Adesh, affirming that he had followed the direct inspiration of God. Strange as this defence was, no one, even among his adversaries, called in question his sincerity, which is certainly one of the highest tributes of respect that could have been paid to his character. But his very sincerity merely served to give prominence to the dangers of such a system and to show the necessity for its open repudiation.

Of the fifty-seven Somâjes which expressed an opinion on this subject, fifty censured Keshub's conduct and twenty-six of them demanded his immediate deposition from office. Finally, on the 21st of March, 1878, at the close of a meeting which Keshub had himself called, the Brahmos of Calcutta passed a resolution declaring "That in the opinion of this meeting he cannot continue in the office of the minister." But he contested the validity of this decision under the pretext of irregularity in the voting, and when on the following Sunday his opponents sought to take possession of the Mandir or Church, he succeeded in repulsing them by calling in the aid of the police.

The dissentients consequently resolved to secede from the Bhâratbharsia Somâj, and to form a new organization, the Sâdhâran Somâj or Universal Church. On the 15th of May the basis of the movement was agreed upon in the following terms, by a meeting of more than four hundred Brahmos:—"We believe that faith in a Supreme Being, and in existence after death, is natural to man; we regard the relation between God and man to be direct and immediate; we do not believe in the infallibility of any man or of any scripture; whatever books contain truths calculated to enoble the soul or elevate the character, is a Brahmo scripture; and whoever teaches such truths is his teacher and his guide. We regard the fourfold culture of man's intellect, conscience, affections and devotion as equally important and equally necessary for his salvation. . . . We look upon the enjoyment of uncontrolled authority by a single individual in any religious community as a calamity, and far from looking upon freedom of thought as reprehensible, we consider it as a safeguard against corruption and degeneracy. We regard the belief in an individual being a way to salvation, or a link between God and man, as a belief unworthy of a Theist and those who hold such a belief, as unworthy of the Brahmo name. We consider it to be blasphemy and an insult to the Majesty of heaven to claim divine inspiration for any act opposed to the dictates of reason, truth and morality."

By the end of September the work of the Provisional Committee was finished, and the Sâdhâran Somâj assumed a definitive constitution, with the double character of being a Brahmo congregation in Calcutta and of forming a centre for affiliated provincial congregations. Besides, the entire organization was formed on the model of the Bhâratbharsia Somâj, except that it entrusted the ultimate direction of its affairs to a committee of forty members, chosen directly by the General Assembly, with an additional delegate from each of the affiliated Somâjes.

The second article of its constitution defined as follows the principles to which its members were called upon to subscribe : (1) The existence of an infinite Creator ; (2) the immortality of the soul ; (3) the duty and the necessity of rendering a spiritual worship to God ; (4) the rejection of the belief that salvation is to be obtained by the intervention of a book or the aid of infallible men.[1]

On the 22nd of January, 1881, the members of the Sâdhâran Somâj solemnly inaugurated their worship at the vast mandir they had built for themselves, in Cornwallis-street, Calcutta. The congregation met at dawn, in their temporary place of worship, where, after prayers, the pandit Sevanâth Sâstri reminded them how they must sing the name of God in the streets, without making a parade of it. This introductory service being over, the congregation betook themselves to the new church, in procession, singing suitable hymns as they went. As they proceeded their numbers increased so much that, to use the language of an eye-witness, the procession formed "a sea of uncovered heads surging slowly onwards." From 1,200 to 1,500 were constantly present at the devotional exercises and the ceremonies of inauguration, which extended over two entire days.[2]

The reader will be able to judge from all this how far the members of the Sâdhâran Somâj merit the appellation of *Secular* Brahmos, which Keshub's friends have contemptuously styled them. On the

---

1. *The New Dispensation and the Sâdhâran Brahmo Somâj*, by the pandit Sevanâth Sâstri. Madras, 1881. P. 90.
2. *The Brahmo Year Book* for 1881.

contrary, indeed, it is they who represent the genuine idea of Brahmoism in all its integrity. It is but just to add, moreover, that they have already reproduced or developed the principal agencies of reform which had grouped themselves around the Bháratbharsia Somáj. These consist of schools and colleges for both sexes, libraries, *sanghat sabhás*, missions and lectures, philanthropical societies, journals in several languages, associations of women, &c. In relation to the emancipation of women, they are even in advance of the Bháratbharsia Somáj, which while demanding for young girls the advantages of a complete education, does not, however, go so far as to grant them the freedom of action which characterizes Western civilization.[1] Finally, they completely organized, as we have seen, the principle of self-government in the affairs of the Church.

---

1. Savanûth Sástri. *Op. Cit.* Page 74.

CHAPTER XIV.

THE SYNCRETISM OF THE NEW DISPENSATION.

Increasing influence of Keshub among his followers after the secession of the dissentients—Am I an inspired prophet?—India asks: Who is Christ?—The motherhood of God—Proclamation of the New Dispensation—Borrowings from the rites and symbols of Hinduism—Invocation of Hari—The sacrifice of Homa—Mystic dances—Keshub's judgment of Hinduism—Extension of his syncretism to the doctrines and practices of other religions—The Eucharist and Baptism in the New Dispensation—Ecclesiastical vows—Borrowings from the Religion of Humanity—Communion of saints and subjective pilgrimages—The theatre of the New Dispensation—Keshub as a juggler—Criticisms urged against his mixed system of rites—Max Müller's Letter to the *Times*—Keshub's death on the 6th of January, 1884—Keshub's religious ideal and the doctrine of Adesh—The true scope of his syncretism—Antecedents and future of his attempt.

Whilst the Sâdhâran Somâj was thus taking in hand the cause of true Brahmoism, the mother Church continued to develop itself in the opposite direction. As was to be expected, the secession of those who were hostile to Keshub resulted in an increase of his ascendancy over the minds of the Brahmos who remained faithful to him, while it, at the same time, permitted him to follow out his mystic tendencies without any counteracting influence. During the whole of 1879, he never ceased to urge, both in his sermons and in his principal organ, the *Indian Mirror*, that he had been favoured with special divine inspiration. Taking up in a direct way the thorny question: Am I an inspired prophet?—in his anniversary address on the 22nd of January, he did not hesitate to range himself among the sinners rather than among the saints of the world, and to speak of himself as being unworthy to touch the shoes of the last of the prophets: but at the same time he described himself as an "extraordinary" man, invested with a divine mission and favoured by mysterious communications with the ancient prophets, and even with God himself. "The Lord said I was to have no doctrine, no creed," he added, "but a perennial and perpetual inspiration from heaven."

On the 9th of April he gave a lecture in English at the Calcutta Town Hall, under the title—India asks: Who is Christ? This left an impression upon certain of his audience that he was shortly

T

about to become a convert to Christianity, or at least to a sort of Hindu Arianism. In fact, however, if he declared, on that occasion, his acceptance of Christ, it was—as he distinctly added—in the spirit of the Hindu scriptures, that is in harmony with the eclectic principle which makes of Christ a great religious reformer, but refuses to give him the absolute pre-eminence and the unique mission ascribed to him by the Christian sects. "In Christ you see," he continued, "true Pantheism. . . . Behold Christ comes to us as an Asiatic in race, as a Hindu in faith, as a kinsman and a brother, and he demands your heart's affection. Will you not give him your affection? . . . For Christ is a true Yogi, and he will merely help us to realize our national ideal of a Yogi." In the month of September he instituted an order of religious teachers, in which he enrolled himself with Protâb Chunder Mozoumdar and three missionaries. The distinctive badge of the brotherhood was a dress of yellow cloth, known in India by the name of *gairic bastra*.

Some time afterwards, Keshub solemnly proclaimed the "Motherhood of God," as an idea correlative with that of the divine Fatherhood. "Many are ready to worship me as their Father," he makes the Divinity say. "But they know not that I am their Mother, too, tender, indulgent, forbearing and forgiving. Ye shall go forth from village to village, singing my mercies and proclaiming unto all men that I am India's Mother."[1] As a result of this, a band of twenty-five persons, among whom were nine missionaries, quitted Calcutta on the 24th of October, and travelled over about 250 miles in five weeks, preaching everywhere the Motherhood of God.[2]

Meanwhile, as early as the month of November, the *Indian Mirror*, the official organ of the Somâj, announced for an early date, one of those special manifestations of the divine will, such as the world receives every time it feels the need of them, and, it was added, that Keshub would be "a part, a large part, the central part" of this manifestation. As a matter of fact, the manifestation, in question, took place on the 22nd of January, 1880, when Keshub announced *urbi et orbi* the birth of a child destined to receive the heritage of every revelation and every religion. The child was the Nava Bidhân

---

1. *Indian Mirror* of the 12th of October, 1879.
2. *Brahmo Year Book* for 1880.

(the New Dispensation), which claims to be a fusion or rather a synthesis of every form of faith.

It should be noted that Brahmoism has always aimed at the establishment of a universal worship with principles common to every religion. The Brahma Dharma claims, in a certain sense, to form the residuum which persists, after the gradual elemination of everything contradictory and consequently false, in special systems of religious belief. Wholly different from this eclecticism is the attitude of the New Dispensation: it virtually contends, not that there is truth in all religions but that every religion is true.[1] Keshub compares it, in turn, to the thread which holds together the pearls of a necklace, to the ray of light in which the colours of the prism are blended, to the symphony produced by an accord of musical instruments, and to the dissolving chemical which reduces all bodies to a single substance.[2] Protáb Chunder Mozoumdar further explains, that it really is a question of a Dispensation, since in common with all religion it is a gift of God—and of a New Dispensation—not that it had created new truths, but because it presents in a new light the truths partially proclaimed in other religions.[3]

All religious practices, rites, ceremonies, and even all the pretended revelations, possess an analogous value in this conception, so far as they serve for symbols, means, or agencies in the soul's effort to rise towards God: the devotees of Chaitanya, for instance, delight to sing hymns in honour of Hari (he who blots out sin), a personification of Vishnu. Very well, then! Keshub will go through town and country and sing the praises of Hari, with banners, trumpets, and cymbals, whilst the crowd prostrate themselves on his way, and, with their heads in the dust, cry, "*Hari, Hari, bol!*" The old Aryans, again, and the Agnihotri Brahmans of to-day delight in the special sacrifices to Agni, "the resplendent God of Fire;" hence Keshub will celebrate the *Homa* by ostentatiously pouring clarified butter on the flame of the

---

1. *Sunday Mirror* of October the 3rd, 1881.
2. *We Apostles of the New Dispensation.* Calcutta, 1881.
3. *Theistic Quarterly Review* of January, 1881. Here, moreover, is the programme which Keshub assigns to his new creation, in the first number of his organ, *The New Dispensation*. "One God, one scripture, one Church. Eternal progress of the soul. Communion of prophets and saints. Fatherhood and Motherhood of God; brotherhood of man and sisterhood of woman. Harmony of knowledge and holiness, love and work, Yoga and asceticism in their highest development. Loyalty to the Sovereign."—(*The New Dispensation* of March the 24th, 1881.)

sanctuary.[1] And further, in the worship of Vishnu, the Hindus are accustomed to perform mystic dances before their idols: Keshub will therefore organise a ceremony in which young men, dressed in garments of different colours, will dance in concentric circles around the "Invisible Mother," within the mandir, and he himself will set them an example by dancing before his vêdi (pulpit), as David did formerly before the Ark.[1]

Does it follow, as some have maintained, that Keshub thus effected a return to Hinduism? To assert this is to misunderstand the thought which dictated his bearing toward the faith of his fathers. Here, indeed, is a passage from an article in which he made a special effort to demonstrate that there is something in Hinduism which is neither to be despised nor rejected:—

"Hindu idolatry is not to be altogether overlooked or rejected. As we explained some time ago, it represents millions of broken fragments of God. Collect them together and you get the indivisible Divinity. . . . We have found out that every idol worshipped by the Hindus represents an attribute of God, and that each attribute is called by a different name. The believer in the New Dispensation is required to worship God as the possessor of all those attributes, represented by the Hindu as innumerable as three-hundred-and-thirty millions. To believe in an undivided God without reference to those aspects of his nature, is to believe in an abstract God, and it would lead us to practical Rationalism and Infidelity. Nor can we worship the same God with the same attribute investing Him. That would make our worship dull, lifeless, and insipid. If we are to worship Him, we should worship him in all his manifestations. Hence we should contemplate Him with these numerous attributes. We shall name one attribute, Sârasvatê, another Lakshmi, another Mahadeva, another Yagadhatri, &c., and worship God each day under a new name, that is to say, in a new aspect. We do not worship Him as Yogi for ever, or as Father or as Mother, or as Lakshmi, or as Sârasvatê. But now the one and then the other, and so on, beholding our Hari in a new garb and in new holiness for ever. How bewitching the prospect, how grand the picture!"—(Quoted from an article *The Philosophy of Idol Worship*, in the *Sunday Mirror* of the 1st of August, 1880.)

---

1. See a curious description of this ceremony in *The Brahmo Year Book* for 1881.

This conception is doubtless perfectly reconcilable with Hinduism, for Vishnu expressed himself long since in these eclectic terms: Those who, full of faith, worship other divinities honour me also, although apart from the ancient ordinance; for it is I who receive and preside over all sacrifices. Only they do not know me in my true nature.

But the originality of the New Dispensation consists in the fact that its syncretism overleaps the limits of Hindu creeds, to place in juxta-position with them the beliefs and ceremonies held and practised by all the other religions, beginning with Christianity. Even at the time of his visit to Birmingham in 1870, Keshub took occasion to state to the representatives of the different sects, who were discounting his speedy conversion to Christianity: "I wish to say I have not come to England as one who has yet to find Christ. When the Roman Catholic, the Protestant, the Unitarian, the Trinitarian, the Broad Church, the Low Church and the High Church all come round me and offer me their respective Christs, I desire to say to one and all: Think you that I have no Christ within me? Though an Indian, I can still humbly say: Thank God that I have my Christ." It is no matter for surprise, therefore, that like Mohammed, he should have accepted Christ as one of the prophets of the New Dispensation, and that he should have paid considerable attention to the principal rites of Christianity in his liturgy, notably to those of Baptism and the Lord's Supper. It should be added, however, that he baptized in the name of the Vedāntine Trinity as well as in that of the Christian Trinity, and, as to the Eucharist, he administered it by means of rice and water.

The description of these ceremonies shows clearly the amount of freedom with which Keshub treated the rites he drew from other faiths to enrich his liturgy.[1] I shall confine myself to the reproduction of the story of his own baptism "in the waters of the Jordan," from *The New Dispensation* of the 16th of June.[1]

His followers being told that they had to reach the banks of the Jordan, betook themselves in procession to a tank or pond situate on some property which belonged to him. The banks were decorated with foliage and flowers; the flag of the New Dispensation was floating in

---

1. Sivanāth Sāstri, *The New Dispensation and the Sādhāran Brahmo Somáj*, pages 56 and *seq.*

the wind. When they had all taken a place on the steps of the reservoir, in the broiling sun, the minister, seated on a tiger's skin, addressed the following prayer to the great Varuna, the Source of Life:

"O thou great Varuna, Water of Life! Sacred Water, mighty expanse of Seas and Oceans and Rivers we glorify thee. Thou art not God but the Lord is in thee. Thou art full of the beauty and glory of Heaven; each drop revealeth the Divine face. Thou art the Water of Life. A most helpful friend art thou unto us. From the clouds above thou comest in copious showers to quench the thirst of the parched earth, and to fertilize its soil. Thou fillest rivers, seas, and oceans. Thou causest the dry earth to become fruitful and thou producest plentiful harvests, fruits and corn in abundance for our nourishment. O friend of the human race, thou satisfiest our hunger, thou appeasest our thirst. Thou cleansest our body and our home, and washest away filth and impurity. O thou great Purifier, thou healest disease and thou givest health. Cooler and comforter, daily we bathe in thee and feel refreshed and comforted. Ships, freighted with riches, float upon thy bosom and bring us affluence from distant shores. O serene pacifier, thou extinguishest all agony and refreshest the troubled head. O true friend and benefactor, our venerable ancestors loved thee, and honoured thee, and adored thee. And to-day, as in days gone by, the Ganges, the Jamouna, the Narmadá, the Godáveri, the Kaveri, the Krishna, and all the sacred streams in the land, are greatly revered by the people. Say, mighty Varuna, didst thou not suggest to Buddha the idea of Nirwâna, O thou extinguisher of the fire of all pain and discomfort. And Jesus, too, magnified thee, and he praised thee as none ever did before. For he saw and found in thee new life and salvation. In the holy Jordan was the Son of God baptized. We praise thee, we bless thee, Holy Water! Rain and river, lakes, seas, and oceans, we bless and magnify thee!"

Keshub then read the chapter in which the Evangelist Matthew describes the baptism of Jesus. Having done this he explained that Jesus desired to be baptized "because the water was full of God;" then anointing himself with a delicate oil, he walked down the steps of the reservoir, praying as he went in a loud voice, and immersed himself three times up to the neck, saying successively: "Glory be to the Father, to the Son and to the Holy Ghost." After this, in order to specially honour the Trinity, he plunged a fourth time into the water, uttering the words: "Blessed be Sacchidânanda" (the Vêdántine Trinity, Truth, Wisdom and Joy). He then left the water, but not till he had filled a vase that was handed to him. This water he used to sprinkle the heads of his followers, crying as he did so: "*Sânti!*" (peace), "*Sânti! Sânti!*" While he was changing his clothes, a part also of the audience bathed in the reservoir; then all withdrew, carrying away the Water of Peace (Sântijal), in earthen or metal vessels. In the afternoon the women and children did the same.

A few days later Keshub's organ, *The New Dispensation*, insisted upon the essentially independent and original character of this ceremony. "There was no mimicry," said the writer, "no vulgar or mechanical imitation of Europeanism or of foreign Christianity. The whole thing was a Hindu festival."

It is from the Roman Church that Keshub seems to have borrowed the solemn vows of chastity and poverty, which on several occasions he caused his missionaries to take, appearing however to assign to them only a temporary and partial character. He drew from every source, even going so far, it would appear, as to borrow from Comte, whom he seems to have imitated in making a distinction between an abstract form of worship and one of a concrete kind for every day of the year, the former addressing itself to general truths and social aggregates, the latter to persons considered as types. Thus the *Brahmo Pocket Almanac* for 1883, assigns respectively to each day of the week, a double religious purpose, which is indicated by the following arrangement:—

"I. HARMONY OF THE PROPHETS.—Monday is dedicated to the Rishis; Tuesday to Chaitanya; Wednesday to Moses; Thursday to Socrates; Friday to Buddha; Saturday to men of learning; Sunday to Jesus Christ.

"II. ORDER OF DUTIES.—Monday is dedicated to the family and to children; Tuesday to servants; Wednesday to benefactors; Thursday to enemies; Friday to the inferior creatures; Saturday to the poor; Sunday to the holy dead.

In the same order of ideas we find what Keshub termed the "communion of saints," which is one of his most curious creations, and was conceived of and carried out in the following manner: The pious Brahmos choose some celebrated historical personage—Moses, Mohammed, Socrates, Chaitanya, Theodore Parker, &c., and during a week they occupy themselves exclusively in the study of his works or in meditating upon his career. This done, they meet in a place transformed for the occasion into some noted locality in Palestine, Greece, Arabia, or America. There the prophet or philosopher is invoked in imagination: an attempt is made to recall the conditions and surroundings of his life; a conversation is entered upon respecting the true sense of his teaching; and finally opinions are expressed as to what he would say and do if living in our day. These are what Keshub called subjective pilgrimages.

"We have been asked," he says, "to explain what we mean by these pilgrimages. They are simply a practical application of this principle of subjectivity which characterizes the New Dispensation. As pilgrims we approach the great saints, killing the distance of time and space. We enter into them and they enter us. In our souls we cherish them and we imbibe their character and principles. We are above the popular error that materializes the spirits of the departed saints and clothes them again with the flesh and the bones which they have for ever cast away. Nor do we hold these spirits to be omnipresent. We believe they still exist; but where they are we cannot tell. Wherever they may be, it is possible for us earthly pilgrims, if we are only men of faith and prayer, to realize them in consciousness. If they are not personally present with us, they may be spiritually drawn into our life and character. They may be made to live and grow in us."

The founder of the New Dispensation called even the theatre into requisition, by organizing at Calcutta the representation of a drama, entitled "The Harmony of Religions," which was due to the pen of one of his followers. Keshub himself appeared on the scene as a juggler.[1] Among other "tricks" which he performed before the public, was that of the instantaneous fusion of a cross, a crescent, the *Om* (the sacred symbol of the Védântines), the trident of Siva and the Khunti of the Vishnuites into a single symbol. Another feat consisted in showing the body of a bird, taken to represent the sacred dove which "descended from heaven eighteen centuries ago, and has been struck down to-day by the blows of human reason." Suddenly,

---

1. *Brahmo Year-Book* for 1882, page 56.

the dead bird disappeared, and a living bird came down, as from heaven, bearing on its neck a card or ticket, with this inscription :— *Narva Bidhāner jai, Satya Dharma Samanvaia* ("Victory to the New Dispensation! Let there be a harmony of all religions.")[1]

All this exuberance of symbolism greatly shocked not only the Brahmoists of the old school, who had passed their life in combatting the rites and ceremonies of idolatry, but also the Hindus and the orthodox Christians, who were scandalized by this eccentric use and, in a sense, parody of their most sacred ceremonies. In England, above all, Keshub brought about the final alienation of those who had formerly felt the warmest sympathy with his movement, among whom Miss Collet may be specially mentioned. Max Müller and Dean Stanley, perhaps, stood alone in asking the public to be on their guard against any hasty condemnation of a movement which it was very difficult, they urged, to judge of impartially at a distance. "It is the old story over again," wrote the eminent Indianist of Oxford, to *The Times* of the 24th of March, 1880. "Nothing is so difficult for a reformer, particularly for a religious reformer, as not to allow the incense offered by his followers to darken his mental vision, and not

---

1. The hymns of the New Dispensation reveal the same mystic eclecticism. Here is a specimen of them, "The Mystic Dance," borrowed from *The New Dispensation* of the 24th of March, 1881 :—" Chanting the name of Hari, the saints in heaven dance. My Gouranga (Chaitanya) dances amid a band of devotees : how beautiful his eyes which shower love! Jesus dances; Moses dances with hands upraised; Devarshi Nárad dances, playing on the harp. Old King David dances, and with him Janak and Yudhisthir. The great Yogi Mahádeo dances in joy, and with him dances John, accompanied by his disciples. Nának and Prahlád dance ; dances Nityánanda ; and in their midst dance Paul and Mohammed. Dhruba dances ; Suk dances ; dances Haridás ; and in their company dance all the servants of the Lord. Sankar and Wásudeb dance—Rám and Sákya, Muni, Yogis, devotees, ascetics, workers and wise men. Dádu and Confucius dance—Kabir and Toolsy ; Hindus and Mussulmans dance, on their lips the smile of love. The sinner dances; the saint dances; the poor and the rich dance together; the women sing 'Glory, glory,' with sweet voices. Renouncing the pride of caste and rank, the Brahmin and the Chandál dance embracing each other. Surrounded by saints, in the centre is Sri Hari, the Lord of all, and all dance unitedly, with hands round each other's neck. And in this holy company dance the believers in the New Dispensation, killing the distance of space and time. The fishes dance in the sea, and the fowls in the air; and the trees and plants dance, their branches sporting with the wind. The Bible and the Védas dance together with the Bhagavat ; the Purán and the Koran dance, joined in love. The scientist and the ascetic and the poet dance, inebriated with the new wine of the New Dispensation. The world below and the world above dance, chanting the name of Hari, as they hear the sweet Gospel of the New Dispensation."

to mistake the divine accents of truth for a voice wafted from the clouds. In this respect, Keshub Chunder Sen has shared in the weakness of older prophets; but let us not forget that he possesses also a large share of their strength and virtue. . . . His utterances of late have shown signs, I am sorry to say, of an overwrought brain and of an over-sensitive heart. He sometimes seems on the verge of very madness of faith. But I fear for his health and his head far more than for his heart, and I should deeply regret if any harsh words from those who ought to know best how to make allowance for the difficulties and dangers of all religious reformers should embitter a noble life already full of many bitternesses."

The eminent sanscrit scholar divined but too truly what was about to take place. So great was the spiritual exaltation of Keshub's life, that it could not fail to rapidly wear out his exceptionally nervous organization, and as early as 1882 he suffered from the first attacks of the malady which suddenly became more acute in the autumn of 1883, and carried him off on the 6th of the following January, when he had but just entered upon his forty-fifth year. Among the last persons who had an opportunity of conversing with him on his sick bed, were, by a strange and significant coincidence, the venerable Debendra Nâth Tâgore, the Anglican Bishop of Calcutta, and the Hindu Paramhansa of Dakhinaswar, that is to say the principal representatives of the three great religions which he had specially attempted to fuse together in the New Dispensation.

His death was regarded throughout India as a national misfortune. The entire press of England as well as of India, spoke in sympathetic terms of the high moral character and the eminent services of the deceased. At the same time expressions of condolence were received from all parts of the country and even from Europe. Queen Victoria, for instance, telegraphed to the family an expression of her sympathy and regret. Even the Sâdhâran Somâj, putting aside its hostile opinions, passed a resolution in acknowledgment of the long and faithful services rendered by the deceased to the cause of the Brahmo Somâj. Finally, the students of Calcutta met and decided to commence a subscription in order to raise a monument to his memory.

The second day after death, the body, which was literally hidden by flowers, was carried on a bier to the place of cremation on the banks of the Ganges. The banner of the New Dispensation was borne at the head of the procession, and behind the corpse there was a vast crowd who joined in singing the hymn: "*Jai, jai, Satchita Nandun jai,*" (Glory to him who has a pure heart.) The bier was placed on a pile of sandal-wood, whilst the Upadhyâyâ chanted the mantras of the Brahmoist ritual. As the orb of day was sinking beneath the horizon, the eldest son of the deceased, Karvuna Chunder Sen, placed the torch to the funeral pile, pronouncing these words: " In the name of God I convey the sacred fire to these last remains. Let the mortal part burn and perish; the immortal part will survive. O Lord, the liberated soul rejoices in thee, in thy blessed abode." The flame then rose in the quiet evening air, whilst all present repeated the verse: "Glory to the Redeemer who is Truth, Wisdom and Joy. Divine grace alone prevails. Peace! *(sânti),* Peace! Peace!" By about eleven o'clock, all was over. The ashes of the late minister were placed in an urn and carried provisionally to the Chapel adjoining Lily Cottage.

Is the day come for justly estimating Keshub's work? For my own part, I do not hesitate to assert that the path upon which he had entered was full of equivocal positions and dangers. With the tendency of the Hindu sects to deify their *gurus*, it is quite possible that the founder of the New Dispensation may be raised to the dignity of an Avatar, and his Church become a simple variety of the Vishnu sects. All those who have studied the past of India know, as M. A. Barth has so well said, that the history of religious reforms among the Hindus, is a story of perpetual and painful re-commencement. Vigorous efforts and high purpose mark the early stages, which are soon followed by irremedial decay; while the final result is another sect and a new superstition.[1]

Already, indeed, certain of the ceremonies which Keshub introduced into his Church have proved how much his teaching tended to develope the spirit of contemplation and renunciation, which has always been a scourge for India; whilst others were but regrettable landmarks along the road which leads to the creation of theocracies. And further, it is very clear that the excess of his symbolism was calculated to absorb the activity of his disciples in a multitude of odd and heterogenous rites, absolutely at variance with the requirements of the modern spirit, if we take up the European stand-point.

---

1. A. Barth, *Les Religions de l'Inde.*

But regard must be had to the external circumstances under which a religious reform is carried on. It remains to be seen, therefore, whether the New Dispensation, with all its mystic and ritualistic exaggerations, is not better fitted to act upon the popular mind of India, than the sober and more enlightened faith of the Adi or even of the Sâdhâran Somáj.

Keshub, and this point cannot be too strongly emphasized, was, in spite of his errors and eccentricities, a person of superior power, one of those men who may become a Buddha, a Mohammed, or a Luther, according to the nature of their surroundings. To have seen him or even to have taken note of his work, was sufficient to explain the ascendancy he possessed over his followers, and which he also exercised upon the minds of the masses. On more than one occasion, I have severely condemned his acts, and almost despaired of his future. But whenever I turned to his discourses and writings, I again felt in some measure under the charm which arose from his personalty and genius.

The following *critique* of Keshub's character by one of his principal opponents, Sivanáth Sástri, the missionary of the Sádháran Somáj, will probably not be without interest:—" Throughout his career, Mr. Sen has been distinguished for three things: a proud and indomitable spirit, a fine and powerful intellect, and a strong and vigorous will. . . . Added to these, there is an earnest, fervid, and enthusiastic temperament. . . . Like every other proud nature, he is shy to strangers, but full of pleasant humour to friends, mild and affable to inferiors, but haughty and untractable to the least show of superiority in others, and specially under opposition, conceiving his plans in silence and carrying them out with but half-revealed purpose. He does not condescend to take into his confidence even his immediate associates about his plans, and has no friend properly so-called. He is not altogether above the art of over-reaching an enemy by clever shifts or of trying to compromise him by unfair and ungenerous means. At times he is carried away by his wounded pride to use harsh and abusive epithets against his opponents. Yet he has been an example to many of us of purity of private conduct, earnestness of purpose and of devotedness to noble pursuits. Many of his ways have been certainly those of a man of faith, and many of the principles of action he enunciated for his Church show considerable depth of spiritual insight and keenness of moral perception. . . . But Mr. Sen has, in the meantime, allowed himself to be led astray by an unfortunate idea—the idea of being a singularly inspired man."[1]

It is incontestable that the religious ideal which Keshub set before his disciples lacks neither in opportuneness nor in elevation. He formulated it himself, in a somewhat eccentric fashion, by making the subjoined parallel between the old and new man, which was published in the second number of his journal, *The New Dispensation:*—

"THE OLD MAN.	"THE NEW MAN.
Asiatic or European.	Asiatic and European.
Hindu or Christian.	Hindu and Christian.
Mystical recluse and sleepy Quietist.	Mystical philanthropist and practical Quietist.
Trinitarian, who hates Unitarian.	Unitarian, who believes in the trinity of Unitarian manifestations.
Sectarian, who excludes all other sects.	Eclectic, who includes all sects.
Mechanical combination of truths and characters by the intellect.	Chemical fusion in life.
Exceptional inspiration.	Universal inspiration.
Believes in invisible spirit or visible idols.	Beholds the Spirit-God.
Honours Christ, but reviles Socrates and Chaitanya.	Honours all prophets in Christ.
Sees multiplicity and confusion.	Sees unity and harmony.
Destructive.	Constructive.
Sees only errors in others, and frets.	Sees only their virtues, and improves.
Decrepit and cold."	Always fresh and young."

The really questionable feature of the New Dispensation is the doctrine of Adesh. When, in accordance with the doctrine of Kant, we seek the voice of God in the intuitions of conscience, we are simply acting upon an ennobling and fruitful theory, as evidenced by the American Transcendentalists. Still it must be on the condition

---

1. *The New Dispensation and the Sádáran Brahmo Somáj*, page 58.

that we subject our impulses to the control of observation and reason. Keshub, in truth, seemed to admit that in order to constitute Adesh, inspiration must be based upon certain "objective considerations," resulting from some particular set of circumstances and leading to the same conclusion. As regards the marriage of his daughter, for instance, these were: the political necessities of Couch-Behar; the personal merits of the young Mâhârajah; the advantages to Brahmoism which were likely to result from this union, &c. But if objective indications are to concur with inspiration, to determine any given line of conduct, what purpose is served by the Adesh? And if they do not thus concur, what is to decide between them? To see the dangers of this system, it suffices to listen to the extreme champions of the New Dispensation, such as the Pandit Dourgâ Dâs Rây, who, in urging the uncertain and relative character of the moral laws, denies to conscience the right to decide in matters of inspiration, and declares that the commands of God are independent of the "so-called common morality,"[1] or further, like the writers of the *Theistic Record* of Dacca, who expressed themselves thus in 1881: "Nothing with a Brahmo is 'good' which is not a command of God, and nothing is His command unless every man receives it directly from Him. We have no scripture, no revelation, no Shastrâ, no Véda, save His words: every little thing of our life—whether we should eat pumpkins on the first day of the month or go towards the north on a Tuesday—should be regulated by His living command. Here then is something peculiar, something new. We Brahmos have to go to God for every trifle that we do, while people of other religions have books, men and their own conscience for their guides."[2] This is the stumbling-block at which the New Dispensation will fall and be dashed to pieces, if the most enlightened of Keshub's followers do not, now their leader is gone, hasten to correct his theory of Adesh, by restricting it on the one hand to super-sensible things which transcend experience, while extending it on the other, in a certain measure, to the whole human race, and subordinating it to the authority of reason, which is also of divine origin.

With the exception of this unfortunate theory which is not, indeed, an essential element of the New Dispensation, Keshub does not

---

1. *Brahmo Year-Book* for 1880, page 100.
2. *Brahmo Year-Book* for 1881, page 95.

appear to have abandoned the Rationalistic method in spite of his exaggerated mysticism. Among the ceremonies and discourses to which I have alluded, there are certain details which may provoke a smile, as does the language of all religious and social symbolism of an unfamiliar character. Then again, it seems to me that the excess of ritualism has proved obnoxious, above all in England, to persons who from education and surroundings feel a profound repugnance for everything that savours of a sacerdotal or even of a sacramental order. It is but just to remark, however, that such is by no means the characteristic of the rites originated or reproduced by Keshub. He has told us so himself in formal terms :—" Do we mean to establish the Rice Ceremony (the Sacrament of Communion) and the Flag Ceremony as permanent institutions in our Church? No. They are meant to explain and spiritualize and fulfil corresponding ordinances in the older Churches. As the pulpit of the New Dispensation expounds texts in the ancient Scriptures, so are these novel ceremonies offered as practical sermons on the deep philosophy of the rites observed in previous dispensations."[1]

. Nor can Keshub be charged even with having aimed at the establishment of an esoteric form of faith, to be allegorically interpreted by its adepts and accepted literally by the crowd. He let no opportunity pass, indeed, of explaining the real significance of his symbolism. " We do not believe," he added, in the article from which I have just quoted, "in lifeless ceremonies. Read *absorption* in place of 'rice,' and the *kingdom of God* in lieu of 'banner,' and our metaphors will become clear."

We have already seen the meaning he attached to his celebration of baptism and to his communion of saints. When celebrating the *Arati* according to the rites of the Vishnuites and the Sikhs, he was accustomed to place on the altar the traditional *panchadripa* (a lamp with five branches which the devotees are in the habit of swinging before their idol), and he would explain it, at once, as the symbol of the five inner lights which permit the worshipper to rise to the contemplation of the divine countenance : purity, love, faith, *bhakti*, and knowledge. As to the sacrifice of the *Homa*, Protâb Chunder Mozoumdar thus reveals to us its significance: "The recent Hom ceremony performed by the minister and missionaries of the Brahmo

---

1. The second number of *The New Dispensation*, 31st of March, 1881.

Somáj of India, represents only the idea of burning the passions in effigy. The bundle of dry hard sticks represented the lusts of the flesh tied to the heart by a knot which cannot be loosened, each passion strengthening the neighbouring ones, and all of them together forming a mass of impenetrable obstruction to piety and holiness, able to resist strong and repeated attempts to break through. Nothing but fire can destroy such a heap of tough unbreakable wood. That fire is the fire of holy will, kindled and breathed upon by the Spirit of the eternal fire of holiness. The wind and clarified butter that aid the flame are our prayers and aspirations, the great aid of a pure human will."[1]

We may not care for allegories, nor, speaking generally, for symbolism at all; but in this respect the New Dispensation does not differ from an institution which is most extended and most popular in all Anglo-Saxon countries: Freemasonry, which also symbolizes by external rites the traditions of its history and the principles of its humanitarian philosophy.

And if the ceremonies instituted by Keshub, instead of being drawn from a single system of religion, are borrowed indifferently from all, is there any ground for blaming him in this which is, in reality, a pledge and a proof of toleration? The fusion of all the forms of faith into a single religious synthesis, has been, in every age, the dream of many a large and enlightened mind in advance of its time. Aristotle, Cleanthes, Seneca, Maximus of Tyre, Confucius, Kabir, the neo-Platonists, the Authors of the Upanishads, the Sofis of Persia, as well as German Idealists and the contemporary students of comparative theology, have all shown the identity of the religious sentiment under the multiplicity of its manifestations. A few thinkers such as Proclus, Jambilicus and Alexander Severus in antiquity, Akbar in India during the Middle Ages, and, to a certain extent, Auguste Comte in our own day, have even attempted to found a universal religion—not, indeed, by eliminating the differential elements of the principal forms of faith, after the manner of English Theism and American Transcendentalism—but by commingling either the rites and symbols or the names and forms under which their adherents conceived the Supreme object of worship.

Such, too, was the work commenced by Keshub, and if there is

---

[1]. *The Theistic Review and Interpreter* of 1881, page 15.

any difference, it is that the author of the New Dispensation succeeded in founding a religion, while his predecessors scarcely did more than carry their syncretism beyond the sphere of individual conception. Roman Polytheism stands alone, perhaps, as the only instance of an ultimate amalgamation of this kind; but even in that case, it was a juxta-position, rather than a synthesis of the various forms of religion practised in the Empire. It was reserved for the New Dispensation to offer us a living Church formed, as a single conception, with materials drawn from the most diverse faiths, and this is not one of the characteristics which contribute least to render its development so interesting to all who are engaged in the study of religious history.

CHAPTER XV.

BRAHMOISM AND THE RELIGIOUS FUTURE OF INDIA.

Present strength and ramifications of Brahmoism—Dayánanda Sarasvati Sivámi and the Védántine movement of the Arya Somájes—The Theosophic Society of India—Orthodox Associations of the Dharma Sabhás—Religious movements beyond the pale of Hinduism—The Anjumans—The Guru Jurgi among the Bhils—Disintegration of Hinduism: What will take its place?—Condition and prospects of Islamism in India—Negative result of Christian missions—Parallel of religious progress between the Aryans of the East and of the West—Satisfaction offered by Brahmoism to the aspirations of the Hindu mind and the requirements of modern civilization—Affinity of Hindu speculation to our most recent scientific theories—The idea of the Unknowable in Brahmoism—Re-action of Oriental genius upon the religious culture of Western society—Professor Tyndall's prediction to Protáb Chunder Mozoumdar—Max Müller and Von Hartmann's opinions as to the influence which the beliefs of India are destined to exercise on the religious future of the West.

It was to be feared that the divisions of Brahmoism would prove fatal to the cause of religious Rationalism in India. From the inevitable confusion of such schisms, more than one superficial observer has come to the conclusion that the work of Rám Mohun Roy is about to disappear by the return of some to the bosom of Hinduism, and the conversion of others to European scepticism. Isolated cases may have justified this double prediction; but the signs of disorganization have been of short duration, and to-day, Brahmoism has resumed its former progressive course. In 1877, on the eve of the secession of the Sádháran Somáj, its Churches were 107 in number. To-day they exceed 173;[1] and its journals or periodical publications have increased by ten within the same period.[2]

---

1. *Brahmo Year Book* for 1872. It must be borne in mind, however, that some of these new Somájes are due to schisms in the old congregations, as a result of the events of 1878.

2. Taking into account the entire number, there are seventeen printed in Bengali; four in English; one in both these languages; one in Urdu; one in Canara; two in both Tamoul and English; two in Telugu and English; and one in English and Marathi. A single one of these organs appears daily: the *National Paper* of Calcutta; and eight are weekly. Among the monthly publications in Bengali, there is one for women, another for workmen, and a third, which is illustrated, for the use of children. (See the *Brahmo Year Book* for 1882.)

The Brahmos may be divided at present into four groups:

I. The Somájes which have accepted the New Dispensation. They consist of about twenty of the old congregations which remained faithful to Keshub, together with a certain number of recent formation. Some of these Somájes vie with the Calcutta congregation in their life and fervour. This is specially true of that at Dacca, which is distinguished by the number and originality of its publications; that of Chittagong, which has become a centre of active proselytism among the masses of the people; and that of Bhagalpour, where the new mandir bears on its facade both a cross and a crescent, interwoven with symbolic representations belonging to Buddhism and to the various Hindu faiths. At Calcutta, too, Keshub attracted larger and larger numbers down to the close of his work.[1] Meanwhile, and it is a happy augury, there is a new growth of the institutions designed to promote educational and social reform, which were more or less neglected for several years. The principal educational establishment, the Albert School, which was affiliated to the University of Calcutta in 1881, contained at that date 667 pupils. The Indian Reform Association has laid the foundations of an Institution for the superior education of women, which was opened in 1883. *The Indian Mirror* has been replaced by a journal that is better edited, *The Liberal*, with a supplement devoted exclusively to religious questions.

II. The congregations which constitute the Sádháran Somáj. This association represents, as we have seen, the true tradition of Brahmoism, and it has taken up, as a part of its work, all the institutions intended to promote religious and social reform, which had long been the monopoly of the Bháratbharsia Somáj. The Somájes which it comprises within its pale are twenty-nine in number. Its principal organ in the English language is *The Brahmo Public Opinion*, which discusses, from an elevated stand-point, religious and political questions relating to India. The President of the Association is a contemporary and friend of Rám Mohun Roy, the Babu Chib Chunder Seb.

III. The Adi Somáj. One result of the crisis described in the previous chapter, has been to recall public attention to the Adi Somáj of Debendrá Náth Tágore. This latter, who could hardly have imagined a more striking form of revenge in relation to Keshub Chunder Sen,

---

[1]. *Brahmo Year Book* for 1881, page 11.

spontaneously approached the Sâdhâran Somâj, and in 1880, the oldest Church of Brahmoism was seen joining with the youngest to celebrate in a fitting manner the fiftieth anniversary of the Rajah Râm Mohun Roy. It is now several years since the venerable Debendrâ Nâth Tâgore withdrew to the Himalaya Mountains, where he enjoys well-earned repose. From time to time he quits his retreat in order to preside over certain religious ceremonies in neighbouring Somâjes, and he is always welcomed with sympathy and respect by both the old and new Brahmos. His successor in the presidency of the Association is the Babu Raj Narain Bose, a speaker and writer of great merit, who has been engaged since 1880 in the publication of the complete works of Râm Mohun Roy in the English Language.[1] The Adi Somâj professes the same religious principles as the Sâdhâran Somâj; but it maintains a certain reserve as to the abandonment of ancient social usages.[1]

IV. A certain number of congregations which share the religious opinions of the Sâdhâran Somâj, but have remained on good terms with the New Dispensation, since they have refused to take sides with either of the two groups and have welcomed with the same heartiness missionaries from both.[2]

V. The Prârthanâs Somâjes (Associations for Prayer) of Eastern India. These are, generally speaking, congregations which, while they wholly reject the authority of the Vêdas, display a conservative tendency both as to doctrines and ceremonies. The chief of them, the Prârthanâ Somâj of Bombay, has even inscribed over the door of its place of worship, the celebrated motto of the Vêdântine Pantheism: *Ekam eva advitijam* (a single Being without a second.)[3] The same state of things is to be met with in some of the Somâjes of the South, as for example at Madras, where the Brahmo Somâj of Southern India, while treating Brahmoism as a simple form of universal religion, yet considers it to be the logical development of Hinduism, and chooses its devotional readings exclusively from the Hindu Scriptures.[4]

Finally, these 173 associations form so many centres for the spiritual

---

1. The first volume, which is the only one that has yet appeared, is in 8vo., and consists of 816 pages.
2. *Brahmo Year Book* for 1880, page 120.
3. Monier Williams, *Hinduism*, page 150.
4. *Brahmo Year Book* for 1882, page 56.

regeneration of India, and though they may differ as to questions of form and method, and even of principle, they none the less represent, as a whole, the power of religious Rationalism among the Hindus.[1]

Still, Brahmoism does not figure as the only agency of reform which is exciting the attention of the populations of Hindustan. "Ramifications of this sect and kindred sects moving in a parallel direction," recently wrote Sir Richard Temple, "have spread through the three Presidencies of Bengal, Madras and Bombay."[2]

In addition to the groups which have taken up a Rationalistic stand-point, there have been formed in several localities, and particularly in the Punjaub, what are called Arya Somájes, whose members have adhered to that phase of Vedaic infallibility, which was given up

---

[1]. It may be well to note here one or two points, which will bring the history of the Brahmo movement down to a later date than that referred to in the text. To begin with the New Dispensation Church at Calcutta : After the death of Chunder Sen, a schism took place among his immediate followers, owing to the determined opposition of the majority of his missionaries to Protáb Chunder Mozoumdar's desire to occupy the deceased minister's pulpit. Three of these missionaries and the majority of the congregation sided with him, but the opposition party prevailed and, after more than a year's interval, a compromise was arrived at which was, in reality, destructive of Mozoumdar's claim, the pulpit being left vacant in memory of Keshub.

Happily a feeling of reconciliation between the different sections of the Brahmo Church is manifesting itself. It may be mentioned in illustration of this, that Mozoumdar has advanced nearer to the Sádhárán Somáj, and even took part in their anniversary services last January (1885) for the first time. There has been, indeed, as I learn from Miss Collet, a gradual tendency during the last two or three years towards the healing of the divisions caused by the Couch-Behár and New Dispensation schism. At Lahore and Madras, for instance, the two severed Somájes have been re-united, while in several other towns where the rival Somájes have not officially coalesced, the feeling between them has become far more friendly. This desirable change would seem to be in some measure the result of Chunder Sen's death, for he forbade his missionaries to preach at Somájes which had protested against his New Dispensation—a prohibition which has since been relaxed.

At present the state of the Brahmo Somáj generally is fairly prosperous, and the Sádhárán Somáj is doing extremely well. The number of registered members belonging to the latter in January, 1885, was 829, while the aggregate number of Brahmos belonging to the different sections of the Church is estimated at about 4,000. These belong to or form over 190 different Somájes in various parts of India. Over forty journals are now edited by Brahmos, and are, more or less, devoted to the advocacy of their principles. Hence, though the number of avowed adherents of the Brahmo Church may seem small in comparison with the vast population of India, it must not be forgotten that many a Somáj is a centre of life and light in its own locality, so that the magnitude of the movement is not to be estimated by mere statistics. Besides, there is evidently a strong under-current of interest flowing on in the minds of many unavowed adherents. Signs of this have been frequent in the history of the movement, and they were not lacking at the

more than thirty-five years ago by Debendrâ Nâth Tâgore and the Adi Somâj. These associations, which claim to occupy the platform of Revelation while they reject Polytheism, are due to the initiative of a Brahman of the Guzerat, Dayânanda Sarasvatî Sivâmî, who for several years travelled through India from North to South and preached a purely spiritual worship, founded on the existence of one God, the maintenance of the doctrine of metempsychosis and the infallibility of the four Vêdas.[3] Mr. H. G. Keene stated, in an article in *The Calcutta Review* of April, 1879, that the Arya Somâj was gradually extending in India and had connected itself with a Theosophic Society imported from the United States.

There exists at New York, an association which, under the title of The Theosophical Society, claims to be in possession of profound

meetings held at the beginning of the present year (1885) to celebrate the fifty-fifth anniversary of the foundation of the Somâj. Speaking of the meetings in question, the *Indian Messenger* of February 1st says:—" By the grace of God, the fifty-fifth annual festival of the Brahmo Somâj has passed off very successfully. These are occasions when we feel ourselves specially drawn towards God. Every soul turns to Him with great expectancy. Friends meet from all parts of the country, and forgetting all the littlenesses of life, join soul to soul in prayer and thanksgiving to their common Father. What a beautiful sight is this, of hundreds of men and women gathering at a common spiritual feast! Yes, it has been a veritable spiritual feast to us, and the Bread and Water of Life have been freely served by the All-holy Spirit. A blessed spirit of unity and brotherly sympathy pervaded the whole proceedings, and made them really sweet to the soul. We felt our hard hearts melting under the inspiration of the living God; and young and old, men and women, all felt themselves embraced within the loving arms of God."

At one of the meetings on this occasion a lecture was delivered by the pandit Sivanâth Sâstri, on "The New Life and its New Responsibilities," of which the journal just mentioned contains the following very interesting summary:—" The lecturer tried to show that the contact of the East and the West had given birth to a new life, and had called into existence new forces, many of which had been dormant in the race, and some of which had been altogether absent from the constitution of the national mind. Under the operation of the new spirit, time-honoured customs and institutions were fast dissolving, and a rapid process of disintegration was visible on all sides. The new spirit had brought on many changes. Not the least—perhaps the most serious—of them was the decay of the natural spirituality of the race. Our educated young men were becoming secularized in their sympathies and tendencies. They were fast losing the old religious instincts and traditions of their forefathers. This secularization of thought, the lecturer said, was something appalling in its consequences. No one knew whither the rising generation of the educated Indians was drifting. The Brahmo Somâj was doing its best to foster the new spirit, to help in the development of the spirit of liberty which, like a solvent, was slowly doing the work of destruction in the mass of old customs and usages. Consequently it was the duty of the Somâj to infuse spirituality into the minds of the people, which alone could safely conduct liberty to a happy and successful issue. Liberty without moral self-knowledge preserved from ancient times in certain colleges of Tibet. The "brothers," as the initiated are called, state their object to be as follows: (1) The establishment of a universal fraternity; (2) the study of ancient language, science, and religion; (3) the investigation of the hidden mysteries of nature, as well as the psychic forces latent in man. The first and second of these objects form esoteric theosophy, the third constitutes its exoteric form. As regards religion, they reject the doctrine of a Personal God, declare that men ought to consider themselves but a transient effect of a self-existent, universal, and infinite Cause, abandon the supernatural, and take their stand on the ground of pure science. But, at the same time, they admit that together with the facts established by the ordinary processes of observation and induction, there exist phenomena and occult laws, the knowledge of which is only to be obtained by a certain exercise of the will, with contemplation, abstraction, fasting and eastacy.[1]

This doctrine seems to be rather Hindu than American. Hence there is no room for surprise that it should have met with marks of favour among the adherents of Védántism, when in 1879 the Theosophic Society of the United States sent four of its members to India, among whom were Colonel H. Olcott and the Countess Blavatsky.[5]

control and without the operation of the nobler moral and spiritual impulses of the soul, runs to license. But real moral self-control springs from deep spiritual convictions. Hence spirituality is the real legitimate guide of liberty. It was the duty of the Brahmo Somáj to develop this guiding principle."

It will be seen from the foregoing statements and extracts that the great work of the Brahmo Somáj is still silently but surely progressing as a harmonizing and regenerative influence in the midst of the complex forms of Hindu civilization, and that it is at least preparing the way for that new form of faith which will ultimately take the place of the ancient beliefs and superstitions of the country.—*Translator*.

2 "Political Effect of Religious Thought in India," in *The Fortnightly Review* of January, 1883.

3. Monier Williams, *Hinduism*, page 150; Garcin de Tassy, *Revue de la Littérature Hindoustanie*, 1876, page 92, and 1877, page 91.—The Arya Somáj of Lahore, 710 members in 1878 (*Theistic Annual* for 1878).

4. *Hints on Exoteric Theosophy*. Calcutta, 1882. *The Theosophical Society and its Founders*. Bombay, 1882. See also W. C. Fink, *Theosophy, Exoteric and Esoteric*, in *The Calcutta Review* of April, 1883.

5. A notice of a work by this lady, *Isis Devoilée*, which must have been published at New York, informs us that the authoress, who was born in Asia, passed her childhood among the Kalmucks, Tartars, Persians, and other Oriental peoples, and her ripe age with the Hindus, the Tibetans, the Cingalese, and the Egyptians, and that she had thus an opportunity of studying the languages, literatures, traditions and mythologies of Oriental peoples.—Vide *La Revue Politique et Littéraire* of the 24th of November, 1877.

These "missionaries" had assigned to themselves the task of preaching "the majesty and glory of all the ancient religions," as well as that of warning the Hindu, the Cingalese, and the Parsi against the substitution of a new faith for the teachings of the Védàs, the Tri-Pitaka and the Zend Avesta. Their activity was not restricted to India proper, and impartial observers state that in the island of Ceylon they brought back to Buddhism thousands of natives who had been converted to Christianity.[1] The Theosophical Society of India takes the lead in this propagandism to-day, and its organ is *The Theosophist*, which is published in Madras.

It is quite possible there are further movements which might be described, not only in Hinduism but also in the other faiths of India. There have been formed, for instance, at several places and above all among the Brahmans, societies called Dharma Sadhàs (Associations of the Law), whose object is a return to the ritual and traditions of the Védàs. This has the appearance of an orthodox revival; but in point of fact these organizations, as Mr. Barth shows, are the result of the critical spirit, and their aim is to develop sciences which tend to destroy superstition.[2] As much may be said of the Anjumans, semi-literary and semi-religious societies, which have been established among the Mussulman population of India, for the spread of literary and artistic tastes, the cultivation of poetry and the study of the sciences which relate to religion.

Together with every other section of the community, even the non-Aryan and as yet but half civilized populations, are being roused by the need for religious reform. Thus, while one portion of them are gradually abandoning their Fetishistic beliefs to accept Islamism, Catholicism or Hinduism, there has been recently seen to spring up

---

1. Fifty-eighth Annual Report of the British and Foreign Unitarian Association, London, 1883; page 48.—The Buddhist section of the Theosophist Society has recently published a Buddhist Catechism for the use of the Cingalese, with a preface by Colonel Olcott, who says: "There are abundant reasons to believe that of all the great religions of the world Buddhism is destined to be the religion which will be spoken of most in the future, and which will be found to present the least antagonism to nature and law. Who would venture to affirm that Buddhism will not be the religion of the world's ultimate choice?" This Catechism, which is written in Cingalese and English, is invested with the approbation of the High Priest of Sripada. (*Revue de l'Histoire des Religions.* Tome VIII. No. 1. 1883.)

2. A. Barth, *Op. Cit.*, page 62.

among the Bhils, a tribe of the Vindhyas mountains, a guru named Jurgi, who is preaching the existence of but one God, forbidding the use of strong drinks and condemning the destruction of any living creature.[1]

What will be the result of this fermentation of ideas? Hindu Polytheism, though still numbering two hundred millions of adherents, presents unquestionable signs of decay. It is possible, and even probable, that its death agony will be of long duration; but its days are none the less numbered by the progress of civilization. The moment will come therefore when we shall have to face this question, which M. Barth asked without attempting to answer it: "What will be the faith of India when its old religions, which are already condemned to perish but tenaciously cling to life, have been finally swept away?"[2]

Here we must avoid a tendency which is nowhere more calculated to vitiate any estimate we may form of the future. I refer to the unfortunate habit which so often leads us to reason from the particular to the general. Thus, because a native of ability—Dwarka Nath Mitter—had devoted speech and pen to the service of Comtism, it was hastily predicted that India was about to pass at a bound from idolatry to the religion of Comte.[3] In the same way, English Secularists are apt to imagine that India will be an early conquest to their opinions, simply because there exists at Madras a small group of native Free-thinkers, which is affiliated to the National Secular Society. And finally, every time any Christian Church succeeds in making a few converts of higher social standing than usual, it is contended that India is on the eve of embracing that form of Christianity, be it Catholic or Protestant, which the converts have adopted.

It is clear that the various forms of Christianity—and even Comtism and Secularism—are influencing, and will continue to influence, the

---

1. Garcin de Tassy, *Revue de la Littérature Hindoustanie*, 1876, page 92.
2. A. Barth, *Op. Cit.*, page 175.
3. Dwarka Nath Mitter died near Calcutta in 1874. The Positivist Church of London erected a tablet to his memory, with the following inscription:—

"Dwarka Nath Mitter,
1832—1874,
Principilo della Santa Milizia
Nell Oriente."

religious evolution of the Hindu mind; but it is hardly likely that this evolution will borrow from any one of these factors its general and ultimate form.

The introduction of European ideas, by overthrowing the ancient beliefs of India, has produced, in more than one instance, comparative religious indifference, and specially among the literary classes. In some cases, the result is a disdain of the ideal and an exclusive search for material enjoyment, which finds its earlier expression in the materialistic philosophy of the Cārvākas.[1] On the other hand, India has always had a weakness for theories of universal illusion—the Māyā—which are to be met with at the heart of Atheistic as well as Pantheistic conceptions of the world. Hume himself and his existing disciples do not go so far in their philosophic nihilism as the author of the *Byom Sār* and of the *Souni Sār*, the contemporary poet Bhaktāwar. We read in the first of these compositions: "From nothing all things are born; in nothing all things perish. Even the illimitable expanse of sky is all hollowness. What alone has no beginning, nor will ever have an end, and is still of one character, that is vacuum." The *Sourni Sār* is still more explicit: "All that is seen is nothing, and is not really seen. Lord or no Lord, it is all one. Māyā is nothing; Brahm is nothing. All is false and delusive. . . . The teacher is nothing; the disciple nothing; the *ego* and the *non-ego* are alike nothing. The Temple and the God are nought; nought is the worship of nought, and nought the prayer addressed to nought."[2]

The majority, however, of the educated classes have remained profoundly religious at heart and in the tone of their thought. What has been said of the Germans may be said of the Hindus: that even when they profess to be Materialists or Atheists, they still remain Metaphysicians, Idealists, or, in some measure, Mystics. Those who, fascinated by European science, profess to accept one of the systems of thought at present in vogue among us, seem to be specially influenced by the synthetic aspect of its doctrines. Even the Vēdāntine school appears to have been endowed with new life from its contact with European culture,[3] and there is no reason why it should not

---

1. Monier Williams, *Hinduism*, page 225.
2. F. S. Growse, *Mathura, a District Memoir*. Agra, 1874, part I., page 19.
3. See an interesting defence of the Vēdāntine philosophy, published by Prof. Pramadā Dāsa Mittra, in the 10th volume of the *Journal of the Royal Asiatic Society*, 1878.

completely emancipate itself from popular superstitions without losing any of its religious aspirations or even of its mystic tendencies.

It may be asked, therefore, whether the Hindus will not confine themselves to replacing their ancient faith by one or other of the religions which at present exist in India. Let us consider, then, the relative importance of these creeds and their chances of predominance in the future.[1]

The Parsees constitute too small a group for comparison in a consideration of this kind. Besides, the religion of Zoroaster, which is perhaps the oldest in the world, shows no signs of proselytism. The Sikhs, again, are little more than a sect of Hinduism. As to the Buddhists, who also form to-day but a very small minority of the Hindu population, they could only regain an ascendancy by complying with a two-fold condition: on the one hand, a radical reform of the Buddhist Church; on the other, a general development of Pessimist tendencies, of which there are no signs at present.—There remain the religions of the Koran and the Bible.

Islamism numbers fifty millions of adherents in British India, which has led to the statement that England is the first Mussulman power in the world. As the reader may be aware, the followers of Mohammed are divisible to-day into three great sects: the Sunnites, by far the most numerous who render allegiance to the spiritual authority of the Sultan of Constantinople; the Shiites or partisans of Ali, who specially predominate in Persia; and the Wahabis of recent origin, whose principal centre is in Arabia. These sects hold in common: (1) The belief in One God, the Creator and Sustainer of the Universe; (2) the belief in a future life in which the good will be rewarded and the wicked punished; (3) the doctrine of a Divine

---

[1]. Here are, as regards religion, the results of the Decennial Census taken in British India on the 17th of February, 1881, the Independent States being excluded from the computation:—

Hindus (believers in Hinduism)	187,937,450
Mohammedans	50,121,585
Buddhists	3,418,884
Christians (including foreigners)	1,862,634
Sikhs	853,426
Fetishists	6,426,511
Other faiths, or those without any specified religion	4,279,026
Total	254,899,516

Revelation by the intervention of the Prophets, and in the last place of Mohammed—a Revelation, indeed, which relates not only to spiritual matters but to all the forms of human activity; (4) the conviction that the Koran is the literal Word of God.

The Sunnites go so far as to extend the gift of inspiration to the first Caliphs and to the principal doctors of Islam; thus they consider themselves pre-eminently orthodox; they possess, however, a liberal school, the Shafites, who admit the possibility of religious progress, and profess, with regard to unbelievers, a toleration based upon universal morality. The Shiites refuse all special authority to the decisions of the Caliphs who succeeded Mohammed; they proclaim the rights of individual interpretation with regard to the text of the Koran; but they seem less strictly attached to Monotheism, inasmuch as they believe in the personification of the twelve principal divine attributes, and count on the advent of the Messiah. It is from their ranks that the Sofis of Persia have sprung, whose Mystico-Pantheistic doctrine is not without resemblance to the Védántine Philosophy. The Wahabis, who have been called, and not improperly, the Puritans of Islamism, accord authority to nothing beyond the Koran and the utterances of the Prophets; they condemn pilgrimages as well as the worship of saints and holy relics; and their ideal is the return of the Islamic world to the position it occupied at the death of Mohammed.

India scarcely contains more than five millions of Shiites. As to the Wahabis, however small their numbers, they have had more than once to endure the rigours of the English Government in consequence of their fanaticism. Speaking generally, the Islamism of the lower classes is more or less imbued with Hindu superstitions; among the educated Mussulmans, on the other hand, a certain spirit of liberalism prevails, and this has powerfully contributed to the development of the Anjumans. Not only is there to be found among these a most decided taste for the study of the sciences, but also a sincere desire to purify the religion of Mohammed by freeing it from its parasitical excrescences, with a certain religious eclecticism, kept, it is true, within the limits of the sects of Islam. In 1877, for instance, one of the most distinguished Indian Mussulmans, Saïd Ahmed Khan, a former judge at Benares, founded at Aligurth, a large Oriental college for both Shiites and Sunnites. He was followed in this course by the lamented Salar Yung, the Nizam's Minister, who did so much for the moral and material well-being of the kingdom of Hyderabad.[1]

It is difficult to foresee where this movement of intellectual emancipation will end. Islamism has to take but a single step to find itself in full sympathy with the Rationalistic Monotheism of the West. But it could not make this advance, which consists in the rejection of the supernatural origin of the Koran, without losing its distinctive characteristic, and so long as it abstains from taking this step forward, neither persuasion nor force will gain an acceptance for it among the masses of the Hindu people—even though we should be called upon to witness the restoration of a vast Mussulman power in India, as Mr. W. S. Blunt predicts.[2]

Will Christianity be more fortunate? If Christian missionaries were not addicted to hope against all hope, they would have been long since discouraged at the uselessness of a propagandism which, after immense sacrifices and the constant efforts of half a century, has merely resulted in the conversion of a few hundred thousand natives out of a population of two hundred and fifty millions. This unsatisfactory state of things is admitted by the Anglican Bishops of India, in their collective letter to the English Clergy, of May, 1874. "There is nothing," said they, "that can at all warrant the opinion that the heart of the people has been largely touched, or that the conscience of the people has been affected seriously. There is no advance in the direction of faith in Christ; . . . the condition is one rather of stagnation."

This avowal should not surprise us. When the missionaries begin to teach the Hindus the infallibility of the Scriptures, the Divinity of Christ, or the mystery of the Trinity, they either have to address themselves to the Orthodox, who, possessing analogous dogmas in their own theology, see no reason for exchanging them for beliefs which are more unfamiliar to their race, without being more in harmony with their reason; or else they have to deal with Rationalists, who, having outgrown the traditions of Hinduism by means of free inquiry, are anything but disposed to subject themselves to the yoke of a new Revelation. Thus Râm Mohun Roy said that, after giving

---

1. Garcin de Tassy, *Revue de la Litterature Hindoustanie*, Année 1877.
2. W. S. Blunt, *The Future of Islam*. London, Kegan Paul, 1882.

up the belief in a plurality of Gods or Divine Persons, which is held by several sections of Hinduism, he could not conscientiously and logically adopt an analogous system, however purified it might be.

According to writers like Monier Williams and Garcin de Tassy, Indian missionaries, in order to be successful, should be drawn from that enlightened section of the clergy who possess a complete knowledge of the religions which they are called upon to oppose. But it is just here that the difficulty lies, for the moment the missionary acquires a taste for the study of comparative theology, it is no longer, in his eyes, mere Pagan superstition which he subjects to the criterium of scientific methods, and the end is that he who went out to convert others, returns converted himself. As illustrations of this, take the career of Mr. F. W. Newman in Syria, that of Bishop Colenzo among the Caffirs, and that of the Rev. — Adams in India, to mention merely the most noted cases. The only form of Christianity which succeeds in impressing the Hindu is its moral and humanitarian side. But Christianity, reduced to this element, is scarcely represented by any but the modern Unitarians—that is to say, by Brahmoism with an English name.

In perusing the extracts I have given in the course of this work, the reader must have been struck by the resemblance between Brahmoism and liberal Christianity, both in doctrine and history. Certain views of truth which are expressed every day in Unitarian pulpits and in the works of liberal Protestants, might be met with in the utterances of Brahmoists—just as passages are to be found in the publications of the Brahmo Somáj which would do honour to the pen of a Channing or a Parker. When Keshub Chunder Sen, and, at a later time, Protáb Chunder Mozoumdar, preached in certain Unitarian churches of Great Britain, their hearers, as one of them told me himself, might have easily imagined themselves listening to their customary ministers, who had become slightly Orientalized in manner and expression by a long residence on the banks of the Ganges. Doubtless, there is something both impressive and remarkable in this contact of two currents of religious thought which, having originated in Central Asia and moved in opposite directions with the Aryan migrations five or six thousand years ago, are thus meeting on the common ground of an eclectic and rational faith as the result of a like evolution. Still, if this synthetic faith is to spread in India, will it not be in its native form and with its national badge?

Brahmoism has retained the elements which are indispensable for satisfying the traditional exigencies and the characteristic conceptions of the Hindu genius. I shall restrict myself to mentioning, on this head, the importance which it attaches to the divine immanence, to a recognition of the claims of duty towards all living creatures, to the conviction that the struggle for truth and justice is continued after death, and finally to the influence of an element of the religious life which has almost fallen to a minimum in our Western civilization: the love of God.

Whether it be a question of the Adi Somâj, the Sâdhâran Somâj, or of the New Dispensation, there is unanimity of opinion on this last point. Here is a passage from a somewhat interesting pamphlet dedicated to the English Unitarians by the existing President of the Adi Somâj, Raj Narain Bose, "in the hope of aiding them in some measure, to give to their Church a tone more in harmony with the spirit of Theism:"

"If I were to describe Theism in one word, it would be the word love. Theism can be divided into—firstly, a belief in the love of God to his creatures; secondly, our love of God; thirdly, doing the work he loves. It was love that created the world. God wanted to diffuse happiness to other beings and he created the world. It is God's love that still preserves the world. It is love of God to man that makes him take personal interest in him. It is love of God to man that entitles him to the appellations of Father and Friend. It is the love of God to man that makes him near and easily accessible to man. It is the love of God to man that leads him to grant prayers and reveal religious truth to him. It is the love of God to man that leads him to promote the progress of his soul in a future state. It is an instinctive love of God that first draws man towards God. It is like the love of the new born insect for the honey in the flower, which it has not yet tasted. It is love of God that makes man perform the works which God loves. Morality is nothing but love. What does morality say? Morality says love your neighbours, love your country, love the world, love the right. Love also implies knowledge. As we cannot love a friend if we do not know his merits, so if we do not know the perfections of God, which constitute his lovliness, how can we love him? If we do not know what is right, how can we love the right? All religion, therefore, is included in the word love. What is leading a religious life, but leading a life of love, thinking love, speaking love, diffusing an atmosphere of love around us?"[1]

The Constitution of the Prârthanâ Somâj of Surat declares that religion consists of devotion *(bhakti)*, in union with morality *(niti)* and love *(prem)*. It adds, moreover, that devotion is a combination of faith *(crâddhâ)*, contemplation *(prâsanâ)*, and virtuous conduct *(sadâchâr)*.[2]

Even the Sâdhâran Somâj, though due to a re-action against the mystical excesses of Keshub, asserts that "the way to salvation is not through Pantheism, which regards sin and misery as delusions; not through Asceticism, which aspires to uproot the desires and subjugate the body; but through love, which teaches the soul to seek the will of the Father as the highest good."[3]

The entire history of the Hindu people bears witness to their invincible repugnance to every form of faith which is not based upon an exalted sentiment of Divine love and upon the possibility of attaining to an intimate communion with God: in other words, upon the *bhakti* and the *yoga*. But if we are to take into account this double tendency when estimating every attempt made to transform the beliefs of India, we must also admit that the spirit of the age lends itself to other methods and processes, even in the matter of religion and on the banks of the Ganges. Christianity, or, if the expression be preferred, the influence of Christian civilization, has developed in India an element which Mohammedanism was unable to create: a need of intellectual and moral activity, which has also its religious side, revealing itself in missionary, moral and philanthropic efforts, but which readily comes into antagonism with the different forms of contemplation and ecstasy. The doctrine most fitted to reconcile these contradictory elements is assuredly that which would have the best chance of acceptance among the Hindus.

---

1. Raj Narain Bose, *The Hindu Theist's Brotherly Gift to English Theists*. Calcutta, 1881, page 16.

2. *Brahmo Year Book* for 1882, page 84.

3. Sivanâth Sâstri, *The New Dispensation and the Sâdhâran Brahmo Somâj*, page 91. See also, on the same subject, an article of the *Brahmo Public Opinion*, reproduced by Miss Collet in her Annual for 1880, page 92.

This is a truth which the different sections of Brahmoism have recognized, with varying degrees of clearness. "Communion *(yoga)*," said *The Brahmo Public Opinion* on the 26th of February, 1880, in an article dealing more or less with the New Dispensation, "sharpens the eyesight of the spirit. Through it we grow familiar with the verities of the spiritual world; through it objects of faith become objects of spiritual perception. But communion, if practised as the only means of spiritual culture, begets moral inanity and deadens the active energies of the soul. Like communion, religious frenzy *(bhakti)* has also its use and its dangers. A state of frenzy can never be the normal condition of the soul. . . . It can be, and often is, induced by purely external and adventitious causes. . . . Besides, there is not much connection between such ecstatic display and real excellence of character. In the spiritual culture of a Brahmo, active and prayerful work should form the ground plan, the other two supplementing it for perfection." "The ultimate object of religion," says another number of the same journal (January 23, 1879), is to be at one with God, not only in sentiment, but in action, too. We are required not merely to worship, but also to serve God. Love is practical in its nature. If genuine, it must come out in action. Love that is not active is no love at all."

It is equally necessary to take into account the changes which the diffusion of Western scientific knowledge will produce in the Hindu mind. Sir H. Sumner Maine said at the University of Calcutta in 1865: "In the fight which the educated Hindu and the Christian missionary wage against error, such success as has been gained, such as will be gained, evidently depends on physical knowledge. . . . Happily some fragment of physical speculation has been built into every false system. Here is the weak point. Its inevitable destruction leaves a breach in the whole fabric, and through that breach the whole armies of truth march in."

The different sections of Brahmos have already had an opportunity of showing, by their educational institutions, how fully they have realized the necessity of founding the regeneration of Modern India on the diffusion of scientific knowledge. The cultivation of science is placed by the Brahmo Dharma in the list of duties towards God, and Keshub himself did not differ on this subject from Parker and Emerson. "A Theist," said he, "must love science with warm and enthusiastic love, for science is God's Scripture, written by his own hand, infallible and sacred."[1]

Up to the present Brahmoism has remained faithful to our spiritual and transcendental Theism. But there is no reason why it should not, in imitation of the Unitarian Church, adapt itself equally well to the ideas which tend to predominate in the philosophy of evolution. It must not be forgotten indeed that all our present systems of thought have their equivalents in the ancient speculations of the Brahmans. Before our era, for instance, the Sânkhya school taught that the universe had arisen by a gradual evolution, from an incoherent, indeterminate and homogenous substance, *Prakriti*, and had differentiated and developed itself by its own inherent forces. This system seems to have been at first Atheistic and Materialistic, and therefore more analogous to the doctrine of Haeckel than to that of Spencer. But the impossibility of explaining the transformation of matter into spirit, led later advocates of this bold speculation to admit the existence of spiritual energies, not to be traced back to the material manifestations of the Prakriti, and which had to be conceived of as uniting with the latter in the evolution of the universe.[2] Then again the difficulty of accounting for the relative and finite without assuming an Absolute substratum led them, as it has led the evolutionists of our epoch, to concede the existence of the Unknowable, the mysterious power from which matter and spirit alike emanate. There is a passage in the Upanishads which describes God as unknown by those who profess to know him, and known only by those who put forward no such claim.[3] A profound remark this, and one which even Herbert Spencer himself would not disavow.

Does it follow that religion and worship disappear with the possibility of defining the Absolute Being? The Brahmos have resolved this problem which is occupying so much attention in Christian society, and have given it the solution which tends to prevail in the most

---

1. *Essays Theological and Ethical*, page 37.

2. *Sânkhya Tatwa Kaumoudi* of Vachaspati Misra commences with these words: "The Pratrika is one; it is self-existent and in a state of equilibrium. It is the source and mother of all life. Souls (puroushas) are multiple, uncreated and associated with matter; after a certain time they quit this material envelope and depart."

3. It was in order to clearly mark the indeterminate nature of the Absolute Being that the Brahmans used the neuter gender in speaking of the Supreme.

advanced liberal Protestantism: "In our religious culture, said the *Brahmo Public Opinion* of the 2nd of January, 1879, we should lay greater stress on the spiritual side of it than on the theological; in other words we should distinguish between knowing God and loving God. All our attempts to know God, to divine and explain his purposes, to fathom the depths of his wisdom and goodness, are vain and fruitless. But we can always approach him from the side of love. Love is life; this is rigorously true for our spiritual life. It is, moreover, the Key of Paradise."

Doubtless, it is impossible to state with certainty that Brahmoism under one or other of its forms, is destined to become the future religion of India, or even that it is the approaching faith of the enlightened Hindus, as Sir Richard Temple, one of those best acquainted with the country, has recently said of it.[1] But what may be affirmed, as it seems to me, is: first that the reform of Hinduism will come, not from without but from within; and further, that of all the religious movements observable in India, Brahmoism is the one which seems to most closely correspond with the present direction of Hindu thought.

After having thus considered the influence which European thought has been able to exert on the beliefs of India, it would be of interest to inquire, both as regards the present and the future, whether the genius of India is not destined, in its turn, to re-act upon the philosophical and religious ideas of the Western world.

It is only by way of suggestion that I refer here to individual conversions of Europeans to the faiths of India. More frequent than might be supposed, on *a priori* grounds, they none the less form the exception.[2] Nor shall I dwell upon the modifications which the direct

---

1. *Fortnightly Review* of January, 1883.

2. Garcin de Tassy, who kept an account of these "perversions," as he called them, mentions the occurrence of seven in 1874 and of nine during 1875; among others he refers to the case of an English captain, who had adopted the Mussulman faith at Bangalore. He also speaks of a young Englishman who had become a Yogui and had placed himself under the spiritual direction of the officiating minister of the Hindu Temple at Mount Jago. (*Revue de la Littérature Hindoustanie* for 1874, 1875, 1876.) Less calculated to arrest public attention, but more significant and more numerous are the conversions to the philosophical ideas of India. Speaking from personal experience, I may mention the case of two English officials whose hospitality I shared during my journeys through the interior. Alike

and continued contact of native ideas cannot fail to produce on the religious convictions of enlightened and independent minds. But when the problem is considered from a more general point of view, it becomes apparent that even to-day the influence of the two countries has been reciprocal; and if we see in Brahmoism the Hindu equivalent of the views in favour among the more advanced minds of the Christian Churches, it would be unjust to under-rate the influence which has been exercised on the latter by the knowledge of the religious and spiritual systems due to the genius of Oriental peoples.

Of all the religious literature of the East, our fathers knew only the rigorously Monotheistic Scriptures of the Semitic peoples—the Bible and the Koran. Suddenly, just where they imagined there was nothing but incoherent superstitions or indecipherable ruins, science began to reveal the profound, consistent, and, in some instances, sublime conceptions of the various systems embodied in the sacred books of the Brahmans, the Buddhists, and the Parsis, as well as among the tablets of Egypt and Babylon. Those who have unexpectedly found themselves in presence of the treasures of the Zend-Avestâ, the Pitakas, and, above all, of the Vêdâs, are alone able to understand, from their own feeling of astonishment and admiration, the importance of the possibly unconscious transformation of thought, which the works of Orientalists have produced upon the intellectual and theological conceptions of Western society. If we have perchance awakened to activity the dogma of Divine transcendence among the Hindu reformers, has not India, on the other hand, aided in bringing before the Monotheists of the West the conception of Divine immanence, which restores God to Nature, or rather Nature to God? Where, in these days, do we find any trace of the cold and abstract Deism of last century, which, after having suppressed miracles, did not know what to do with its Divinity, who was inert and superfluous, having no relation to either nature or humanity? And if, in the majority of modern schools of religious thought, this Deism is replaced by

---

versed in the languages of the country, they had distinguished themselves by profound researches, the one on the Buddhists of the Himalaya and the other on the legend of Krishna. At the time when I made their acquaintance, the former a Protestant by birth, had become a disciple of Schopenhauer, if not of Buddha; the latter, who at first became a convert to Catholicism, had absolutely adopted the Védântine philosophy of the Bhavagad Gîtâ, which he sincerely believed he could reconcile with Catholic theology.

more synthetic and living conceptions, which re-open the fountains of religious emotion while they facilitate the reconciliation, not of science with religion, but of religion with science, is not this change due, in some measure, to that philosophical literature of the East, which is pervaded by so profound a sentiment of close relationship between the three great factors of the religious idea—God, nature and humanity?

Just before leaving Europe on the occasion of his first visit, Protáb Chunder Mozoumdar had a long conversation with Professor Tyndall, who had just shocked orthodox England by his open avowal of religious scepticism at the Belfast meeting of the British Association. "Working in the cold light of the understanding," said the eminent English physicist, "we feel here the want of the fire and vigour of the religious Life. This is all but extinct in England. In saying so, and in not accepting it at the hands of those who have it not, I have become unpopular. Let those who have the Life give it unto us. To you, therefore, in the East we look with real hope. Life came from those regions once before, and it must come again."[1]

I cannot say whether we are to accept this compliment of the English scientist to the Brahmoist reformer in the light of a prediction, but its realization would not surprise those who have studied the present state of India, as well as the general history of religious thought, apart from all sectarian prejudices.

Professor Max Müller has shown in one of his finest works what the religious sentiment of Europe may borrow from India.[2] In a work of a more speculative order, Von Hartmann has gone so far as to predict that the religion of the future will be a Pantheistic Monism, which will borrow the conception of the Divine immanence from India, and that of the Divine unity from the Judeo-Christian tradition. "Viewed from the stand-point of religious history," says he, "the aim we propose to ourselves can only be attained by a synthesis of the development of the Hindu and Judeo-Christian religions, in a form which will unite the advantages of these two tendencies of the human mind, and which, by remedying their mutual defects, will also be able

---

1. Protáb Chunder Mozoumdar, *Missionary Operations in England*, in the *Theistic Annual* for 1875.
2. The conclusion of the lectures on *L' Origine et le Développement de la religion etudiés à la lumiere des religions de l'Inde*, translation by M. J. Darmesteter. Paris, Reinwald, 1879, page 327.

to replace both, and to thus become, in the proper sense of the word, a universal religion. Such a Pantheistic Monism, whose metaphysical foundations are in perfect harmony with reason, would lend itself, in other respects, to the liveliest action on the religious sentiment, and would thus give to morals a solid vantage-ground more nearly allied to what is called religious *truth* than anything to be found in any other system."[1]

This truth Brahmoism thinks it has found, or is at least assured of its discovery, and its various Churches, however divided they may be among themselves, are agreed in accepting the words of Protâb Chunder Mozoumdar, when he says, in his apology for the New Dispensation, "We have not now a doubt in our minds that the religion of the Brahmo Somâj will be the religion of India—yea, of the whole world, and that those who really care for God, for piety, for purity, for human brotherhood, for salvation and for eternal life, will have, in one way or another, under one name or another, to accept the faith and the spirit that a merciful God is perpetually pouring into the constitution of our Church."[2]

Without professing to share this absolute confidence, which is the gift of faith, we may nevertheless come to the general conclusion that, if the Hindu spirit continues to advance along the lines now forming its course, the world will yet witness more than one curious interchange of religious, as well as of moral and scientific ideas, between the two great branches of the Aryan race. Was it not from analogous interchanges between the ancient Pantheism and the Semitic Monotheism in the crucible of Neo-Plationism, that Christianity itself took definite form in the second century of our era? If India helps us to pass through the religious crisis which is now troubling society, and it is perhaps in a condition to do this, it will have deserved well of all those who are interested in the harmonious development of civilization.

---

[1]. Von Hartmann, *La Religion de l'Avenir*, ch. ix. M. von Hartmann has subsequently developed the same idea in his work, *Das Religiöse Bewusstsein der Menscheit im Stufengang seiner Entwickelung*. Berlin, 1882, 1 vol.

[2]. *Brahmo Year Book* for 1881, page 137. Protâb Chunder Mozoumdar visited England again during the summer of 1883, when he preached in several Unitarian Churches with the same acceptance as at the time of his first visit. In truth the position he has taken up belongs less to the New Dispensation than to the general principles of Brahmoism, in other words, to Transcendental Theism.

SUMMARY AND CONCLUSION.

In beginning this work, I at first described how the moral and spiritual emancipation of which Luther gave the signal in his first cry of revolt against Rome, came into collision in England with the popular life of the day, and even with the motives which had led to the reform effected by Henry VIII. I showed in the second place how these obstacles were gradually smoothed away, partly by the natural and legitimate development of the Protestant principle, and partly by the intellectual and political influences at work in secular society. The reader was also enabled to follow the course of that evolution which manifested itself in turn by the progress of religious neutrality in civil legislation, of Rationalism in the prevalent modes of thought, and of liberalism in the constitution of the Churches.

Is it to be inferred that the existence of religion is threatened by this general repudiation of theocracy? I have shown that though certain sects in the Protestant Churches pride themselves on ignoring the discoveries of science and the aspirations of their age, and though others persist in seeking the means of reconciling the data of science with the belief in miracles by means of specious compromises, on the other hand, a large number of religious people and many congregations have been able to meet all the claims of the modern spirit, without breaking the continuity of religious thought. This extension of the theological horizon, which is taking place more or less in all sections of Christendom, open to a modification of their dogmas, is specially manifest in those Churches which rest, not upon uniformity of beliefs, but rather upon identity of sentiment. It is the Unitarian Church which perhaps offers us the most perfect type of the latter condition.

Anglo-Saxon Protestantism might be compared, indeed, to the division of an army which is executing a forward march. Day after day the main body pitch their tents on the very spot occupied by the advanced guard the night before, and this interchange of position is so fully maintained between detachment and detachment that at length the rear-guard takes up the position evacuated by the centre. Each corps loses as a matter of course a few stragglers on the march, and sometimes also a few scouts; but while the latter disappear from the field of battle, the former simply increase the strength of the columns immediately in their rear. Thus the relative positions remain unchanged, although the entire division keeps advancing nearer and nearer its goal.

As we have seen, this progressive movement has not been restricted to the limits of liberal Protestantism, but has manifested itself beyond the pale of Christian communions in a two-fold direction—the one religious the other philosophical.

In the first place, the progressive elimination of dogmatic elements has produced a "free religion" after creating a "free Christianity," on the basis of a distinction between religious sentiment and religious belief, to be henceforth regarded as absolute. Sometimes, as in the case of Mr. Moncure D. Conway's congregation, this radical conception assumes the form of an æsthetic worship rendered to the human ideal. At other times, as among the Free Religious Congregations of the United States, it tends to practical applications and religious reform. Regarding it in this latter aspect, we have stated the results it is attaining, from a theoretical point of view, in the Comtist scheme of worship, as this is organized in London; and from a practical standpoint in the recently-formed "Societies for Ethical Culture" in New York, Chicago and Boston, which are already surrounded with institutions making them true Churches of humanity. It should be remarked, moreover, that when in our day it is a question of carrying out some common philanthropical or moral aim, even the most creed-bound sects put aside their differences in order to unite, not only among themselves, but even with Agnostics and sceptics.

In the second place, the rejection of a supernatural Bible has brought Theists of Christian antecedents into union with the emancipated minds of Jewish and Hindu origin. When it is remembered that this Theism rests on principles long since accepted as the essence of natural religion—in other words, the existence of God, the immortality of the soul, the imperative authority of the moral law and the spiritual value of personal piety, it would appear that we must really have found the final expression of religion, the supreme synthesis of all the reforms carried on in the name of reason and conscience. Thus we can hardly fail to be astonished that only some few isolated congregations, such as Mr. Voysey's in London and Mr. Samuel Johnson's at Lynn, U.S., should have sprung from this school. Nor will this surprise be diminished when it is remembered that Theism, more or less the result of reflection, constitutes to-day the dominant faith of the enlightened classes in England and America.

It is because Theism is above all things a personal faith that we meet with this result. With some, it represents merely the spiritual residuum left after the progressive elimination of orthodox dogmas. With others, it is the direct product of the intuitive method brought to bear upon the materials furnished by consciousness. But in the one case as well as in the other it leads to isolation rather than to religious grouping. As to the Theists who feel the need of spiritual fellowship, they often find sufficient to satisfy this without leaving the historic Church in which they have been brought up, as happens at times among the advanced Unitarians, the liberal Friends, the Reformed Jews, and even with certain sections of the Congregationalists and Presbyterians. It is only in India that pure Theism has produced a whole net-work of fervent congregations; and this result is doubtless as much due to the mystical temperament of the Hindu race as it is to the successive failure of all attempts to regenerate the old native creed.

Transcendental Theism, which seemed about to endow America with a new religion half a century ago, would have merited this brilliant success had it been merely a question of the elevation of its principles and the fruitfulness of its teachings. But, like German Idealism, whose most mystical tendencies it represented, this movement, which Parker and Emerson rendered illustrious, fell a victim to its own excesses the very day it encountered its old adversary, Sensationalism, supported this time by the marvellous discoveries of the positive sciences.

It is difficult to predict where victory will ultimately declare itself, in this conflict between the two philosophies which have always struggled for the mastery in the human mind. Rendered more circumspect by their reciprocal vicissitudes, they both seem to be approaching a common stand-point to-day, possibly with a view to making a permanent compromise, by the adoption of some system which, while it admits that positive knowledge is limited to the phenomenal world, shall proclaim the absolute existence of a transcendent Reality.

This double thesis, it should be added, was long since adopted by Kant, and the success of the works which the centenary of the illustrious German philosopher has called forth, seems to indicate that his school after sustaining, without submission, one of the most violent assaults known to the history of philosophy, is still capable of resuming an ascendency over modern thought, or at least offering a starting point for some new synthesis of the Universe, in conformity with our present scientific knowledge. It is the *Critique of Pure Reason* which directly inspires an influential section of the so-called Agnostic school, and it is perhaps owing to its having sounded in time a retreat upon Kant, that English Theism has not shared the fate of American Transcendentalism.

If we seek to ascertain what modern criticism has not been able to shake in the sphere of the super-sensible, we shall hardly find more than can be summed up in the four following propositions:—

(1) The positive existence of a Supreme Reality which reveals itself in consciousness but which transcends all definition.
(2) Our constant state of dependence upon this Reality, in which we live, move and have our being.
(3) The certainty that this Power manifests its action by fixed and general laws.
(4) A connecting link of some kind between this action and the tendency which prompts us to do our duty.

The reader must not mistake the scope of this enumeration. It assuredly falls far short of the principles generally looked upon as the essence of natural religion. It fails, indeed, in my opinion, to embody all the beliefs which are to be reconciled with the existing affirmations of science. I have not made, for instance, any allusion in it, to the continued existence of the soul, although that hypothesis, as Mr. James Sully formally asserts, has not been rendered untenable by all the attacks of positive science. Even more, it seems difficult to accept the last two propositions without deducing from them, as a corollary, the existence of a mysterious end towards which, not only humanity, but also the whole economy of Nature is tending—whether we employ the term Final Cause or not, to indicate this goal. But I make no claim whatever to utter the last word of science in its bearing on religion ; my object has simply been to summarize the truths relating to a super-sensible order of things, which may be looked upon as generally admitted by contemporary scientists and thinkers in, at least, the Anglo-Saxon world.

Now—apart from the advocates of the old physiological Materialism, who are every day becoming more rare, and the small sceptical school entrenched within the universal Phenominalism of Hume, together with the group of orthodox Positivists who systematically refuse to discuss the question of the Unknowable—it may be affirmed that these four propositions are accepted by all who are in any way capable of exercising an influence on modern culture, from the liberal theologians of the Anglican Church and of the Dissenting sects to the evolutionists in harmony with Spencer and the critical thinkers of the Kantian school. We may see in them, therefore, not the faith of to-morrow, but its first outlines, the indestructible basis of every edifice of religious thought, the crypt, " still so narrow and obscure" in which Professor Max Müller shows us the Hindu, the Buddhist, the Mussulman, the Jew, and the Christian, each bringing the truest and purest elements of his creed to serve as materials for erecting the Church of the future.

Even now, the Churches are not alone in furnishing either materials or workmen for this process of reconstruction. For though in the course of this volume I have been compelled to register the blows dealt by contemporary science at the old mode of argument in support of spiritual religion, I have also been able to relate the happy efforts of the Anglo-Saxon mind, either to strengthen the foundations of rational theology by new arguments, or to find fresh sources of religious inspiration in the harmony of the cosmos and the mystery of the Unknowable. It is not merely Christian ministers such as Dr. Martineau, Mr. Savage, Chadwick and Heber Newton or leaders of Free Congregations like Voysey, Conway, and Potter, or, indeed, literary men such as Prof. Seeley, Mr. Graham, Matthew Arnold, &c., who have devoted themselves to this task. It is also the principal representatives of English science from Darwin to Herbert Spencer, with Wallace, Jevons, Tait, Balfour Stewart, Tyndall, and Dr. Carpenter—those whom preachers sometimes treat as Atheists as well as those who glory in the profession of Christianity.

"There is no more remarkable feature in the philosophy of our day, wrote Prof. Fairbairn in the *Contemporary Review* of July, 1881, than its endeavour to baptize its highest ideals in the emotions or even enthusiasms of religion, to penetrate its ultimate doctrines with something of the Theistic spirit and power. This, perhaps the most common and characteristic tendency of all our modern systems, is due to many causes—to the nobler and more reverent spirit of the age; to the sense of weakness deepening in man, with his growing consciousness of the immense energies he has, but the still immense work they have to do; to the larger sense of humanity that marks our culture, making men sensitive to human misery, conscious of a kinship with the suffering millions that have suffered in the past; to the new feeling of the omnipotence of the order that reigns around us, the almightiness of the law that binds into an ordered and organized universe the infinitude of material atoms and the multitude of spiritual units, each by itself so feeble and wayward, but altogether so mighty and glorious. But, however the tendency may be explained, it is there, urging men of all systems to find a symbol or substitute for Deity, a field and law for religious emotions."

Mr. O. B. Frothingham indicated the same tendency in the United States, when he said in the preface of his *Freedom and Fellowship in Religion:* "The destructive period is about passed by; the constructive period has begun. In science the greatest men are distinguishing themselves by positive generalizations. In philosophy, the lines are converging towards certain central principles. . . . For a long time yet the relentless armour must be worn; but sentiment and imagination, recovering from the shock occasioned by the fall of their old idols are rallying courageously to do their part in peopling the new heavens with worshipful ideals and clothing in robes of glory the august forms which the seraphs at the gate of knowledge allow passage to the upper skies."

There is in all this a sort of second edition of the intellectual phenomena, which occurred at the time of the Antonines. In a parallel of this kind it is, of course, necessary to take into account the special characteristics of each epoch. Ancient civilization was all at the surface; it was not based upon a co-ordinated sum of positive knowledge; it did not extend down to the humbler classes by the intervention of popular education; it was restricted to a small area of the globe and therefore liable to be destroyed in any social cataclysm of a partial or local character. It might be compared, indeed, to a fine majestic oak which yields to a few strokes of the axe, applied to its roots. Our civilization, however, rather resembles those banyan trees of India, whose branches reach down to the soil and put forth rootlets which give rise to new trunks, so much so that to cut down a tree it would be necessary to uproot a forest.

Then again printing and, above all, journalism, have wholly changed the conditions of religious propagandism. Controversy has reached new strata of society, and it has become more difficult to close the ears of the pious world to any storm of criticism which may be raging beyond the pale of the Churches. Superstitions, again, have to run the risk of being tested in the light of thought, and impostures of being exposed before they have had time to crystalize into legends and dogmas. On the other hand, religious proselytism has seen its sphere of action increased tenfold, and the journalist tends to replace the missionary.[1]

But all these social differences only serve to render more striking the analogy, if not of the facts and doctrines at least of the situations and tendencies, between contemporary society and the Pagan world during the first three centuries of our era.

Then, as now, the old popular theology had been superseded by the progress of reason; a natural reaction had led to the successive predominance of the sober and correct Deism of Cicero; the Materialism of Epicurus as sung by Lucretius; and the system of humanitarian morality of which the Stoics made themselves the brilliant interpreters; it might have been supposed that Scepticism was about to gradually invade all classes of society. But after having measured the insufficiency of purely negative solutions, the best minds found themselves once more, by a sort of fatality, in the presence of the enigmas of the Sphinx, which has devoured so many religions and philosophies; the

---

[1]. In 1783, eleven years after the death of Swedenborg, two clergymen, who had been converted by the study of his works, inserted an advertisement in the English newspapers, soliciting the co-operation of those willing to join them in founding the New Jerusalem Church. Such was the commencement of Swedenborgianism, which now reckons some thousands of adherents in Europe and America.

insoluable problem of origin and end, the disquieting questions of evil, of duty, and of destiny.

Then, as now, there were champions of the past who attempted to justify the belief in revelations, prophecies and miracles by an appeal to the native incapacity of human reason. There were others again, who, more intelligent in their Conservatism, sought to reconcile the old forms to the new ideas by means of an ingenious symbolism. This solution, which was specially the work of the Mysteries, seemed calculated to make every one satisfied with a religion possessed of neither Bible, Councils nor Pope. Still it failed, as, according to the sincere avowal of Dean Stanley, the attempts to reconcile the letter of Revelation with the discoveries of science have failed in our own day.

Looking at the question from another point of view, the knowledge of foreign systems of faith and worship—which, in reproducing itself in our day, has so largely contributed to the extension of our theological horizon—had produced in the Roman Empire an Eclecticism eminently favourable to new metaphysical and religious conceptions. Not that it created many new forms of faith; Paganism, at the time of Alexander Severus, was sufficiently broad to open its Pantheon to all the gods. But under cover of old traditions, and often within the shadow of ancient sanctuaries, new theological ideas tended, as they do to-day, to direct to worthier objects that reverence which was no longer given to the old divinities.

Meanwhile, there was being developed in the lowest strata of society, a fermentation of religious sentiment which, finding its ancient channels obstructed, now over-flowed in some popular eccentricity—now assumed the form of a vague philosophical Mysticism. It was the same "hunger for spiritual food," to use the expression of an American observer,[1] which is showing itself to-day even in the populations of the Far West, and which so often assumes there the form of a belief in Spiritualism. Besides, whether we consider the calling up of spirits, the prophetic mutterings of a few eccentric heretics, or the extravagances of the Salvation Army, it suffices to glance at such works as *Heterodox London*, by Maurice Davies, *New America*, by Hepworth Dixon, or simply the miscellaneous reports of the Press

---

[1]. See the passage which refers to the annual meeting of the Free Religious Association in 1881.

in the two hemispheres, in order to see that the Anglo-Saxons have no cause to envy the Syrian miracle-workers or the Egyptian Theosophists. The wonders wrought by the medium, Slade, are quite on a par with those of Simon the Magician. The badge adopted by Joe Smith has not found less sincere adherents than the Sybilline literature, and "General" Booth has made more recruits than Alexander the Paphlagonian or Apollonius of Thyana. It might be supposed, indeed, if we confined our attention to these superficial aspects, that while religions pass away superstitions remain.

Happily, the analogy is not restricted to these lower manifestations of religious activity—the mere dross of the transfusion being effected in religious beliefs. There came a time, in the life of the ancients, when the old philosophical schools of Plato, Aristotle, and Epicurus ceased to satisfy the requirements of criticism as well as the needs of faith. Stoicism, after finishing its work of intellectual sanitation and of humanitarian propagandism, found itself, like the school of Littré and Mill to-day, insensibly absorbed by systems of thought which were more complete or at least bolder in their claim to interpret the universe. Now, the philosophers of that epoch had so refined away the idea of God, by attempting to reduce it to the idea of Absolute and of Substance, that they had dug an impassable abyss between man the Author of things. After the Judeo-Alexandrians, who had made of the Divinity a pure spirit, came the early Neo-Platonists, who declared this supreme principle to be above intelligence, as indeed superior to life and motion, and therefore beyond and above all conception. They admitted, however, that man, as a finite being, could enter into union with God by the self-obliteration of voluntary renunciation, and they sought, in the Oriental theory of emanation, which explained nature by the fall of spirit into matter, the metaphysical bridge so much needed to cross from the Unconditioned to the finite, from pure spirit to the phenomenal world. But their successors taught that God is as inaccessible as He is ineffable.

Towards whom then could the prayers of the masses or the smoke of the sacrifices ascend? Who then remained in the height of the heavens to respond to the aspirations and to sympathize with the anguish of the human heart? As all communication with the Unknowable was now cut off, search had to be made for a mediator or "second God." Each brought his Demiurgus. The Greek and the Persian offered to the masses the Sun, under the form of Apollo or of Mithra. The Egyptians turned to their god Hermes; certain Jews suggested the Wisdom of the Eternal. Simon of Gitto proposed his Helen. Philo put forward the *Logos*; the Apostle Paul the Christ of the Nazarenes, and the Evangelist John these two conceptions united. The reader knows the result of this competition, which decided for a period as yet incomplete, the religious destiny of Western civilization.

Now, here again, after the long slumber of the Middle Ages, modern criticism has resumed the work of ancient philosophy. For a second time human reason has striven to reduce God to the conception of an indefinable and inaccessible existence, without attributes common to the phenomenal world, and destitute of all possible relation to the human mind. Hence speculation has hastened to begin a search for some intermediate agency to fill the void which the soul seems to hold in horror.

Herbert Spencer admits that men will always have recourse to symbols to represent the Unknowable. But he abstains from proposing or recommending any.

The Unitarians would retain a mediator in the person of a Jesus modified according to the demands of critical thought.[1]

The Transcendentalists of Europe, America, and India trust to conscience, which they regard as representing the Divine Word in man.

Professors Tait and Balfour Stewart, returning by the path of science to a sort of Neo-Platonism, suppose that between God and the world there exists an invisible and eternal universe, of which phenomenal nature is in some measure a transitory materialization.

Keshub Chunder Sen seemed inclined to resuscitate the doctrine of the hermetic chain which made all great reformers special messengers of the Divinity, and his disciples of the New Dispensation appear to follow him in this tendency.

Felix Adler and Moncure D. Conway offer for the veneration of their followers the ideal which the human mind forms of absolute perfection.

---

1. This is only true of the older and more conservative school of Unitarians.—*Translator*.

Finally the orthodox disciples of Comte reserve their homage for Humanity personified in its noblest types, and if the majority of Comtists refuse to express an opinion respecting the existence of a Supreme Reality, some among them, in imitation of Mr. W. Frey, claim to reconcile their creed with the philosophy of evolution, by making the Great Being Humanity the minister and mediator of the Unknowable.

Now we might be tempted to see in these views the last gasp of a dying religion. But he who studies them closely and impartially will not fail to recognize in them the first signs of a new faith. If there is any conclusion to be drawn from the present work it is that religion is neither dead nor dying in the Anglo-Saxon race; but that on the contrary, it has never been more tenacious of life nor more fruitful, and perhaps never nearer an entire renovation.

Does it follow from this that we are even now in possession of the formula of this regeneration, and that in order to find the needed organism we have only to look round among the Churches which have sprung from the Rationalistic movement and select the one best fitted to absorb and outlive its rivals? Logic and history alike bid us be on our guard against so hasty a conclusion.

If it had been a question of fixing upon the form of religion destined to take the place of Paganism, when, about the middle of the first century, the Government of Tiberius expelled from Rome, as Suetonius tells us, the disciples of one Chrestus, who had created a disturbance in the Jewish quarter, some would have doubtless turned their eyes towards the Academy or the Portico; others would have mentioned the Mysteries of Isis, Eleusis or Mithra; a certain number would have suggested the philosophical schools of Rome and Alexandria; and the most daring spirits would have perhaps alluded to the Dualism of Persia or the Buddhism of India. No one, however, would have fixed upon a miserable handful of Jewish innovators, disowned by their fellow-countrymen; or even, somewhat later, would have turned to those alleged Atheists who were beginning to attract the attention of the police by their mysterious meetings in the subterranean vaults of the imperial town.

With all deference to human pride, be it said, everything in nature is of humble origin, and no one can say to-day whether the unconscious mission of the publicans and fishermen who grouped themselves around a sweet and mystic idealist on the shores of Lake Tiberias eighteen centuries ago, will not be renewed to-morrow in our midst by some band of Spiritualists holding their séances in a recess of the Rocky Mountains; by some gathering of enthusiasts discussing Socialism in a back parlour in London; or by some confraternity of ascetics meditating, like the Essenes of old, on the miseries of the world in a jungle of Hindustan. Perhaps their only need would be to find another Paul on the road to Damascus, in order to enter upon the ways of the age under his direction.

Powerless as we are to predict the name or even the form of the religion of the future, can we not at least conceive of the needs it must satisfy and the tendencies to which it will have to adapt itself? As early as the first century of our era, an impartial observer could have predicted with certainty that the approaching system of religion would have to manifest the sentiments of humanity, fraternity and universal charity: that it would have to preach gentleness, humility and continence, with a scorn for riches and pleasure; that it would have to emphasize the promises of a future life as a recompense for the ills and injustices of the present; and, lastly, that it would have to re-act against the old anthropomorphic theogonies, by presenting for the adoration of men a God who should be Spirit, Purity and Love.

To-day those aspects of the Divine which seem to specially attract us are Science, Law, Harmony, and consequently Justice: The faith of the future will have to take note of the movement which has prevailed in the realm of science; it will have to adapt its theology to the ideas of immanence, continuity and uniformity in the order of the universe.

But a religion is not merely the dramatized reproduction of a cosmical system. From the very fact that it is a reflex of the ideal, it also represents a reaction against the moral imperfection of the environment in which it exists.

Thus Christianity has looked upon matter with an excess of scorn: the coming faith will have to rehabilitate the Beautiful, sanction all rational pleasures and re-establish the communion of man with nature.

Our metaphysical speculations have long turned the attention of the highest and most generous minds from the consideration of social problems: the new faith will have to relegate the contemplation of super-sensible things to the second rank, in order to concentrate the chief activity of society upon the amelioration of the present world.

Our positive sciences tend more and more to the crushing of the feeble by the strong in the struggle for existence: the faith of the future will have to react against this apotheosis of force and to establish on a religious foundation the rights of the individual.

Our economic science has not answered to the hopes that our fathers for a while cherished: the future faith will not only have to present us with its solution of the problem of evil, but it must likewise provide us with a remedy, so that more justice may be brought into the relations of men.

If in developing these indispensable elements of a progressive and harmonious culture, this faith succeeds in retaining the principles of sincerity, spirituality, and fidelity to duty, together with the devotedness and enthusiasm which have constituted the glory and led to the success of its predecessor, why need we concern ourselves about the name and the symbol under which it may be manifested in order to secure the peace of the human soul and the regeneration of the world!

INDEX.

INDEX.

Abbot, F. E., his propositions at Syracuse, 186. His editorship of *The Index*, 187. His secession from Unitarianism, 194. His pamphlet, 212. His sermons, 220. His idea of God, 221.

Academy of Concord, Description of, 210. Its Hegelianism, 213.

Acontius, J., his list of doctrines, 18. His synthetic method, 24.

Adams, President, his reference to the extension of Unitarianism, 160.

Adams, Rev. W., his religious meetings in Calcutta, 233. His adoption of Liberal Christianity, 303.

Adesh, a theory of inspiration, 261. Keshub Chunder Sen's use of it, 269. A doctrine of the New Dispensation, 285, 286.

Adi Somáj, its opposition to the Hindu Marriage Act, 249. Chunder Sen's secession from it, 261. The faith of, 284. Its belief in the infallibility of the Vedas, 295. Its agreement with the other Somájes, 304.

Adler, Felix, his presidency of the Free Religious Association, &c., 191-195. Reference to his opinions, 205. The beliefs of his followers, 210. His views of morality, 216. His belief in the Absolute, 221.

Advaita, the doctrine that the world exists in God, 227.

Adventists, believers in the second coming of Christ, 77. One of the American sects, 205 (note).

Affirmation Bill, Mr. Gladstone's, 34.

Agnostics and Agnosticism, a negative school, 4. Its development from Unitarianism, 6. The origin of the word, 47. Their presence in Parliament, 73. Their estimate of science, 145. Its relation to Spiritualism, 201.

Ahmed Khan, his judicial position at Benares, 301.

Akbar, The syncretism of, 231. His comprehensive aims, 288.

Akhai Kumar Datta, his editorship of a Hindu journal, 238.

Alcott, A. B., his connection with the Transcendental Club, 174. His special work, &c., 180, 181. His neo-Pythagorean views, 210.

Alexander the Great, The victories of, 41.

Alexander the Paphlagonian, The adherents of, 321.

Alexander Severus, The opinion of, in relation to universal religion, 288. Paganism in his time, 320.

Alexandria, The school of, and its doctrine of pure spirit, &c., 321-323.

Allah, The edifices devoted to the worship of, 226. A personal God, 233.

Alliance, Evangelical, its growing liberality, 80.

Anabaptists, The persecution of, in the sixteenth century, 19. Their opposition to ecclesiastical functions, 21. Their origin, 82. Their exclusion from New England, 157.

Anjumans, semi-religious societies of India, 297. Their development, 301.

Antinomians, their exclusion from New England, 157.

Apollonius of Thyana, The followers of, 321.

Arati, The celebration of, 287.

Arians, the progress of their ideas, 19. When first known in England, 82. Their views of Christ, 85. The Hindu form of the doctrine, 274.

Aristotle, The influence of, 52. Dedication of a month to him by Comte, 132. His large views of religion, 288. The school of, 321.

Army, Salvation, The practices of, 5. Its band, 15. Its various divisions, &c., 58, 59. Its adherents drawn from the lowest classes, 75. Its extravagances, 320.

Arminianism and Arminians. The doctrines of, 19. Relation to Unitarianism, 93. Antagonism to Predestination, 160. Doctrines of, held by the Campbellites, 205.

Antonines, the intellectual condition of their age, 318.

Armstrong, Rev. R. A., The sermon of, 89.

Arnold, Dr., The influence of, 64. His views of Sacred History, 65.

Arnold, Matthew, his definition of God, 9, 50. His views of the functions of a Church, 69. What he sees in the Unknowable, 220. His relation to the new school of thought, 317.

Articles, The Thirty-nine, when formed, 16. The doctrines of, 66, 67. How accepted by Chillingworth, 71. The probable disappearance of, 72.

Arya Somájes, their belief in Vedaic infallibility, &c., 294, 295.

Aryans, the two branches of family, 7. Conception of neo-Platonic Word, 169. Races of India, 227. Their genius, 236. Their ancient sacrifices, 275. Their migrations, 303.

Assises, Francis of, his place in the Comtist ritual, 135.

Association of Congregational Ministers at Brooklyn, their resolution, 207.

Atheists, their place in Mr. Gladstone's classification, 4. Excluded from Parliament, 33, 73. Relation to Herbert Spencer's doctrine, 43. Their doctrines in the last century, 84. The profession of, a crime, 159. Relation to Spiritualism, 201. The pessimistic, in India, 236. Mysticism of, in India, 299. The ancient systems of, 307.

Atmiya Sabhá, a religious society formed by Rám Mohun Roy, 233.

Bacon, Lord, establishes the experimental method, 23.

Baltimore, Lord, founded Maryland, 159 (note).

Bancroft, his *History of the United States*, 156 (note). His relation to Transcendentalism, 180.

Baptists, the sections and numbers of, 58, 59. Their position and churches, 75. Gradual change of old congregations, 93. Their relative importance in America, 203.

Barth, A., quoted from, 283, 297, 298 (notes).

Bartol, C. A., his Transcendentalism, 174.

Beecher, Rev. H. Ward, his salary, 202 (note). His liberal teaching, 205. His popularity, 206 (note). Estimate of his heresy, 207. His speech at the banquet given to Herbert Spencer, 218.

Beesley, Professor, a champion of Comtism, 136. His views of the future of society, 137.

Bellows, Rev. Dr., his desire for union, 185.

Berkeley, Bishop, his work of emancipation, 22.

Bernard, Claude, the place of his teachings, 214.

Besant, Mrs., her connection with *The Freethinker*, 32 (note).

Bhagavad Gitá, The poem of, 229. The philosophy of, 309 (note).

Bhakti, The doctrine of, 229. The school of, 247.

Bhárat Assam, a boarding-house founded by Chunder Sen, 251.

Bháratbharsia Somáj, the name for the Somáj of India, 244. The Secretary of, 245. Its Church, 247. Its organization and minister, 248, 250. The congregations affiliated to it, 254. The unity of the, 255. The progress of the, &c., 261-292.

Bhils, The spirit of reform among the, 298.

Biddle, John, his heretical views, 82. His death, 83. His idea of Christ, 85.

Bisbee, Mrs. Clara, her religious work, 188.

Black, Dr. Patrick, one of Mr. Voysey's Committee, 112 (note).

Blavatsky, Madame, her connection with the Theosophical Society, 296.

Blount, his teaching, 24.

Blunt, Mr. W. S., Prediction of, respecting Mussulman power, 302.

INDEX. 331

Bolingbroke, Lord, The natural Monotheism of, 24.
Booth, "General," his statement, 75 (note). His recruits, 321.
Bruno, The religious susceptibilities of, 143 (note).
Buddhism and Buddha, his relation to Moses, &c., 185, 187. Mr. Potter's reference to, 191. Rise of, 227. Incarnation of, 228. The difficulties of, 229. The adherents of, 232. The social insurrection of, 243. The sects of, 250 (note). Numbers in India, 300. Existence of, in the time of Christ, 323.
Bowring, Sir J., his connection with Mr. Voysey, 105, 112.
Bradlaugh, his statement about the *Freethinker*, 32. His exclusion from Parliament, 34, 97. Editor of the *National Reformer*, 148.
Brahm or Brahma, The sleeping states of, 41. The neuter of the name, 234.
Brahma-Dharma, means, "the rule of Theism," 238, 239. The saving truths of, 245. The eclecticism of, 257-271. Its claims, 275.
Brahmans, their privileges, 227. Their adoption of Buddha, &c., 228, 229. Rám Mohun Roy's reference to, 232. Their position in the Brahmo Somáj, 234. The tradition of the, 243. Their opposition to reform, 249-253. The societies of the, 297. Their sacred books, 309.
Brahmoism and Brahmoists, The different schools of, 2. Sympathy for among the Transcendentalists, 202. Their worship, 226. Their numbers, 235. The constitution of, &c., 238 (note), 239. Their divisions, &c., 244-294. The utterances of, &c., 303-311.
Brahmo Somáj, its origin, 234. Loses its leader, 235. The new comers to, 236. Breaks with the tradition of Hinduism, 238, 239. Social reforms of the, 241-255. The anniversary of the, 259. Its danger, 263. The crisis, 265, 266.
Brahmo Somáj, of Southern India, its devotional readings, 293.
Brahmo Public Opinion, the principal organ of Brahmo movement, 292. Its reference to the *New Dispensation*, 306. Its views of religious culture, 308.
Brahmostab, a Brahmoist festival, 246. Conference at time of the, 253.
Bridges, Dr., his connection with Comtism, 133.
Bright, John, The Parliamentary struggles of, 120.
British and Foreign Unitarian Association, The Scotch correspondent of, 78. The annual sermon of, 94 (note). When founded, 96. Reprints life of Ezra Stiles Gannett, 161 (note). Annual meeting of, and Dr. Putnam's address, 220.
British Secular Union, its formation, 148, 149.
Brooke, Stopford, his change to Unitarianism, 93, 94.
Brownson, Orestes, The religious changes of, 174.
Büchner, his Materialism, &c., 219.
Butler, Bishop, supported a liberal theology, 25.
Byom, Sâr, its philosophic Nihilism, 299.

Calvin, Calvinism, reference to by John Hales, 19. The central doctrine of, 28. Its Puritan baldness, 62. Rehabilitated by Professor Drummond, 67 (note). Held by the Baptists, 75. Insists on the humanity of Jesus, 85. God of, 108. The principles of, in the United States, &c., 155-165. Is losing its dogmatic authority, 181. Impossible to be reconciled with evolution, 218 (note).
Campbellites or Disciples, The liberal movement of, 205.
Carlyle, the influence of his writings, 27. Teaches German Idealism, 30, 31, 163. Taine's reference to, 36. His saying about Dr. Newman, 63. Religious susceptibilities of, 143 (note). Influence in India, 257.
Carpenter, Dr., his British Association address, 49. His relation to the new theology, 317.

Carvâkas, The Materialistic philosophy of, 299.
Castelar, his belief in religious reconstruction, 3.
Chambers, his *Vestiges of Creation*, 37.
Calas, pro-totypes of, in New England, 158.
Catholicism, the desire to retain it in English Ritual, 16. Number of adherents, 59. No halting place between it and irreligion, 63. Persecution in New England, 157. The power of, 195. Relative importance of in United States, 203. Seeks to enlarge its influence, 207. Mention of by Chunder Sen, 277.
Chadwick, J. W., his definition of Christianity, 195. Value of his lectures, 220. His position, 317.
Chaitanya, his efforts to reform Hinduism, 229. The followers of, 247. Brahmoist estimate of, 257. Invoked in imagination, 280. Formerly reviled, 285.
Channing, Dr., The words of, 20. His influence in the Unitarian Church, 86. His estimate of dogma, 95. Ezra Stiles Gannett, a disciple of, 161 (note). His position and work, 162-164. The sermon of, at Baltimore, 174. His power as a writer, 303.
Channing, Rev. W. H., the Transcendentalism of, 174. His lectures, 211. His fidelity to the Transcendental school, 213.
Charles the First, The fall of, 17.
Cherbury, Lord Herbert of, the father of English Deism, 24, 25.
Chib Chunder Seb, the contemporary of Râm Mohun Roy, 292.
Child, Lydia, her Transcendentalism, 213.
Chillingworth, a founder of the Latitudinary party, 19, 20. His view of clerical subscription, 71.
Christ, The traditional, 26. Redemption by the blood of, 61. The supernatural, 74. The Divinity of, 83, 85, 302. The miracles of, 84. Theistic view of, 88-90. Mr. Conway's estimate of, 126. Name of, omitted by Comte, 132. The pre-existence of, 168. The nature of, 174. The moral teaching of, 185. The disciples of, and free inquiry, 186. Relation of teaching to the doctrine of evolution, 217. Accepted by the Vishnuites as the last incarnation of their god, 228. Regarded as a reformer, 258. Chunder Sen's opinion of, 273, 274, 277. How honoured, 285. Preached as the Divine Word, 322.
Christians, The, a Protestant sect, 74, 161.
Christians of the New Connection, 205.
Celsus, his attacks on religion, 178.
Christadelphians, a sect who deny the Trinity and the immortality of the soul, 77. Referred to by Mr. Spears, 205 (note).
Chubb, one of the Deists, 24.
Church, Anglican, its signs of progress, 6. Attitude towards Rationalism, 21. Coleridge takes orders in the, 26. Subject to the state, 31, 32. The oath of adherence to, 34. Description of, 39-74. Secessions from, to Unitarianism, 83, 84. Mr. Voysey's expulsion from, 108. The persecutions of, 157.
Church for Foreigners, founded by Cranmer, 18.
Church of Scotland, the baldness of, 62. The Free Kirk secession from, 76 (note). Address by a minister of, 79.
Church, Greek (in London), its symbolism, 14.
Church, Episcopal (in Ireland), its suppression of the Athanasian Creed, 72. Its resources, 74.
Church, Episcopal (in the United States), its rejection of the Athanasian Creed, 72. Its adoption by the higher classes, 195.
Church, Reformed Episcopal, its extension in England, 61. The schism of in America, 205.
Cicero, the Deism of, 319.
Clarke, James Freeman, his acceptance of German Idealism, 174.
Cleanthes, the religious aims of, 288.
Cobbe, Miss F. P., her representative position as a Theist, 30, 31. Her opinion of the Reformed Jews, 118, 119.

Cobden, The Parliamentary struggles of, 120.

Colenso, Bishop, his acquittal by the Privy Council, 64, 71. His sincerity, 64. His conversion to liberal opinions, 303.

Coleridge, The early career of, 26, 27. His Transcendental teaching, 30, 31. The doctrine of the Trinity re-habilitated by, 63. His liberal influence in Anglicanism, 86. Influence of in the United States, 168. Influence of, in India, 257.

Coleridge, Lord, his reference to Mr. Bradlaugh's trial, 32.

Collet, Miss S. D., the historian of Brahmoism, 226. Her remembrance of Rám Mohun Roy, 234. Her estimate of Theism, 242. Her reference to Hindu hymns, 247. *The Year Book* of, 251. Her description of the activities of a Somâj, 254. Thinks that fervour saved Brahmoism, &c., 261, 262. Opposes Keshub, 281. Believes that the old divisions are being healed, 294 (note). Article re-produced by, 305 (note).

Collins, a member of the Deistical school, 24.

Comtism, Comte, his opinion of the power of passion, 10. His philosophy, 39. The Worship of Humanity established by, 129-145. Marriage ceremony of, 151. Relation to Religion of Ethics, 194. M. Littré and the doctrines of, 210. The aims of, 288. Its chances of success in India, 298. Its relation to the Philosophy of Evolution, 323.

Condillac, The Sensationalism of, 36.

Congregationalists, The, their numbers, 59. The historical descendants of the old Independents, 53. Constitution of their churches, 158. Their relative importance in America, 203 (note). Their progress represented by Henry Ward Beecher, 218. Attitude of the advanced to the old dogmas, 315.

Confucius, The enlightened views of, 288.

Congreve, Dr., his adoption of Comte's religious system, 133. The liturgy of, 134, 135. Rejects the authority of M. Lafitte, 136.

Constant, Benjamin, his works read in America, 168.

Conway, Moncure D., his opinion of the Ritualists, 62 (note). His contribution to the *Index*, 65 (note). His chapel licenced for marriages, 115. His theological opinions and position, 119-128. The practical teaching of, 146. Form of worship in the congregation of, 314, 322. The free congregation of, 317.

Clair, Rev. G. St., The transition state of, 93.

Cooper, John, The Unitarian teaching of, 83.

Copernicus, The cosmogony of, 28.

Coquerel, Athanase, his Free Christian sympathies, 95.

Corrano, Antoine, his rejection of the Trinity, 19.

Cosmas, The curious views of, 28.

Cosmism, The Divinity of, 3. The description of, 205-221.

Courtauld, Samuel, his connection with Mr. Voysey, 112.

Cowie, T. H., his decision as Attorney-General of India, 248.

Cranmer, Archbishop, invites scholars to England, 18.

Crompton, H., his championship of Comtism, 136.

Cromwell, his treatment of Biddle, 83.

Couch-Behâr, The Mahârâjah of, marries Chunder Sen's daughter, 264, 265. The personal merits of, 286.

Curteis, Rev. Canon, The Boyle lectures of, 70 (note). His part in the Spencer-Harrison controversy, 143 (note).

Cousin, The writings of, in America, 168.

Dalton, The study of, in Boston, 214.

Darmesteter, J., his translation of Max Müller's lectures, 310 (note).

Darwin, The hypothesis of, 37, 38, 40. His action against the persecution of the Jews, 80 (note). His sympathy with Mr. Voysey, 112. His new views of religion, 317.

Darwin, Erasmus, a member of the Voysey Committee, 112.

Dawson, Mr. George, The transition stage of, 93.

Davies, Maurice, his description of heterodox congregations, 67, 320.

Dayânanda Sarasvati Sivâmî, The missionary labours of, 295.

Dean, Rev. Peter, his confession of faith, &c., 88, 92.

Debendra Nâth Tâgore, his personification of the Brahmo movement, 231. The tendencies of, 236, 237. Throws overboard infallibility of Scriptures, 238. Compared with Keshub, 241. His preaching by example, 243, 244. Visits Chunder Sen, 282. His connection with the Adi Somâj, 292, 293, 295.

Deism, Deists, of the 18th century, originated with Lord Herbert of Cherbury, 24, 25. The writings of, largely sold, 84.

Descartes, The disciples of, 28. A month dedicated to, by Comte, 132.

Dharma Sabhâs, The object of, 297.

Dial, The, the organ of the Transcendentalists, 174.

Dissenters, The persecutions of, 22. Helped to overthrow the Stuarts, 32. Formerly excluded from Parliament, 34. *The Christian Standard*, an organ of the, 67. Their legislation for the Church, 73. The denominations of, 77. The trust deeds of, 80. The theological progress of, 317.

Dix, Rev. William, the large salary of, at New York, 202 (note).

Dixon, Mr. W. Hepworth, his estimate of the Spiritualists, 200, 320.

Döllinger, Dr., The position of, in the Old Catholic party, 62 (note).

Dourgâ Dâs Rây, The ethical views of, 286.

Drummond, Professor, The theological views of, 67, 68 (note).

Dwarka Nâth Mitter, his championship of Comtism, 298.

Dwarka Nâth Tâgore, the father of Debendra Nâth Tâgore, 235.

Dordrecht, The Council of, 19.

Edward VI., The reign of, 18. His hospitality to the Italian and Spanish Protestants, 82.

Elizabeth, Queen, The Calvinists in the reign of, 21. Puritan movement in the reign of, 155.

Eliot, George, her estimate of James Thomson, 147 (note).

Emerson, The religious susceptibilities of, 143 (note). His comparison of superstition and principle, 149 (note). His opinions and influence as the "Prince of Transcendentalists," 170-173, 315. Both a philosopher and poet, 180. His Christianity contested, 185. His connection with the Free Religious Association, 202. Heard in the Academy of Concord, 211. His prediction of a religious interregnum, 212. His definition of God, 221.

Emory, Professor, one of the Transcendentalists, 211.

Encampment of Christian philosophy, The, at Greenwood, 211.

Epicurus, The doctrines of, 227. The Materialism of, 319. The philosophical school of, 321.

Falkland, Lord, his house like a university, 19.

Fairbairn, Professor, The opinions of, 318.

Feuerbach, his Atheism, 36. His attacks upon religion, 178.

Fichte, The subjective Idealism of, 167, 168. His definition of religion, 214, 215.

Firmin, Thomas, his love of Socinian ideas, 83.

Fiske, Professor, develops the synthesis of evolution, 214. His conception of God, 221.

Foote, his imprisonment, 32 (note).

Fox, W. J., the minister of South Place Chapel, 120. His hymns, 121. Succeeded by Mr. Conway, 127.
Francis, Professor, a Transcendentalist, 174.
Free Religious Association, formed by Mr. Abbot, 186. The object of, 187. Its propagandism, 188. Comparison with Society for Ethical Culture, 191; with Unitarianism, 194, 195. Its report, 197. Its relation to Spiritualism, 201. Its Committee, 202. Its work, influence, &c., 211-219.
Free Christian, the movement, 194, 195.
Free Church of England, numbers forty congregations, 61.
Free Church of Scotland, The formation of, 75.
Free Religious Congregations at Providence, 189; at Florence, 215 (note); at New Bedford, 214; at Dorchester, 188.
Freie-Religiöse Gemeinde, formed by the Germans, 200.
Frey, W., his attempt to reconcile the doctrines of Comte and Spencer, 140-146, 323. His non-dogmatic Comtism, 210.
Frothingham, O. B., the historian of Transcendentalism, 169. President of the Free Religious Association, 187. His estimate of the Spiritualists, 200. His speech, 219. Value of his lectures, 220. His views of the constructive period, 318.
Froude, Mr., his part in the Tractarian movement, 62.
Fuller, Margaret, carries Transcendentalism into criticism, &c., 180, 212.
Furness, W. H., a Transcendentalist, 174.

Gannett, Ezra Stiles, his opinion of Dr. Ware, 161. The biography of, 207.
Gannett, W. C., his father's biographer, 161 (note). His opinion of Channing's Baltimore sermon, 162, 174. On the Committee of Free Religious Association, 202. His views of science and religion, 219-221.

Garcin de Tassy, The reference of, to Râm Mohun Roy, 231 (note), 234, 235 (note). Reference to his work on Hindustan, 296, 302 (notes). His views of missionary work in India, 303. His account of the "perversions" from Christianity 308 (note).
Garfield, Mr., the candidature of, 206.
Gibbon, the last of the Deists, 25.
Guizot, his estimate of Mr. Fox's eloquence, 120.
Gladstone, The Right Hon. W. E., his description of the various schools of religious thought, 4. His Affirmation Bill, 34. His estimate of the religious value of Mr. Spencer's philosophy, 45.
Glanvil, one of the Latitudinarian party, 22.
Glassites, The, their holy kiss, 77.
Goethe, The scientific hypothesis of, 37. The religious susceptibilities of, 143.
Gotheil, Dr., a liberal rabbi, 195.
Gouri, a Hindu divinity of marriage, 267.
Graham, W., his remarkable work, 50. Sees in the Unknowable an ordaining Power, 220. The broad views of, 317.
Grandier, Urbain, a prototype of New England persecution, 158.
Guebres, Islamism has borrowed from the, 231.

Haeckel, The scientific faith of, 143 (note). The doctrine of, 227, 307.
Hales, John, brought liberal opinions to England, 19.
Hall, Rev. E. P., his translation of Bonet-Maury's work, 19.
Hall, Rev. John, The salary of, 202 (note).
Hamilton, Sir W., his doctrine of the Unknowable, 40.
Hari, a Hindu divinity of marriage, 267. The god who blots out sin, 275, 276.
Harris, Prof., edits the *Journal of Speculative Philosophy*, 211.
Harrison, Frederic, President of the London Positivist Society, 136, 137. His views of the evolutionary philosophy, 138. Controversy with Herbert Spencer, 139-143 (note).

Hartley, his influence on Priestley, 85.
Harte, Bret, The stories of, 120.
Hartmann, Von, his definition of religion, 10. His prediction as to religion in the future, 310, 311.
Hawthorne, his power of psychological analysis, 181.
Hegel, Hegelianism, The doctrine of, 36. Expounded at Concord, 211, 213.
Henry the Eighth, progress of thought since his reign, 5. The ideas of his time, 17. The reform effected by, 313.
Hebrews, The Monotheism of, 29.
Herder, The works of, studied in America, 168.
Hepworth, Rev. G., his religious conservatism, 194.
Higginson, Colonel Wentworth, his Transcendentalism, 174. Preaches in Mr. Conway's chapel, 122. His connection with the Free Religious Association, 202. His fidelity to old beliefs, 213.
Hinkley, Rev. F. A., examined as to the nature of "Free Religion," 189. His view of God, 215 (note).
Hinduism and Hindus, The mysticism of, 7, 259. The monuments of, 173. The faith of, 191. The idols of, 226. The intellectual character and vitality of, 227, 228. The temples of, sacked, 230. The superstitions of, 231. The practices of, 243, 248. Marriage among the, &c., 249-281. Its possible absorption of Brahmoism, 291. The Rationalism of, 294. The movement of thought among, 297. The religious character of, 299. Sects of, &c., 300-303. The lofty sentiments of, &c., 305-309. The emancipated minds of, 314. Relation to other faiths, 317.
Hobbes, destroys foundations of religion, 22. His theory of the Church, 31. The Materialism of, 36. The criticisms of, 209.
Holyoake, Austin, The death of, 148.
Holyoake, G. J., aids in founding National Secular Society, 148. His preaching in Unitarian pulpits, 150, 195.

Holmes, Oliver Wendell, a writer and humorist, 180.
Homa, the sacrifice of fire, 266. Chunder Sen's observance of, 275.
Hooker, his work of emancipation, 22.
Hopps, Rev. J. P., The special services of, 101 (note).
Howe, Mrs., her lectures at Concord, 211.
Hugo, Victor, a vice-president of the British Secular Union, 150.
Humanitarians, The, a description of, 114-117.
Hume, his universal scepticism, 25, 36, 317. The life of, 51. The philosophic nihilism of, 299.
Huxley, his lay sermons, 46. His article on Evolution, 51. His description of Positivism, 131. The scientific faith of, 143 (note). His works read in Boston, 214.

Idealism, German, taught by Coleridge, 26. Its effect in England, 30. 64. Produces the Transcendental school, 170. See Transcendentalism.
Independents, their demand for religious freedom, 21. Their support of Cromwell in the amnesty to Biddle, 83. See Congregationalists.
Independent Religious Reformers, their lifeless Theistic services, 114.
Indian Reform Association, founded by Chunder Sen, 250.
Ingersoll, Colonel R., his extreme utterances, 204.
Incarnation, The dogma of, 27.
Irvingites, The, their symbolism, 14. Their churches, 77.
Islamism. See Mohammedanism.

Jackson, Dr., succeeded by Dr. Temple, 65.
Jacobi, The doctrine of, 167. His works read in Boston, 168.
Jacquemont, Victor, his description of the English, 226.
Jaina, The, religion, 250.
James the First, Persecutions in the reign of, 156.

INDEX. 337

Jamblicus, a thinker in antiquity, 288.
Játkarma, a form of thanksgiving, 245.
John, St., the Evangelist, his Logos doctrine, 322.
Jevons, his relation to the newer thought, 317.
Johnson, Samuel, the individualism of, 174. His church at Lynn, Mass., 213, 315.
Jones, Dr., his lectures at Concord, 211.
Jones, Rev. Jenkins L., edits *Unity*, 197.
Jouffroy, The works of, in America, 168.
Jourgi, a reformer among the Bhils, 298.
Jowett, Prof., his connection with Essays and Reviews, 65.
Jews, Reformed or Progressive, the doctrine of, 117-119. Their attitude toward the past, 199. The Theists among, 315.
Judas Iscariot, Parker's reference to, 176.
Jumpers, The eccentricities of, 14.

Kabir, substitutes a spiritual faith for Vêdas and Koran, 230. The enlightenment of, 288.
Kant, The theory of, 27. Theistic school traceable to, 31. His relation to the doctrine of evolution, 36. The religious feelings of, 143 (note). The school of, 165, 184. Combats negative psychology, 167. His teaching the basis of Transcendentalism, 174, 177, 316. The postulates of, 192. The doctrine of, 285.
Karvuna Chunder Sen, the son of Keshub, 283.
Kaspary, Joachim, the leader of the Humanitarians, 115, 116.
Keble, his connection with Dr. Pusey, 62.
Keene, Mr. G. H., his article in *The Calcutta Review*, 295.
Kegan Paul aids Free Christian movement, 95.
Kemp, his connection with *The Freethinker*, 32.
Kempis, Thomas à, The spiritual power of, 99 (note). In great favour with orthodox Comtists, 134 (note).

Keshub Chunder Sen, his communication with the Transcendentalists, 202. Personifies Brahmoism, 231. Changes Brahma-Dharma into a religion, 239. His family, 241. His views of Theism, 242. Dines with Debendra and loses caste, 243. A similar violation of caste and the secession of, 244. Is made Secretary of the Bháratbharsia Somáj, &c., 245-263. His daughter's marriage, &c., 264-269. His New Dispensation, &c., 273-289. The old congregation faithful to, 292. Changes occasioned by death of, 294 (note). His preaching in Unitarian churches, 303. His relation to the doctrine of the hermetic chain, 322.
Kingsley, Canon. The sincerity of, 68.
Koran, Passages from, in the *Sacred Anthology*, 121. Kabir's treatment of, 230. The Monotheism of, 233. The religion of, 300, 301, 309. Supposed origin of, 302.
Krishna, his worshippers, 229. Temple dedicated to, 231. The legend of, 309 (note).
Krishna Bihari Sen officiates at marriage of Keshub's daughter, 266.
Kuenen, Professor, Banquet to, 65 (note). Represents school of modern Protestantism in Holland, 91.

Laboulaye, Ed., quoted from 159 (note). His opinion of American Democracy, 160.
Lafitte, P., accepted as leader by Comtists, 133. His authority rejected, 136.
Labarre, a prototype of New England persecutions, 158.
Lamarck, The hypothesis of, 37.
Laplace, The generalizations of, 28.
Laugel, M. Aug., his reference to Herbert Spencer, 45, 46, 138 (note).
Laveleye, Emile de, his views of American Democracy, 160.
Lecky, W. S. H., The opinions of, 22, 49 (note). His reference to the Rationalists, 130. His reference to religious liberty, 84.
Leibnitz, The doctrine of, 36.
Leroux, Pierre, The system of, 115.

Y

Lewes, G. H., The writings of, in America, 214.
Lindsey, Rev. Th., his leaving the Established Church, 84.
Littré, The opinion of, 8. The Positive school of, 138, 210, 321.
Locke, his explanation of mental phenomena, 23. The Sensational school of, 24-26, 29. Influenced by prejudice, 85. Priestley a disciple of, 85. The theology of, 164. The philosophy of, 184, 185.
Lollards, The old leaven of, 16. Attempts to connect Unitarianism with the, 82.
Lily Cottage, The ashes of Chunder Sen deposited in, 283.
Longfellow, his place in American literature, 170, 181.
Longfellow, Samuel, The hymns of, 174. His fidelity to old opinions, 213.
Low, A., The profession of faith of, 185.
Lucretius, the Materialism of, 319.
Luther, The Reform inaugurated by, 16, 313.
Lyell, Sir Ch., his service to science, 28. The funeral of, 65. His sympathy with Mr. Voysey, 105, 112.
Lytton, his rule in India, 252 (note).

MacDonald, Rev., The liberal opinions of, 78.
Mádhava, an Indian reformer, 229.
Maine, Sir H. Sumner, his bill relating to Hindu marriages, 248-250. His speech at Calcutta, 306.
Man, Singh, The Rajah, 231.
Mansel, Dean, referred to by Mr. F. Harrison, 142 (note).
Mariano, the higher thought of, 3.
Martineau, Dr. James, a Unitarian, 3. Quoted from, 29, 30, 54. Compared with Dean Stanley, 66. His opinion of existing theological changes, 78. Reference to works of, 86, 87 (notes). His "Ten Services," 91, 105. Interest in "Free Christian" movement, 95. Channing's letter to, 170. A leader in the new theology, 317.

Materialism, Materialists, a monistic solution of the world, 52. Relation to Spiritualism, 201. Quarrel with religion, 214. Remain Idealists in India, 299. The old physiological, 317. The, of Epicurus, 319.
Maximus, of Tyre, his Platonic philosophy, 11. The enlightened opinions of, 288.
May, Thomas Erskine, his history, 26, 32 (notes).
Medard, St., The contortions of, 14.
Methodists, The, their numbers, 59. The origin of and condition, 74, 75. Mr. Conway's connection with, 119. Relative position in America, 203. Movement of thought among, 205.
Miall, Rev. W., connected with "Free Christian" movement, 95.
Middleton, The liberal theology of, 25.
Mill, J. Stuart, The psychology of, 39, 40. Positivists of the school of, 119, 138. His modification of Posivitism, 133. The school of, 321.
Milton, The theological opinions of, 84.
Missions, Christian, in India, their want of success, 302.
Mohammed, Mohammedanism, the spirit of, 14. Mussulman inspiration from, 144. Compared with Buddha, &c., 185, 187, 257. An Asiatic faith, 191, 251. Accepted Christ as a prophet, 277. Chunder Sen and the name of, 280. The position of in India, 300-305.
Moses, Mr. Conway and name of, 126. Comte and name of, 132. Compared with Mohammed, &c., 185. Rám Mohun Roy's veneration for, 233. Chunder Sen and name of, 280.
Moleschott, his words and influence, 219.
Monotheism, The natural, among the Deists, 24. The introduction of among the Hebrews, 29. Among reformed Jews, 117. The strict, of the first Evangelists, 169. A return to, 221. The rigid, of the Mohammedans, &c., 230 et seq. Of the West, 309. The Semitic, 311.
Montaigne, The statement of, 3.
Montefiore, Claude, his article, 117 (note). His opinions of reformed Judaism, 118.

Montesquieu, his estimate of religion in England, 152.
Moravian Brethren, their numbers, 77.
Morrison, J. Cotter, The Comtism of, 136.
Mormons, The, the places of worship of, 77.
Morse, Rev. Dr., his charge against liberal ministers, 162.
Mott, Lucretia, the Transcendentalism of, 202.
Müller, Prof. Max, his reference to Indian faiths, 228 (note), 310. His sympathy with Chunder Sen, 281. His opinion of the common basis of religions, 317.
Mussulmans, The Deity of, 226. Claimed the body of Kabir, 230. The Indian, 301.

Námkaran, The choice of a name, 245.
Nának Shah, his efforts at religious reform, 230. The services of, 257.
National Secular Society, The Freethinkers of, 298.
Native Marriage Act, passed to satisfy the Brahmos, 250. Keshub's disregard of, 264.
Nava, Bidhán (The New Dispensation), reference to, 238 (note). The syncretism of, 273-289. Relation to the Sádháran Somájes, 293, 294. Description of, by the *Brahmo Public Opinion*, 306. Chunder Mozoumdar's apology for, 311. Doctrine of hermetic chain in, 322.
Neal, his history referred to, 17 (note).
Newman, Cardinal, one of the Tractarians, 62. Enters the Roman Church within ten years, 63. Opposes persecution of the Jews, 80 (note).
Newman, Prof. F. W., a representative of Theism, 30. Joins Unitarian Association, 87. The career of in Syria, 303.
Newton, The generalization of, 28. The theological opinions of, 84. The mind of, 178 (note).
Newton, Rev. Heber, his admiration of Emerson, 172. The new views of, 317.

Northbrook, Lord, his estimate of Brahmoism, 252.

Ochino, Bernard, The proscription of, 18.
Olcott, Col. H., his connection with the Theosophical Society, 296, 297 (note).
Old Catholics, mentioned by Mr. Gladstone, 4.
Owen, Robert Dale, his connection with the Free Religious Association, 202.

Paganism, ancient, The believers in, 4, 48, 49. Mr. Savage's definition of, 218. Its comprehensiveness in the time of Alexander Severus, 320. The place of, 323.
Paine, Thomas, his influence in America, 209.
Paley, the liberalized theology of, 25. The teleological combination of, 39.
Pantheism, Pantheists, The negative position of, 4. A form of, held by Servetus, 18. The Brahminic, 41. The hour of, struck, 48. Its philosophic conception, 52. Idealistic, held by advanced religious teachers, 88. Emerson's, 171. Hindu, 227-233. Chunder Sen's estimate of, 260, 274. Opinion of, by Sádháran Somáj, 305. The ancient, 311.
Parker, Theodore, from John Robinson to, 160. His Transcendental opinions and teaching, 174-185. Church erected to memory of, 214. Chunder Sen, and 280. The eloquent pen of, 303. His position in the Transcendental movement, 315.
Parsees, the differences of, with Brahmans, 249. But few in number, 300. The sacred books of, 309.
Parris, George Van, The martyrdom of, 19.
Pasteur, a vice-president of the British Secular Union, 150
Pattison, Mark, his description of the Positivist service, 135.
Paul, St., compares the earth to a tabernacle, 28. The writings of, 194. His bearing towards the Athenians, 113.

INDEX.

Quoted from, by Mr. Conway, 121. Comte's use of name, 132. His view of Christ, 322. Another needed, 324.
Pease, Mr., The election of, 34.
Peculiar People, The, their notoriety, 77.
Penn, William, his charter, 159.
Philo, The Logos of, 322.
Picton, J. Allanson, The opinions of, 97 (note).
Pierpont, John, his Transcendentalism, 174.
Pillon, M., his description of the hymn to Varuna, 237 (note).
Plato, admired by the Transcendentalists, 174. The school of, 321.
Playfair, his influence on the interpretation of Genesis, 28.
Plymouth Brethren, The, their exclusive claim, 77.
Potter, W. J., is made secretary of the Free Religious Association, 187. His religious opinions, 190, 191 (note). Comparison of words with Mr. Beecher's, 205. The followers of, 210. His estimate of the future, &c., 213-215. The lectures of, 220. His definition of God, 221. His Free Congregation, 317.
Prakriti, the primordial substance of things, 307.
Pramada Dasa Mittra, Prof., his defence of Vedantine philosophy, 299 (note).
Prárthanás Somájes, their aim and position, 293, 305.
Presbyterianism and Presbyterians, in Elizabeth's time, 21. Their numbers, 59. The Calvinism of, 76. Progress among, 78, 205. Their part in the overthrow of Charles the First, 156. Relative position in America, 203. Resemblance to neo-Brahmos, 245. The advanced, 315.
Pitakas, The literary treasures of, 309.
Prescott, The Transcendentalism of, 181.
Priestley, Dr., his views of Revelation, 85. The sensational theology of, 185.
Pritchard, Andrew, one of Mr. Voysey's committee, 112.
Proclus, The great religious aims of, 288.
Protab Chunder Mozoumdar, his messages from the Transcendentalists, 202. His description of Theism, 241. Of the Brahmostabs, 246. Complains of Keshub's tendencies, 263. Explains the New Dispensation, 275, 287, 311. His claim, 294 (note). His preaching in England, 303. Conversation with Tyndall, 310.
Puranas, the popular Bible of the Hindus, 237.
Puritans, The, their looking to the primitive Church, 85. In New England, 155, 160. Mr. Potter's Church and the, 190. Influences unknown to, 206. The, of Islamism, 301.
Pusey, Dr., his name associated with Tractarian movement, 62.
Putnam, Dr., the address of, 220.
Pym, his view of Church and State, 17.
Pythagoras, admired by Bronson Alcott, 174.

Quakers, or Friends, The, their opposition to ecclesiasticism, 21. The persecution of, 32. The affirmation of, 34. Their numbers, 77. Their colonization of Pennsylvania, 155. Excluded from New England, 177. The liberal position of, 187, 202, 315.
Queensberry, Lord, the connection of, with British Secular Union, 150.
Quinet, Edgar, his opinion of the Brahmans, 237.

Raj Narain Bose, his ability, &c., 293. President of the Adi Somáj, 304. His work, 305 (note).
Rám Mohun Roy, the founder of Brahmoism, 226. His descent, labours, and character, 231-235. Nature of his organization, 236. His family similar to Chunder Sen's, 241. The work of, &c., 291-293. His statement respecting Christianity, 303.
Rámánda, the philosopher, 230.
Rámánuja, a Hindu Reformer, 229.
Ramsey, Mr., his connection with *The Free-thinker*, 32 (note).
Rawlinson, Mr. G. F., his statistics of Catholicism, 63 (note).
Rawson, Mr. L., the Free-thinkers' Report, 201 (note).

Renan, Ernest, The constructive tendency of, 3. His lecture, 90 (note). The religiousness of, 143 (note). A Vice-President of the British Secular Union, 150.
Renouvier, The constructive tendency of, 3.
Reville, Albert, An article by, 64 (note). His opinion of Calvin and the Divinity of Christ, 85.
Reynolds, The work of, 69, 70 (note).
Ripley, George, The Transcendentalism of, 174. His fortune spent, 181. The fidelity of, to old opinions, 213.
Ripon, Lord, The rule of, in India, 252.
Robespierre, The failure of, 25.
Robinson, John, his address to the first emigrants, 156. The continuous development from, 160.
Rosencranz, Professor, The death of, 211.
Rothschild, Lionel de, his election annulled, 34.
Rousseau developed Deism in France, 25.

Sabellius, The opinions of, 18 (note).
Sacchidánanda, the Védántine Trinity, 279.
Sádháran Somáj, A description of, 238 (note). The secessions of, 269, 291. The constitution of 270. Takes up cause of true Brahmoism, 273. A *critique* of Keshub by the missionary of, 284. Its congregations, 293. Agreement with the other Somájes, 304.
Safford, Mary A., a ministress, 194.
Salar Yung, his good influence, 302.
Salter, W., his work for the Society of Ethical Culture, 194.
Sandemanians, see Glassites.
Sankhya, The school, 307.
Sargent, John J., connection with Free Religious Association, 202.
Savage, Rev. M. J., his Unitarianism, 3. The broad views of, 195, 202. His desire to harmonize religion and evolution, 214-221, 317.
Shelley, The religiousness of, 143 (note).
Schelling, his theory of the Trinity, 64. His philosophical ideas, &c., 167, 168.
Schiller, his estimate of scepticism, 150 (note).

Schliermacher, The works of, in America, 168. His ideas of religion, 167.
Secularists, Secularism, The negative position of, 4. The rudimentary worship of, 6. The aims and character of, 147-152. Their opinions in India, 298.
Seekers, The, their anti-ecclesiasticism, 21.
Seeley, Professor J., his work, "Natural Religion," 47. The stand-point of, 49.
Seneca, The enlightened aims of, 288.
Schopenhauer, The opinions of, adopted, 309 (note).
Servetus, Michael, his heretical views, 18, 19. Sent to the stake, 67 (note). His idea of Christ, 85.
Shafites, a school of Islamism, 301.
Shaftesbury, Lord, The natural Monotheism of, 24.
Shakers, The, see Jumpers.
Shiites, a Mohammedan sect, 300, 301.
Shakespeare, The works of, 41. Mr. Conway and the name of, 126. A Comtist month dedicated to, 132.
Schrádha, a Hindu funeral service, 245.
Schunemann-Pott, his interest in Free Religion, 202.
Sidgwick, Professor, The opinions of, 53.
Sikhs, The, their origin, 231. Their present character, 300.
Simon the Magician, The wonders wrought by, 321.
Siva, the god personifying destructive agencies, 234. The trident of, 280.
Sivanath Sástri, The New Dispensation described by, 270, 277, 305 (notes). His description of Keshub, 284.
Slade, The wonders wrought by, 321.
Smith, Joe, The badge of, 321.
Society for Ethical Culture, formed by Mr. Adler, 191, 192. Its aims, 193. A branch of, at Chicago, 194. Its practical stand-point, 314.
Socinianism, Biddle and the doctrines of, 82. Dangerous to preach, 84. Forms one extreme of Unitarianism, 89. Readily followed Arminianism, 160.
Sofis of Persia, 288. Their Mystico-Pantheistic doctrine, 301.

Sonnesheim, Rabbi S. W., connects Free Religion with Reformed Judaism, 200.

Souni Sâr, its philosophic Nihilism, 299.

Southcote, Johanna, The believers in, 77.

Spears, Rev. Robt., The Unitarian Martyrology published by, 82. The origin of half the Unitarian Churches according to, 93. His estimate of the American Churches, 202, 205.

Spencer, Herbert, his conception of an omnipresent Power, 8, 50. Identifies "force" and "energy," 36 (note). The philosophical system of, 39-46. All our conceptions symbols, according to, 71, 322. The writings of, 88. His belief in the kinship between man and the Unknowable, 101. Positivists hostile to the writings of, 138-145. His doctrines developed by Professor Fiske and Mr. Savage, 214-220. His philosophy not materialistic, 307. Views of the evolutionists in harmony with, 317.

Socrates, use of name by Mr. Conway, 126. By Chunder Sen, 280. Formerly reviled by Christians, 285.

Spiritualism and Spiritualists, their connection with the Free Religious Association, 187. Their numbers, &c., 200-202. The statement of a, 212.

Spinoza, The religiousness of, 143 (note.)

Stanley, Dean, his words at Sir C. Lyell's funeral, 65. Opinions of, compared with Dr. Martineau's, 66. The sincerity of, 68. The liberality of, 79. His sympathy with Mr. Voysey, 112. His generous opinion of Chunder Sen, 281. His reference to the reconciliation of science and revelation, 320.

Stebbins, G. B., his statement about Spiritualists, 201.

Stephen, Fitzjames, introduces "Brahmo Marriage Act," 249, 250.

Stewart, Balfour, his return to neo-Platonism, 50, 322. The large views of, 317.

Stansfield, Judge, a supporter of Mr. Voysey, 112.

Stephens, Sir James, his part in the Spencer-Harrison controversy, . 143 (note).

Strauss, the naturalistic idealism of, 214.

Suetonius, his allusion to the Jewish quarter in Rome, 323.

Suffield, Rev. R. R., his sermon: "Why I became a Unitarian," 99.

Sully, Mr. James, his article on evolution, 50-54.

Sumner, Charles, The Transcendentalism of, 180.

Sunnites, The, their allegiance to the Sultan, 300. Their views of inspiration, 301.

Swedenborgians, their congregations, 79. Origin of the, 319.

Tabernacle Ranters, The eccentricity of, 14

Taine, M., his description of Deism in France, 25 (note). Traces present current of thought to Germany, 36.

Tait, Prof. P. J., The neo-Platonism of, 50, 322. A representative of English science, 317.

Tattva Bodhini Sabhâ, a Brahmoist association, 235, 238.

Tayler, J. J., his work referred to, 17, 21, 29, 30 (notes). Dr. Martineau's introduction to the work of, 54. Work referred to, 78, 82 (notes).

Taylor, Rev. J., The advanced opinions of, 92.

Taylor, Jeremy, his connection with the Latitudinarian party, 19, 20.

Temple, Dr., a writer in *Essays and Reviews*, 65. The sincerity of, 68.

Temple, Sir Richard, the reference of, to Hindu sects, 294, 308.

Test Act, The, its injustice to Dissenters, 34.

Theism, the eclectic of India, 6. The school of in England, 30. 87, 257, 288, 316. Rejected by Spencer, 43, 45. The principles of, and evolution, 50. A vague form of, accepted. 55. Mr. Voysey's, 107, 117. Mr. Conway's advance beyond, 120. The great axioms of, 169, 314. Mr. Adler accepts foundation of, 192. Protab Chunder Mozoomdar's description of, 242. The Sâdhâran Somâj and, 270. Described by Raj Narain Bose, 304. The Transcendental, of Brahmoism, 307. A personal faith, 315.

INDEX. 343

Theophilanthropes, The, the comprehensive aims of, 103.
Theosophical Society of New York, The, its claims, 295. Of India, the propogandism of, 297.
Thomson, James, his description of Secularism, 147, 149 (note).
Tiberius, the government of, 323.
Tindal, The natural Monotheism of, 24.
Tocqueville, The prediction of, 221.
Transcendentalism, The phase of, passed through in America, 6. Name given by Americans, 165, 257. The description of, 168-185. Represented in the Free Religious movement, 202. The happy influence of, 213, 285. The method of, 288. The fate of, 316. Its trust in conscience, 322.
Trinity, the dogma attacked in Italy, 18 (note). Omitted by Antoine Corrano, 19. The theory of, and Coleridge, 64. Dean Stanley and Dr. Martineau's view of, 66. Unitarian revolt against, 81, 161. The Védantine, 277. The mystery of, 302.
Tri-Pitaka, the teachings of, 297, 309.
Tübingen, The school of, its negative criticism, 29.
Tudor, Mary, The Protestants proscribed by, 21.
Tyndall, Prof., his estimate of the religious question, 1. The Belfast address of, 46. His sympathy with persecuted Jews, 80. His description of Emerson, 172. Influence of, in America, 214. His conversation with Chunder Mozoumdar, 311. His large views, 317.
Tulloch, Principal, the work of referred to, 20 (note).

Underwood, Mrs. Sarah A., her view of religious speculation, 210.
Underwood, Mr. B. F., an editor of the *Index*, 187. The Agnosticism of, 195. His views of the spread of the evolution doctrine, 214.
Unitarian General Conference, held at Liverpool and Birmingham, 97.
Unitarian National Conference in America, its concession to Universalists,
186. Messrs. Potter and Abbot's secession from, 194-196.
Unitarianism, Unitarians, Mr. Gladstone's classification of, 4. The origin of, 22. Passed through by Coleridge, 26. The profession of, a blasphemy, 32. The numbers of, 59. Represented at the banquet given to Professor Kuenen, 65 (note). The position of, 67, 77. General description of, 81-102. The methods of, 126. The growth and character of, in America, 161-186. Its relation to the Free Religious Association, 194-198, 202. Its revolt against orthodox dogmas, 221. Rev. W. Adams converted to, 233. Chunder Sen's reference to, 277. Its relation to Brahmoism, 303. Its undogmatic church, 313. The advanced, 315. Their view of Jesus, 322.
Universalists, The classification of, 4. Their doctrine, 77, 161.
Upanishads, religious readings from, 233, 235. The authors of, 288.

Vachaspati Misra, his philosophy, 307.
Vallabhácárya, a Hindu reformer, 229.
Védânta, The Pantheism of, 227. Its two doctrines, 233. The adherents of, 296.
Védas, Mr. Conway's extracts from, 221. The hymns of, 227. Their esoteric texts, 234. The direct breath of God, 236. Women according to, 249. Chunder Sen's reference to, 281. The infallibility of, 294. The traditions of, 297. The treasures in, 309.
Vicence, an association in Italy, 18.
Vishnu, Buddha an incarnation of, 228. The worshippers of, 229, 231. Personifies the world's preservative forces, 234, 237. Chunder Sen's early worship of, 241. Hari, a personification of, 275. The worship of, 276. The eclecticism of, 277.
Voltaire, carries Deism into France, 25. His reference to English sects, 57. Use of name by Mr. Conway, 126. The criticisms of, 209.
Voysey, Rev. Ch., The Theism of, 3. His Church and teaching, 104-113.

His retention of prayers for Queen, &c., 121. His Church compared with Mr. Conway's, 127. The isolated position of, 315. The large views of, 317.

Wahabis, a Mussulman sect of recent origin, 300, 301.
Walker, James, The philosophical views of 168.
Wallace, his theory of natural selection, 37, 38. A representative of English science, 317.
Walters, Rev. F., his address on the progress of Rationalism, 79. The views of, 92.
Ware, Dr., his position in Harvard University, 161.
Wasson, his fidelity to Transcendentalism, 213. The writings of, 220.
Watts, Ch., The secular liturgy of, 150.
Webster, Daniel, his position as an orator, 181.
Weiss, John, his Transcendentalism, 174. His connection with the Free Religious Association, 202.
Welchman, The heresy of, 82.
Wesley, John, The influence of, 26. The Methodists sprang from, 74. The hymns of, 99. The God of, and Mr. Voysey's services, 108.
Wette, De, The writings of, studied, 168.
Whitfield, The influence of, 26.

Whittier, The poetry of, 180.
Wicksteed, Rev. P. H., his translation of Dutch works, 91.
Wightman, The martyrdom of, 19.
Wilberforce, his connection of Arminianism with Deism, 160.
Williams, Professor Monier, The opinions of, referred to, 227, 229, 296, 303 (notes). His description of Hinduism, 228. His estimate of Rám Mohun Roy, 232.
Williams, Roger, founds the State of Rhode Island, 159, 189.
Williams, Roland, The sincerity of, 68.
Winnebrenner, John, The followers of, 205.
Wise, Rabbi Isaac, his connection with the Free Religionists, 202.
Woolston, The natural Monotheism of, 24. The loss of his Fellowship, 84.
Wordsworth, The religiousness of, 143. The Transcendentalism of, 168.
Wycliff, The aspirations of, &c., 16.

Yoga, The teachings of, 262 (note). Its nature and influence, 305, 306.

Zend Avesta, readings borrowed from, 245. The treasures of, 309.
Zoroaster, his equality with Moses, &c., 185. The religion of, 300.

OPINIONS OF THE PRESS

ON

THE WORK IN THE ORIGINAL.

LIBRAIRIE EUROPÉENNE C. MUQUARDT

MERZBACH & FALK, ÉDITEURS

LIBRAIRES DU ROI ET DE S. A. R. LE COMTE DE FLANDRE

45, RUE DE LA RÉGENCE, A BRUXELLES.

L'ÉVOLUTION RELIGIEUSE
CONTEMPORAINE
CHEZ LES ANGLAIS, LES AMÉRICAINS & LES HINDOUS

PAR

Le comte GOBLET D'ALVIELLA

Professeur d'histoire des religions à l'Université de Bruxelles

---

OPINIONS OF THE PRESS.

"Will be read with interest both in England and in America."—*The Athenæum.*

"A careful and interesting book."—*Saturday Review.*

"His study of the various divisions of religious England was evidently intelligent, close and liberal."—*British Quarterly Review.*

"The best summary of Brahmic history accessible to non-Oriental readers and marked throughout by an earnest desire to present a faithful picture of the reality."—Miss S. D. COLLET, *Modern Review.*

"A minute yet vivid picture."—*Christian Life.*

"Worthy of the highest praise, rich in instruction and very interesting."—*Inquirer.*

"Elaborate, comprehensive, accurate and impartial."—ROD. SUFFIELD, *Christian Herald.*

"The first of its kind."—*The Jewish World.*

"The author possesses surprising knowledge."—*The Nation*, of New York.

"Strong in statistics and other details, rich in original generalisations and lucid conceptions, and singularly tolerant, devout and hopeful in its spirit, the book must be read carefully from beginning to end, in order to gain any fair idea of its rare merit."—*Boston Index.*

"Of deep interest to the philanthropist and thinker."—*Boston Commonwealth.*

"Lucid, genial, altogether fine and fascinating."—N. GILMAN, *Christian Register.*

"A really valuable contribution to the history of modern thought; especially welcome to the Indian reader for the light it throws on the religious evolution actually occurring in our midst, but which we, therefore, do not properly appreciate."—*Times of India.*

"We conclude with the hope that some able writer would translate the book into English and unfold its perspicacity and its beauty to everyone of our readers." *Indian Messenger.*

"Tells us all we want to know on the subject."—*The Liberal,* of Calcutta.

"Les chapitres sur le rationalisme américain et sur le rationalisme hindou, outre ce qu'ils contiennent de renseignements qui seront pour le lecteur européen de véritables révélations, sont en même temps autant de chapitres de critique et de philosophie d'une grande portée qui constituent dès à présent, comme on dit, des documents du plus rare intérêt pour l'histoire religieuse contemporaine."—*Revue des Deux Mondes.*

"Montre que les questions d'histoire contemporaine, quand on sait se dégager des passions de parti et les remplacer par la haute curiosité d'un esprit désireux de comprendre, prennent un intérêt et une signification qu'on ne leur soupçonnait pas. Cette étude de la religion contemporaine, saisie dans les tressaillements de sa vie quotidienne, est d'une haute portée."—MAURICE VERNES, *Revue de l'histoire des religions.*

"C'est, si je ne me trompe, le premier travail d'ensemble qui ait encore été fait sur ce grand mouvement, et il est tracé avec une ampleur de lignes, une intelligence des nuances, une clarté et une simplicité de vues que la critique religieuse de nos jours semblait avoir oubliées."—JAMES DARMESTETER, *Revue critique d'histoire et de littérature.*

"Personne ne s'est mieux rendu compte de la gravité de la crise at de l'effet produit sur notre génération par les résultats acquis de l'immense mouvement scientifique de notre siècle."—E. DE PRESSENSÉ, *Revue politique et littéraire.*

"Expose avec une lumineuse clarté l'état religieux de l'Angleterre et de l'Amérique. Aucun écrivain français n'a mieux tracé, sans confusion, avec un ordre logique et facile à retenir, ce tableau chargé de tant de détails."—E. POUSSET, *Polybiblion.*

"Récit fort instructif."—A. BOYENVAL, *La Réforme sociale.*

"A le rare talent d'exposer brièvement, clairement les différents systèmes philosophiques ou religieux sans les mutiler."—*La Renaissance, organe des Eglises réformées de France.*

"Impossible de faire preuve de plus d'objectivité, de plus de largeur et d'impartialité."—ALBERT REVILLE, Correspond. parisienne de la *Flandre libérale.*

"L'impartialité de la critique indique assez que les faits ont été bien observés et sincèrement exposés."—ROUXEL, *Journal des Economistes.*

"Destiné à rendre un grand service à l'œuvre de synthèse et de reconstruction après laquelle, bien que peu d'esprits en aient conscience, l'humanité entière aspire." —CH. FAUVETY, *Bulletin de la Société scientifique d'études psychologiques.*

"Plein de faits, écrit sans parti pris, avec une grande élévation et dans une méthode toute scientifique."—*La Nouvelle Revue.*

"Très important ouvrage."—*Revue britannique.*

"D'une incontestable utilité."—*Journal des Débats.*

"Du plus haut intérêt pour tous ceux que préoccupe le même problème de la conciliation de la religion et de la raison."—*Journal de Genève.*

"Intéressant, riche de faits, d'un style animé."—*Gazette de Lausanne.*

"C'est ici un livre pour le grand public, non pas seulement pour les savants."—JEAN REVILLE, *L'Alliance libérale.*

"Sera lu par tous les esprits élevés auxquels l'histoire du rationalisme religieux ne peut être indifférente."—*Indépendance belge.*

"Ce livre est d'une utilité singulière et dans notre pays il peut rendre de grands services."—*Flandre libérale.*

"Ouvrage sérieux et considérable."—*La Gazette.*

"Il n'y aura qu'une voix pour admirer la lucidité de l'exposition et la solide facture d'un style éminemment approprié à l'exposé philosophique et religieux."—*Echo du Parlement.*

"Attachant, suggestif, sincère et bien écrit; tous ceux qui voient dans l'avenir religieux de l'humanité un intérêt primordial ont quelque chose à y apprendre."—*Athenæum belge.*

"Marquera une date dans l'histoire des idées religieuses de notre temps."—*La Chronique.*

"Dans des voyages réitérés en Angleterre, aux Etats-Unis et aux Indes, l'auteur s'est mis en communication avec les chefs des principales sectes religieuses de ces pays. Ses observations personnelles lui ont permis de communiquer à son livre cet intérêt vif et piquant d'une description faite d'après nature."—*La Revue catholique.*

"Ce livre est un des meilleurs ouvrages d'histoire religieuse qui aient paru en ces dernières années. Ecrit dans un style excellent, correct, élégant et d'une très belle allure."—E. DE LAVELEYE, *Bulletin de l'Académie royale.*

"Ce qui ressort du livre avec une clarté sans égale c'est que la religion n'est pas par essence réfractaire au progrès."—H. PERGAMENI, *L'Avenir.*

"Par son attrait de nouveauté, par le talent d'exposition de l'auteur, par l'élévation et la sincérité de pensée qui y éclatent à chaque page, il laissera une trace profonde."—*La Meuse.*

"Quel tableau instructif, attrayant!"—*Journal de Liège.*

"Oeuvre d'un écrivain et d'un penseur."—*Organe de Mons.*

"Tous ont quelque chose à apprendre dans ce livre."—*Gazette de Charleroi.*

"Très-intéressant ouvrage."—Professor C. P. TIELE, *Manuel de l'histoire des Religions,* 2ème edition.

"Beau livre."—A. BARTH, *Bulletin des Religions de l'Inde,* 1885.

"Pages éloquentes."—Professor J. BONET-MAURY, *Etude sur Akbar.*

"Man darf das hohe Verdienst des Verfassers nicht verkennen."—*Allg. Zeitung des Judenthums.*

"Alle Schilderungen bieten uns deshalb ebenso zuverlässiges als schwerzugängliches material für die neueste Kirchengeschichte.—*Literarischen Centralblätter.*"

"La erudicion del libro es vasta y el talento conque esta escrito inne gable."—*Revista Contemporanea,* de Madrid.

"Rivela grande attitudine, ingegno e studio non commune."—B. LABANCA, *La Cultura,* de Rome.

"Een merkwaardig boek."—*Het Vaderland,* de La Haye.

www.ingramcontent.com/pod-product-compliance
Lightning Source LLC
Chambersburg PA
CBHW020224240426
43672CB00006B/413